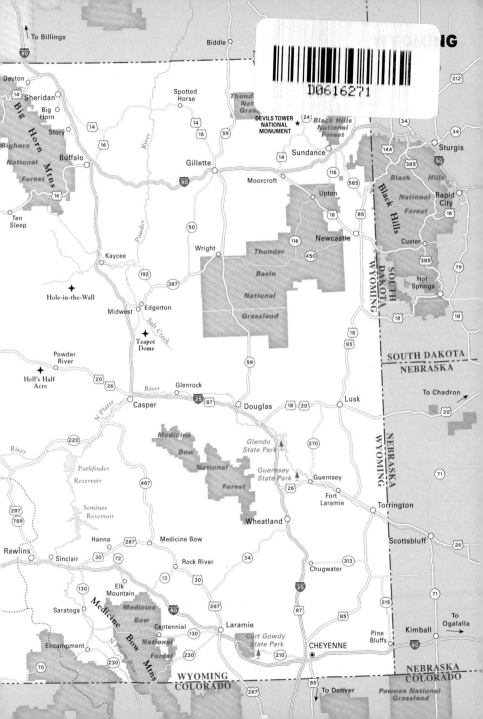

YELLOWSTONE AND GRAND TETON NATIONAL PARKS

Contents

DISCOVER

Wyoming

Embodied by the bucking bronco on its license plates, Wyoming is a child's cowboy fantasy come to life, with rodeos aplenty and dude ranches where even city slickers can try their hand at riding and roping.

But what strikes people most about Wyoming is its authenticity. The harsh climate and isolation that make Wyoming the least populated state in the union result in an uncommon grace in its residents. It's expressed not just in the weathered creases on their faces but in the way they do business and welcome visitors. There is glitz here too, in places like Jackson Hole and Cody, but it doesn't distract from the essence of Wyoming. Those towns are but a flash of silver, the shiny buckle on a well-worn belt.

The landscape—from soaring mountains to narrow valleys and sweeping plains—was carved over eons by water, wind, fire, and ice. The culture was also shaped by conflict: between those who were from here and those who were not; those who valued the land itself and those who sought only its riches. Its distinct histories, both natural and cultural, are evident everywhere, not just tucked away in dusty museums, as the state continues to define itself.

Clockwise from top left: Shoshone National Forest; aspens in fall; Old Faithful in Yellowstone National Park; Mormon Row in Grand Teton National Park; ancient lava fields in Hell's Half Acre; Yellowstone's Upper Geyser Basin area.

Planning Your Trip

Where to Go

Yellowstone National Park

This magnificent park is constantly in motion; nothing here is static. See abundant wildlife, including **bison, elk, bears, and wolves;** marvel at geothermal features like the legendary **Old Faithful;** and stay in marvelous historic lodges like the **Old Faithful Inn** and rambling **Lake Yellowstone Hotel and Cabins.** Perimeter communities, including **West Yellowstone, Gardiner,** and remote **Cooke City,** should not be missed.

Grand Teton National Park

Grand Teton packs a punch, particularly when it comes to **mountain splendor.** Twelve peaks in the Teton Range soar above 12,000 feet. While there are only 100 miles of roads in the park, there are twice as many **miles of trails,** leaving hikers endless options for adventure. Favorite landmarks include picturesque **Jenny Lake,** vast **Jackson Lake,** drive-to-the-summit **Signal Mountain,** and serene **Oxbow Bend.**

Jackson Hole, Cody, and the Wind Rivers

Wyoming's northwest corner is far more than a gateway to Yellowstone and Grand Teton National Parks. **Jackson Hole** is a destination in and of itself, with **glitzy galleries** and boutiques, gourmet eateries, **luxe accommodations,** and a sensational art scene in immediate proximity to world-class **ski resorts** and **white-water rafting.** The **National Museum of Wildlife Art** and the **National Elk Refuge** are major draws for animal enthusiasts. In **Cody** the cowboy is still king, and the sun rises and sets on the **Buffalo Bill Center of the West** and its five museums. Farther south, outdoor enthusiasts will find **hot springs** and **mountain meccas.**

Bison roam in Yellowstone National Park.

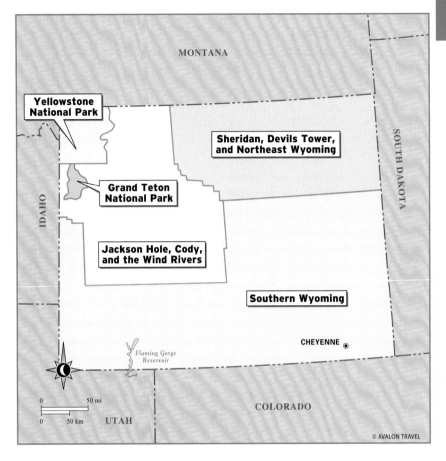

Sheridan, Devils Tower, and Northeast Wyoming

Where the prairies meet the mountains, cowboy culture comes alive. This is where you'll find **dude ranches** and **Sheridan,** one of the most charming and authentic Western towns in the state. The spectacular **Cloud Peak Skyway Scenic Byway** climbs into the mountains toward the pictograph-rich **Medicine Lodge State Archeological Site** and more mysterious **Medicine Wheel National Historic Landmark.** The isolated and enigmatic **Devils Tower National Monument** draws climbers, geologists, and Native Americans who consider it a sacred site.

Southern Wyoming

Southern Wyoming contains everything from **sweeping deserts, sand dunes,** and **wild mustang herds** to **lush river valleys** and **green mountains.** The southwest corner is noted for fabulous recreational opportunities along the Green River and in the **Flaming Gorge National Recreation Area.** It's also home to three of the state's largest cities: capital **Cheyenne,** synonymous with its legendary **Frontier Days** rodeo, college town **Laramie,** and onetime frontier town **Casper.**

When to Go

Summer is the easiest and busiest time to travel the roads, both front- and backcountry. Thoughtful planning and advance reservations, particularly for hotels and campgrounds, are essential. Hotel rooms are particularly hard to find during local events such as Frontier Days in Cheyenne.

Rates for accommodations are generally lower and rooms more available when snow is on the ground, except around ski areas, but **winter road travel** can be challenging because of the inevitable storms and possible closures.

The **shoulder seasons** can be a delightful time to travel. The **national parks** are heavenly and much less crowded in **autumn,** but keep in mind that winter comes very early at high elevations. There are also little-known ways to enjoy the parks by bicycle in the **spring,** before they open to cars. Opening and closing times for the parks can vary by year (weather and federal budget too), so make sure to check with the parks before travel.

Don't try to see too much in too short a time; this cannot be overstated. Don't spend so much time on the road that you miss the small details—idyllic hikes, roadside burger joints, the locals who give small towns their true character—that make Wyoming what it is.

Even coyotes look cold when the wind blows in winter.

Explore Yellowstone and Grand Teton

Don't spend your trip stuck behind the wheel. See and experience this breathtaking region without exceeding 200 miles of travel in a single day.

Day 1: Cody

After breakfast, head out on the hour-long **Cody Trolley Tour,** which can include tickets to the **Buffalo Bill Center of the West.** Spend most of the day exploring its five museums. Before dinner at the celebrated **Irma Hotel,** grab a cocktail and step outside to watch the **Cody Gunfighters.** After dinner, head over to the **Cody Nite Rodeo** for a two-hour action-packed show with local cowboys and cowgirls.

Day 2
Cody to Tower Junction
111 MILES, 3 HOURS

On your way out of town, stop by **Old Trail Town.** Then head farther west on the **Buffalo Bill Scenic Byway** toward the east entrance of **Yellowstone National Park.** Stop for a bite at Buffalo Bill Cody's historic **Pahaska Tepee** resort. Once inside the park, check out the phenomenal **Grand Canyon of the Yellowstone** and the wildlife-rich **Hayden Valley** on your way to **Tower Junction** and the classic **Roosevelt Lodge Cabins.** Arrive in time to ride horseback (or travel by covered wagon) to the **Old West Dinner Cookout.** Then retire to your rustic cabin under the stars.

Day 3
Tower Junction to
Paradise Valley
59 MILES, 1.5 HOURS

Early birds will delight in a sunrise drive through the famed **Lamar Valley** for amazing opportunities to spot wildlife, including wolves and bears. Consider a hike up to **Trout Lake** or maybe

Yellowstone's limestone terraces mimic the curves of the clouds at sunset.

meander along the trout waters of **Slough Creek.** Turn around and head back north to **Mammoth and the Mammoth Hot Springs Terraces,** where you can amble around the colorful geothermal features. For lunch, try the bison or trout tacos at the **Mammoth Hotel Dining Room,** just below the geothermal terraces. On your way out of the park, perhaps you'll want to soak in the **Boiling River.**

Day 4
Paradise Valley to Lake, Wyoming
91 MILES, 3 HOURS

Backtrack through the park's northern entrance. River rats should take a morning **raft trip** on the Yellowstone River through Yankee Jim Canyon. Inside the park, head to **Norris** for another education in geology and supervolcanology. Then head to **Canyon**—check out the canyon or the falls from another angle, or even on a trail like **Uncle Tom's Trail,** which will take you to the spectacular **Lower Falls.** Wind up your day with a cocktail on the porch and a relaxing dinner at the idyllic **Lake Yellowstone Hotel and Cabins.**

Stay or dine at the Lake Yellowstone Hotel and Cabins.

Day 5
Lake to Jackson
95 MILES, 2.5 HOURS

After a morning stroll at water's edge, head down to **West Thumb Geyser Basin,** an incredible selection of geothermal features. From there, continue south to **Grand Teton National Park.** You'll pass this way again in two days, so don't feel pressured to stop at every scenic turnout. Grab lunch along the way and try a hike along the gentle **Lakeshore Trail** at Colter Bay. Continue down to Jackson and settle in at the **Anvil Motel.** Walk just a few blocks for small plates and communal seating at **Bin 22,** or sit down to a long and sumptuous meal at the **Snake River Grill.** Before tucking in for the night, stop for a nightcap at the famous **Million Dollar Cowboy Bar.**

Day 6
Jackson Hole

Hit the local favorite—**The Bunnery**—for a hearty breakfast. White-water enthusiasts will have no shortage of options on the **Snake River.** Mountain bikers and hikers can hit the

Appreciating wildlife is as much a part of the culture as mountains are part of the landscape. The most obvious choice for prime wildlife viewing is Yellowstone National Park, where animals have the right of way; just try telling a herd of rutting bison that you have to be somewhere. Grand Teton National Park is also a great bet, although the restricted roads and dense forests can limit visibility. Wyoming has seven national wildlife refuges that offer prime habitat to any number of species.

- Just outside **Jackson,** the **National Elk Refuge** is home to 6,000-7,000 elk throughout the winter months.

- In **Dubois,** the **National Bighorn Sheep Interpretive Center** offers winter tours of the nearby **Whiskey Mountain Habitat Area.** Self-guided tours take visitors into prime sheep country, where waterfowl, raptors, and moose can often be seen as well.

- Just north of **Rock Springs,** the **White Mountain Herd Management Area** is home to 1,100-1,600 wild mustangs. Pronghorn, sage grouse, coyotes, and eagles also frequent the region.

- North of **Green River,** the wetland habitat

National Elk Refuge

of the **Seedskadee National Wildlife Refuge** hosts some 200 bird species, including Canada geese, great blue herons, and swans.

---

alpine slopes at either **Snow King** in town or off the fabulous **gondola** at **Jackson Hole Mountain Resort,** or consider **horseback riding.** If you have the energy in the afternoon, visit the **National Museum of Wildlife Art** before grabbing a margarita and some Mexican fare at **Pica's Mexican Taqueria.** Wednesday and Saturday nights you can catch the **Jackson Rodeo.**

Day 7
Jackson to Old Faithful
98 MILES, 2.5 HOURS
After breakfast, head north toward Grand Teton and Yellowstone. Stop at **Jenny Lake** for a hike to **Hidden Falls and Inspiration Point,** a boat

ride, or just a picnic. Continue north through **Grand Teton,** checking out the sights you missed on the way down. Once in **Yellowstone,** drive north and west to Old Faithful and stay at the **Old Faithful Inn** for the night. There are great trails along the way, including an easy jaunt to **Lone Star Geyser.** Explore the area before settling in for dinner and a bed at the inn. If you can keep your eyes open, Old Faithful eruptions in the moonlight are pretty unforgettable.

Day 8
Old Faithful to West Yellowstone
32 MILES, 0.75 HOUR
After a leisurely morning, head north and then west to the town of West Yellowstone. Enjoy this

The clear waters of Jackson Lake are a stunning mirror for the Tetons.

small but dense section of the park on your way out. Don't miss the opportunity to swim in the thermally heated waters of the **Firehole River.** In West Yellowstone, check out the **Grizzly and Wolf Discovery Center** and the adjacent **Yellowstone Giant Screen Theatre.** Grab a bison burger at **Buckaroo Bill's Ice Cream** or a gourmet meal at **Bar N Ranch** before calling it a night in a cozy safari tent at **Yellowstone Under Canvas.**

Cowboys, Hot Springs, and Wide Open Spaces

This 10-day road trip includes two tried-and-true cowboy towns, a geological wonder, an outdoors mecca, four days at a working ranch, and all the beautiful and historical sights in between.

Day 1: Sheridan

Ease into your cowboy experience with a visit to the **Trail End State Historic Site.** Check out the Western duds at the legendary **King's Saddlery,** and don't leave without a **King Ropes baseball cap,** which is de rigueur in the West. Wander around town, nosing into some of the shops and galleries along **Main Street.** Then enjoy a hearty dinner at **Wyoming's Rib & Chop House.**

Wind things down at the classic **Mint Bar** and find a comfy bed at the **Mill Inn.**

Day 2
Sheridan to Thermopolis
160-205 MILES, 3 HOURS

To get from Sheridan to Thermopolis, there are a couple of starkly beautiful drives, both offering access to interesting sights and countless trails in the **Bighorn National Forest.**

The **Bighorn Scenic Byway** (about 205 miles) climbs up and over the mountains past such sights as the **Medicine Wheel National Historic Landmark.** This route follows

Highway 14 to Lovell and then south toward Thermopolis.

The shorter route (about 160 miles) is higher but no less scenic. It heads south to **Buffalo** past the impressive **Fort Phil Kearny State Historic Site,** then over the **Cloud Peak Skyway Scenic Byway** through Ten Sleep to Worland and eventually south to Thermopolis.

As you pull into Thermopolis, head to the colorful and otherworldly **Hot Springs State Park.** Stroll along the **Spirit Trail** or stop into the historic **State Bath House** for a swim before checking into the **Best Western Plaza Hotel.** For dinner, grab a burger at the **Front Porch Deli and Grill.**

Day 3
Thermopolis to Casper
134 MILES, 2 HOURS

Spend the day in Thermopolis, exploring the park and soaking in the medicinal waters. Arrange for a tour of **The Wyoming Dinosaur Center and Dig Sites.** You can even participate in its **archaeological digs.** Fill your belly at the **Black Bear Café** before heading south through

Thermopolis is a town built on thermal features.

some of the oldest rock formations on the planet. Consider planning a **white-water excursion** with the Wind River Canyon Whitewater and Fly Fishing, the only outfitter licensed to operate on the Wind River Reservation. Keep your eyes peeled for **bighorn sheep.** At Shoshoni, head east toward Casper. After a thick steak at the **FireRock Steakhouse,** or surprisingly good pan-Asian food at **Dsasumo,** settle in for two nights at the **Sunburst Lodge** on **Casper Mountain.**

Day 4
Casper

Wake up to wilderness on **Casper Mountain.** There are endless options for ways to enjoy it: Hike or bike the trails, or fish on the well-recovered **North Platte River.** For a more cultural experience, head to the **Nicolaysen Art Museum and Discovery Center** and wonderful **National Historic Trails Interpretive Center.** Lunch at **The Cottage Café** or **Sherrie's Place,** and plan for dinner at **Guadalajara.** Back on the mountain, if the **Crimson Dawn Museum** is open, stop in to drink in the lore of the mountain.

The culture and lives of indigenous people have powerfully defined the identity of Wyoming. There are tremendous opportunities for those interested in learning about and experiencing Native American history, traditions, and contemporary culture.

WIND RIVER RESERVATION

Wyoming's only reservation is home to about 8,600 Northern Arapaho and some 3,900 Eastern Shoshone Indians. Sights of interest include the **Shoshone Tribal Cultural Center** and the grave sites of the two most prominent Shoshone Indians, **Chief Washakie** and Lewis and Clark's guide, **Sacagawea.**

The best time to visit is during the annual three-day powwows. The largest Shoshone powwow is the **Eastern Shoshone Indian Days Powwow and Rodeo,** held the fourth weekend in June. The largest Arapaho powwow is the **Ethete Celebration,** usually held in late July.

MEDICINE WHEEL NATIONAL HISTORIC LANDMARK

This mysterious carved stone wheel has spiritual but unexplained significance to many Native American tribes. Interpretive tours are offered by local Native American guides.

DEVILS TOWER NATIONAL MONUMENT

This iconic rocky sentinel, the first national monu-

Native Americans celebrate during a powwow.

ment in the country, is considered sacred by numerous tribes, all of whom have unique origin stories for it. A voluntary climbing closure is in effect each June out of respect for various Native American ceremonies.

Day 5
Casper to Buffalo
115 MILES, 1.5 HOURS

Head north on I-87, which runs parallel to the old **Bozeman Trail.** This is stark open country, with the Thunder Basin National Grassland sweeping out east of the highway. In Buffalo, belly up to the bar in the historic **Occidental Hotel** for a meal and a cozy room for the night. For a little exercise, hit the 13-mile **Clear Creek Trail System.** If

you're lucky, you'll be able to catch the weekly **Cowgirl Rodeo,** on Tuesdays, at the Johnson County Fairgrounds.

Day 6
Buffalo to TA Guest Ranch
14 MILES, 0.5 HOUR

Rise early and hightail it to the historic **TA Guest Ranch,** south of Buffalo off Highway 196, where you'll spend the next four days. This is where cowboy culture comes to life.

Blue sky, yellow flowers, and white peaks signal the start of summer in the Northern Rockies.

Days 7-9
TA Guest Ranch

Spend the next three nights enjoying an **authentic ranch experience.** Activities range from riding to fly-fishing, hiking, biking, and golf. You'll visit tipi rings and Bozeman Trail sites on the property, plus important battlefields nearby. Expect to work and play hard.

Day 10
TA Guest Ranch to Sheridan
61 MILES, 1 HOUR

Trade your saddle for a bucket seat and head north to Sheridan. Consider a stop at **Fort Phil Kearny State Historic Site** and the tiny town of **Big Horn** to see the **Bradford Brinton Memorial and Museum.** Enjoy a last meal—Wyoming gourmet—at **Frackleton's** on Main Street in Sheridan.

It's hard to drive through Wyoming without running into rodeo action somewhere. Stop. Buy a ticket. The bleachers are fine. These small-town rodeos offer a unique window into life here: Locals wear their Sunday best, and no one seems to mind the dust. Sitting on a sun-baked wooden bench, a beer in one hand and a bag of popcorn in the other, is the best first date in small towns, where they show off their best without hiding what's real.

THERMOPOLIS COWBOY RENDEZVOUS (WEEKEND AFTER FATHER'S DAY)

From tailgate parties and a Western dance to a pancake breakfast and parade, the small-town rodeo in **Thermopolis** ushers in the pro rodeo circuit for the Big Horn Basin with plenty of action and family fun.

CODY STAMPEDE RODEO (JULY 1-4)

With all the showmanship one would expect from a town named after Buffalo Bill **Cody,** this professional rodeo lets the town shine with all of the classic events including bareback riding, roping, steer wrestling, barrel racing, saddle bronc and bull riding. The rest of the summer, visitors can get a true sense of small-town rodeo at the Cody Nite Rodeo.

TEN SLEEP FOURTH OF JULY RODEO (TWO DAYS OVER FOURTH OF JULY)

With a rodeo history that dates back to 1908 and includes some of the biggest names in the sport, **Ten Sleep** boasts rodeo action throughout the summer. Special events at the annual Fourth of July

Rodeos advertise however possible.

shindig include a Pony Express Ride from nearby Hyattville, a Main Street parade, an old-fashioned rodeo, fireworks, and a sometimes-bloody wild horse race.

SHERIDAN WYO RODEO (USUALLY THE SECOND WEEK IN JULY)

This is the biggest week of the year for **Sheridan.** There is a golf tournament, art show, rodeo royalty pageant, carnival, Indian relay races, parade, and street dance on top of four nights of pro-rodeo action.

Yellowstone National Park

Look for ★ to find recommended
sights, activities, dining, and lodging.

Highlights

★ **Boiling River:** In a stretch of the Gardner River at the park's north entrance, hot water flows over waterfalls and via springs, mixing with the river water to create a perfect soaking temperature (page 36).

★ **Mammoth and the Mammoth Hot Springs Terraces:** The travertine terraces here look like an enormous cream-colored confection. Since the springs shift and change daily, a walk around the colorful terraces is never the same experience twice (page 40).

★ **Grand Canyon of the Yellowstone:** The sheer cliffs and dramatic coloring of this canyon have inspired millions of visitors. In the summer, get a rare bird's-eye view of several osprey nests (page 41).

★ **Watching the Wolves:** The wolves put on a spectacular show—with at least one reported sighting daily since 2001. The sagas of the 10 packs are dramatic, heart-wrenching, and captivating (page 46).

★ **Lamar Valley:** Known as the "Little Serengeti of North America," this scenic, glacially carved valley offers spectacular wildlife-watching year-round (page 48).

★ **Yellowstone Lake:** This beautiful lake was touted by early mountain men as perhaps the only place where you could catch a fish and cook it without ever taking it off the line (page 55).

★ **Old Faithful:** If you can see just one thing in Yellowstone, make it this world-famous geyser that erupts every 45-90 minutes (page 56).

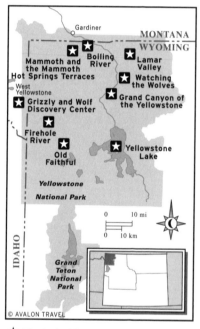

© AVALON TRAVEL

★ **Firehole River:** This river offers a stunning, heated swimming area surrounded by cliffs. The twists and turns of the cascading canyon are worth seeing even if you don't get wet (page 57).

★ **Grizzly and Wolf Discovery Center:** You're guaranteed an up-close look at two of the park's biggest and most fascinating predators at this home to grizzly bears and wolves that can't survive in the wild (page 62).

Yellowstone National Park is at the heart of our country's relationship with wilderness. It's also the largest intact ecosystem in the Lower 48—all of the species that have roamed this plateau are still (or once again) in residence.

Yellowstone was our nation's first national park. Signed into being by President Ulysses S. Grant after a series of important and legendary scouting expeditions through the area, the region's history is lengthy and very much alive, from its prehistoric supervolcanic eruptions, to its occupation by the U.S. Army in the 1880s, to the controversial reintroduction of wolves in the 1990s and the more recent snowmobile-usage, bison, and grizzly delisting quagmires. The stories, both far-fetched and true, and characters that have emerged from the park are as colorful and compelling as the landscape itself.

A vast 2.2 million acres, Yellowstone is indeed a wonderland, filled with steaming geysers and boiling mud pots, packed with diverse and healthy populations of wildlife, and crisscrossed by hundreds of miles of hiking and skiing trails. A stretch of the park called the Lamar Valley is known as the "Little Serengeti of North America," and for

good reason: At certain times of the year, in a single day visitors can spot grizzly and black bears, moose, wolves, bison, elk, coyotes, bald eagles, and the occasional bighorn sheep or mountain goat. In fact, the opportunities for viewing wildlife in the park are unparalleled anywhere in the United States, and although Yellowstone may not be as picturesque as Glacier or the Tetons, it is magnificent in its wildness and uniquely American.

Seeing Yellowstone from the back of a cramped station wagon—or these days, a decked-out Winnebago—is almost a rite of passage in this country. What parent doesn't dream of hauling their children out West to see Old Faithful erupt or to catch a glimpse of a grizzly bear? And what kid doesn't want to swim in the Boiling River or lie awake in a sleeping bag, listening to the howl of coyotes? It is not exactly the last frontier that it once was—there are convenience stores, beautiful old hotels, and even places to get a decent

Previous: skiers on the road from West Yellowstone; the Boiling River near the park's north entrance.
Above: Old Faithful.

Yellowstone National Park

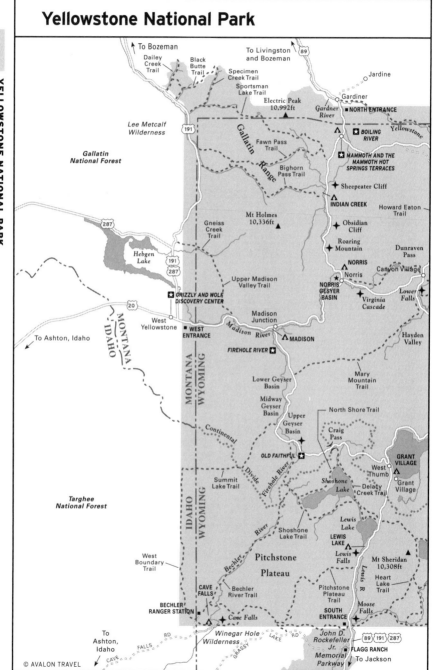

© AVALON TRAVEL

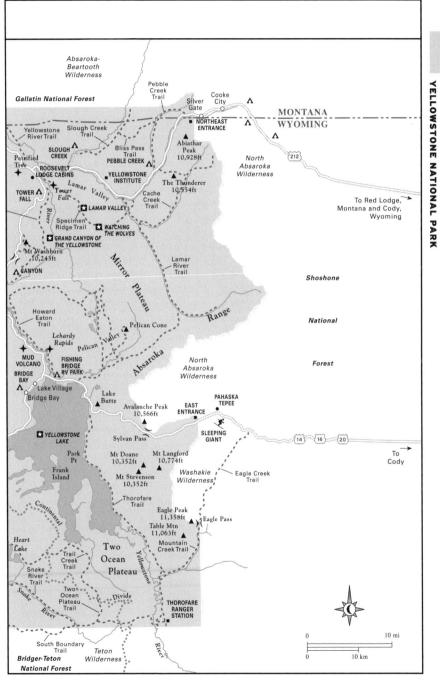

Absaroka-
Beartooth
Wilderness

Gallatin National Forest

Pebble
Creek
Trail

Silver
Gate

Cooke
City

MONTANA
WYOMING

NORTHEAST
ENTRANCE

212

Yellowstone
River Trail

Slough Creek
Trail

SLOUGH
CREEK

Bliss Pass
Trail

PEBBLE CREEK

Abiathar
Peak
10,928ft

North
Absaroka
Wilderness

Petrified
Tree

ROOSEVELT
LODGE CABINS

YELLOWSTONE
INSTITUTE

The Thunderer
10,554ft

To Red Lodge,
Montana and Cody,
Wyoming

TOWER
FALL

Tower
Fall

Lamar Valley

Cache
Creek
Trail

LAMAR VALLEY

Specimen
Ridge Trail

WATCHING
THE WOLVES

GRAND CANYON OF
THE YELLOWSTONE

Lamar
River
Trail

Mt Washburn
10,243ft

CANYON

Mirror

Plateau

Shoshone

Howard
Eaton
Trail

Pelican Cone

Lehardy
Rapids

Pelican Valley

Range

National

MUD
VOLCANO

FISHING
BRIDGE
RV PARK

Absaroka

North
Absaroka
Wilderness

Forest

BRIDGE
BAY

Lake Village

Bridge Bay

Lake
Butte

Avalanche Peak
10,566ft

EAST
ENTRANCE

PAHASKA
TEPEE

YELLOWSTONE
LAKE

Sylvan Pass

SLEEPING
GIANT

14 16 20

To
Cody

Park
Pt

Frank
Island

Mt Doane
10,352ft

Mt Langford
10,774ft

Mt Stevenson
10,352ft

Washakie
Wilderness

Eagle Creek
Trail

Thorofare
Trail

Eagle Peak
11,358ft

Eagle Pass

Continental

Table Mtn
11,063ft

Mountain
Creek Trail

Heart
Lake

Trail
Creek
Trail

Two
Ocean
Plateau

Yellowstone

Snake
River
Trail

Two
Ocean
Plateau
Trail

Divide

THOROFARE
RANGER
STATION

Snake

River

South Boundary
Trail

Teton
Wilderness

Bridger-Teton
National Forest

0   10 mi

0   10 km

latte—but Yellowstone still occupies its own corner of our national imagination; classified somewhere between American wilderness and family vacations, it conjures up foggy but perfect memories.

HISTORY

Evidence from archaeological sites, trails, and even oral histories suggests that humans inhabited the region of Yellowstone as far back as 11,000 years ago. And although the land is rich with history, one can argue that not much has changed since the park was created in 1872, the invaluable blessing of having been protected as the nation's first national park. The unique geothermal features, pristine lakes and waterfalls, abundant and varied wildlife, and the different ecosystems have endured through the years.

As with all of the West, Yellowstone was traversed by various Native American tribes, including the Crow, Blackfeet, Nez Perce, and Shoshone, whose oral history teaches that they originated in this area. Although these nomads passed through the area, only a branch of the Shoshone, known as the "Sheep Eaters," made Yellowstone their home. The first Europeans to have visited the area were most likely fur traders and trappers who seem to have missed the unusual geothermal activity. Lewis and Clark's expedition bypassed the region completely. On their return voyage in 1806, however, John Colter separated from the group and ventured alone into the region. He is considered the first non-Native American to have seen the wondrous thermal features in the park. When Colter returned home three years later, his stories were considered suspicious. His tales of "bubbling ground," "mountains made of glass," and rivers where you could catch a fish and cook it without ever removing it from the water seemed preposterous to Easterners. Colter's descriptions of fire and brimstone quickly earned the place the nickname of "Colter's Hell." However, as more fur traders moved into the region, the stories of boiling mud, steaming land, and hot pools of water continued. Jim Bridger explored the

area in 1856 and is considered by some the "first geographer" of the region. He too shared wild descriptions that were met with similar skepticism.

The first organized expedition into the Yellowstone area was made in 1869 by David E. Folsom, Charles W. Cook, and William Peterson, who witnessed the breathtaking Tower Falls, Mud Volcano, Yellowstone Lake, and the geyser basins of the Firehole River. The Washburn-Langford-Doane expedition followed in 1870. It was the 1871 government-sponsored expedition into the region led by Ferdinand Vandeveer Hayden, however, that produced a detailed account of the area. The Hayden Geological Survey was accompanied by William Henry Jackson photographs and artwork by Henry W. Elliott and Thomas Moran. Photographs and spectacular paintings and drawings were splashed across magazines and newspapers around the East so that people could see the wonders of the region for the first time. It was this report, coupled with the earnest pleas of the men who had seen the area, that prodded Congress to grant the region national park status in 1872. That year, the park had 300 visitors.

Nathaniel Langford was the park's first superintendent, but without proper funding and staff he had difficulty protecting the land. Poachers and vandals exploited the park's natural resources, creating a state of general lawlessness. By 1886 the U.S. Army had entered the park to help regain control of the region. They built park structures, strengthened and enforced regulations, encouraged visitors, and made sure the land and wildlife were protected. Transportation infrastructure improvements also helped attract more visitors to the park. The Northern Pacific Railway extended to the town of Cinnabar, north of modern-day Gardiner, near the northern entrance of the park, and in 1915 automobiles were allowed into Yellowstone, making it more accessible to the masses. Following World War II, car travel exploded, and more than one million visitors came to the park in 1948.

The Army's leadership was not a long-term

The Sheep Eaters of Yellowstone

During the early 18th century, the horse was introduced to many of the Native American tribes that frequented the Yellowstone area. With the acquisition of this new, strong, and agile animal, people were able to spread out across the plains, traveling farther and longer to follow the bison. Hunting and warfare became more efficient almost overnight. A small group of Shoshone chose not to use horses or guns, however, and instead remained committed to their traditional mountain living.

The Sheep Eaters, also known as the Tukudika, were forest dwellers considered to be the only Native Americans to have inhabited Yellowstone year-round. They lived in *wikiups*—temporary shelters made of aspen poles, pine boughs, and other brush—rather than animal-hide tipis, and they traveled the mountain ridges rather than the river paths as their counterparts on the plains did. Living in small bands of 10-20 people, they relied on their wolf dogs to help them move provisions up and down the mountains. They were named for the animal whose migration they followed: the bighorn sheep. The Sheep Eaters developed highly effective sheep traps, the remains of which can be seen around Dubois, Wyoming, and they utilized the animal for both food and tools. They heated the sheep's horns in the hot springs of Yellowstone to mold them into exquisite and strong bows, powerful enough to drive an arrow through a bison. The reputation of these bows spread to other tribes and were highly sought-after. The European outsiders who made their way into the park during the early and mid-1800s described the Sheep Eaters as destitute and forlorn, not owning or seeming to want the modern trappings of the Plains Indians. Contemporary views suggest that these people revered their environment and ancestors' way of life and were more intent on maintaining their customs than competing and conquering.

Unfortunately, their traditions did not allow the Sheep Eaters to escape the same ultimate fate as other Native Americans. Devastated by smallpox and considered an obstacle to westward expansion, the Sheep Eaters fought the U.S. Army in the last Indian war in the Pacific Northwest. Unfairly accused of murdering five Chinese miners, the last remaining Sheep Eaters, a group of 51 people that included woman and children, were relentlessly pursued in the Idaho wilderness along the Middle Fork of the Salmon River in the fall of 1879. When the Army purportedly captured a woman who had just given birth, the remaining members of the tribe surrendered, exhausted, on October 1, and were sent to the Wind River Shoshone Reservation in Wyoming and Fort Hall Shoshone Bannock Reservation in Idaho.

solution to managing the new national park, and in 1916 the National Park Service was created. (The birthday of the Park Service is still celebrated every year on August 25 with free admission to Yellowstone for the day and a smattering of hilariously decorated Christmas trees around the park.) The rangers took responsibility for management of the park in 1918. Since then, the park's boundaries have been redrawn to encompass 2.2 million acres (roughly equivalent in size to the state of Connecticut), and wildlife management has been continuously refined as new science emerges. One fundamental change came as a result of the 1963 Leopold Report, which suggested that "natural regulation" was superior to the long-held unnatural management in which park managers controlled animal populations and altered the course of naturally occurring events like fire. The Ecological Process Management, as it has come to be called, is still the core philosophy behind park management today.

Yellowstone was named an International Biosphere Reserve in 1976 and a United Nations World Heritage Site in 1978. Both the grizzly bear and the gray wolf (reintroduced to the park in 1995) have seen enormous improvements to their endangered status due to Yellowstone's wildlife policies. In 1988 the park experienced the largest wildfires in its history, affecting more than a third of its land, and once again sparking furious debates about management of public resources and the value of natural ecosystems. In the spring of 2016, the U.S. Fish and Wildlife Service proposed removing grizzlies from the endangered species list in the Greater Yellowstone Ecosystem, a controversial decision that will likely be tied up in courts for years to come.

Modern-day Yellowstone is every bit as spellbinding as it was for John Colter and Jim Bridger and the scores of Native Americans who had traveled through the park long before them. But it is increasingly complex. Issues like bioprospecting, bison management in the face of the disease brucellosis, and the delisting criteria of endangered species loom large. Despite the fact that, thankfully, the physical features of Yellowstone—its mountain-scapes, geothermal features, and wildlife populations—remain largely untouched, an area of this size with more than four million visitors annually (nearly three times the populations of Montana and Wyoming combined!) cannot be immune to human influence. The challenge as we move forward is to determine a way to let Yellowstone age and evolve in its own way, on its own time, while giving people around the world access to this truly unique and spectacular place. It is we, the visitors, who have an opportunity to be changed forever by time spent in Yellowstone, and not the other way around.

PLANNING YOUR TIME

One could quite literally spend a lifetime in Yellowstone without being able to cover every last corner of this magnificent wilderness, but the reality is that most visitors only have a couple of days, at best, to spend exploring the park. Something like 98 percent of visitors never get more than a mile from the road, but it's easier than you might think—and incredibly worthwhile. Three days in the park is ideal, but if you have less time, there are ways to maximize every minute.

One important consideration in planning your time in Yellowstone is to know the season you'll be traveling. Summer offers magnificent scenery, usually good weather, and the inevitable "bear jam," when drivers hit the brakes as soon as someone spots anything resembling a brown furry creature. Summer visitors to Yellowstone need to plan for traffic and often for road construction delays. Fall and spring are fantastic times to see wildlife, but the weather can change in a heartbeat—at Yellowstone's high elevation, blizzards can strike nearly any month of the year. Winter is a magical time in the park, but cars are only permitted on one road in the northeast corner. All other travel is done via snow coach, guided snowmobile tour, or on skis and snowshoes. There is no wrong time to visit the park, but knowing the advantages and disadvantages of the various seasons will help you manage your expectations.

Assuming you'll be in Yellowstone when the roads are open to car traffic, there are five entrances and exits to Yellowstone, making loop trips relatively easy. From Montana, you can enter or exit the park from the northeast at Cooke City, from the north at Gardiner, or from the west at West Yellowstone. From Wyoming, you can enter the park from the east entrance nearest Cody or from the south through Grand Teton National Park. If you're going from one state to the next, there is no more spectacular route than through the heart of Yellowstone.

A cursory glance at a Yellowstone map will reveal the main roads, which form a figure eight in the heart of the park, and the access roads leading to and from the entrances. The majority of the park's big-name highlights—**Old Faithful, West Thumb Geyser Basin, Fishing Bridge, Grand Canyon of the Yellowstone, Norris and Mammoth Geyser Basins**—are accessible from the main loops. Depending on your time and your plan for accommodations, you could easily spend a full day driving each of the two loops. A third day would permit an opportunity for deeper exploration—perhaps a hike—and a leisurely exit from the park.

If time won't permit even one night in the park, it is still well worth driving through, just to get a sense of this magnificent and tremendously diverse place. Consider choosing one feature and pursuing it. To give yourself the best chance of seeing wolves, traveling between the north and northeast entrances is an excellent route during non-summer months. Geothermal aficionados will have no shortage of choices for seeing the park's impressive features, but to swim in them, try the **Boiling River,** a stretch of the Gardner River near Mammoth, which is swimmable year-round except during spring and early summer runoff. The **Firehole River** also offers excellent summer swimming not far from Old Faithful. Landlubbers might prefer a short hike into a less-famous geyser like **Lone Star,** just a few flat miles from Old Faithful.

The best advice is this: Get off the road, get out of your car, be smart, and come prepared to give yourself the opportunity to see and understand what makes Yellowstone America's first wonderland.

INFORMATION AND SERVICES

The best resource to familiarize yourself with the park and to help plan your trip is the **National Park Service** (307/344-7381, www.nps.gov). On the website, click on the link titled Plan Your Visit. The site also posts information about the different **Ranger Programs** being offered, including educational lectures and hikes.

Park Fees and Passes

Admission to the park is $30 per vehicle for seven days, $25 for motorcycles, and $15 for hikers and bicyclists. In 2016, entrance fees to the park were waived on 16 days, including January 18 (Martin Luther King Jr. Day), April 16-24 to celebrate National Park Week, August 25-28 for the National Park Service centennial, September 24 for National Public Lands Day, and November 11 for Veterans Day. Check the Yellowstone website before you travel to see if any fee-free days are on the horizon. The park is open year-round, but during the winter, cars can only access the park through the north and northeast entrances.

Visitors Centers

There are 10 visitors centers in and around the park. Since days and hours vary seasonally, it's a good idea to check the website (www.nps. gov) before you go into the park.

The **Albright Visitor Center at Mammoth Hot Springs** (307/344-2263) is open daily year-round and houses a bookstore, wildlife and history exhibits, and films on the park and its early visitors. The **Canyon Visitor Education Center** (307/344-2550) is open daily mid-April-early November and offers the best overview of the park's geology, including phenomenal supervolcano exhibits and a dynamic film. The **Fishing Bridge Visitor Center** (307/344-2450) is open daily late May-early October and is home to a bookstore, birds and wildlife exhibits, plus information on the lake's geology. The **Grant Village Visitor Center** (307/344-2650) is open daily late May-early October and offers information on fire in Yellowstone. The **Madison Information Station and Trailside Museum** (307/344-2821) at Madison Junction is open daily late May-late September and provides a bookstore as well as detailed information on the **Junior Ranger** program. The **Museum of the National Park Ranger** (307/344-7353) is located one mile north of Norris Geyser Basin and gives a good history of the park ranger profession. It is open daily late May-late September. The **Norris Geyser Basin Museum & Information Station** (307/344-2812) is open daily late May-early October and gives visitors an excellent overview of the hydrothermal features in the park. The **Old Faithful Visitor Education Center** is open daily mid-April-early November and includes exhibits, information, films, a bookstore, and geyser eruption predictions (307/344-2751). The **West Thumb Information Center** (307/344-2876) is open daily late May-early October and offers information about the West Thumb Geyser Basin on the shore of Yellowstone Lake. In West Yellowstone, the **West Yellowstone Visitor Information Center** (307/344-2876) is open daily May-September and early November-April, and on weekdays only October-early November. The center hosts a National Park Service desk, plus information and publications.

Entrance Stations

Yellowstone National Park is open 365 days a year, 24 hours a day. There are five entrance stations, three in Montana and two in Wyoming. The **North Entrance,** at Gardiner, Montana, is the only one open year-round to wheeled vehicles. The **Northeast Entrance** is located near the small communities of Cooke City and Silver Gate, Montana, and is generally open late May-mid-October depending upon weather and road conditions. The **West Entrance** is located in West Yellowstone, Montana, and is open to wheeled vehicles normally the third Friday in April-first Sunday in November. The **South Entrance,** 49 miles north of Jackson, Wyoming, at the border between Grand Teton National Park and Yellowstone, is open to wheeled vehicles typically the second Friday in May-first Sunday in November, and to snow coaches and snowmobiles mid-December-mid-March. The **East Entrance,** 53 miles west of Cody, Wyoming, is generally open to wheeled vehicles the first Friday in May-first Sunday in November. All entrances can be closed at any time due to weather and unscheduled changes. Visit www.nps.gov before your trip for up-to-date information, or call 307/344-2117 for recorded road and weather information.

Services

Xanterra Parks and Resorts (307/344-7901, www.yellowstonenationalparklodges.com) is the official concessionaire of Yellowstone, and all reservations for lodging, dining, and special activities in the park can be made through them.

If you encounter an **emergency** when traveling through the park, dial 911, but be aware that cell coverage is spotty. Emergency medical services are attended to by rangers. There are three **urgent care facilities**

inside Yellowstone. The clinic at **Mammoth** (307/344-7965) is open year-round, and the clinics at **Lake** (307/242-7241) and **Old Faithful** (307/344-7325) are open in the summer.

TRANSPORTATION
Getting There
BY AIR
Yellowstone is about 90 miles from the airports in Bozeman and Billings, 49 miles from the airport in Jackson Hole, and 52 miles from the airport in Cody. The **Yellowstone Airport** (WYS, 607 Airport Rd., West Yellowstone, www.yellowstoneairport.org, 406/646-7631) is served by **Delta** (800/221-1212, www.delta.com) and is only open late May-late September.

BY CAR
The North Entrance at Gardiner, which is the only entrance open year-round to cars, is 83 miles south of Bozeman and 170 miles southwest of Billings. The Northeast Entrance at Cooke City is 124 miles, including the spectacular Beartooth Highway, from Billings. The West Entrance at West Yellowstone is 90 miles south of Bozeman. The East Entrance is 53 miles west of Cody. The South Entrance is 49 miles north of Jackson, Wyoming.

BY BUS
Bus service with **Karst Stage** (800/845-2778, www.karststage.com) is available from Bozeman to West Yellowstone year-round and to Gardiner during the winter and summer seasons.

Getting Around
PRIVATE VEHICLES
Your best bet to see the park on your own terms is to go by car. The nearest car-rental agencies are **Budget, Avis,** and **Big Sky Car Rentals** (800/231-5991), available in West Yellowstone. Cars can also be rented from airports in Billings, Bozeman, Cody, and Jackson Hole.

When planning your drive through

Yellowstone, it is best to fill up your tank outside the park. Once inside, the gas prices you'll encounter tend to be extremely high, and options are quite limited. Gas stations are located within the park at Canyon, Fishing Bridge, Grant Village, Mammoth, Upper and Lower Old Faithful, and Tower Junction. They are generally open late spring-early fall.

One of the things that makes Yellowstone so wild and enchanting is its utter unpredictability—something that relates to wildlife, weather, and, unfortunately, road conditions. A 20-year $300-million plan is currently afoot to address the structural deficiencies of Yellowstone's roads. Plan to keep a close watch on road closures and delays that can happen any time of year because of construction, bad weather, or even fire. For a 24-hour road report, check **Road Construction Delays and Closures** (307/344-2117, www.nps.gov). Information on state roads is available from the **Montana Department of Transportation** (800/226-7623, www.mdt511.com) and the **Wyoming Department of Transportation** (888/996-7623, www.wyoroad.info). **National Weather Service** (www.crh.noaa.gov) reports are available for Yellowstone and Grand Teton National Parks.

TOURS

Xanterra (307/344-7311, www.yellowstonenationalparklodges.com) offers a variety of different bus tours of the park during the summer, including historic Yellow Bus tours that range 1-12 hours. The Grand Loop Tour departs daily from Gardiner and Mammoth and covers the entire park in one day. Other options include early morning or evening wildlife tours, lake sunset tours, geyser gazers, Lamar Valley wildlife expeditions, photo safaris, boat tours, fishing trips, and custom guided tours.

Depending upon your particular interests, there are a range of companies outside the park that offer specialized tours of Yellowstone. The only one inside the park, and an outstanding option, is the **Yellowstone Association Institute** (406/848-2400, www.yellowstoneassociation.org). Courses are broken into summer and winter semesters, and course fees begin around $150 with a tuition discount for YA members. The courses are engaging and are taught by experts in their fields. Using Yellowstone as their classroom, the instructors concentrate on "individual aspects of the ecosystem." During the summer, you can take the "Behind the Scenes of Wolf Management and Ecology" course led by a wolf biologist, or "Mammal Signs: Interpreting Tracks, Scat, and Hair" with an animal tracker. Classes also focus on flora with courses such as "The Art of Wildflower Identification"; other options include "Yellowstone's Geoecosystem" and "Wilderness First Aid." The institute can provide unique (and inexpensive) lodging in its two field campuses, in Gardiner and the Lamar Valley. Or it can include standard hotel lodging at park hotels. If you take the time to browse through the course catalog, you will likely find something geared to your interests. This is one of the best ways to get an in-depth insider's view of Yellowstone.

Other tour operators that offer a range of excursions in the park include **Yellowstone Tour & Travel** (800/221-1151, www.yellowstone-travel.com), a full-service travel agency in West Yellowstone that can book everything from accommodations and tours to complete packages, and **Yellowstone Alpen Guides** (555 Yellowstone Ave., 406/646-9591 or 800/858-3502, www.yellowstoneguides.com, from $90 adults, $85 seniors, $80 children under 16), also in West Yellowstone, which offers a fantastic array of naturalist-guided tours year-round.

PLANTS AND ANIMALS

Yellowstone is a living, breathing, evolving ecosystem that is home to a diversity of high alpine, subalpine, and forest plants (more than 1,000 native species of flowering plants) and an extraordinary number of animals (including 67 mammal species). It is fascinating to understand how the flora and fauna relate—and react—to one another throughout the park.

Plants

What makes the plant life in Yellowstone so interesting is neither the abundance nor the variety but rather the relationship between the plants and their environment and the way they are determined and shaped by forces of geology, climate, fire, insect infestation, drought, flood, and not least of all, wildlife. In various places throughout the park, for example, visitors will notice small fenced areas where grazing animals like elk, deer, and bison do not have access. The flora is decidedly different when it is protected from herbivores. The massive burns of 1988 have given rise to a plant-lover's paradise where hot pink fireweed is among the first to recolonize the blackened areas. The geothermal areas have their own rare and unique plant communities. And the reintroduction of wolves caused the movements of elk to be more sporadic as they tried to avoid being eaten, which led to an increase in the number of willows and a resulting increase in various animals, including beavers, that thrive on willows. These chains of events linking plants, animals, and the natural forces that control the park are endless and fascinating.

Animals

For many, the fauna in Yellowstone is the main event. With large mammals such as elk, bison, bighorn sheep, pronghorn, bears, wolves, and mountain lions, Yellowstone is among the best areas in the country to see wildlife in its natural habitat. For those willing to get up early and be patient enough to wait, sometimes for hours, Yellowstone is like the Discovery Channel brought to life.

There are a few species of reptiles and amphibians known to inhabit the park—10 in all—thanks to Yellowstone's cool, dry climate, and some 330 species of birds have been documented since the park's 1872 founding, ranging from tiny calliope hummingbirds to majestic trumpeter swans.

But it's the big animals that draw more than four million people to the park annually. The omnipresent bison are the largest animal in the park, with males (bulls) weighing upwards of 1,800 pounds and females (cows) averaging about 1,000 pounds. Yellowstone is the only place in the Lower 48 where wild bison have existed since prehistoric times. The herd dropped to near-extinction levels at the turn of the 20th century with only 50 animals within the park boundaries. The importation of 21 bison from private herds and the subsequent 50 years of repopulation efforts led to a marked increase in numbers. By 2006 some 3,500 of these wild, woolly behemoths once again roamed the high prairies of Yellowstone, but significant population fluctuations occur, primarily because of fears surrounding the disease brucellosis. In a given year, the bison population in Yellowstone ranges 2,300-5,000 animals, with the population in 2015 hovering around the high end at 4,900.

The most recent official count in 2014 placed the number of grizzly bears in the park at 150, with another 674-839 living within the Greater Yellowstone Ecosystem, and likely three to four times as many black bears. Gray wolves were reintroduced to the park (after being entirely killed off in the area) in 1995, and in 2014 there were 95 wolves in 10 packs living primarily within the park boundaries, and as many as 500 living in the Greater Yellowstone Ecosystem. Wolverines and lynx live within the park but are rarely seen. Coyotes are plentiful and often visible from cars, andsomewhere between 26 and 42 mountain lions inhabit the park. Elk populations soar in the summer months to 10,000-20,000 animals in six or seven herds, compared to the roughly 5,000 elk that winter in the park, while moose, hard hit by the fires of 1988, number fewer than 200. In the northern Yellowstone area, there are 421 bighorn sheep, with roughly 200 in the park. There are also 208 nonnative mountain goats in and around Yellowstone.

Finding the animals means knowing their habitats, being willing to wait during the

The Ecology of Fire

In 1988, wildfires blazed through Yellowstone National Park. To quell the flames, the largest firefighting effort in U.S. history was organized, involving 25,000 people and $120 million, but it was the first snowfall of the season that would eventually rein in the fire. The fires began in July and burned until November. More than 793,000 acres, roughly one-third of the park, were affected, 67 structures were destroyed, and 345 elk and 63 other large mammals died as a direct result of the fire. The entire nation watched in horror as the first national park burned. The park's fire management plan consequently came under intense scrutiny. The question on everyone's lips was, "How could this have happened?"

During the first half of the 20th century, it was widely believed that nothing good came of wildfire. In the 1940s and 1950s, all fires that occurred in the park, whether of natural origin or caused by people, were immediately suppressed. During the 1960s, however, the tide shifted subtly as the ecological benefits of fire were studied. Findings showed that fire was a natural condition that helped maintain balance in the wild. Fires cleaned out understory and residual dead plant matter, creating less competition between tree species for important nutrients and natural elements. It was determined that, until humans got involved, wildfires had always been a part of the ecosystem and in fact necessary to preserve healthy and continuous life cycles of plants and trees. The lodgepole pine, for example, which makes up an enormous percentage of Yellowstone's forests, has two kinds of cones, one of which is called a serotinous cone. The pitch sealing the serotinous cone needs to be heated by fire in order to release the seeds and continue the species. Without fire, the tree would not be able to regenerate as successfully.

By the 1970s, the park decided to allow wildfires caused by lightning to burn under controlled conditions. From the time the park established this natural fire policy until 1988, they had allowed 235 fires to burn; only 10 of those were larger than 100 acres, and in total 33,759 acres had been burned. In June 1988 the park was experiencing a drought, and it turned out to be the driest year in the park's history. Early summer storms produced lightning without rainfall, and 20 fires erupted. Eleven of them self-extinguished, and the rest were monitored; by mid-July only 8,500 acres had burned. Within a week, park managers agreed to extinguish the fires because of the extremely dry conditions. Strong winds made that impossible, however, and within a week 99,000 acres had burned. By September, in order for emergency workers to battle the blaze, the park had to close to visitors for the first time in its history.

When spring came, no one knew what to expect. It was with some trepidation that people went into Yellowstone. Miraculously, the earth was green and vibrant amid the fire-blackened swaths. With the exception of the moose, which lost a significant portion of their forested habitat, the animal populations appeared as if nothing had ever happened. Elk were even reported munching on the burned bark. Yellowstone, it seemed, was different—better and healthier.

As visitors marveled at the park's rebirth, park managers reevaluated their fire management policy and updated it in 1992 with stricter guidelines for managing natural fires. In 2004 they made further additions by defining clear parameters for fires, including size, weather conditions, and the potential for danger. The overriding philosophy today is that naturally occurring fire maintains a balance in the natural ecosystem of Yellowstone and that the land, which has adapted to large wildfires, ultimately reaps its benefits.

edges of daylight, and oftentimes just plain getting lucky. A number of excellent wildlife spotting guides are available through the **Yellowstone Association** (www.yellowstoneassociation.org), but the most obvious place to start is by asking any of the rangers at the park's various visitors centers. They can tell you about recent predatory kills, bear and wolf activity, elk and bison migrations, and the most up-to-date sightings of any number of animals.

As is true with nearly every feature of the park, the importance of safety in the face of wildlife cannot be overstated. Just check out

YouTube for any number of videos highlighting ill-advised visitor interactions with wildlife. Be certain to stay at least 25 yards away from bison and elk and at least 100 yards away from bears, wolves, and other predators. If the animals change their behavior because of your presence, if they stop eating to look at you, for example, you are too close and are creating a significant and perhaps even life-threatening hazard for both the animal and yourself. Always remember that you are the visitor here and they are the residents; show proper respect.

Geothermal Features

If the animals are what bring people to Yellowstone, the geothermal features are what transfix them and lure them back year after year.

The world's largest concentration of thermal features—more than 10,000 in all—Yellowstone bursts to life with geysers, hot springs, fumaroles (steam vents), and mud pots. There are six grand geysers, of which **Old Faithful** is the most famous, and more than 300 lesser geysers. Throughout the park are a number of basins where visitors can see all four types of thermal features, including **Norris Geyser Basin.**

The thermal features in Yellowstone are an indication of the region's volcanic past, present, and future, and as such they are in constant states of change. Small but daily earthquakes cause shifts in activity and temperature. The travertine **Mammoth Terraces** are literally growing and changing on a daily basis to the point that the boardwalks have had to be altered to protect visitors from different flows of searing hot water.

As miraculous as these water features are to see—with dramatic color displays and water dances that put Las Vegas's Bellagio fountains to shame—and to smell (think rotten eggs), what you can't see is perhaps even more compelling: thermophiles, heat-loving

A Yellowstone bear lumbers down the road.

microorganisms that inhabit the geothermal features throughout the park. A source of ongoing scientific study, these thermophiles are modern examples of the earth's first life forms and are responsible for the discovery of DNA fingerprinting.

As spellbinding as they are, particularly in winter when the warm steam beckons, it is critically important to stay on boardwalks in geothermal areas and never touch the water. In addition to being boiling hot, many features are highly acidic or alkaline and could cause extreme chemical burns. The ground around the features is often thin and unstable, occasionally allowing animals to break through and be cooked. Twenty-one people have died in Yellowstone's thermal features, including one man who strayed off the boardwalk in 2016 to get a closer look and broke through the thin crust; the water was so hot that by the time help arrived, there were no remains to collect.

Yellowstone's Supervolcano

It's always interesting to watch visitors' expressions when you tell them that in Yellowstone National Park they are standing atop one of the world's largest active supervolcanos . . . and that it is overdue for an apocalyptic eruption. While these facts are true, the reality is much less threatening. Indeed there have been three phenomenal eruptions over the course of the last two million years, and the patterns do indicate that the volcano is overdue to erupt. But scientists agree that the chances of a massive eruption in the next 1,000 or even 10,000 years are very slight. For the time being, anyway, the supervolcano that gives rise to Yellowstone's extraordinary geothermal features is all bark and no bite—thankfully.

The first supervolcanic eruption 2.1 million years ago was 6,000 times more powerful than the 1980 eruption of Mount St. Helens, spouting rock and ash in every direction from Texas to Canada, Missouri to California. The eruption emptied the magma chamber located just underneath the park and caused a massive sinking of the earth, known as a caldera, within the confines of what is now the park. Small lava flows filled in the perimeter of the Huckleberry Ridge Caldera over the course of hundreds of thousands of years.

The second major, but smaller, eruption occurred 1.3 million years ago and created the Henry's Fork Caldera. The most recent massive eruption took place roughly 640,000 years ago and created the Yellowstone Caldera, which is 30 by 45 miles in size. The perimeter of the Yellowstone Caldera is still visible in places throughout the park. Hike up Mount Washburn on Dunraven Pass between Canyon and Tower, look south, and you will see the vast caldera formed by the most recent eruption. The caldera rim is also visible at Gibbon Falls, Lewis Falls, and Lake Butte. As you drive between Mammoth and Gardiner, look at Mount Everts to the east and you will see layers of ash from the various eruptions.

But volcanic activity is not a thing of the past in Yellowstone. The magma, which some scientists think is just 5 miles beneath the surface of the park in places as opposed to the typical 40, has created two enormous bulges, known as resurgent domes, near Sour Creek and Mallard Lake. The Sour Creek Dome is growing at an impressive rate of 1.5 inches per year, causing Yellowstone Lake to tip southward, leaving docks on the north side completely out of the water and flooding the forested shore of the south side. In addition, there are roughly 2,000 earthquakes every year centered in Yellowstone, most of which cannot be felt. In 2014, however, a 4.8-magnitude quake occurred four miles from Norris Geyser Basin. The earthquakes shift geothermal activity in the park and keep the natural plumbing system that feeds the geyser basins flowing. They also suggest volcanic activity. In early 2010, a series of more than 3,200 small earthquakes (the largest registered 3.8 on the Richter scale) rocked the park, with 16 quakes registering a magnitude greater than 3.0. A 1985 swarm recorded more than 3,000 earthquakes over three months, with the largest registering at 4.9 on the Richter scale.

Still, the scientists at the Yellowstone Volcano Observatory have no reason to suspect that an eruption, or even a lava flow, is imminent. For more than three decades, scientists have been monitoring the region for precursors to volcanic eruptions—earthquake swarms, rapid ground deformation, gas releases, and lava flows—and although there is activity, none of it suggests anything immediately foreboding. Current real-time monitoring data, including earthquake activity and deformation, are available online at http://volcanoes.usgs.gov. The bottom line is that the volcano is real and active, but certainly not a threat in the immediate future, and not a reason to stay away from this awe-inspiring place.

Gardiner

Named rather inauspiciously for a cannibalistic mountain man who allegedly got rid of his wives year after year by, ahem, eating them, Gardiner (population 875, elevation 5,314) is actually a cute little town with plenty of places to stay, eat, and stock up, and has ideal proximity to the park. The only year-round entrance to Yellowstone for automobiles, this scrubby little tourist town has a charm and an identity all its own. The Yellowstone River cuts a canyon beside the main drag, which allows for plenty of river-runner hangouts. Few other places in the world have elk congregating in the churchyard or on the front lawns of most of the motels in town. And where else do high school football players have to dodge bison dung as they're running for a touchdown? The town's architecture is a combination of glorious wood and stone "parkitecture" buildings alongside old-school Western-style buildings complete with false fronts. The towering Roosevelt Arch, built in 1903 and dedicated by Yellowstone champion Teddy Roosevelt himself, welcomes visitors to the park with its inspiring slogan, "For the Benefit and Enjoyment of the People." Yes, Gardiner is built around its proximity to the park, but the town has maintained its integrity by preserving its history and making the most of its surroundings.

SIGHTS
★ Boiling River

Halfway between Gardiner and Mammoth Hot Springs, straddling the Montana-Wyoming border and the 45th parallel, the halfway point between the equator and the North Pole, is the Boiling River, one of only two swimmable thermal features in Yellowstone. From the clearly marked parking area, visitors amble upstream along a 0.5-mile rocky path running parallel to the Gardner River. Where the trail ends and the steam envelops almost everything, a gushing hot spring called the Boiling River flows into the otherwise icy Gardner River. The hot and cold waters mix to a perfect temperature that can be enjoyed year-round. The area is open during daylight hours only, and all swimmers must wear a bathing suit. The Boiling River

The town of Gardiner is just outside the northern entrance of the park.

is closed each year during spring and early summer runoff, when temperature fluctuations and rushing water put swimmers at risk. Alcohol is not permitted.

Kids and adults alike marvel at the floating Day-Glo green algae. The water should not be ingested. Bison and elk frequent the area, and despite the frequent crowds of people (note that 20 people constitute a crowd in this part of the West), this is one of the most unique and unforgettable ways to enjoy a few hours in Yellowstone.

ENTERTAINMENT AND EVENTS

The biggest event of the year in this gateway community is the **Annual NRA Gardiner Rodeo** (406/848-7971, $10 adults), usually held in June over Father's Day weekend. The rodeo is held in the Jim Duffy arena at the northern end of town off U.S. Highway 89 and includes the usual competitions such as bull riding and bareback bronc riding. Women and juniors compete in barrel racing and break-away roping. The first night of the rodeo is followed by a dance at the Gardiner Community Center, and the following day the chamber of commerce hosts a parade downtown. This is a great small-town rodeo.

But Gardiner is far from a one-event town. The **Annual Chomp & Stomp** (406/848-7971, www.gardinerchamber.com) in late February is a chili cook-off with live bluegrass music that benefits the Gardiner Community Center. Also in late February, the **Jardine Ski Run** is a 5-mile groomed track race where outlandish costumes are appreciated as much if not more than speed. Another worthwhile pursuit for the active is the **Park to Paradise Triathlon** in early May, which includes a 17.5-mile bike, 4-mile run, and 7-mile river paddle. The much less demanding and very family-friendly **Annual Brewfest** (406/848-7971, $10 entrance pays for 2 free tastings, $2 each additional tasting) happens in mid-August and raises money for the local chamber with live entertainment, food, crafts, microbrews,

and fun kids' activities like soda-tasting, face-painting, horseshoes, and kites. For more information on these events, contact the Gardiner Chamber of Commerce (406/848-7971, www.gardinerchamber.com).

SPORTS AND RECREATION
Fishing and Boating

The Yellowstone is the longest free-flowing river in the Lower 48, and as such it offers excellent boating and fishing opportunities. With the river plunging through town on its way to Yankee Jim Canyon, Gardiner is home to several outfitters that can whet your appetite for adventure, trout, or both. The **Flying Pig Adventure Company** (511 Scott St., 888/792-9193, www.flyingpigrafting.com, May-Sept., 2-hour raft trip $42 adults, $32 children 12 and under) is a full-service outfitter offering guided white-water rafting, horseback rides, wildlife safaris, and cowboy cookouts. **Yellowstone Raft Company** (111 2nd St., 406/848-7777 or 800/858-7781, www.yellowstoneraft.com, May-Sept., half-day raft trip $42 adults, $32 children 6-12) was established in 1978 and has an excellent reputation for experienced guides and top-of-the-line equipment. For adrenaline junkies, Yellowstone Raft Company offers sit-on-top kayak instruction and adventures.

For anglers eager to wet a line in or out of the park in search of native cutthroats or brown trout, **Park's Fly Shop** (202 2nd St. S., 406/848-7314, www.parksflyshop.com, 9am-5pm Mon.-Sat, 10am-4pm Sun., extended hours in summer) is the best place to start. This is an old-school shop with a 1920s cash register—nothing fancy here. It offers half-day trips for two people starting around $350, and full-day trips for two from around $495. Anglers can pick up their licenses and any supplies in the retail shop, which stays open year-round. And since Park's has been serving the area since 1953, its guides are keenly aware of the spots where the fish greatly outnumber the anglers.

Hiking

Yellowstone is a hiker's paradise, and unless you have a pet that needs to stretch its legs, hiking just outside the park is like spending the day in the Disney World parking lot. Not that there isn't stunning country in every direction, but there is something particularly alluring about hiking within the boundaries of the park.

That said, some 4.7 miles south of the terraces at Mammoth Hot Springs, on the left-hand side after the Golden Gate Bridge, is the **Glen Creek Trailhead** and a small dirt parking lot. A range of wonderful hikes start from this point. Across the street on the west side of the road, a trail leads through **The Hoodoos,** massive travertine boulders that look otherworldly in this setting, and down the mountain 3.8 miles back to Mammoth. If you cannot arrange either a drop-off at the trailhead or a shuttle, the return trip, another 3.8 miles, climbs constantly for nearly 1,000 vertical feet. Another more ambitious hike is the 9.2-mile round-trip to **Osprey Falls.** The first 4 miles are easy and flat, following an abandoned roadbed popular with mountain bikers. A blink-and-you'll-miss-it spur trail off the south side of the road leads hikers down into Sheepeater Canyon and the remaining 0.6 mile to the mesmerizing 150-foot falls. Relax, have a snack, and save your energy for the 800-vertical-foot climb back up to the road. **Bunsen Peak** offers hikers an interesting walk through an entirely burned forest and all of its colorful rebirth, as well as a stunning view from the 8,500-foot summit. The climb is steep: 1,300 vertical feet over 2.1 miles. Try to ignore the hum of the radio tower near the summit, easily accomplished when the summit view fills your senses.

FOOD

Known since 1960 for its "Hateful Hamburgers" and the huge personality of its owner, Helen, this fabulous burger joint was sold to the Wild West Rafting Company and is now known as ★ **Wild West Corral** (Hwy. 89 S., across from the Super 8 Motel,

406/848-7627, 11am-11pm daily May-Oct., burgers $7-14). Even without Helen, this is still the kind of place you might easily drive 100 miles to for the burgers, shakes, and old-school ambience. The limited seating is mostly outside, and there is often a line of people waiting to order. But none of that will matter when you take your first bite of a bison bacon cheeseburger or a perfectly grilled elk burger. Wild West Corral even managed to improve on Helen's by expanding the menu and cleaning the place up a bit. This is still a little slice of hamburger paradise—if you like that sort of thing.

Just over the river toward the park, the **K-Bar Pizza** (202 Main St., 406/848-9995, www.kbarmontana.com, 4pm-9:30pm Mon.-Thurs., 4pm-10pm Fri., 11am-11pm Sat.-Sun., large pizzas $18-24) is a classic bar that's been dishing up surprisingly good homemade pizza since 1953. **The Raven Grill** (118 Park St., 406/848-9171, 5pm-10pm daily mid-Apr.-mid-Oct., $10-28) boasts a small but excellent menu long on comfort food and made from scratch. It also serves cocktails, including a mean Montana Huckleberry Moscow Mule. For a good, hearty breakfast, excellent pastries, fresh Mexican food, and burgers, the **Yellowstone Grill** (404 Scott St., 406/848-9433, 7am-10pm Tues.-Sun., $6-10) is sure to please. Remember though, this is small-town Montana. Sometimes the place closes when short-staffed. Or when the owners' youngest son has a Legion baseball game. Be glad for that; the important stuff still matters here. You can always have a late lunch.

ACCOMMODATIONS

Gardiner is built to accommodate the overflow from the park, but in reality, many of the little motels have more charm and much better value, particularly in non-summer months, than those inside the park. For the most part, it's hard to go wrong in Gardiner. There are plenty of small cabins and larger vacation rentals in the area. The folk Victorian ★ **Gardiner Guest House** (112 Main St. E., 406/848-9414 or 406/848-7314, www.gardinerguesthouse.com, $90-400 depending on season and number of rooms) welcomes both children and pets and offers three modest but comfortable guest rooms and a cabin. Owners Richard and Nance Parks are longtime residents and an extensive source of information on the area. His fly shop and guiding company, **Park's Fly Shop** (202 2nd St. S., 406/848-7314, www.parksflyshop.com), is one of the oldest businesses in town. **Yellowstone Park Riverfront Cabins** (505 S. Yellowstone, 406/570-4500, www.cabinsontheyellowstone. com, $225-299) offers comfortable cabins in a quiet location above the river. Another option for small, basic, and reasonably priced cottages right in town is **Hillcrest Cottages** (400 Scott St., 406/848-7353 or 800/970-7353, www.hillcrestcottages.com, early May-mid-Oct., $92-170). The **Flying Pig Raft Company** (511 Scott St. W., 866/264-8448, www.flyingpigrafting.com) offers a host of higher-end vacation rentals ranging from cozy canvas wall tents on a nearby ranch ($150) and cabins ($190-275) to an enormous private lodge ($599) that can sleep up to 15. **Above the Rest Lodge** (8 Above the Rest Ln., 406/848-7747 or 800/406-7748, www.abovetherestlodge.com, cabin $135 for 2 people) is hardly glamorous, but it is comfortable, and the views over the river and into the park are breathtaking.

For more standard hotels, there is a decent selection ranging from the riverfront **Absaroka Lodge** (310 Scott St., 406/848-7414, www.yellowstonemotel.com, $150-175), where each room has its own balcony, and the **Comfort Inn** (107 Hellroaring St., 406/848-7536 or 800/424-6423, www.comfortinn.com, $218-296) to the barebones but clean and pet-friendly **Super 8** (702 Scott St. W., 406/848-7401, www.yellowstonesuper8.com, $75-221) and recently renovated **Rodeway Inn &**

Suites (109 Hellroaring St., 406/848-7520, www.travelodge.com, $244-349).

CAMPING

The difference between camping outside the park and inside Yellowstone is simply that you need to focus on reservations and availability instead of permits and regulations. There are six campgrounds in Gardiner—four national forest campgrounds and two private ones. The **Yellowstone RV Park & Campground** (121 U.S. 89 S., 406/848-7496, May-Oct., 46 sites including pull-through and tent sites) is ideally situated on the Yellowstone River just 1.3 miles north of the park entrance.

Those in search of a more rustic experience might enjoy the pack-in, pack-out **Bear Creek Campground** (Forest Rd. 493, 10.5 miles northeast of Gardiner, 406/848-7375, 4 sites with no services, mid-June-late Oct. depending on weather, free) or the **Timber Camp Campground** (Forest Rd. 493, 9.5 miles northeast of Gardiner, 406/848-7375, no services, mid-June-late Oct. depending on weather, free), both of which are small, isolated, and pleasantly rustic.

INFORMATION AND SERVICES

For information on Gardiner and the area around it, the **Gardiner Chamber of Commerce** (222 Park St., 406/848-7971, www.gardinerchamber.com, 9am-5pm Mon. and Wed.-Thurs., 9am-noon Tues. and Fri., extended summer hours) is an excellent and welcoming resource. Just a couple of doorways down, the headquarters of the **Yellowstone Association** (308 Park St., 406/848-2400, www.yellowstoneassociation.org, 8am-8pm daily) offers information about the park, as well as its own phenomenal educational tours. A great gift shop also is on-site, and the nicest bathrooms you have likely seen in a while.

The Northern Loop

With striking panoramas, wonderful thermals, plentiful wildlife, and year-round vehicle access between the north and northeast entrances, this is one of the most underappreciated parts of the park. The accommodations and dining are not as fancy as elsewhere, but the crowds are more manageable, and the experience is just as good or better. Phenomenal highlights include Mammoth Hot Springs, the Lamar Valley, Tower Falls, Dunraven Pass, the Grand Canyon of the Yellowstone, and Norris Geyser Basin.

SIGHTS
★ Mammoth and the Mammoth Hot Springs Terraces

Just five miles into the park and up the road from Gardiner, Mammoth is the primary northern hub of Yellowstone National Park. It is also an interesting little community in its own right, with a small medical center, the most beautiful post office in the West, and a magnificent stone church. The town of Mammoth, once known as Fort Yellowstone, was essentially built by the U.S. Army during its 1886-1918 occupation. Thinking they were on a temporary assignment, the soldiers erected canvas wall tents and lived in them through five harsh winters. In 1890, Congress set aside $50,000 for the construction of a permanent post, a stately collection of stone colonial revival-style buildings, most of which are still in use today.

The recently renovated **Albright Visitor Center** (307/344-2263, 8am-7pm daily late May-Sept., 9am-5pm daily Oct.-late May) is a must-see. There are films, history and wildlife exhibits, and a small but excellent selection of books and videos in the shop run by the Yellowstone Association (406/848-2400, www.yellowstoneassociation.org). While at the center, don't miss seeing some of the artwork produced during the 1871 Hayden Geological Survey of the park, including quality reproductions of painter Thomas Moran's famous watercolor sketches, and original photographs by William Henry Jackson. Rangers on staff can usually give you up-to-date animal sightings and activity reports. The flush toilets (the last for a while) are located downstairs.

The primary ecological attraction in Mammoth (other than the elk often seen lounging around and nibbling on the green grass) can be found on the **Mammoth Hot Springs Terraces.** Since the days of the earliest stagecoach trails into the park, they have been a visual and olfactory marvel for visitors. The Hayden Expedition named the area White Mountain Hot Spring for the cream-colored, steplike travertine terraces.

Beneath the ground, the Norris-Mammoth fault carries superheated water rich in dissolved calcium and bicarbonate. As the water emerges through cracks in the surface, carbon dioxide is released as a gas, and the carbonate combines with calcium to form travertine. The mountain is continuously growing as travertine is deposited and then shifted as the cracks are sealed and the mineral-laden water emerges somewhere else. For frequent visitors to the park, vast changes are noticeable from one visit to the next. In addition to changes in shape and water flow, the colors at Mammoth can vary dramatically from one day to the next. Not only does travertine morph from bright white when it is new to cream and then gray as it is exposed to the elements, the cyanobacteria create fabulous color shifts too—from turquoise to green and yellow to red and brown, depending on water temperatures, available sunlight, and pH levels.

Liberty Cap, at the base of the terraces, is an excellent example of a dormant spring, where all but the core cone has been eroded away. **Minerva** and **Canary Spring and Terrace** are two other springs worth seeing.

Their temperatures average around 160°F, and when they are flowing they often put on marvelous color displays.

Tower Falls

Eighteen scenic miles down the road from Mammoth Hot Springs—past **Undine Falls** and **Blacktail Plateau,** where you can see deer, elk, and bison along with some impressive lookouts—is **Tower Junction** and the breathtaking Tower Falls. The waterfall itself cascades 132 feet from volcanic basalt. A popular spot with visitors and just steps from the parking lot, this is not the ideal place for solitude, but it is lovely to see.

Dunraven Pass

Between Tower and the dramatic Grand Canyon of the Yellowstone is one of the most nerve-racking and perhaps most beautiful drives in the park. Climbing up the flanks of **Mount Washburn,** Dunraven Pass is the highest road elevation in the park. The spectacular summit of the road tops out at 8,859 feet and offers impressive views of Yellowstone's caldera rim. Eagle eyes can also spot the nearby Grand Canyon of the Yellowstone. Hikers will have no shortage of trailheads to start from. The whitebark pines that grow along the road are a critical and dwindling food source for grizzly bears, so keep your eyes open. Because of its extreme altitude and relative exposure, Dunraven Pass is one of the last roads to open in the spring and one of the first to close when bad weather hits. For current road information, call 307/344-2117.

★ Grand Canyon of the Yellowstone

Yellowstone's most recent volcanic explosion, some 600,000 years ago, created a massive caldera and subsequent lava flows, one of which was called the Canyon Rhyolite flow, in the area that is now known as the Grand Canyon of the Yellowstone. This particular lava flow was impacted by a thermal basin, which altered the rhyolite and created the beautiful palette of colors in the rock through constant heating and cooling. Over time, lakes, rivers, and glaciers formed in the region, and the relatively soft rhyolite was easily carved away. Roughly 10,000 years ago, the last of the area's glaciers melted, causing a rush of water to carve the canyon into the form it has today. The 20-mile-long canyon is still growing thanks to the forces of erosion, including water, wind, and earthquakes. A number of

You can practically watch limestone form as the water cools at the Mammoth Hot Springs Terraces.

terrific lookouts are on both the North and South Rims of the canyon.

Before setting out for the canyon itself, visitors are advised to visit the new **Canyon Visitor Education Center** (307/344-2550, 8am-8pm daily late May-early Sept., 8am-6pm daily early Sept.-late Sept., 9am-5pm daily early Oct.-early Nov.), which has an outstanding and vast exhibit on Yellowstone's supervolcano, geothermal activity, and other natural history. In fact, this should be a mandatory stop for every visitor who might otherwise have no appreciation for the region's fascinating geology.

On the **North Rim,** don't miss **Inspiration Point,** a natural viewing platform that gives a bird's-eye view both up and down the river. Nathaniel Langford, who would go on to be the park's first superintendent, stood in the same spot with the Washburn Expedition in 1870. He wrote:

> Standing there or rather lying there for greater safety, I thought how utterly impossible it would be to describe to another the sensations inspired by such a presence. As I took in the scene, I realized my own littleness, my helplessness, my dread exposure to destruction, my inability to cope with or even comprehend the mighty architecture of nature.

Look down, if you dare, among the nooks and crannies of rock to try to spot nesting ospreys.

Another phenomenal viewing platform can be found at **Lookout Point,** where visitors can gaze from afar at the thundering Lower Falls of the Yellowstone. Visitors who want to get closer to the spray of the falls and don't mind a long hike down, and back up again, can head toward the base of the falls at **Red Rock Point.** It's a 0.5-mile trip one-way that drops more than 500 vertical feet. There is another platform at the top of the 308-foot falls aptly named the **Brink of the Lower Falls.** This lookout also involves a 0.5-mile hike and a 600-foot elevation loss. The **Upper Falls** are just over one-third the size of the lower falls, at 109 feet, but they are worth a gander and can be easily accessed at the **Brink of the Upper Falls.** Mountain man Jim Bridger purportedly regaled friends with tales of the Upper Falls as early as 1846 and urged them to see it for themselves.

From the **South Rim,** visitors can see the Upper Falls from the **Upper Falls Viewpoint.** A trail that dates back to 1898, **Uncle Tom's Trail** still takes hardy hikers to

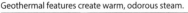
Geothermal features create warm, odorous steam.

the base of the **Lower Falls.** The trail down loses 500 vertical feet through a series of 300 stairs and paved inclines, but what goes down must come up again. From **Artist Point,** one of the largest and most inspiring lookouts, visitors get a glorious view of the distant Lower Falls and the river as it snakes down the pinkish canyon. It was long thought that Artist Point was where painter Thomas Moran made sketches for his 7- by 12-foot masterpiece *Grand Canyon of the Yellowstone.* More likely, say historians, he painted from a spot on the North Rim now called **Moran Point.**

Norris Geyser Basin

Both the hottest and the most unpredictable geyser basin in the park, Norris Geyser Basin is a fascinating collection of bubbling and colorful geothermal features. A 2.25-mile web of boardwalks and trails leads visitors through this remarkable basin. From the **Norris Geyser Basin Museum** (307/344-2812, 9am-6pm daily mid-Apr.-Sept., 9am-5pm daily Oct.-early Nov., free), which carefully unravels the geothermal mysteries of the region, there are two loop trails guiding visitors safely through the basin. The 1930s log-and-stone building that houses the museum has been designated a National Historic Landmark. There is also an information desk and a Yellowstone Association bookstore inside the building.

Porcelain Basin is a stark, barren setting with a palette of pink, red, orange, and yellow mineral oxides. Some of the features of note include **Africa Geyser,** which had been a hot spring in the shape of its namesake continent and started erupting in 1971. When it is active, **Whirligig Geyser,** named in 1904 by the Hague Party, erupts in a swirling pattern for a few minutes at irregular periods with a roar and hiss. The hottest steam vent in the hottest geothermal basin in the park is **Black Growler,** which has measured 280°F. The second-largest geyser in Norris, **Ledge Geyser** erupts irregularly to heights up to 125 feet.

In Norris's **Back Basin** you'll find the world's tallest geyser, **Steamboat Geyser,** which can erupt more than 300 feet in the air. Minor eruptions of 10-40 feet in height are more common. The eruptions can last 3-40 minutes and be separated by days or decades (in the past, Steamboat has gone more than 50 years without an eruption, but in 1964, it erupted 29 times). The most recent major eruption, in September 2014, happened at 11pm and was witnessed by a park ranger. Prior to that, the last major eruption occurred

Catch a view of the Grand Canyon of the Yellowstone's rocky walls.

in 2013, and before that in 2005. Just down the boardwalk, **Cistern Spring** is linked to Steamboat Geyser and drains in advance of a major eruption. The color is a beautiful blue, enhanced by as much as 0.5 inch of gray sinter deposited annually. By comparison, Old Faithful only deposits 0.5-1 inch of sinter every century. **Echinus Geyser** is the world's largest acid geyser and is almost as acidic as vinegar. Eruptions since 2007 have been rare and unpredictable, typically lasting about 4 minutes.

SPORTS AND RECREATION

Yellowstone is indeed a hiker's paradise, with ubiquitous brown signs pointing to trailheads. Look for them anytime your legs need a stretch. In the northern loop, there are some fantastic trails in an otherwise nondescript stretch between Norris and Canyon. Drive east of Norris Junction 3.5 miles (or 8.5 miles west of Canyon Junction) to the **Ice Lake Trailhead** on the north side of the road. It is a fairly popular 4.5-mile loop with minimal elevation gain. In fact, the entire trail to Ice Lake is wheelchair accessible and leads to the only wheelchair-accessible backcountry campsite in the park. Avid hikers will want to continue on to **Little Gibbon Falls,** a 25-foot waterfall that is not even on the USGS topographic map. Another way to see this hidden gem is to find the Little Gibbon Falls Trailhead 0.4 mile east of the Ice Lake Trailhead. There is a small pullout on the south side of the road. The trail starts about 100 feet east of the pullout on the north side of the road. From here, Little Gibbon Falls is a 1.2-mile out-and-back hike.

FOOD

By far the most unique meal available in the park is the ★ **Old West Dinner Cookout,** which departs daily early June-mid-Sept. from the Roosevelt Lodge and is served in Yellowstone's wilderness. The hearty steak-and-potatoes dinner with all the cowboy trimmings can be attended on horseback (1-hour rides from $80 ages 12 and over, $69 children

8-11, 2-hour rides from $89 ages 12 and over, $82 children 8-11) or via covered wagon (from $60 ages 12 and over, $48 children 3-11, free for children under 3).

Breakfast, lunch, and dinner are served daily throughout the season in the **Roosevelt Lodge Dining Room, Canyon Lodge Dining Room, Cafeteria, and Deli,** and the **Mammoth Hotel Dining Room and Terrace Grill** (866/439-7375, www.yellowstonenationalparklodges.com). Each restaurant has its own flair—Roosevelt Lodge tends to be heartier, with options like barbecue beef, bison chili, and Wyoming cheesesteak, while Mammoth is known for elaborate buffets and inventive small plates like goat cheese sliders, mini trout tacos, and Thai curry mussels. Canyon offers burgers, sandwiches, and an extensive soup and salad bar. Breakfasts include entrées ranging from pancakes and eggs to biscuits and gravy ($6-12). Lunches range $9-16, and dinners are generally $12-36. The most reasonably priced spot for dinner is the Canyon Lodge Cafeteria, with menu options that include hot dogs, hamburgers, rice bowls, and pasta entrées ($4-12). Generally, breakfast is served 6:30am-10am, lunch 11:30am-2:30pm, and dinner 5:30pm-10pm. Hours vary seasonally by restaurant and are subject to change. Call ahead for reservations or to check on hours; menus are available on the website.

ACCOMMODATIONS

There are three accommodations in the northern loop. The largest is the **Mammoth Hot Springs Hotel and Cabins** (late Apr.-early Oct. and mid-Dec.-early Mar., $98 budget cabin, $160 frontier cabin, $90 hotel room without bath, $150 standard room, $262 hot tub cabin, $499 suite), which has 211 spartan but perfectly decent guest rooms and another 116 cabins, some with hot tubs. Mammoth is undergoing a two-phase renovation that will close the facilities to overnight guests in winter through the spring of 2018. After the renovation, all rooms will have a private bathroom and rates are sure to rise. Set amid

Be Safe and Smart in the Backcountry

Hiking and camping in the Yellowstone backcountry is undoubtedly the best way to understand and appreciate this magnificently wild place. But with this remarkable opportunity comes the very important responsibility to keep yourself safe, protect the animals from human-caused altercations, and preserve this pristine environment.

When hiking, prevent erosion and trail degradation by hiking single file and always staying on the trail. Don't take shortcuts or cut corners on switchbacks. If you do have to leave the trail, disperse your group so that you don't inadvertently trample the vegetation and create a new, unwanted trail.

Chances are good that you will encounter some kind of wildlife in the backcountry, so you need to be prepared to react. Never approach an animal: Remember to always stay at least 25 yards away from all wildlife, and at least 100 yards away from predators, including bears. Make noise as you hike along to give animals the opportunity to depart before an encounter. Do not hike at the edges of day—dawn or dusk—or at night, as these are the most active times for bears and other predators. Always be aware of your surroundings. Look for overturned rocks and logs, dug-out areas, and, of course, carcasses, all of which suggest bear activity.

If you do encounter a bear, know what to do. If there is some distance between you and the bear, give the bear an opportunity to leave, or take the opportunity to redirect your own party. If you run into a bear at close range, be as nonthreatening as possible. Talk calmly and back away. Never turn your back, and never run. Make sure you have your bear spray accessible. If the bear charges, stand your ground. Bears will often bluff charge to determine whether you will run and are thus prey. If the bear does attack, keep your pack on, fall to the ground on your belly, protect your head and neck with your arms, and play dead. When the bear leaves, get up and retreat. In the very uncommon circumstance that a bear provokes an attack or enters a tent, fight the bear with every resource you have.

Go to great lengths to avoid attracting bears by hanging all food, cooking utensils, and scented items (toothpaste, deodorant, other toiletries, and trash) in a bear bag in a tree or atop a bear pole. Designate a separate cooking and eating area away from the sleeping tents. Dispose of your trash and personal waste properly.

You need to plan your trip carefully and secure all permits and backcountry campsites through any one of seven backcountry permit offices: Bechler Ranger Station, Canyon Visitor Center, Grant Village Visitor Center, Bridge Bay Ranger Station, Mammoth Visitor Center, Old Faithful Ranger Station, South Entrance Ranger Station, Tower Ranger Station, and the West Yellowstone Visitor Information Center (307/344-2160, www.nps.gov, permits available 8am-4:30pm daily June-Aug., $25 annual pass, $3 pp over 9 years old per night). Some of Yellowstone's roughly 300 backcountry campsites can be reserved in advance either in person, by fax, or through the mail. Backcountry Use Permits are required for all overnight stays and can only be attained in person no more than 48 hours before your trip. A park booklet titled *Beyond Road's End* is available online and will help familiarize you with the backcountry regulations and restrictions.

historic Fort Yellowstone, Mammoth provides convenient access to restaurants, gift shops, a gas station, and the visitors center, so guests may forget they're somewhat out in the wild. Despite human and car traffic in Mammoth, wolves have been known to sneak onto the green watered lawns at night to take down an unsuspecting well-grazed elk. You can imagine the surprise when early risers spotted the carcass on their way to get a breakfast burrito.

Named for Yellowstone champion Theodore Roosevelt, the ★ **Roosevelt Lodge Cabins** (mid-June-early Sept.) offer a timeless rustic setting reminiscent of a great old dude ranch in a quiet corner of the park. The Roughrider Cabins (from $89) usually offer double beds and a wood-burning stove. What they lack in amenities they make up for with charming authenticity. Toilets and communal showers are available nearby. The

Frontier Cabins (from $142) are slightly larger and include a private bathroom with a shower, toilet, and sink.

Set adjacent to the spectacular Grand Canyon of the Yellowstone, **Canyon Lodge & Cabins** (early June-late Sept.) is the largest single lodging property in the park. The facilities were built in the 1950s and 1960s, and added onto and renovated significantly in 2016 to total more than 500 rooms and cabins. In the lodges, there are standard rooms ($140), premium rooms ($230), superior rooms ($255), superior lodge rooms with patios ($265), and suites ($499). The modest Western Cabins ($204) are basic motel-style units with private full bathrooms.

Reservations for all hotels inside the park should be made through **Xanterra Parks & Resorts** (307/344-7311 or 866/439-7375, www.yellowstonenationalparklodges.com). Nature is the draw here: There are no televisions, radios, or air-conditioning. Internet access can be purchased in the public areas of most hotels in the park.

CAMPING

The only campground in the park's northern loop that can be reserved in advance, operated by Xanterra, the park's concessionaire, is the 270-site **Canyon** (307/344-7901 for same-day reservations, 307/344-7311

for advance reservations, late May-early Sept., $28 nightly rate includes two showers/night), which has 15 public restrooms with flush toilets, faucets with cold running water, and pay showers. The other six sites—at Mammoth, Tower Falls, Slough Creek, Pebble Creek, Indian Creek, and Norris—are available on a first-come, first-served basis and cost $15-20. These sites fill up quickly; your best bet is to arrive before 11am. Mammoth is the only campground open all year; all the campgrounds have some RV sites. A great feature on the Yellowstone website shows current availability and also what time any given site closed the day before (www.nps.gov).

In addition to the campgrounds, more than 300 backcountry campsites are scattered throughout the park. Overnight permits, which are available at all ranger stations and visitors centers, are only issued in person up to 48 hours in advance; they are required for all the sites. Backcountry campsites can be reserved January 1-October 31 by paying a $25 reservation fee. All requests to reserve sites must be made in person, faxed, or mailed in. Pertinent forms and information for backcountry camping in Yellowstone are available online at the National Park Service Backcountry Trip Planner (www.nps.gov).

The Northeast Corner

With arguably the best wildlife viewing in the park, especially in winter, this region is known as the "Little Serengeti of North America." The wide-open spaces of the Lamar Valley and much of the northeast corner of the park also offer some pretty dramatic mountain vistas. There is excellent fishing and hiking in the region, and just outside the park's northeast entrance is Cooke City, a cool little community with tremendous appeal to backcountry skiers, snowmobilers, and other outdoor enthusiasts.

★ WATCHING THE WOLVES

When visitors list the animals they most want to see in Yellowstone, wolves rank second, right behind grizzly bears. Since their return to Yellowstone in 1995, wolves have surprised park-goers and wildlife experts alike by being much more visible than anyone anticipated. In fact, since their reintroduction, wolves have been spotted in Yellowstone by at least one person nearly every day. Much of that is thanks to wolf researchers, including the

Camping in Yellowstone

As accommodations cannot meet the demand of Yellowstone's four million visitors each year, camping is an excellent option, particularly for those spontaneous souls who want to see the park without planning months in advance. More than 2,000 campsites spread over 12 campgrounds are located in the park. The five largest—Bridge Bay, Canyon, Fishing Bridge RV, Grant, and Madison—are run by Xanterra; all inquiries and reservations should be made by calling Xanterra (same-day reservations 307/344-7901, advance reservations 307/344-7311); these campgrounds have additional sales and utility tax fees. The other sites are assigned on a first-come, first-served basis. Try to arrive early to secure your spot; sites often fill up by 11am, especially in the busy summer months. Yellowstone also has more than 300 backcountry campsites, which require permits.

Campground	Number of Sites	Dates (Approx.)	Fees	RV Sites
Bridge Bay	432	late May-early Sept.	$23.50	call for availability and reservations
Canyon	273	late May-early Sept.	$28	call for availability and reservations
Fishing Bridge RV Park	less than 325	early May-mid-Sept.	$47.75	call for availability and reservations
Grant Village	430	mid-June-mid-Sept.	$28	call for availability and reservations
Indian Creek	70	mid-June-mid-Sept.	$15	14 for 30-foot, walk through to assess site
Lewis Lake	85	mid-June-early Sept.	$15	25-foot limit
Madison	278	late Apr.-mid-Oct.	$23.50	call for availability and reservations
Mammoth	85	year-round	$20	most pull-through, 30-foot limit
Norris	111	late May-late Sept.	$20	2 50-foot, 5 30-foot
Pebble Creek	27	mid-June-late Sept.	$15	some long pull-throughs
Slough Creek	23	mid-June-early Sept.	$15	14 for 30-foot, walk through to assess site
Tower Falls	31	late May-late Sept.	$15	all 30-foot or less; hairpin turn

indefatigable Rick McIntyre, who is out in the field an average of 11 hours per day seven days per week, and the ever-passionate wolf watchers (who tend to follow Rick), armed with massive scopes and camera lenses that look strong enough to spot wildlife on other planets.

The bad news is that there are roughly 95 wolves in 10 packs, plus a few lone wolves, roaming throughout Yellowstone, an area that is approximately the size of Connecticut. It's always a good idea to bear those figures in mind when you have only a couple of hours and a keen desire to spot one of these majestic canines.

But there's good news too. If seeing the wolves is a high priority for you, here are five ways to improve your odds:

· **Visit in winter.** Wolves are most active and most visible (nearest to the roads and against a white backdrop) in the winter when they have significant advantages over their prey, including elk and bison. Spring and fall can offer viewing opportunities as well, but summer visitors are at a disadvantage because the wolves are often way up in the high country, far from roads. Whenever you go, don't forget your binoculars or a scope if you have one.

· **Do your homework or hire a guide.** Stop at the visitors center in Mammoth in winter (or any of the visitors centers at other times of year) and inquire about recent activity. Rangers can often tell you where packs have been spotted, if kills have recently occurred, and so forth. You could also consider hiring a guide that specializes in wolf watching. **Yellowstone Wolf Tracker** (406/223-6634, www.wolftracker.com, $575/day for 1-2 people, $625 for 3-5 people, $750 for 6-14 people) offers 6-8-hour tours led by wildlife biologists. The **Yellowstone Association Institute** (406/848-2400, www.yellowstoneassociation.org) offers a variety of courses that focus on wolves.

· **Visit the Lamar Valley.** The only road

open to car traffic year-round, the stretch of asphalt that winds through the Lamar Valley takes visitors through the heart of some of the park's best winter wolf terrain. There are numerous pullouts along the road for viewing, but be sure to park safely out of traffic without blocking other visitors. In the summer, along the stretch of road near the confluence of the Lamar River and Soda Butte Creek, the road is often closed to stopping thanks to a wolf-denning site not far from the pavement. Your chances to see a wolf—even pups—is good.

· **Wake up early.** Like most wildlife, wolves are most active at the edges of day. Putting yourself in the heart of the Lamar Valley before sunrise greatly improves your odds of seeing the wolves. The same is true at sunset. In this game, patience pays.

· **Watch for the wolf watchers.** They often have significant advantages, including radio telemeters that allow them to track collared wolves. These people know much about the wolves and can regale you with dramatic sagas of individual animals and entire packs. Don't be shy about pulling over when you see them; they are often willing to let you peer through their scopes. But do be safe and courteous; turn off your engine and remain quiet.

★ LAMAR VALLEY

One of my favorite corners of the park, the **Lamar Valley** is stunningly beautiful with wide valleys carved by rivers and glaciers as well as views to the high rugged peaks around Cooke City. Generally uncrowded (save for the ever-growing number of bespectacled and bescoped wolf watchers), some of the best hiking, fishing, and camping can be had at Slough Creek. And the wolf watching, particularly in the winter, is unrivaled anywhere else in the world. There are also grizzlies, black bears, mountain lions, coyotes, red foxes, elk, bison, bighorn sheep, and pronghorn in the area. In early summer, on occasion, there can be as many as 2,000 bison dotting the wide green expanse; it's a miraculous sight.

Cinderella: The Real-Life Fairy Tale of Wolf 42

In 1926 the last known wolf in Yellowstone was killed, bringing to a conclusion a decades-long campaign to rid the region of an animal widely considered a worthless pest. The murderous eviction was a tragic end to a noble creature. It took nearly 70 years for wolves to be seen not only for their intrinsic worth but their value in making the Yellowstone ecosystem whole again. This was their home, after all, and they had been unnaturally removed. Thirty-one Canadian gray wolves—*Canis lupus*—were reintroduced to the park in 1995-1996 with loud cheers and simultaneous objections.

Among the wolves brought into the park from Canada was a female who would come to be known as wolf number 42. Her sister, wolf 40, was the alpha female of the Druid Peak pack and known to rule the pack with an iron paw. She was suspected of running off her mother, number 39, and her sister, number 41. Number 42, the pack's beta female, managed to stay in the pack, likely as a result of her unmatched speed and excellent hunting ability, but she could not get into her sister's good graces. The two fought constantly for four years. Both bred with wolf 21, the pack's alpha male, and wolf 40 reportedly killed her sister's first litter of pups in 1999. Wolf watchers nicknamed 42 "Cinderella" and flocked to the Lamar Valley to watch the drama unfold. Much of Cinderella's life was captured on film by Bob Landis for two *National Geographic* specials.

In a story that plays out like a fairy tale, wolf 42 got her nieces to den with her in 2000 when she had another litter of pups with 21, and after researchers saw wolf 40 approaching the den just before the pups were weaned, ostensibly to kill this second litter of pups, 42 and her nieces attacked. Wolf 40 was found dying of her wounds, and 42 not only rose to alpha status overnight, paired for life with wolf 21, but also moved into 40's den and adopted her dead sister's seven pups as her own. That year 42 and 21 raised 20 pups.

Over the course of her life—eight years, which is more than double wolf lifespan averages—she birthed 32 pups and held her alpha-female status over the Druid Pack, which climbed to 37 members in 2000, one of the largest wolf packs ever recorded. She was noted for her faithful and patient parenting, even coaching younger wolves in the middle of an elk hunt. When she was killed by another pack in February 2004, wolf watchers noted wolf 21, her constant companion, atop a ridgeline howling for two days straight. The wolf watchers mourned along with him.

After receiving a mortality signal from 42's radio collar, chief park wolf biologist Doug Smith hiked up the 9,000-foot Specimen Ridge on a blustery winter day. There he found Cinderella dead. She was the last remaining member of the 31 wolves imported from Canada, but her legacy and story will be forever entwined with the Yellowstone wilderness and the saga of *Canis lupus* finally coming home.

Yellowstone Association Institute

An arm of the Yellowstone Association, the **Lamar Buffalo Ranch Field Campus** of the **Yellowstone Association Institute** (406/848-2400, www.yellowstoneassociation. org) is located away from the large crowds (of two-legged creatures, anyway) in the idyllic Lamar Valley. The institute offers field seminars at this private and unique campus year-round. If you bring your own sleeping bag and pillow, you can stay at the ranch in one of its log cabins ($36 pp shared cabin in summer, $85 for 1-2 people private cabin in winter, sleeping bag and pillow rental $20). Propane heaters, a communal bathhouse with individual showers, and a fully equipped kitchen are located in the common building. It's quite comfortable but not fancy. The best part is waking up each morning in the Lamar Valley, an opportunity very few people have. You can also stay in a nearby campsite or hotel while taking a course at the ranch. Field seminars also take place at hotels throughout the park. The institute holds rooms in various lodges until 30 days before the course.

COOKE CITY

Named for a miner and populated by hard-core modern-day prospectors in search of snow, **Cooke City** (population 75, elevation 7,600) is a jumble of old buildings and some fairly salty characters, all with true Western flavor. At the end of a one-way road for most of the year (except during the height of summer when the Beartooth Highway leads visitors up and over the towering peaks), Cooke City has a remarkable sense of community, unlimited recreational opportunities, plenty of accommodations, and some excellent places to fill your belly. Nearby **Silver Gate** is equally scenic and even quieter, the Connecticut to Cooke's New York City. Pilot, Index, and Beartooth Peaks are three of the impressive summits that loom over these twin settlements, beckoning adventurers.

A gray wolf is a marvel to watch.

Entertainment and Events

Among the biggest events of the year in Cooke City is the annual **Sweet Corn Festival,** a gathering for backcountry skiers and snowboarders usually held in April on the weekend after the nearby ski hills have closed for the season. The weather is often sublime—think blue skies, cold nights, and warm afternoons—and the snow is like, well, sweet corn. Accommodations are not easy to come by this weekend (even floor space is pretty much spoken for), so plan ahead or bring a tent. Plenty of snowmobilers are on hand to act as taxis, enabling telemark skiers not to have to earn their turns for once. With some of the best backcountry skiing in the West when the conditions are right, this is a welcome event.

The **Annual Hog Roast** happens in mid-March and attracts a throng of hungry snowmobilers, backcountry skiers, and more recently, a healthy number of cross-country skiers to Cooke City. The event includes an auction, dinner, and live music.

The popular **Firemen's Picnic** is held annually on July 4, just east of town, with a good old-fashioned parade on Main Street, food, kids' games, and fireworks after dark.

For some culture on the periphery of Yellowstone's wilderness, check out **Shakespeare in the Parks** in Silvergate Park in July or August. Or for some good history, on Thursday nights in July at 6pm is **Joe's Campfire Program** (held behind the visitors center at 206 W. Main St., rain or shine), which features regional historians talking about a range of subjects, from fur trapping to bear history to the Great Depression. There's also an open mic night for local storytellers.

For more information on any of these events, call or visit Donna—who is as knowledgeable as she is friendly—at the chamber-run **visitors center** (206 W. Main St., 406/838-2495, www.cookecitychamber.org, year-round, hours change seasonally), on the west end of town on the north side of the street; the center also has flush toilets.

Sports and Recreation

The northeastern corner of the park and the area just outside it is a natural playground for

The Brucellosis Problem

Yellowstone is the only place in the continental United States where bison have existed since prehistoric times. Current policy mandates that the animals stay within the park's unfenced boundaries, and how best to enforce this is a matter of constant debate.

The park's management of the bison has changed throughout the years, just as bison numbers have fluctuated. Prior to 1967, park authorities would trap and reduce the herd to keep it manageable. After 1967, however, the guiding philosophy changed, and the bison were managed by nature alone. By 1996 the number of bison in the park had grown to 3,500. The size of the herd, coupled with winters that brought significant snowfall, led many of the bison to migrate out of the park in order to find better grazing and calving grounds. The problem of brucellosis played out on the national stage.

Brucellosis is a bacterial infection present in the bison and elk in the Greater Yellowstone area. The disease can cause spontaneous abortions, infertility, and lowered milk production in the infected animal, but the Yellowstone elk and bison populations seem relatively unscathed by the disease, despite the number of animals infected. The same tolerance of the disease is not common among cattle, however. The overwhelming fear is that bison exiting Yellowstone could infect neighboring cattle; this would be gravely detrimental to Montana, Wyoming, and Idaho beef production. Brucellosis cannot be treated in cattle and can be passed on to humans in the form of undulant fever. The government created a fairly simple inoculation program to eradicate the disease in cattle as early as 1934, but brucellosis has never been eliminated from wildlife.

Starting in the 1980s, when more than 50 percent of the park's bison tested positive for the disease, the park's approach was to control the borders with hazing to limit the number of bison that left the park. When hazing was unsuccessful, the bison were shot. The winter of 1996-1997 brought record cold and snow, and bison left the park in large numbers to forage for food; 1,079 bison were shot and another 1,300 starved to death inside the park's boundaries. This incident magnified the problem of maintaining a healthy herd while preventing the spread of brucellosis.

The National Park Service, the U.S. Department of Agriculture, and Montana, Wyoming, and Idaho are working together to see how brucellosis can be eliminated and free-roaming bison protected. A vaccination program has been implemented, with a 65 percent success rate, and the use of quarantine has proven fairly successful. Local bison rancher and wildlife advocate Ted Turner has agreed to accept some of the quarantined bison on his property. A small and highly regulated hunting season on bison is carried out each winter just outside the park boundaries.

But while there are no easy or obvious solutions, there are questions: What about elk, which also carry the disease and have been identified as the source of brucellosis outbreaks among horses in Wyoming and cattle in Idaho? No efforts to limit their natural migration in and out of the park have ever been attempted. Why are bull bison—who can carry the disease but cannot spread it through milk or birthing fluids as females do—quarantined and killed? For now, it seems, we watch, wait, and hope for a healthy, wild, and free-roaming bison population.

fishing, hiking, cross-country skiing, and snowmobiling.

HIKING AND FISHING

One short but worthwhile hike can be found 1.8 miles west of the Pebble Creek Campground at **Trout Lake.** The hike itself is short and steep, just 1.2 miles round-trip, and leaves from the Trout Lake Trailhead on the north side of the road. Anglers can bring a rod after July 15 when it opens to catch-and-release fishing for native cut-throats. In late spring-early summer, trout can be seen spawning in the inches-deep inlet, a fairly miraculous sight. There is an excellent trail around the 12-acre lake and shallow inlet and a decent chance of spotting playful otters, but hikers should take great care not to disturb the fish, especially during spawning. Bear awareness and a can of bear spray are necessary, as the bruins like fish too.

Another great place to combine fishing,

hiking, and wildlife watching—perhaps the perfect Yellowstone trifecta—is along the trail at **Slough Creek.** East of Tower Junction 5.8 miles (or west of the northeast entrance) is an unpaved road on the north side of the road leading to Slough Creek Campground. The trailhead is 1.5 miles down the road on the right side, just before the campground. The trail itself is a double-rutted wagon trail that leads to Silver Tip Ranch, a legendary private ranch just outside the park. The trail is maintained for 11 miles (one-way) and only gains 400 feet in elevation. All along the trail there is world-class fishing in slow-moving Slough Creek, home to a healthy population of native cutthroat trout. You may meet elk, bison, wolves, and even grizzlies along the trail, so be prepared and be safe.

WINTER RECREATION

With an average of 500 inches of snowfall each year, mountainous terrain with elevation that ranges 7,000-10,000 feet, and a nearly interminable winter, Cooke City is a winter mecca with 60 miles of groomed snowmobile trails and endless acres of ungroomed terrain for skiing and snowmobiling. Some favorites trails are **Daisy Pass, Lulu Pass,** and **Round Creek Trail.**

A number of places in town rent snowmobiles and all the necessary gear. Most important, you'll need to talk with experts about local conditions, trail closures, and avalanche dangers. **Cooke City Motorsports** (203 Eaton St., 406/838-2231, www.cookecitymotorsports.com, snowmobiles from $215/day) and **Cooke City Exxon** (204 Main St., 406/838-2244, www.cookecityexxon.com, snowmobiles from $225/day) are obvious choices in town.

The **Silvertip Mountain Center** (115 U.S. 212, Silver Gate, 406/838-2125 or 800/863-0807, www.silvertipmountaincenter.com) has an impressive collection of equipment for purchase and for rent, including skis, snowshoes, ice-climbing and rock-climbing equipment, tents, and more. Staff members are local experts in various passions and are

A road goes through Yellowstone to Cooke City.

a great resource for ideas about any type of adventure you're inclined to plan.

Food

There are a million ways to work up an appetite in and around Cooke City. Be assured you won't go hungry (or thirsty, for that matter). ★ **Beartooth Café** (14 U.S. 212, 406/838-2475, www.beartoothcafe.com, 11am-10pm daily end of May-end of Sept., lunch $6-13, dinner $9-29) offers excellent mountain fare—think steak and trout—with just a hint of Mexican flair. The front-porch outdoor dining is a treat. The **Loving Cup** (Main Street, 406/838-2412, 7am-4pm daily Feb. 1-Oct. 1, closing hours may vary, $4-10), which used to be the Bike Shack and is still a local hangout, got rid of the bikes to focus more on the coffee and food. It serves breakfast and lunch and offers free Wi-Fi. Another great spot for a quick bite anytime (except April and November when it's closed) is the **Bearclaw Bakery** (309 E. Main, 406/838-2040, 5am-11am daily, rolls and coffee served from 5am, hot breakfasts from 6am), which makes from-scratch baked goods, full hearty breakfasts, and light lunch. The bakery also offers ice cream and a full coffee bar.

The **Prospector Restaurant** (210 U.S. 212, 406/838-2251, www.cookecity.com, 7am-10pm daily, breakfast $7-13, lunch $11-15, dinner $13-35), inside the Soda Butte Lodge, is open year-round and is particularly known for steak and prime rib—not a stretch in these parts. Finally, for those wanting to pick up some supplies, the ★ **Cooke City Store** (101 Main St., 406/838-2234, www.cookecitystore.com, 8am-8pm daily mid-May-Sept, hours may vary slightly based on customers and local activity) is as much a local museum and community center as it is a place to pick up some bread and a bottle of sunscreen. It's a wonderful place and worth a visit; plus the nearest grocery store is 90 minutes away.

Accommodations

For a town with a population that rarely surpasses 100, Cooke City has an impressive number of places to hang your hat. Lodging runs the gamut from cabins and vacation rentals to roadside motels, chain hotels, and small resorts, although not all of them are open year-round. Most of the photo galleries on the accommodations' websites are images of moose and bears or snowmobiles buried in powder rather than pictures of beds and baths. Clearly, Cooke City has morphed from a mining town into a tourist destination.

Big Moose Resort (715 U.S. 212, 406/838-2393, www.bigmooseresort.com, $100-150) is three miles east of town and a great place to set up a base camp if you want to explore the region's trails and rivers. Open year-round, the lodge has a collection of seven old and new cabins, all of which are quite comfortable and

can accommodate up to four people. There are no phones in the cabins (and no cell service in the area), but free Wi-Fi is provided, and you can schedule a Swedish massage on-site.

In the heart of bustling Cooke City is the **Soda Butte Lodge** (210 E. Main St., 406/838-2251, www.cookecity.com, $100-145), a full-service hotel with 32 guest rooms, a saloon, and a restaurant. The guest rooms are basic, but you didn't come to Cooke City to hang out in your hotel room.

In nearby Silver Gate, ★ **Silver Gate Lodging** (109 U.S. 212, 406/838-2371, www.pineedgecabins.com, $72-300) offers 29 great cabins, plus motel rooms and a big lodge that can accommodate any size group and welcomes pets. The setting is both quiet and communal, with barbecue grills, horseshoe pits, and a playground. And because this is Yellowstone, you can also rent scopes, which will come in plenty handy.

Camping

Three Forest Service campgrounds are located in the vicinity of Cooke City. **Soda Butte** (406/848-7375, www.fs.usda.gov, July 1-Sept. 7 depending on weather, $9/vehicle) is one mile east of Cooke City on U.S. Highway 212. It has 27 sites, restrooms, and drinking water, and fishing is available nearby. Please note that due to bear activity, this is a hard-sided campground only, and advance reservations are not accepted. Also strictly a hard-sided campground, **Colter Campground** (406/848-7375, www.fs.usda.gov, July 15-Sept. 7 depending on weather, $8/vehicle) is just two miles east of Cooke City and gives campers access to 18 sites, restrooms, drinking water, and nearby fishing and hiking trails. Reservations are not accepted, so arrive early and have a backup plan in place.

The Southern Loop

Some of the park's biggest highlights are found in the southern loop, along with a significant number of visitors and plentiful wildlife. There are a lot of trees, many of them burned, and not as much dimension to the land as elsewhere, but the southern loop is what many people think of when they think of Yellowstone. From the sweeping Hayden Valley and the otherworldliness of West Thumb Geyser Basin to the sheer size of Yellowstone Lake and the well-deserved hubbub around Old Faithful, this section of the park has an abundance of dynamic features—some world-famous, others hidden gems—for every visitor.

SIGHTS
Hayden Valley

South of Canyon is the expansive and beautiful Hayden Valley, a sweep of grassland carved by massive glaciers, named for the famed leader of the 1871 Hayden Expedition, and occupied by copious amounts of wildlife that includes grizzly bears, wolves, and in summer, thundering herds of bison. The Yellowstone River weaves quietly thorough the valley, and because the soil supports grasses and wildflowers instead of trees, this is one of the most scenic drives in the park, especially during the bison rut and migration in late summer. Besides driving, hiking is an excellent way to explore the valley, either on your own (pay very close attention for signs of bear activity) or with a ranger on weekly guided hikes (4-5 hours, early July-late Aug., free). The hikes are limited to 15 people, and reservations must be made in advance at the **Canyon Visitor Education Center** (307/344-2550, daily late May-mid-Oct.) in Canyon Village.

Fishing Bridge

What was once the epicenter of Yellowstone fishing is today a relic of the past and a touchstone for the ongoing struggle between nature and human meddling. Fishing Bridge was built in 1937 and for years was considered the best place to throw a line for native cutthroat trout. Humans were not the only ones fishing in the area, and human-grizzly encounters led to 16 grizzly bear deaths. To protect the

The vast Hayden Valley is a lush paradise in summer.

the year—the lake bottom is littered with faults, hot springs, craters, and the miraculous life forms that can thrive in such conditions. There is also a rather large bulge, some 2,000 feet long, that rises 100 feet above the rest of the lake bottom. The uplift is related to the ever-present geothermal activity beneath Yellowstone. Whether the bulge is gaseous or potentially volcanic in nature is the subject of ongoing research.

Aside from its geological significance, Yellowstone Lake also offers plenty of recreational opportunities, primarily in the form of boating and fishing. The water is bitter cold, though, typically 40-50°F, and not suitable for swimming. Outboards ($52.50/hour) and rowboats ($10/hour, $45/day) can be rented mid-June-early September at **Bridge Bay Marina** (307/344-7311 or 866/439-7375), just south of Lake Village or 21 miles north of West Thumb. There is great fishing for native cutthroat trout as well. It's worth mentioning that early visitors to the park loved to tell stories about catching fish at the edge of the lake and then dipping their catch in the hot springs at West Thumb Geyser Basin to cook them without taking the fish off the line—a practice that would be seriously frowned upon today.

The rambling pale-yellow **Lake Yellowstone Hotel** was built in 1891 and is an elegant reminder of Yellowstone's bygone era. The lobby and deck, which overlook the lake, are worth seeing, even if you are not staying here. Grab an iced tea and soak in the views; this is a stunning spot. If you can, stay for a meal and enjoy the live piano music. The crowds will fade as you gaze on the idyllic scenery, both natural and artificial.

West Thumb Geyser Basin

On the western edge of Yellowstone Lake is the stunningly eerie West Thumb Geyser Basin, a collection of hot springs, geysers, mud pots, and fumaroles that dump a collective 3,100 gallons of hot water into the lake daily. An excellent boardwalk system guides visitors through the area, but there have been

Yellowstone Lake

bears and the fish, fishing in the vicinity was banned in 1973. Today, because of the sharp decline of cutthroat as a direct result of the introduction of nonnative lake trout, grizzlies are not seen as often fishing in the river.

There are some services—an RV park, a gas station, and a general store—and a 1931 log and stone structure that serves as the **Fishing Bridge Visitor Center** (307/242-2450, 8am-7pm daily late May-Sept., 9am-5pm daily early Oct.). On the National Register of Historic Places, the visitors center has a collection of stuffed bird specimens worth seeing and an exhibit on the lake's geology, including a relief map of the lake bottom.

★ Yellowstone Lake

Covering 136 square miles, Yellowstone Lake is North America's largest freshwater lake above 7,000 feet. In addition to being spectacularly scenic—both when it is placid and when the waves form whitecaps—the lake is a fascinating study in underwater geothermal activity. Beneath the water—or ice, much of injury-causing bison and bear encounters on the boardwalk, so keep your eyes open.

Abyss Pool is a sensational spring, some 53 feet deep, that transforms in color from turquoise to emerald green to brown and back, depending on a variety of factors. Similarly beautiful, **Black Pool** is no longer black because the particular thermophiles that caused the dark coloration were killed in 1991 when the water temperature rose. **Big Cone** and **Fishing Cone,** surrounded by lake water, are the features that led to the stories of fishing and cooking the catch in a single cast. Called "Mud Puffs" by the 1871 Hayden Expedition, **Thumb Paint Pots** are like miniature reddish mud volcanoes (depending on rainfall, after which they can get soupier) and are an excellent example of mud pots. Throughout the last several years, the mud pots have been particularly active, forming new mud cones and even throwing mud into the air. **Surging Spring** is fun to watch as the dome of water forms and overflows, unleashing a torrent of water on the lake.

Grant Village

Located on the West Thumb of Yellowstone Lake, Grant Village is a fairly controversial development dating to the 1970s and built in the heart of grizzly bear habitat and among several cutthroat spawning streams. The architecture is ugly, and the location is better suited to wildlife than visitors. In addition to the **Grant Village Visitor Center** (307/344-2650, 8am-7pm daily late May-Sept., 9am-5pm daily early Oct.), which houses an exhibit dedicated to fire in the Yellowstone ecosystem, accommodations, a campground, and food services are available.

★ Old Faithful

Though often crowded, the **Old Faithful** complex brings together so many of the phenomena—both natural and human-made—that make Yellowstone so special: the landmark geyser and the incredible assortment of geothermal features surrounding it, the wildlife, the grand old park architecture of the Old Faithful Inn, and even the mass of people from around the world who come to witness the famous geyser.

An obvious stop at the Old Faithful complex is the **Old Faithful Visitor Education Center** (307/545-2750, 8am-8pm daily Memorial Day-Sept., 9am-5pm daily Oct.-early Nov., 9am-6pm mid-Apr.-late May), which showcases Yellowstone's hydrothermal features. The $27 million facility hosts

Visitors walk the boardwalks around Old Faithful.

Firehole River offers thermal swimming.

2.6 million visitors annually. Efficient travelers (who are fighting an uphill battle here most of the time) can call ahead for a recorded message about daily geyser eruption predictions (307/344-2751).

Known as the **Upper Geyser Basin,** the area surrounding Old Faithful is the largest concentration of geysers anywhere in the world. By far the most famous is Old Faithful because of its combination of height (although it is not the tallest) and regularity (although it is not the most frequent or most regular). Intervals between eruptions are generally between 60-110 minutes and can be predicted according to duration of previous eruptions. Eruptions can last anywhere from 90 seconds to five minutes. It spouts 3,700-8,400 gallons of hot water at heights of 106-184 feet. Signs inside the nearby hotel lobbies and the visitors center, and a Twitter feed (www.twitter.com/geysernps), keep visitors apprised of the next expected eruptions, of which there are an average of 17 in any 24-hour period. Keep in mind that Old Faithful doesn't stop being

predictable just because people go to bed or the weather turns cold—some of the most magical eruption viewings can happen without crowds. Choose a full-moon night, any time of year, and be willing to get up in the middle of the night. The vision of Old Faithful erupting in winter with snow and ice, frost, and steam in every direction is remarkable.

If you take the time to come to Yellowstone to see Old Faithful, take the time—an hour or more is ideal—to walk through the other marvelous features of the Upper Geyser Basin. **Giantess Geyser** can erupt up to 200 feet high in several bursts. The irregular eruptions happen 2-6 times each year and can occur twice hourly, continuing 4-48 hours, and changing the behavior of many of the other geysers in the region. **Doublet Pool,** a colorful hot spring with numerous ledges, is lovely and convoluted. You can actually hear Doublet vibrating and collapsing beneath the surface. Looking something like a fire hose shooting 130-190 feet in the air, **Beehive Geyser** typically erupts twice daily, each eruption lasting 4-5 minutes. **Grand Geyser** is the world's tallest predictable geyser, erupting every 7-15 hours, lasting 9-12 minutes, and reaching heights up to 200 feet. Visible from the road into the Old Faithful complex if you look back over your shoulder, **Castle Geyser** is thought to be the park's oldest. It generally erupts every 10-12 hours, reaches 90 feet in height, and lasts roughly 20 minutes. A 30-40-minute noisy steam phase follows the eruptions.

★ Firehole River

Since swimming in Yellowstone Lake is not an option unless you are a trained member of the polar bear club, a dip in the heated (but far from hot!) waters of the Firehole River is one of the nicest ways to spend an afternoon. The designated and somewhat popular swimming area is surrounded by high cliffs and some fast-moving rapids both upstream and downstream, so the area is not recommended for new or young swimmers. The water temperature averages 80°F, but this avid swimmer would argue that the temperatures are more likely in the 70s. Though quite limited, parking is accessible from Firehole Canyon Drive, which leaves the main road south of Madison Junction, less than 1,000 feet after crossing the river. There is a toilet available but no lifeguards, so you will be swimming entirely at your own risk.

Midway and Lower Geyser Basins

Between Old Faithful and Madison Junction, along the pastoral Firehole River, are the Midway and Lower Geyser Basins, technically considered part of the same basin. In 1889, Rudyard Kipling dubbed Midway Geyser Basin "hell's half-acre" for its massive hot springs and geysers. Among the most significant features at Midway is **Grand Prismatic Spring,** a colorful and photogenic spring that was immortalized by painter Thomas Moran on the Hayden Expedition. It releases some 560 gallons of water into the Firehole River every minute. At 250 by 380 feet, Grand Prismatic is the third-largest hot spring in the world and the largest in Yellowstone. Now dormant, **Excelsior Geyser Crater** was once the largest geyser in the world, soaring up to 300 feet high. Major eruptions in the 1880s led to a dormancy that lasted more than a century. In 1985, Excelsior erupted continuously for two days but never topped 80 feet. Today, acting as a spring, it discharges more than 4,000 gallons of heated water every minute.

Compared to the much smaller Midway Geyser Basin, the Lower Geyser Basin is enormous, spanning 12 square miles and including several clusters of thermal features. Among them are the notable **Fountain Geyser,** a placid blue pool that erupts on average every 4.5-7 hours for 25-50 minutes and sprays up to 50 feet high, the temperamental **White Dome Geyser,** the almost-constant **Clepsydra,** and the **Pocket Basin Mud Pots,** which are the largest collection of mud pots in the park. **Great Fountain Geyser** in the Firehole Lake area is the only predictable geyser in the Lower Geyser Basin and erupts

every 10 hours and 45 minutes, give or take two hours, for up to an hour, reaching heights of 70-200 feet.

SPORTS AND RECREATION
Fishing and Boating

Some 80,000 anglers are lured to Yellowstone each year by the promise of elusive trout, and they are seldom disappointed by the offerings at Yellowstone Lake. In addition to the prized native cutthroat, the lake is home to a population of nonnative lake trout that is sadly devastating the cutthroat. Introduced in 1890 into Lewis and Shoshone Lakes by the U.S. Fish Commission, the lake trout were first documented in Yellowstone Lake in the mid-1990s; scientists believe they were illegally introduced from a nearby lake in the 1980s. The average lake trout live and spawn in deep waters, feeding on as many as 40 cutthroat each year. By comparison, cutthroat trout spawn in the shallow tributaries of the lake, making them an important food source for a variety of creatures that include eagles and bears. Since the lake trout have no enemies in the deep waters of Yellowstone Lake, they are creating a serious food shortage by devouring the cutthroat. All lake trout caught in Yellowstone Lake must be killed. Pick up your **fishing permit** at one of the visitors centers along with a copy of the Yellowstone fishing regulations.

There are a number of ways to see Yellowstone Lake by boat. Scenic or fishing boat tours as well as outboard motor ($52.50/hour) and rowboat ($10/hour, $45/day) rentals are available from Bridge Bay Marina, south of Lake Village or 21 miles northeast of West Thumb. Hour-long cruises ($17 adults, $10 children 3-11, free for children under 3) depart regularly from the marina mid-June-mid-September. Reservations can be made with Xanterra (307/344-7311 or 866/439-7375, www.xanterra.com).

Hiking

The southern loop of the park offers plentiful

hiking opportunities, most of which can be combined with other interests. The **Hayden Valley** has great trails for wildlife lovers, but precautions against bear encounters must be taken. The **Alum Creek Trail,** 4.4 miles south of Canyon at the north end of the Hayden Valley, is a good hike. Wide open and relatively flat, the trail offers a 10-mile out-and-back trip through prime bison and grizzly habitat. There are also some thermal features along Alum Creek.

Among the geysers in the Upper Geyser Basin is **Lone Star Geyser,** named for its lonely location 5 miles from Old Faithful. An old once-paved road leads to the geyser and makes a nice level hike or bike trip. The entire out-and-back trip is 4.6 miles. There is parking at the trailhead on the south side of the road, 3.5 miles east of the Old Faithful interchange. Lucky viewers will get to see a 30-50-foot eruption, which happens every 2-3 hours and tends to last 10-15 minutes.

FOOD

As the southern loop is generally the most heavily traveled section of the park, there are plenty of dining opportunities. In the park restaurants, breakfast and lunch are on a first-come, first-served basis, but reservations are strongly recommended for dinner, particularly if 5pm or 9pm are not your ideal dining hours. In almost all the venues, you will find some good vegetarian options and many items made with sustainable or organic ingredients; these are identified on each menu. If you are planning a day activity away from the center of things, the restaurants or cafeterias offer box lunches for travelers to take with them. Place your order the night before, and it will be ready in the morning. The Yellowstone General Stores at Grant Village, Lake Village, and Old Faithful also have fast-food service, groceries, and snacks.

The **Grant Village Dining Room** (866/439-7375, 6:30am-10am, 11:30am-2:30pm, and 5pm-10pm daily late May-early Oct., breakfast $3.50-10.50, lunch $7-16, dinner $15-30) offers a pleasant view of the lake,

good service, and a nice variety of American cuisine. In addition to the à la carte menu for breakfast, a buffet is available ($13.50 adults, $6.95 children). Lunch and dinner include inventive dishes such as bison meatloaf, trout three ways, or grilled vegetable cannelloni. Reservations are required for dinner. The **Lake House** at Grant Village (6:30am-10:30am and 5pm-9:30pm daily high season, shortened hours early/late seasons, $9-12) sits right on the lake and is a low-key option. Breakfast ($13.50 adults, $6.95 children) is buffet only, and the dinner menu consists primarily of Asian food including rice or noodle bowls and *banh mi* (Vietnamese-style) sandwiches.

The ★ **Lake Yellowstone Hotel Dining Room** (866/439-7375, 6:30am-10am, 11:30am-2:30pm, and 5pm-10pm daily mid-May-early Oct., reservations required for dinner, breakfast buffet $15.25 adults, $6.95 children, entrées $6-13, lunch $10-16, dinner $14-42) is the most elegant dining room in the park, with a gorgeous view of the lake. The restaurant is committed to creating dishes with fresh, local, organic, and sustainable ingredients. Lunch is a good way to sample some of the gourmet fare without putting too large a dent in your pocketbook. Try the delicious organic lentil soup or lobster ravioli. Dinner at the hotel is sure to be a memorable experience with options like brown butter lobster sliders and grilled quail. Directly inside the hotel is the **Lake Hotel Deli** (6:30am-9pm daily mid-May-early Sept., shortened hours early/late seasons), which serves a nice selection of soups, salads, and sandwiches. The **Lake Hotel Cafeteria** (6:30am-10pm daily early June-late Sept., shortened hours early/late seasons) is a casual place for a quick bite. It serves great breakfast burritos, paninis, plenty of kids' favorites, and comfort food dishes ranging from pot roast to lasagna.

Five eateries are located in the Old Faithful complex, but by far the most desirable is the **Old Faithful Inn Dining Room** (866/439-7375, 6:30am-10am, 11:30am-2:30pm, and 4:30pm-10pm daily early June-early Sept., shortened hours in May, Sept., early Oct.), which offers a buffet for each of the main meals daily (breakfast buffet $13.50 adults and $6.95 children, lunch buffet $15.95 adults and $7.95 children, dinner buffet $29.50 adults and $11.50 children) as well as an à la carte menu (breakfast $5-10, lunch $10-16, dinner $16-27). You can dine in the historic inn while enjoying its distinct rustic architecture and Western-style ambience. Lunch is a "Western buffet" with items such as farm-raised pan-fried trout, chopped barbecue chicken sandwiches, and bison chili. If you don't opt for the dinner buffet (featuring prime rib and trout), you could try grilled quail or the smoked bison and pheasant with chicken sausage. Reservations are required for dinner. The **Bear Paw Deli** (6am-9pm daily late May-early Sept., shortened hours early/late seasons, $4-9), also located in the inn, is perfect for on-the-go meals. It offers a continental breakfast including bagel sandwiches, and sandwich and salad deli fare for lunch, as well as serves up several flavors of ice cream. In addition to these two eateries at the inn, there is a cafeteria and bakeshop in the lodge, and a dining room and grill in the Old Faithful Snow Lodge.

ACCOMMODATIONS

★ **Lake Yellowstone Hotel and Cabins** (mid-May-early Oct., rooms $237-425, suites $572-690, cabins $157) is both grand and picturesque, perched on the shores of Yellowstone Lake. Originally built in 1891 and restored in the 1990s to its 1920s elegance, the hotel houses the nicest rooms in the park. As is true everywhere in the park, though, the appeal comes from the location and the views, not the amenities, which are basic. If you are staying in the hotel, request a room with a view of the lake. There is an annex that offers more modest rooms; individual cabins are located behind the hotel. These duplexes were remodeled in 2004 and are simple and modest.

The **Lake Lodge Cabins** (mid-June-late Sept., $204 Western cabin, $138 Frontier cabin, $88 Pioneer cabin) are clean and simple, and many underwent renovation in 2016. Located just off the lake, the cabins are clustered around the main lodge, which is an inviting common area for guests to gather. It has a large porch that beckons guests to take a seat in one of the rocking chairs and soak in the view, as well as two fireplaces, a gift shop, and a cozy lounge. The Western cabins are a bit more spacious, with two beds and a shower-tub in each bathroom. The Pioneer cabins are older and more spartan, with shower-only bathrooms and 1-2 double beds. The setting is tranquil and quiet, and early risers may spot a herd of bison wandering through the property.

The ★ **Old Faithful Inn** (early May-early Oct., $572 suites, $503 junior suites, $243-254 premium rooms, $229 standard rooms, $115-220 with shared bath) is the most popular lodging inside the park, and for good reason. The original part of the lodge, known as the Old House, was built in 1904 by acclaimed architect Robert Reamer. Situated close to the Old Faithful geyser, the lodge epitomizes rustic beauty, originality, and strength. It has a large front lobby that houses a massive stone fireplace. The larger rooms are in the wings of the inn, built in the 1920s, while the more modest rooms are in the Old House. The inn has a wide assortment of guest rooms and rates, ranging from two-room suites with sitting rooms and fridges to simple rooms without individual baths. Guest rooms can be booked more than a year in advance, so plan ahead and make reservations.

Located close to the inn is the **Old Faithful Lodge Cabins** (mid-May-early Oct., $88-148), which offers much simpler and rustic lodging. If you are looking for budget-friendly accommodations that put you in the center of park activity, this is a good option. The cabins are small motel-style units that vary in condition. Many of them were renovated in 2016. The lower-priced cabins do not come with baths, but there are communal showers nearby. The cabins are scattered around a main log cabin-style lodge. Built in the 1920s, the main lodge has a large cafeteria, bakery, and fully stocked gift shop, making it popular with park visitors throughout the day.

The **Old Faithful Snow Lodge and Cabins** (late Apr.-mid Oct. and mid-Dec.-late Feb., $264-315 lodge rooms, $163-195 Western cabin, $114-149 Frontier cabin) are the newest accommodations in the park. The original lodge was torn down and a new structure was built in 1999. Its architecture is intended to mirror the Old Faithful Inn, and the lodge won a Cody Award for Western Design. It offers comfortable, modern rooms decorated with Western flair. It also has a few motel-style cabins, built in 1989. The Western cabins are a good value for the money; they're large rooms with two queen beds and a full bath. This is one of only two lodges (the other is Mammoth Hot Springs Hotel, which due to renovation will not re-open for winter guests until December 2018) open during the winter season in Yellowstone.

Grant Village is about 20 miles southeast of Old Faithful on the West Thumb of Yellowstone Lake. Although the accommodations do not have the same rustic feel or character of the other lodges, they do offer a comfortable and modern place to stay away from the crowds. The complex is made up of six small condo-like buildings. Each building has 50 nicely furnished hotel rooms ($230) that come with either two double beds or one queen and full baths.

Reservations for all hotels inside the park should be made through **Xanterra Parks and Resorts** (307/344-7311 or 866/439-7375, www.xanterra.com). Note that there are no televisions, radios, or air-conditioning.

CAMPING

Five of the 12 campsites in the park are located in this southern region: **Bridge Bay** (between West Thumb and Lake, late May-early Sept., flush toilets, $23.50), **Fishing Bridge RV Park** (at Fishing Bridge north of Lake Village, early May-late Sept., the only campground offering water and sewer, with flush toilets and pay showers, for hard-sided vehicles only, $47.75), **Grant Village** (at Grant Village south of West Thumb, late June-mid-Sept., flush toilets, $28), **Lewis Lake** (at Lewis Lake south of Grant Village, early-June-early Nov., vault toilets, $15), and **Madison** (at Madison Junction between the west entrance and Old Faithful, late Apr.-mid-Oct., flush toilets, $23.50). Advance reservations (307/344-7311 or 866/439-7375) or same-day reservations (307/344-7901) can be made at Bridge Bay, Fishing Bridge RV Park, Grant Village, and Madison.

The Old Faithful Inn was designed in 1904 by architect Robert Reamer.

West Yellowstone

West Yellowstone (population 1,321, elevation 6,667 feet) has something of a split personality—hard-core athletes training for the Olympics next to hard-core snowmobilers aiming for high-marking honors; get-too-close tourists alongside bison activists who try to put themselves in the line of fire. The winters are huge, with snow that buries everything but this town's spirit. The region shines with sensational recreational opportunities, from guided snow coach and cross-country skiing excursions to snowmobiling and dogsledding. The winters look interminable with piles of snow still scattered around town well into May and sometimes June, but with so much sun and so much to do, residents never complain about the cold.

The summers tend to be crowded as most people going to Old Faithful come through "West," as the town is known locally. With crystal-clear alpine lakes and rivers in every direction, there is no shortage of summer recreation—fishing opportunities are phenomenal, and there are plenty of places to cycle. As the hub of the region and the busiest entrance to Yellowstone National Park, there is plenty of good grub and lots of comfortable beds in and around town.

SIGHTS
★ Grizzly and Wolf Discovery Center

If you have your heart set on seeing a grizzly or a wolf in Yellowstone, here's my advice: Get it out of the way before you even go into the park, like a first kiss on a first date before you order dinner. The **Grizzly and Wolf Discovery Center** (201 S. Canyon St., 406/646-7001 or 800/257-2570, www.grizzlydiscoveryctr.org, 8:30am-8:30pm daily mid-May-early Sept., 8:30am-6pm daily early Sept.-Oct. and late Apr.-mid-May, 8:30am-4pm daily Nov.-late Apr., $13 ages 13 and over, $12.25 seniors 62 and over, $8 children 5-12, free for children

under 5, admission valid for two consecutive days) is a nonprofit organization that acts something like an orphanage, giving homes to problem, injured, or abandoned animals that have nowhere else to go. Although there is something melancholy about watching these incredible beasts confined to any sort of enclosure, particularly on the perimeter of a chunk of wilderness as massive as Yellowstone, there is also something remarkable about seeing them close enough to count their whiskers. Watching a wolf pack interact from a comfy bench behind floor-to-ceiling windows in the warming hut is an absolutely worthwhile way to spend an afternoon. The naturalists on staff are excellent at engaging with visitors of all ages and have plenty to teach everyone. One fantastic opportunity for curious children ages 5-12 is the **Keeper Kids** program, which is offered twice daily during the summer season. For roughly 45 minutes, the kids learn about grizzly eating habits and behavior. They get to then go into the grizzly enclosure, while the bears are locked away obviously, and hide buckets of food for the bears. When the kids exit and the bears come racing out to search for their treats—overturning massive logs and boulders in the process—the kids (and their parents!) are mesmerized. The center has gone to great lengths to share the personal story of each animal and why it cannot survive in the wild. They also give the bears all sorts of games and tasks—aiding in the design of bear-proof garbage cans is one example. Since these bears do not hibernate, this is a stop absolutely worth making any time of the year. Ultimately, this is a really nice place to learn a lot about bears, wolves, and raptors before heading into the park to look for them in the wild.

Yellowstone Giant Screen Theatre

Montana's first giant screen, the **Yellowstone Giant Screen Theatre** (101 S. Canyon St.,

See a wolf at the Grizzly and Wolf Discovery Center.

information on programs like ranger-led educational Yellowstone National Park afternoon and evening programs and snowshoe walks through the park in winter, free Music in the Park evenings, and weekly West Yellowstone rodeo shows in summer.

The **World Snowmobile Expo** (www.snowmobileexpo.com) is the largest snowmobile exposition in the West. All the major manufacturers descend on West Yellowstone in the early spring to unveil their latest and greatest. The show is combined with racing and evening events.

The **Yellowstone Rendezvous Race** (www.rendezvousskitrails.com or www.skirunbikemt.com), a one-day cross-country ski competition, is the largest event of the year. It usually takes place in early March, and 600-900 skiers come to participate. Six races are held concurrently, based on age and ability, over distances of 2-50 kilometers. The **Kids 'N' Snow Youth Ski Festival** is a newer event held right after the Rendezvous Race. To encourage families to stay after the race, there are a series of ski events (including a relay race, an obstacle course, and even musical chairs) for children 13 and younger. The **Equinox Ski Challenge** (www.equinoxsnowchallenge.com) is the final ski event, held biennially (2017, 2019, 2021) on one of the last weekends in March. Skiers can participate as individuals or in relay teams of up to eight people and compete to see how many laps they can complete in the time allotted. There is a 24-minute Kids Race and 3-hour, 6-hour, 12-hour, and 24-hour races for adults. A potluck and bonfire are held on Saturday night to mark the midpoint of the 24-hour race. All proceeds are donated to local charities.

The **Annual Mountain Bike Biathlon** (406/599-4464, www.skirunbike.com) takes place in June. There are two divisions, and first-timers are welcome to participate. The Match Class is for participants with experience and their own rifles; the Sport Class is for novices. The race covers 7.5 kilometers with two bouts of shooting. If you'd like to get some practice in before the event, you can

406/646-4100 or 888/854-5862, www.yellowstonegiantscreen.com, $9.75 adults, $9.25 seniors, $7 children 4-12) boasts a six-story-high screen with stereo surround sound that makes any subject larger than life. Nature-oriented movies rotate in and out, as do popular movies like *Star Wars* that benefit from the massive screen, but *Yellowstone* is frequently on the playlist and offers an extraordinary introduction to the park's history, wildlife, geothermal activity, and mountainous beauty with giant screen grandeur. The biggest bargain in town is the $0.52 soft serve ice cream available daily at the theater.

ENTERTAINMENT AND EVENTS

There is plenty for visitors to do year-round in West Yellowstone. Before you arrive, you may want to visit the chamber of commerce events calendar (www.westyellowstonechamber.com) to scope out the current happenings. The **West Yellowstone visitors center** (30 Yellowstone Ave., 406/646-7701) also has

West Yellowstone

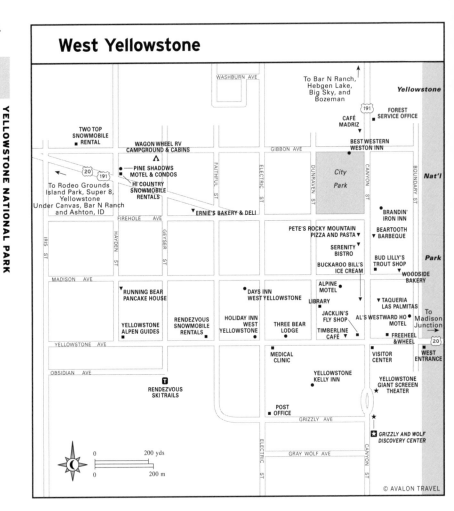

© AVALON TRAVEL

sign up for the **Biathlon Shooting Camp** (406-599-4465).

The **Wild West Yellowstone Rodeo** (406-560-6913, www.yellowstonerodeo.com, $15 adults, $8 children) is another summertime event that runs June-August. Shows begin at 8pm and are held three times each week.

SPORTS AND RECREATION
Fishing

The fishing around West tends to be as plentiful as it is phenomenal. In addition to the big-name rivers like the **Madison, Firehole, Yellowstone,** and the nearby **Henry's Fork** across the border in Idaho, there are all sorts of small streams and beautiful lakes of all sizes. **Hebgen Lake** and **Quake Lake** are two favorites for year-round fishing.

You won't have any difficulty finding guides and gear in the town of West Yellowstone. Among the most respected, and certainly the best-known, is **Bud Lilly's Trout Shop** (39 Madison Ave., 406-646-7801, www.budlillys.com, 7am-7pm daily during the season), which has been outfitting and guiding anglers for 60 years. Another pretty famous name among anglers is Bob Jacklin of **Jacklin's Fly Shop** (105 Yellowstone Ave., 406/646-7336, www.jacklinsflyshop.com, 7am-10pm summer). Both outfitters are licensed to guide in and out of Yellowstone National Park, and both carry an excellent assortment of top-of-the-line gear. Jacklin's Fly Shop also hosts free fly-casting lessons every Sunday evening in summer. Anglers do not need state fishing licenses in Yellowstone, but a Yellowstone fishing permit—available at any of the visitors centers in the park—is required.

Mountain Biking and Cross-Country Skiing

Sandwiched between Yellowstone and the Gallatin National Forest on a high plateau, West Yellowstone offers excellent terrain for mountain biking. Because of its high altitude and location at the top of a reasonably flat plateau, West Yellowstone is also known for its cross-country ski trails. The town's excellent **Rendezvous Ski Trails** (look for the archway at the south end of Geyser St., www.skirunbikemt.com) offer roughly 22 miles of gently rolling terrain, groomed for both skate and classic skiers, which easily converts to a single-track for mountain bikers when the snow melts. Athletes from around the world come to train in West thanks in large part to this trail system. And it should be noted that the proximity to Yellowstone opens up a whole new world of opportunity for both mountain bikers and skiers.

The best bike and ski shop in town—which also has surprisingly stylish clothes, great gear, a pilates studio, and killer coffee—is the **Freeheel & Wheel** (33 Yellowstone Ave., 406/646-7744, www.freeheelandwheel.com, 9am-7pm Sun.-Thurs., 9am-8pm Fri.-Sat.). It rents, sells, and services bikes and skis and can offer any advice you could possibly need on the region's best rides and trails. Front suspension kid and adult mountain bikes ($10/hour, $35/day) and road bikes ($10/hour, $40/

day) can be rented and come with a helmet and water bottle.

Other Winter Recreation

Although snowmobiling inside the park has shifted with the four-stroke engine and guide requirements along with daily entry limits, West Yellowstone is still considered the snowmobile capital of the world for its proximity to the 200 miles of groomed trails in the park as well as hundreds of miles of groomed terrain in the national forests surrounding West.

There are numerous places in town to rent a snowmobile, and since the park mandates that all snowmobilers within park boundaries use a guide, several outfits also offer guiding services both in and out of the park. **Two Top Snowmobile Rental** (645 Gibbon Ave., 800/646-7802, www.twotopsnowmobile. com) has rentals for self-guided tours outside the park from $119 per day and guided tours into the park from $189. It also has licensed guides, Yellowstone-mandated four-stroke engines, and other rental equipment. Another full-service rental outfit in West is **Rendezvous Snowmobile Rentals** (415 Yellowstone Ave., 406/646-9564 or 800/426-7669, www.winteryellowstone.com), renting snowmobiles at $119-188 per day for travel outside the park or $159 inside the park with a guide fee of $50 per snowmobile. For deep-powder backcountry touring options outside the park, **Hi Country Snowmobile Rentals** (229 Hayden St., 406/646-7541 or 800/624-5291, www.hicountrysnowmobile. com) is an excellent bet, with snowmobile rentals from its entirely new fleet each year, guided trail rides, and guided backcountry tours. Rates vary throughout the year, so call for information.

For those who want to explore the backcountry outside Yellowstone National Park in a slightly quieter way, dogsledding might be the perfect choice. **Klondike Dreams** (Yellowstone Rental and Sports, U.S. 20, 8 miles west of West Yellowstone, 406/646-4988, www.klondikedreams.com, $100 over 80 pounds, $50 under 80 pounds) offers

Spring Biking Through the Park

For a few magical weeks between the end of the snowmobile season and the onset of the summer car traffic, Yellowstone's roads are open exclusively to nonmotorized users. This means that bicyclists, walkers, runners, inline skaters, and roller skiers can cruise through the park in near silence with eyes focused on bison traffic as opposed to wide Winnebagos. Depending on the seasonal snow, the road between the west entrance and Mammoth Hot Springs typically opens the last Friday in March and stays open to nonmotorized users until the third Thursday in April. Opening can be delayed in heavy snow years due to the need for plowing.

Sometime in May there is normally a brief period of bicycle-only traffic permitted from the east entrance to the east end of Sylvan Pass, and from the south entrance to West Thumb Junction. The roads between Madison Junction and Old Faithful, and Norris Junction to Canyon, remain closed to all traffic during this spring season for human safety and bear management.

There is something truly spellbinding about being on the open road in the park, the wind whistling through your helmet. The relative silence allows some unrivaled wildlife viewing and necessitates great care. As nerve-racking as it can be to be engulfed by a herd of bison while driving in your car, coming across them on your bike is an entirely different scenario. Still, if you are cautious and respectful, being on your bike can allow you to feel somewhat less like an intruder and more like a resident. You can fall into sync with the flow of the rivers, the movement of the breeze, and the calls of the animals. It is a remarkable way to experience the park.

With that said: Respect, restraint, and absolute caution are of vital importance to your safety and the well-being of the animals. Keep a good distance from all wildlife—25 yards from ungulates and 100 yards from predators. Remember that bison can run at speeds topping 30 mph, and they can jump a six-foot fence. Harbor no illusions about your immunity from an attack. The fact that you have approached silently allows for more of a startle factor for the animals and increases the likelihood of a conflict. Wear a helmet, and dress in layers: Yellowstone in spring can go from blue skies to blizzard conditions in a staggeringly short period of time. Be prepared for anything, and understand that there are no services in the park at this time. Enjoy this spectacularly unique opportunity to enjoy the park up close. For specific information about road openings, call 307/344-2109.

---

two-hour rides and kennel tours featuring its Alaskan huskies with Iditarod bloodlines.

Another amazing way to see the park is on a guided snow coach tour. There are numerous providers, but **Yellowstone Alpen Guides** (555 Yellowstone Ave., 406/646-9591 or 800/858-3502, www.yellowstoneguides.com, from $145 adults, $135 seniors, $110 children under 16, prices do not include national park passes) offers classic 10-passenger Bombardiers, a fantastic array of tours, and some of the best naturalist guides anywhere. Snow coach tours can be combined with some cross-country skiing in the park.

FOOD

For a filling breakfast or lunch, head to the ★ **Woodside Bakery** (17 Madison Ave.,

406/646-7779, www.woodsidebakery.net, 7am-3:30pm Mon.-Sat., $3-12). From the breakfast sandwiches to the cinnamon rolls to the box lunches, everything is made from scratch and delicious. Another great spot for a full breakfast, hot lunch, or terrific sack lunches is the long-standing **Ernie's Bakery & Deli** (409 Firehole Ave., 406/646-9467, www.erniesbakery.com, 7am-3pm daily summer, 7am-2pm daily winter, $7-15). **Running Bear Pancake House** (538 Madison Ave., 406/646-7703, 6:30am-2pm daily, $4-15) offers family-style dining for breakfast and lunch.

For the best soup, salad, and potato bar in town, try the **Timberline Café** (135 Yellowstone Ave., 406/646-9349, 6:30am-10pm daily mid-May-early Oct., breakfast and lunch $6-14, dinner $11-31), an old-school establishment that has been feeding Yellowstone visitors and locals during the summer season since the early 1900s. Don't miss the homemade pie. A real surprise in this tourist town in the wonderful ★ **Café Madriz** (311 N. Canyon St., 406/646-9245, late May-mid-Sept., 11am-2pm and 5pm-9pm Mon.-Sat., $11-30), which serves authentic Spanish dishes, from paella and tortilla española to hot and cold tapas, and makes the most of fresh, local ingredients. The salads are killer.

Another West Yellowstone institution is **Buckaroo Bill's Ice Cream** (24 N. Canyon St., 406/646-7901, 10:30am-10:30pm Mon.-Sat. May-Oct., $6.75-26), which has excellent bison burgers, steaks, and sandwiches in addition to mouthwatering Montana-made ice cream. The joint is popular, though, and it's not always easy to get a seat; the outside patio is a lively place for a meal. **Canyon Street Grill** (22 N. Canyon St., 406/646-7548, 11am-9pm daily May-Oct., seasonal hours vary, $7-13) is a 1950s-style diner with delicious burgers, fries, and milk shakes. **Beartooth Barbeque** (111 N. Canyon St., 406/646-0227, 11am-9pm daily May-Oct., $9-25) serves slow-cooked meat and fried pickles. **Pete's Rocky Mountain Pizza and Pasta** (112 Canyon St., 406/646-7820, 11am-10pm summer, seasonal hours vary, delivery available after 5pm, $8-30) serves up good pizza and hearty pasta dishes like elk sausage spaghetti and Italian buffalo ravioli. If you like Mexican street food, the best place within a day's drive from Yellowstone is, without a doubt, ★ **Taqueria Las Palmitas** (21 N. Canyon St., 406/640-0172, 10:30am-9pm daily early Apr.-mid-Oct., $5-10), known locally as "The Taco Bus." We're talking soft tacos, beans, and more, piled onto paper plates and served in an old-school bus. It couldn't be less fancy or more satisfying.

For a more gourmet experience, **Serenity Bistro** (38 N. Canyon St., 406/646-7660, www.sydneysbistro.com, 11am-3pm and 5pm-close daily May-Oct., $8-30) is undoubtedly the place. It serves excellent, fresh meals utilizing local ingredients whenever possible. Entrées include the bistro burger, Panang chicken, trout escalope, buffalo tortellini, elk tenderloin, and twice-cooked quail. Pasta lovers won't want to miss the butternut squash. The bistro also offers gourmet salads and sandwiches for lunch and boasts the most extensive wine list in town.

Six miles outside of town is the **Bar N Ranch** (970 Buttermilk Creek Rd., 406/646-9445, www.bar-n-ranch.com, 7am-10am and 5pm-10pm daily May-Oct., $15-45), a wonderful place for a meal. With beautiful views all around, you can indulge in terrific Western gourmet cuisine including game burgers, bison stir-fry, steaks, and pasta. In an interesting twist on the meal, one option is to have the restaurant provide the food, but you cook it on an outside grill.

ACCOMMODATIONS

In the summer months there are more than 2,000 hotel rooms to be found in West and about 1,300 when the snow covers the ground. Guest ranches, bed-and-breakfasts, and cabin rentals are also available. **Yellowstone Tour & Travel** (800/221-1151, www.yellowstone-travel.com) is a full-service travel agency in West Yellowstone that can book everything from accommodations and tours to complete packages. The West Yellowstone Chamber of Commerce (406/646-7701, www.destinationyellowstone.com) also has an excellent website that shows all lodging availability.

Just seven blocks from the west entrance to Yellowstone National Park, the pet-friendly **Pine Shadows Motel & Condos** (229 Hayden St., 406/646-7541 or 800/624-5291, www.pineshadowsmotel.com, $69-230) is open year-round and has a selection of motel rooms and newly built, spacious condos, all of which are clean and comfortable. As is true in much of the town, free Wi-Fi is available. Also open year-round, the **Three Bear Lodge** (217 Yellowstone Ave., 406/646-7353 or 800/646-7353, www.threebearlodge.com, $108-264) offers 44 guest rooms in its recently remodeled pet-friendly motel unit and 26 in the lodge, where no two rooms are alike. All guest rooms have a refrigerator, a microwave, an LCD TV, handmade furniture, and fluffy duvets.

The **Alpine Motel** (120 Madison Ave., 406/646-7544, www.alpinemotelwestyellowstone.com, $65-175) is a budget-friendly choice with a variety of units, some including kitchens, just two blocks from the park entrance. The service by owners Brian and Patty is noticeably good. Another good independent property, which is only open mid-May-mid-October, is **Al's Westward Ho Motel** (16 Boundary St., 888/646-7331, www.alswestwardhomotel.net, $109-159), which is just across the street from the park entrance and the Yellowstone Giant Screen Theatre. A couple of blocks farther from the entrance, but a longstanding and reliable choice in town is the 79-room, pet-friendly **Brandin' Iron Inn** (201 Canyon, 406/646-9411 or 800/217-4613, www.brandiniron.com, $76-299).

There are a number of larger, chain hotels in town, including three Best Western options, the nicest of which is probably the **Best Western Weston Inn** (103 Gibbon Ave., 406/646-7373, www.bestwestern.com, $236-550). Other options include **Holiday Inn West Yellowstone** (315 Yellowstone Ave., 406/646-7365 or 800/315-2621, www.ihg.com, $118-409), **Days Inn West Yellowstone** (301 Madison, 406/646-7656, www.daysinn.com, $93-332), **Yellowstone Kelly Inn** (104 S. Canyon, 406/646-4544, www.yellowstonekellyinn.com, $148-339), and, 7.5 miles from town, **West Yellowstone Super 8** (1545 Targhee Pass, 406/646-9584, www.super8.com, $179-269).

CAMPING

With nearly two dozen private and public campgrounds in the vicinity of West, campers have plenty of choices, although most are geared to RV campers. The nearest U.S. Forest Service campground is **Baker's Hole Campground** (U.S. 191, 3 miles northwest of West Yellowstone, 406/823-6961, www.hebgenbasincampgrounds.com, May 1-Sept. 15 depending on weather, $16 for 1 vehicle, $6

for each additional vehicle, plus $6 for electrical sites), with 73 sites set on a scenic oxbow of the Madison River. Basic services such as water and trash pickup are provided, there is firewood for sale, and the fishing is excellent.

Right in town, just six blocks from the park's west entrance, is **Wagon Wheel RV Campground & Cabins** (408 Gibbon Ave., 406/646-7872, www.wagonwheelrv.com, camping May 15-Sept. 30, cabins May 1-Oct. 30, $15 tents, $59-79 full-hookup pull-through sites), offering an ideal forested and quiet setting that is wonderfully convenient. The nine cabins ($149-219), reminiscent of the 1930s and 1940s architecture found throughout the park, are especially charming, but they get booked up quickly and require three- and five-night stays.

For a truly unique experience outside of town, ★ **Yellowstone Under Canvas** (890 Buttermilk Creek Rd., 406/219-0441, www.mtundercanvas.com, Memorial Day-Labor Day) offers "glamping" (glamour-camping) options ($129-439) ranging from modest tipis and safari tents to luxury safari suite tents with king-size beds, private baths with freestanding tubs, and woodstoves. A variety of options are available, from shared bathrooms (the hot water showers are provided by a generator that runs from 6am to 11pm and is not quiet) to private but separate baths, influencing the price. But all of these tents and tipis are set in a mountain-ringed meadow with a creek running through. And the bedding is nothing short of luxurious. The guests here are largely international, and it can be a treat to listen to campfire or next-tent pillow talk in several different languages. The only downside is that snoring is universally annoying, and with all but the most expensive tents situated so close together, light sleepers are bound to hear plenty of snorers. Still, this is comfortable camping without the work.

INFORMATION AND SERVICES

The **West Yellowstone Chamber of Commerce** (406/646-7701, www.

Yellowstone Under Canvas

information you need about the city and the state, and you can even buy your park permits. The visitors center also has a lot of information about the regular and special events held in town.

The **West Yellowstone Public Library** (23 N. Dunraven St., 406/646-9017, 10am-6pm Tues.-Thurs., 10am-5pm Fri., 10am-2pm Sat. May-Oct; 9am-5pm Tues. and Thurs., 10am-5pm Wed. and Fri., 9am-noon Sat. winter) is located between Yellowstone and Madison Avenues. It offers free Wi-Fi and has three computers with Internet access.

The town's only **post office** (209 Grizzly Ave., 406/646-7704, 8:30am-5pm Mon.-Fri.) is located at the corner of Electric Street and Grizzly Avenue.

Swan Cleaners (520 Madison Ave., 406/646-7892, 7am-9pm daily summer, 8am-9pm daily fall-spring) is located just east of the Running Bear Pancake House. It has coin-operated machines and laundry services.

For nonemergency medical care, you can walk into the **Community Health Partners-West Yellowstone Clinic** (11 Electric St., 406/646-9441, 8am-5pm Tues.-Wed. and Fri., 10am-7pm Thurs.). There is 24-hour paramedic emergency service available in town by calling 911.

destinationyellowstone.com), **Montana State Visitors Center,** and **Yellowstone Park Visitors Center** (307/344-2876) are all housed under the same roof at 30 Yellowstone Avenue. You can get all the

Grand Teton National Park

Just south of Yellowstone, Grand Teton National Park is even more dazzling than its more prominent neighbor in mountainous splendor. The Tetons soar skyward, 3 in a sea of 12 peaks topping 12,000 feet.

The mountains are young—still growing, in fact—and utterly spectacular, perhaps the most dramatic anywhere in the Lower 48. The park itself contains approximately 310,000 acres (roughly 15 percent the size of Yellowstone), 100 miles of paved road, and much to the delight of hikers, some 200 miles of trails.

Like Yellowstone, Grand Teton is home to healthy populations of wildlife—this is among the best places in the West to see a moose—but the rugged terrain and limited number of roads affords the animals better places to hide. Still, you always need to be prepared for bear encounters in the park. Beyond the stunning natural and geological history of the region, Grand Teton offers some interesting human-built attractions—including the historic and elegant Jenny Lake Lodge, the Chapel of the Transfiguration, and the Laurance S. Rockefeller Preserve—that are well worth seeing. At the end of the day, though, Grand Teton is a place for nature lovers and outdoor enthusiasts. The vistas are unparalleled, as are the natural features and recreational opportunities.

HISTORY

The history of this region dates back 11,000 years, when it was a seasonal hunting ground for such tribes as the Shoshone, Gros Ventre, Flathead, and Blackfeet. John Colter was likely the first European to explore the region; he is thought to have traveled through the area in 1808, guided by wildlife and Native American trails. By the 1820s the area was widely known for its abundance of beavers, and mountain men arrived with traps in hand. Trapper David E. Jackson spent the winter of 1829 along the shores of Jackson Lake; the valley, the lake, and the nearby town of Jackson bear his name. Many of the park's features were named by the Hayden Geological Survey in 1871.

Previous: the Tetons mountain range; a magnificent view in the Tetons. **Above:** a lake created by retreating glaciers.

Look for ★ to find recommended
sights, activities, dining, and lodging.

Highlights

★ **Cruise to Elk Island:** Lure yourself out of bed and into this wonderland with an early morning cruise that features breakfast (page 80).

★ **Oxbow Bend:** This hairpin curve of slow-moving backwater from the Snake River is perfect for novice boaters, wildlife watchers, and photographers looking to capture the crystalline reflection of Mount Moran (page 82).

★ **Signal Mountain:** Follow this exciting five-mile drive with expansive views of the entire valley (page 82).

★ **Jenny Lake:** Resting like a mirror at the base of the Tetons, this alpine lake is a gem for hikers, boaters, and picnickers (page 87).

★ **Hidden Falls and Inspiration Point:** The glorious views along this popular and scenic hike are worth every step (page 87).

★ **Craig Thomas Discovery and Visitor Center:** This architectural gem—complete with video rivers running beneath your feet and walls of windows that showcase the Tetons—offers a stunning introduction to the park (page 91).

★ **Laurance S. Rockefeller Preserve:** The longtime summer home of the Rockefeller

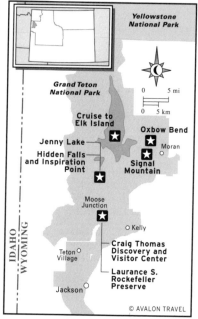

family, this lovely preserve exemplifies the family's commitment to stewardship (page 91).

The region was sparsely settled and farmed due to the climate and the soil, but it was used for cattle ranching in the late 1800s. The area was also well known among hunters and eventually became the setting for a handful of dude ranches.

In 1897, President Grover Cleveland established the Teton Forest Reserve, and the Teton National Forest was created in 1908. The park itself—96,000 acres in its first incarnation—was set aside by Congress in 1929 and included primarily the mountains and alpine lakes. There were some attempts through the 1930s to add to the park, none of which were successful. John D. Rockefeller Jr., however, was quietly purchasing land in the Teton Valley through his Snake River Land Company. Between 1926 and 1946, Rockefeller bought 35,000 acres adjacent to the park, and in 1949 he deeded all but 2,000 acres to the federal government, which had established the 210,000-acre Jackson Hole National Monument under President Franklin Roosevelt in 1943. In 1950, Congress agreed to merge the monument and the Rockefeller-donated land with the park, bringing it to its current boundaries.

PLANNING YOUR TIME

Grand Teton National Park is smaller, and in some ways more manageable, than its northerly neighbor. There are only 100 miles of paved road, all of which can be driven easily in less than a day's time. With fewer accommodations than Yellowstone, Grand Teton lends itself to easy day trips from Jackson Hole, but it is a compelling destination on its own. Grand Teton is a paradise for outdoor enthusiasts. Hikers, bikers, boaters, and in winter, cross-country skiers will have no problem coming up with marvelous weeklong itineraries. Still, for those on a time budget, you can get an excellent sampling of the park in two days, but even if you are just driving through, there are a few places that should not be missed.

While summer is by far the busiest time in the park, spring and fall can be magnificent with wildflowers, golden aspens, and more active wildlife. **Hiking** and **climbing** in the Tetons is best done in summer and early fall, after the winter snow has melted and before it starts flying again. Still, snow squalls and bad weather can surprise hikers any time of year, so come prepared. Park rangers offer marvelous programs throughout the year that are an excellent way to make the most of the time you have. In the fall, for example, drivers can join ranger-led **wildlife caravans** from the Craig Thomas Discovery and Visitor Center that guide visitors to the best places to see wildlife that day. **Ranger-led hikes and eco-talks** are geared to the seasons and offer visitors a wonderful insiders' look at the park.

The National Park Service offers an excellent trip-planning tool online (www.nps.gov), or you can order a booklet by mail by calling 307/739-3600.

INFORMATION AND SERVICES

Visit the website of the **National Park Service** (www.nps.gov) to help plan your trip to Grand Teton. In the section titled Plan Your Visit, you'll find answers to most of your pressing questions. When you enter the park, you will receive a copy of the park newspaper, *Grand Teton Guide*, which has a lot of useful information about park facilities, hours of operation, and programs and specific activities offered daily or weekly. If you need additional information before you go, you can call the **visitors information line** (307/739-3300, ext. 1). For campground information, call the **Grand Teton Lodge Company** (800/628-9988) and for **backcountry** information, contact the permits office (307/739-3309) or book backcountry sites online (www.recreation.gov) in advance.

Park Fees and Passes

Single-entry entrance fees are $30 per vehicle, $15 per person for hikers or bicyclists, and $25 per motorcycle for seven days in both Grand Teton National Park and Yellowstone National Park.

Grand Teton National Park

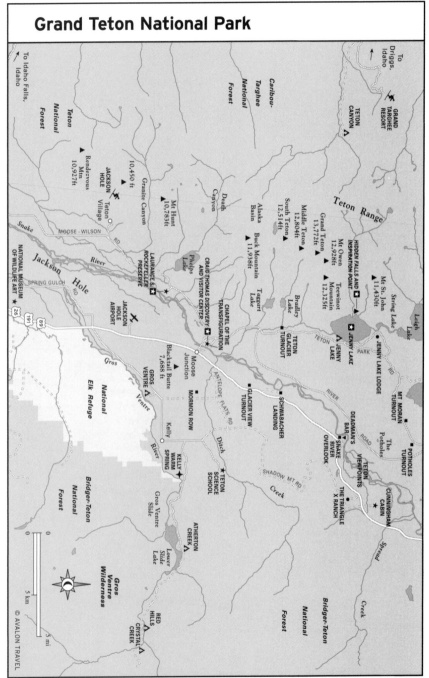

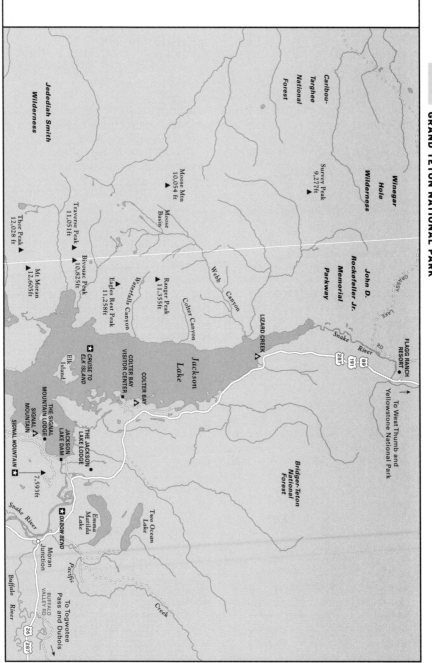

Jedediah Smith
Wilderness

Winegar
Hole
Wilderness

Caribou-
Targhee
National
Forest

Survey Peak
9,277 ft ▲

Moose Mtn
10,054 ft ▲

Moose
Basin

John D.
Rockefeller Jr.
Memorial
Parkway

Thor Peak ▲
12,028 ft

▲Mt Moran
12,605 ft

Traverse Peak ▲
11,051 ft

Bivouac Peak ▲
10,825 ft

Waterfalls Canyon

Eagles Rest Peak
11,258 ft

Ranger Peak ▲
11,355 ft

Webb Canyon

Colter Canyon

LIZARD CREEK

Snake River

GRASSY LAKE RD

FLAGG RANCH
RESORT ●

287
191
89

To West Thumb and
Yellowstone National Park →

Jackson
Lake

Elk
Island

CRUISE TO
ELK ISLAND

COLTER BAY
VISITOR CENTER

COLTER BAY

Bridger-Teton
National
Forest

THE SIGNAL
MOUNTAIN LODGE ●

SIGNAL
MOUNTAIN

THE SIGNAL MOUNTAIN

SIGNAL MOUNTAIN

▲ 7,593 ft

JACKSON
LAKE LODGE ■

THE JACKSON
LAKE DAM ■

Emma
Matilda Lake

Two Ocean
Lake

Snake River

OXBOW BEND

Moran
Junction

Buffalo
River

BUFFALO
VALLEY RD

Pacific

Creek

To Togwotee
Pass and Dubois

26
287

With more than 200 miles of maintained trails in the park, backpacking and backcountry camping provide a unique way to explore the area. Permits ($25) are required and can be obtained in person on a first-come, first-served basis no more than one day before the start of a trip at the Craig Thomas Visitor Center, Colter Bay Visitor Center, or Jenny Lake Ranger Station. Roughly one-third of **backcountry campsites** in heavily used areas can be reserved in advance ($35) January 1-May 15 (877/444-6777 or 518/885-3639 for international calls, www.recreation.gov). All campers are required to use bear-proof canisters below 10,000 feet and at sites without bear boxes. Free canisters are provided when registering for a permit.

Visitors Centers

There are four main visitors centers in the park. The impressive **Craig Thomas Discovery and Visitor Center** (307/739-3399, 9am-5pm daily early Mar.-Apr., 8am-5pm daily May-early June and mid-Sept.-Oct., 8am-7pm daily early June-mid-Sept.) is located 12 miles north of Jackson and 0.5 mile west of Moose Junction. Exhibits include a relief map of the park, an introductory video and natural history displays. The **Jenny Lake Visitor Center** (307/739-3392, 8am-5pm daily late May-early June and early Sept.-late Sept., 8am-7pm early June-early Sept.) is 8 miles north of Moose Junction on Teton Park Road. Visitors' services include guided walks and talks, and exhibits focus on park geology. Half a mile west of Colter Bay Junction is the **Colter Bay Visitor Center** (307/739-3594, 8am-5pm daily early May-early June and early Sept.-early Oct., 8am-7pm daily early June-early Sept.). Four miles south of Moose on the Moose-Wilson Road (which is closed to RVs and trailers) is the **Laurance S. Rockefeller Preserve Center** (307/739-3654, 9am-5pm daily early June-late Sept.), which offers eight miles of hiking trails, fishing and swimming opportunities in Phelps Lake, and unique sensory exhibits. Opening and closing dates for all visitors centers can change annually and are listed online (www.nps.gov).

Entrance Stations

Grand Teton National Park has two official entrance stations, but can be accessed from the south (Jackson), the east (Dubois), and the north (Yellowstone). Although you will be in Grand Teton National Park starting just 5 miles north of Jackson, the southernmost **Moose Entrance Station** is about 20 miles north of town. The eastern entrance at **Moran Junction** is 30 miles north of Jackson and 55 miles west of Dubois, Wyoming, over the Togwotee Pass, which is closed in winter. From the north, visitors enter Grand Teton National Park from Yellowstone; the $30 admission (for private passenger vehicles) is valid for seven days. For $50, vehicles gain access to both Yellowstone and Grand Teton for seven days. Visitors coming in from Yellowstone can stop for information at **Flagg Ranch Information Station** or the **Colter Bay Visitor Center** 18 miles south of Yellowstone.

Services

The main concessionaire in the park is the **Grand Teton Lodge Company** (800/628-9988, www.gtlc.com), which operates lodging, restaurants, tours, and activities. Its website can also be a great aid in planning your visit. The Grand Teton Lodge Company's mission is to preserve, protect, and inspire, and to do so in part by following sustainable business practices. It is responsible for the lodging, restaurants, tours, and activities at Jackson Lake Lodge, Jenny Lake Lodge, Colter Bay Village, Headwaters Lodge & Cabins at Flagg Ranch, and campgrounds throughout the park. The restaurants use free-range, naturally raised meat and dairy, organic coffee and produce, and support sustainable farming practices.

For **medical emergencies** within the park, dial 911. **St. John's Medical Center** (625 E. Broadway, Jackson, 307/733-3636) is open year-round, and the **Grand Teton**

Bear #399 and the Grizzlies of Grand Teton

In July 1975, when mountain bluebells and Indian paintbrush were coloring the Wyoming mountainsides purple and red, grizzly bears were listed as "threatened" under the Endangered Species Act. At that time, and for several years afterward, not a single grizzly was known to wander the wilds of Grand Teton National Park. Estimates put the number of grizzlies in Yellowstone at around 136 at the time, but in Grand Teton, there wasn't even one.

The animal's listing as a threatened species and, thankfully, passionate involvement by good people has changed that. In early 2016, the number of grizzlies in the Greater Yellowstone Ecosystem—which includes Yellowstone and Grand Teton National Parks and their surrounds—hovered somewhere around the 700 mark. And at the end of 2015, Grand Teton National Park was home to some 60 of these totemic animals.

Because it's true that we protect what we love, and love what we know, perhaps no bear has done as much for grizzly protection as #399. First captured and collared in 2001 when she was five years old, #399 has become the most famous grizzly in the world. She has had more than 15 cubs and grandcubs, and has been watched along roadsides by thousands upon thousands of park visitors over the years. "Along with her cubs, she made you want to protect her," said acclaimed photographer Tom Mangelsen, who, with writer Todd Wilkinson, put out a marvelous book on #399 in 2015, *Grizzlies of Pilgrim Creek* (www.mangelsen.com).

Because she is so visible, Bear #399 has shown us the challenges bears face to simply survive. According to Wilkinson, nearly 75 percent of her descendants have died as a result of human encounters—struck by cars, killed illegally by big game hunters, euthanized for preying on cattle or for coming too close to human development. She has lost other cubs to starvation or encounters with dominant males. But it's the day-to-day glimpses of #399, often with her cubs, that endear her to people the world over and give people a vision of something worth fighting for.

Even with postcard bears like #399 and citizen advocates, the fight to protect bears is far from won. After the success of their recovery over the last 40 years, in the early part of 2016, the U.S. Fish and Wildlife Service proposed that grizzly bears be removed from the federal List of Endangered and Threatened Wildlife, which strips away various protective measures and eventually opens grizzlies up for hunting. No doubt the delisting will be debated and appealed for months or years to come, but even as the status of grizzly bears is questioned, their value in our wild world should not be.

While scientists call the grizzly an "umbrella" or "indicator" species—meaning that when the grizzlies thrive, so too do the other plants and animals that inhabit their world—naturalist and writer Doug Peacock, who has dedicated his life to making the world a safer place for grizzlies, goes further in asserting the importance of their survival. "Really, we are as much endangered as the grizzly bears. The fate of humans and grizzlies is a single, collective one," he said.

Twenty years old in 2016, Bear #399 will not be around much longer. But let's hope and fight to make sure grizzly bears still are.

Medical Clinic (307/543-2514 during business hours or 307/733-8002 after hours, 9am-5pm daily mid-May-mid-Oct.) is located in the Jackson Lake Lodge.

TRANSPORTATION
Getting There and Around
BY AIR
Jackson Hole Airport (JAC, 1250 E. Airport Rd., Jackson, 307/733-7682, www. jacksonholeairport.com) is only nine miles from the south entrance to the park and is served by American, Delta, United, and United Express. The schedules change seasonally but include regular flights from Salt Lake City, Denver, Seattle, Chicago, Minneapolis, Dallas, Houston, New York, Washington DC, Atlanta, San Francisco, and Los Angeles.

The airport has on-site car rentals from **Avis, Hertz,** and **Enterprise. Dollar,**

Thrifty, National, and **Alamo** are available off-site.

Somewhat amazingly for this part of the country, Jackson has 30 taxi companies serving the area, including **Broncs Taxi** (307/413-9863, www.jackson-hole-taxi.com), **Snake River Taxi** (307/413-9009, www.snakerivertaxi.com), and **Teton Mountain Taxi** (307/699-7969, www.jacksonholecab.com). Transportation to Jackson from the airport runs roughly $35 for 1-2 people. A taxi to Teton Village averages $60-65.

BY CAR

Grand Teton National Park is 20 miles from Jackson, 195 miles from Bozeman through Yellowstone, 290 miles from Salt Lake City and 550 miles from Denver. Grand Teton National Park is immediately south of Yellowstone and about 100 miles southwest of Cody when the park roads are open and 323 miles in the winter when park roads are closed. If you are driving from Yellowstone, take U.S. Highway 89 south, which will lead you directly into the park. If you are coming from Idaho Falls, from I-15 take U.S. Highway 26 east to Idaho Highway 31 east, continuing to Highway 33 east. This will take you through the scenic Teton Pass, where it becomes Wyoming Highway 22. Continue until you reach U.S. Highway 89, taking it north into the park. An alternate route, flatter but slightly longer, is to take U.S. Highway 26 until it hits U.S. Highway 89 and head north.

BY BUS

Alltrans/Jackson Hole Express (307/733-3135 or 800/443-6133, www.jacksonholealltrans.com) offers shuttles between Jackson Hole, eastern Idaho, and Salt Lake City. The nearest **Greyhound** stop is in Idaho Falls.

Getting Around
PRIVATE VEHICLES

If you are driving through the park, don't forget to keep an eye on your fuel gauge. The only gas station open year-round is at **Dornan's** (gas pumps available 24 hours if paying with a credit card) in Moose. Other gas stations are open May-October and are at Signal Mountain, Jackson Lodge, and Colter Bay.

For up-to-date road information and closures in the park, call 307/739-3614 in summer, 307/739-3682 in winter, or 307/344-2117 for Yellowstone road reports. For Wyoming road information, contact the **Wyoming Department of Transportation** (888/996-7623, www.wyoroad.info).

TOURS

The **Grand Teton Lodging Company** (800/628-9988, www.gtlc.com) offers any number of tours throughout the park, including four-hour tours departing from Jackson Lake Lodge during summer.

A great educational opportunity is provided by the **Teton Science Schools** (307/733-1313, www.tetonscience.org), based in Jackson. The organization is committed to creating a deeper appreciation and understanding of the wilderness and natural ecosystems found in the Greater Yellowstone area. Its experts provide classes and programs to engage every type of learner from small children to adults. The courses focus on everything from ecology and geology to unique plant and animal life. Even if you only plan to be in the park for a day or two, visit the website to see what is being offered. Regular programs can include hikes, campfires, canoe tours, and wildlife viewing. The school also offers renowned **Wildlife Expeditions** (877/404-6626). These can be half-day, full-day, or multiple-day guided tours with professional wildlife biologists who provide you with an up-close and unique opportunity to experience the natural wonders of the park.

Another tour company that focuses on getting visitors up close and personal with the park's wildlife in comfy 4x4 vehicles is **EcoTour Adventures** (307/690-9533, www.jhecotouradventures.com). Guided half-day tours, often at sunrise or sunset, run roughly four hours long and start at $130 for adults and $95 for children 10 and under. Full-day trips last approximately eight hours and can take visitors into Grand Teton and Yellowstone. These tours include lunch at one of the park lodges and start at $225 for adults and $190 for children 10 and under.

PLANTS AND ANIMALS

Despite the fact that every square inch of Grand Teton National Park is at or above 6,400 feet in elevation, there is a remarkable diversity of both plant and animal life in the three main growing zones and four distinct habitat regions. Throughout the short but sublime summer, the valleys are awash in colorful wildflowers. And although animals aren't quite as visible as they are in the vast open spaces or burned-out forests of Yellowstone, wildlife watchers will have terrific opportunities in the park.

All three of Grand Teton's growing zones— alpine, subalpine, and valley—fall between 6,400 feet and 13,770 feet in elevation, meaning harsh climates and a short growing season. Still, upwards of 1,000 species of vascular plants grow in the park. Porous soil allows for an abundance of colorful wildflowers. And even in the high reaches of the mountains, delicate jewels like alpine forget-me-nots grow close to the ground in mats.

Because of the short growing season, the vast majority of trees in the park are conifers—as in Yellowstone, lodgepole pine is the most common tree—but aspens and cottonwoods have chlorophyll in the bark, allowing them to photosynthesize before putting out leaves. As a result, Grand Teton National Park is illuminated in the fall by changing leaves. Sagebrush is everywhere, lending an almost minty smell to the crisp air.

Along with Yellowstone, Grand Teton National Park is a critical part of the more than 11-million-acre Greater Yellowstone Ecosystem, considered one of the last nearly intact temperate ecosystems on earth. As such, it provides critical home habitat and migratory routes for a number of species.

The park's four main habitat types are alpine, sagebrush, forest, and aquatic. The alpine habitat, above 10,000 feet, is home to some of the park's hardiest creatures: yellowbellied marmots, pikas, and bighorn sheep. In the ubiquitous sagebrush areas, with more than 100 species of grasses and wildflowers, wildlife watchers can look for pronghorn, coyotes, bison, badgers, elk, and Uinta ground squirrels. While not as easy to explore, the park's forested regions are home to elk, mule deer, red squirrels, black bears, and snowshoe hares. And finally, in and around the plentiful lakes, rivers, and ponds of Grand Teton National Park are populations of moose, river otters, beavers, muskrat, coyotes, bison, and mule deer.

Flagg Ranch and Colter Bay

Just south of the Yellowstone border, Flagg Ranch was at one time a U.S. Cavalry outpost. Converted to a guest ranch in 1910 and now known as Headwaters Lodge & Cabins at Flagg Ranch, it is ideally situated for visitors looking to explore both Yellowstone and Grand Teton National Parks from one location. In addition to full resort lodging and services, Flagg Ranch offers activities and services—a gas station, a grocery store, a deli and coffee shop—for those just passing through.

One of the busiest spots in the park, with a marina, lodging, a campground, a visitors center, and a museum on the shores of Jackson Lake, Colter Bay is a practical, if not exactly quiescent, place to stay, and it is a worthwhile region to explore.

SIGHTS
Colter Bay Indian Arts Museum
The unassuming **Colter Bay Indian Arts Museum** (307/739-3594, 8am-7pm daily

early June-Labor Day, 8am-5pm daily Labor Day-early Oct., free) is tacked onto the visitors center almost as an afterthought. But the relatively unknown gem includes important Native American artifacts that belonged to tribes across the country. The David T. Vernon collection—which includes more than 10,000 objects ranging from dolls, shields, pipes, and weapons to photography—was donated by the Rockefeller family with the provision that it be displayed permanently in Grand Teton National Park. In 2012, almost the entire collection was sent to a conservation facility but is slowly coming back to the park, at both the Colter Bay and Craig Thomas Visitor Centers. As of 2016, more than 80 objects had been returned to the park, and digital images of many of the artifacts are available online through the Google Cultural Institute (www.google.com/culturalinstitute/). It is a remarkable collection that could just as easily be on display at the Smithsonian were it not for the wishes of an extremely generous family. Meanwhile, Native American artisans practice their crafts in the museum intermittently through the summer, and a number of prominent lecturers and daily educational events are scheduled on-site.

SPORTS AND RECREATION
Boating and Fishing

On the shores of **Jackson Lake,** by far the largest body of water in the park, Colter Bay and the **Colter Bay Village Marina** (307/543-2811 or 800/628-9988, www.gtlc.com) are excellent launching points for a variety of boating expeditions. From the marina, you can arrange cruises, canoe or kayak excursions, motorboat rentals, and guided fishing trips.

Guided fly-fishing tours can be arranged through the marina as well. Guided Jackson Lake **fishing** (307/543-3100) can be arranged from Colter Bay Marina starting at $95 per hour for 1-2 adults with a two-hour minimum and $21 per additional person; day trips start at $465 for 1-2 people for four hours, or $555 for 1-2 people for eight hours.

★ Cruise to Elk Island

Since nothing builds an appetite like time spent on an alpine lake, there are wonderful breakfast cruises and dinner cruises (307/543-3100, www.gtlc.com) departing from the marina that whisk guests across the lake to Elk Island, in the shadow of Mount Moran. Each cruise takes approximately three hours, and

There are plenty of boating opportunities on Jackson Lake.

departure times change with daylight hours. The breakfast cruise ($45 adults, $23 children 3-11), offered daily except Thursday (which can change from year to year), serves hearty fare with eggs and trout, pancakes, pastries, fresh fruit, and the all-important cowboy coffee. The lunch cruise ($44 adults, $20 children 3-11) includes a sack lunch and plenty of time to explore the island. It departs Monday, Wednesday, Friday, and Saturday at 12:15pm. The dinner cruise ($65 adults, $37 children 6-11) is offered daily (except Thursday) and includes such delectable mountain fare as steak and trout, baked beans, corn on the cob, a salad bar, roasted potatoes, and mouthwatering fruit cobbler. Scenic lake cruises ($31 adults, $13.50 children 3-11), which last about 90 minutes and are geared to different aspects of the park (with one cruise designed especially for kids), depart daily at 10:15am, 1:15pm, and 3:15pm.

Hiking and Biking

There is a lot of marvelous terrain in every corner of the park for hiking and biking, and the northern section near Colter Bay is no exception. The hike to **Hermitage Point** is one of the most significant hikes (and long, at nearly nine miles round-trip). The elevation gain is minimal (980 vertical feet), and the trail, which starts immediately across from the boat launch at the southern end of the parking lot, meanders through forest, meadow, and alongside ponds and streams. The easy **Lakeshore Trail** is only two miles long round-trip and circumnavigates Colter Bay with stunning views in every direction.

North of Colter Bay, near the Flagg Ranch, is **Grassy Lake Road,** a 52-mile dirt road—great for mountain biking—that follows an ancient Indian thoroughfare all the way to Ashton, Idaho. Along the way are hiking trails, streams, ponds, and splendid scenery.

FOOD

The main lodge at Headwaters Lodge & Cabins at Flagg Ranch is the center of all activity at the ranch. It has a gas station, a general store, and **Sheffields Restaurant & Bar** (800/443-2311, 7am-10:30am, 11:30am-2pm, and 5pm-9pm daily June-late Sept., breakfast $7.50-11.75, lunch $9-14, dinner $18-32), which serves a solid range of local cuisine—including rustic bison pot pie and Wyoming prime rib—in a family-friendly setting.

The **John Colter Café Court** in Colter Bay Village (11am-10pm daily early June-early Oct., $6.50-11) offers both Mexican and American food. The café has a variety of tacos, burgers, and burritos at reasonable prices, and box lunches are available. So too is a kids' menu. Also at Colter Bay is the **Ranch House Restaurant** (6:30am-10:30am, 11:30am-1:30pm, and 5:30pm-10pm late May-early Oct.). The restaurant offers family-style meals with an emphasis on barbecue. The breakfast buffet ($10-16) can include enchiladas and organic oatmeal, or if you want to order à la carte ($6.50-15), you can easily fill up on the flatiron steak and eggs. Lunch ($10-19) consists of a good selection of salads, burgers, and sandwiches, while dinner ($17-31) offers hearty steaks, chops, and seafood dishes. The bar is open 11:30am-10:30pm daily and has a small food menu as well.

ACCOMMODATIONS AND CAMPING

The **Headwaters Lodge & Cabins at Flagg Ranch** (307/543-2861 or 307/543-3100, www.gtlc.com, June 1-early Oct.) is touted as the oldest continuously operating resort in upper Jackson Hole. It is ideally situated to take advantage of both Yellowstone and Grand Teton National Parks. The accommodations options include deluxe or premium log cabins ($280-299); camper cabins (from $73), which are a four-walled structure with a permanent roof and cots; RV sites (from $70); and campsites (from $35). Log cabins have two queen or one king bed, coffeemakers, private baths, and patios furnished with rocking chairs. The camper cabins (built in 2012), RV sites, and campsites all include access to 24-hour hot shower and laundry facilities.

Colter Bay Village (307/543-3100, www.

gtlc.com, late May-early Oct.) offers some of the park's most affordable lodging and is located on the northern shore of Jackson Lake. The village has charming historic cabins ($165-239), an RV site, and a tent village. The original homestead cabins, purchased by the Rockefellers and moved to the area, have been refurbished but still offer a glimpse into the past. Each cabin displays a description of its own history. While most of the one-room cabins sleep 2, one can sleep up to 6 people, and the two-room cabin can sleep up to 10 with rollaways. Prices vary depending on the number of occupants in the room and the arrangement of double, twin, and rollaway beds. Pull-through RV sites are available for $68. The tent cabins ($69) consist of two log walls, two canvas walls and a canvas roof, a single lightbulb, and a wood-burning pot-bellied stove. Each log wall has two pull-down bunks with thin mattresses; additional cots can be rented. Guests are encouraged to bring their own bedding, but a limited number of sleeping bags can be rented from the cabin office. Each tent cabin has a picnic and grilling area, and showers are located in the launderette with a fee for use. The **Colter Bay Campground** (800/628-9988, late May-late Sept., $25/vehicle, $11 pp for hikers or bicyclists) has 350 sites. All tent cabins, campsites, and RV sites are discounted up to 50 percent with the presentation of a Golden Access Pass.

Located 30 miles north of Moose between Flagg Ranch and Colter Bay Village, the **Lizard Creek Campground** (800/672-6012, mid-June-early Sept., $25) has 60 individual sites and rarely fills.

Jackson Lake Lodge and Signal Mountain

Its stunning setting, coupled with excellent amenities and access to fantastic hiking and sightseeing in the park's northeastern corner, make Jackson Lake Lodge a vacation destination all its own. Though the lodge is not adjacent to Jackson Lake in the way that the Colter Bay Village is, the views over the lake to the Tetons are magnificent. Nearby, the rustic Signal Mountain Lodge is situated immediately on the water, offering unlimited opportunities for enjoying Jackson Lake and its proximity to wonderful hiking and adventuring.

SIGHTS
★ Oxbow Bend

Just southeast of Jackson Lake Lodge on the main road is Oxbow Bend, a picturesque river area created when the Snake River carved a more southerly route. One of the most photographed areas in the park, the slow-moving water perfectly reflects towering Mount Moran. The serenity of the area attracts an abundance of wildlife, including moose, beavers, and otters along with a vast number of birds. White pelicans can occasionally be spotted passing through, as can sandhill cranes, majestic trumpeter swans, nesting great blue herons, and bald eagles. Avid boaters like to paddle the area in their canoes and kayaks. Don't forget your binoculars and your camera.

★ Signal Mountain

One mile south of Signal Mountain Lodge is the turnoff to Signal Mountain Road and one of the greatest viewpoints in Grand Teton National Park. The winding five-mile road is completely unsuitable for RVs and trailers. Along the way, there are ample spots for wildlife viewing—look for moose in the pond on the right as you start up the road, and the pond lilies blooming in June. Two small parking lots are located near the summit. The first offers the best view of the Tetons: Sunsets are sensational. From the second, a short walk takes you down to an overlook with a view of Oxbow Bend. Visitors in August might even have a chance to pick some succulent huckleberries as they ripen in the late-summer sun.

The story of Signal Mountain's name is a rather tragic one. Around the turn of the 20th century, a local rancher named Roy Hamilton got lost when he was out hunting. Rescuers agreed to light a fire on the mountain as soon as anyone found Hamilton. After nine days, a fire was lit atop the mountain, signaling the end of rescue efforts. Tragically, Hamilton's body was found in the Snake River, and some speculated his business partner had suggested he cross the river in a particularly dangerous spot.

SPORTS AND RECREATION
Fishing

Anglers will be pleased with the varied offerings in this stretch of the park. From the lunkers in Jackson Lake, which can be fished on shore or by boat, to the healthy but discerning trout in the Snake River, guided trips can be arranged through **Grand Teton Lodge Company** (307/543-3100, www.gtlc. com), from $95 per hour for 1-2 adults with a two-hour minimum and $21 per additional person; day trips start at $555 per day for 1-2 anglers. From **Signal Mountain Lodge** (307/543-2831, www.signalmountainlodge. com), anglers can go out with experienced guides in pursuit of Jackson Lake's cutthroat, brown, and lake trout for $99 per hour for 1-2 people with a two-hour minimum and $30 per additional person; half-day trips are $299 for 1-2 people and $99 per additional person. Half-day and multiple-day fishing trips on Jackson Lake can also be arranged through **Grand Teton Fly Fishing** (307/690-0910 or 307/690-4347, www.grandtetonflyfishing. com, all-day floats from $575). A Wyoming fishing license is required for all fishing in the park and can be purchased at **Snake River Angler at Dornan's** (12170 Dornan

Rd., 307/733-3699, www.snakeriverangler. com), **Signal Mountain Marina** (307/543-2831, www.signalmountainlodge.com), and **Colter Bay Marina** (307/543-3100, www. gtlc.com). Pick up a fishing brochure from any of the visitors centers to learn about all park regulations.

Boating

With so much beautiful water in the park, boating is a fantastic way to explore. Rafting on the Snake River, canoeing or kayaking on any number of lakes, or cruising across Jackson Lake—there are options for adrenaline junkies and die-hard landlubbers alike.

Scenic 10-mile floats down the Snake can be arranged through **Signal Mountain Lodge** (307/543-2831, www.signalmountainlodge.com, $72 adults, $47 children 6-12), **Grand Teton Lodge Company** (307/543-3100, www.gtlc.com), or **Solitude Float Trips** (888/704-2800, www.grand-teton-scenic-floats.com, $75 adults, $55 children 6-12, $800 for a private boat for up to 12 guests). Most floats on the Snake River inside the park last about two hours. Both GTLC and Solitude offer a wonderful sunrise float, perfect for spotting wildlife. GTLC also offers four-hour luncheon floats daily ($78 adults, $55 children 6-11) and dinner floats (Tues., Thurs., and Sat., $85 adults, $59 children 6-11) with fun riverside cookouts.

Human-powered boats like kayaks and canoes are permitted on Emma Matilda Lake and Two Ocean Lake, east of Jackson Lake Lodge. Jackson Lake is open to motorboats, human-powered boats, sailboats, water-skiing, and windsurfers. Permits are required for motorized boats ($40) and nonmotorized crafts ($10) and can be purchased at the visitors centers in Moose, Jenny Lake, or Colter Bay. A variety of boats can be rented through **Signal Mountain Lodge** (307/543-2831, www.signalmountainlodge.com), including deck cruisers ($129/hour, $675/day for up to 10 people), pontoon boats ($95/hour, $495/day for up to 8 people), fishing boats ($42/hour, $185/day for up to 5 people), canoes ($21/hour, $85/day for up to

Finding a Guide

Setting off into Grand Teton National Park can be slightly intimidating, making guided tours a good option. The Park Service maintains a list of licensed, permitted, and park-approved guides.

For any type of technical **rock climbing,** a guide is as necessary as a helmet and rope. **Exum Mountain Guides** (307/733-2297, www.exumguides.com) has been offering instruction and guided mountain climbing since 1931, making it the oldest guide service in North America and certainly one of the most prestigious. Exum offers numerous programs, from easy day climbing for families with kids to guided expeditions up the 13,770-foot Grand Teton. Detailed information, including climbing routes and trail conditions, can be found at www.tetonclimbing.blogspot.com.

The Hole Hiking Experience (307/690-4453 or 866/733-4453, www.holehike.com) offers a range of **guided hikes** and **snowshoe or ski tours** in and around the park for all interests and ability levels, from sunrise or sunset discovery tours to all-day wildlife-watching hikes. Kids will love the family day hikes with fun survival-like activities that include eating "lemon drop" ants and using butterfly nets. Winter cross-country ski and snowshoe tours are guided by naturalists and show off the best winter has to offer.

There are several options for guided **horseback riding** trips, May-September, from a number of lodges in the park, including Colter Bay Village, Flagg Ranch, and Jackson Lake Lodge. The **Grand Teton Lodge Company** (307/543-3100, www.gtlc.com) can arrange everything from a one-hour ($40-45) or two-hour ($67-75) horseback ride to breakfast and dinner rides ($42-78) to pony rides ($5). All riders in the park must be at least eight years old and under 225 pounds.

With so many varied bodies of water, there are a number of **fishing** outfitters that can guide any type of trip you can dream up. A good place to start is the **Grand Teton Lodge Company** (307/543-3100, www.gtlc.com), which can arrange trips from any of the accommodations inside the park. Fishing trips on the Snake River or Jackson Lake can also be arranged through the lakefront **Signal Mountain Lodge** (307/543-2831, www.signalmountainlodge.com) or **Grand Teton Fly Fishing** (307/690-0910, www.grandtetonflyfishing.com).

Rafting is popular in Grand Teton National Park, and there are 10 licensed outfitters to guide visitors down the Snake River. As with all activities, **Grand Teton Lodge Company** (307/543-3100, www.gtlc.com) can make arrangements for the park's most popular 10-mile scenic float. Other outfitters include **Barker-Ewing** (307/733-1800 or 800/365-1800, www.barkerewing.com) and **Solitude Float Trips** (307/733-2871 or 888/704-2800, www.grand-teton-scenic-floats.com).

Throughout the year, Park Service rangers offer excellent **naturalist-guided tours.** Late December-March, depending on conditions, daily guided **snowshoe hikes** depart from the **Craig Thomas Discovery and Visitor Center** (307/739-3399, reservations required, $5 donation suggested). During the summer months, the range of offerings is vast—from 30-minute map chats and campfire programs to three-hour hikes. For more information on ranger programs, pick up the park newspaper at any of the entrance stations, call 307/739-3300, or check out the visitors centers in Moose, Jenny Lake, Colter Bay, and the Laurance S. Rockefeller Preserve.

3 people), and sea kayaks ($19/hour, $79/day single, or $25/hour, $99/day for 2 people). The **Grand Teton Lodge Company** (307/543-3100, www.gtlc.com) can also arrange various boat rentals throughout the park.

Hiking and Biking

Sandwiched between Jackson, Emma Matilda, and Two Ocean Lakes, the area around Jackson Lake Lodge offers some wonderful scenic hiking. The **Christian Pond Loop** is a relatively flat and easy 4.3-mile round-trip hike through prime waterfowl habitat. The trailhead is east of the parking lot adjacent to the Jackson Lake Lodge corrals. Nearby, **Two Ocean Lake** offers a moderate 6.4-mile round-trip hike around the lake though forest and meadow. **Emma Matilda Lake** offers an even longer 9.1-mile hike, with fabulous Teton views from the north shore ridge.

A nice area for visitors who travel with their bicycles is in the vicinity of **Two Ocean Road,** southeast of Jackson Lake Lodge and northeast of Signal Mountain Lodge. The road itself is just 3 miles long, but the scenery is sublime for a short, sweet ride. **River Road** is 15 miles of gravel running along the west side of the Snake River between Signal Mountain and Cottonwood Creek. Do remember that this is bear country and every precaution—including bear spray—should be taken.

Horseback Riding
The **Grand Teton Lodge Company** (307/543-3100, www.gtlc.com) can arrange one-hour ($45) or two-hour ($75) horseback tours that depart from Jackson Lake Lodge and can include trips to Emma Matilda Lake and an overlook of Oxbow Bend. All riders must be at least eight years old and under 225 pounds.

FOOD
There are a lot of options for dining at the Jackson Lake Lodge. The **Mural Room** (307/543-3463, 7am-9:30am, 11am-2:30pm, and 5:30pm-9:30pm daily mid-May-early Oct., breakfast buffet $19 adults, $12 children, lunch $13-20, dinner $22-46) has unmatched ambience with its windowed wall looking out onto the lake, Mount Moran, and the Teton Range along with the colorful murals by famed artist Carl Routers depicting life out West. The food is upscale and innovative—also known as Rocky Mountain cuisine—and when coupled with the view, it makes this one of the most pleasurable dining experiences in the park. Breakfast includes ricotta and pine nut hotcakes, crunchy French toast, and parfait of organic Teton granola. Lunch is a mix of gourmet burgers and salads as well as regional cuisine such as the buffalo chipotle sausage frittata. Dinner is a hearty affair with delectable main entrée items including molasses-spiced elk loin, grilled Idaho red trout, and whole roasted black angus beef tenderloin direct from the on-site butcher shop. A delightful end to the meal is the flourless dark chocolate cake. Dinner reservations are recommended.

Also in the lodge is the much more casual and less pricey **Pioneer Grill** (6am-10pm daily mid-May-early Oct., breakfast $8-14, lunch and dinner $10-15), a true-to-style 1950s diner; supposedly it has the largest soda fountain counter still in use. A fun place for a meal, the restaurant is decorated with pioneer artifacts. The Pioneer Grill offers American cuisine with a slight gourmet twist (try the garlic parmesan fries) and has a takeout service if you decide you'd rather watch the sunset while munching on your burger. Its famous desserts keep customers returning.

The **Blue Heron Lounge** (307/543-2811, 11am-midnight daily mid-May-early Oct., $8-18) is another casual dining experience in Jackson Lake Lodge. It has a bar menu with a good selection of appetizers and creative sandwiches, and even offer sustainable draft beer from local breweries. Enjoy your meal on the deck while taking in a beautiful view of the mountains.

If you are at the pool or with your kids at the playground, you may want to fill up on the terrific buffet at the outdoor **Pool BBQ** (9am-8pm daily June-Aug. depending on weather, $28 adults, $14 children 12 and under), which serves up sandwiches, salads, burgers, and a baked potato bar during the day and at night offers authentic barbecue of everything from brisket to chicken, ribs, and bison, all accompanied by live Western music.

There are three options for dining at the Signal Mountain Lodge (307/543-2831, www.signalmountainlodge.com) as well. **The Trapper Grill** (7am-10pm daily early May-early Oct., breakfast $8-13, lunch and dinner $7-18) has a large menu for all three meals of the day. It mostly sticks to American fare with some Tex-Mex thrown in. The nachos are a favorite. The breakfast menu is vast, with an egg menu, an omelet menu, and griddle options. The lunch and dinner menu is filled with specialty sandwiches, salads, and burgers, but the restaurant prides itself on its homemade desserts. You may want to share an entrée so that you'll have room for the Kentucky bourbon chocolate pecan pie. **The Peaks Restaurant** (5:30pm-10pm daily early May-early Oct., $18-38) serves delicious dinners and is committed to offering an environmentally sustainable menu. Dine on Snake River Farms steak salad, buffalo-stuffed manicotti, or pecan-crusted Idaho trout. **Leek's Pizzeria** (11am-10pm daily late May-early Sept., $14-23) is located at the marina on Jackson Lake. It serves specialty pizzas and calzones, sandwiches, salads, and microbrews in a fantastic outdoor setting. For a drink, snack, and a glimpse of television, you may want to stop at **Deadman's Bar;** it serves the largest plate of fully loaded nachos you have ever seen. They pair perfectly with a blackberry margarita and a Wyoming sunset.

ACCOMMODATIONS

The **Jackson Lake Lodge** (307/543-3100, www.gtlc.com, mid-May-early Oct., $309-365 cottages, $309-409 lodge rooms, $729-809 suites) is one of the largest resorts in the park and commands an unparalleled view of Jackson Lake and the Teton Range from the lobby's panoramic 60-foot-high windows. There are 385 guest rooms in the main lodge and surrounding cottages, and the grounds also house a playground and swimming pool. The cottages are located in clusters and come in a range of styles. The classic cottage guest room has one king bed and sleeps a maximum of three. The cottage guest room with a view of the Tetons can sleep up to five people and has a mini fridge and a patio or balcony. The mountain-view suite has a spectacular view of Willow Flats, where moose often meander, and the majestic range; it comes with a king bed and a comfortable sitting area. The lodge guest rooms are located on the 3rd floor and also

come in three price ranges. Unlike the cottages, these guest rooms do not accommodate rollaways unless you are staying in the Moran suite, which has two rooms, breathtaking views, a kitchenette, and dining and sitting areas.

The **Signal Mountain Lodge** (307/543-2831, www.signalmountainlodge.com, early May-mid-Oct.) is an independently owned resort on the banks of Jackson Lake with a gorgeous view of the Tetons. It has a variety of options for lodging, ranging from rustic log cabins (1-room cabin $192-217, 2-room $222-252) and motel-style rooms ($243-353) to one- or two-room bungalows ($243-394) on the beach. The two-room lakefront retreats ($353-394) are ideal for families; they overlook the lake with fantastic views of the mountains and have kitchenettes. Many of the rooms in the lodge were remodeled in 2015, and all of them are carpeted and comfortably furnished. There is one three-bedroom cabin aptly named Home Away from Home ($413); if you are lucky enough to get it, you'll have a bedroom, dining area, living room with a gas fireplace, kitchen, and small laundry room all to yourself; the only drawback is that there is no view.

CAMPING

The **Signal Mountain Campground** (800/672-6012, early May-mid-Oct., $24/vehicle, $47 electric site, $10 hikers and bicyclists) is nestled among spruce and fir trees with views of the mountains, lakes, and hillside. It is also wildly popular and often fills up by 10am on a first-come, first-served basis. There are 86 smallish sites, each with a picnic table and fire ring, and RVs up to 30 feet in length are permitted. Restrooms with cold running water are available but no showers.

Jenny Lake and Vicinity

Carved some 12,000 years ago by the same glaciers that carved Cascade Canyon, Jenny Lake is perhaps the most picturesque and popular spot in the park. The hiking—to places like Inspiration Point and the even more beautiful Leigh Lake—is sublime, and the water activities—scenic cruising, canoeing, kayaking, swimming, and fishing—are plentiful. The park's fanciest and most expensive lodging and dining can be found at the historic Jenny Lake Lodge.

In much the same way that Old Faithful embodies the Yellowstone experience for many visitors, so too does Jenny Lake conjure up all that is wonderful about Grand Teton. A scenic drive from North Jenny Lake to South Jenny Lake skirts the water and affords breathtaking views of the Grand Teton, Teewinot, and Mount Owen. Those who are more interested in solitude would be well advised to get off the main drag here, away from the crowds and into the wilderness.

SIGHTS
★ Jenny Lake

In 1872 an English-born mountain man, known widely as "Beaver Dick" Leigh for his enormous front teeth and his penchant for the animal, guided Ferdinand Hayden around the Tetons. Hayden named the alpine lake for Dick's wife, Jenny, a member of the Shoshone tribe. In the fall of 1876, pregnant Jenny took care of an ailing Native American woman, not knowing the woman had smallpox. Jenny and all four of her children became ill. Her baby was born just before Christmas and, along with Jenny and the other four children, died within a week. Beaver Dick buried his family in Jackson Hole.

Despite its tragic namesake, Jenny Lake is indeed one of the most beautiful and visited spots in the park. From cruising across the lake to hiking along its shores, there are an endless number of ways to enjoy this idyllic spot.

★ Hidden Falls and Inspiration Point

One of the area's most popular hikes is to the spectacular **Hidden Falls.** From Jenny Lake's south shore, the hike follows a moderate 2.5-mile trail with 550 feet of elevation gain to the cascade. Visitors who want to put fewer miles on their feet can take the **Jenny Lake Shuttle** (307/734-9227, www.jennylakeboating.com, 10am-4pm mid-May-early June, 7am-7pm early June-early Sept., round-trip $15 adults, $8 children, one-way $9 adults, $6 children), which runs every 10-15 minutes throughout the day, to shorten the hike to one mile with 150 feet of elevation gain. The hike to **Inspiration Point,** a breathtaking overlook 5.8 miles round-trip with 700 feet of elevation gain from the trailhead, or 2.2 miles round-trip with 420 feet of elevation gain from the boat shuttle, earns its name.

Leigh Lake

Named for mountain man "Beaver Dick" Leigh, Leigh Lake is much quieter and perhaps even more beautiful than the more southerly Jenny Lake. The lake offers unrivaled views of Mount Moran, Mount Woodring, and Rockchuck Peak, and it is dotted with sandy beaches ideal for picnics. The 5.4-mile round-trip (out-and-back) trail is flat and weaves in and out of the forest with a constant water view. The Leigh Lake Trailhead is at the northwest corner of the String Lake Picnic Area. The trail can be hiked as early as May or June, depending on snowmelt, and is typically passable well into September. Although popular, Leigh Lake does not attract the crowds that Jenny Lake does.

SPORTS AND RECREATION

Fishing

Fishing is permitted in Jenny, String, Leigh, Bradley, and Taggart Lakes. A Wyoming fishing license is required and can be purchased at **Snake River Angler at Dornan's** (12170 Dornan Rd., 307/733-3699, www.snakeriverangler.com), **Signal Mountain Marina** (307/543-2831, www.signalmountainlodge.com), and **Colter Bay Marina** (307/543-3100, www.gtlc.com). Pick up a fishing brochure from any of the visitors centers to learn about all park regulations.

Boating

Scenic one-hour cruises (noon and 2pm daily mid-May-early June; 11am, 2pm, and 5pm daily early June-early Sept., $19 adults, $17 seniors 62 and over, $11 children 2-11), shuttles to Cascade Canyon hiking trails (round-trip $15 adults, $8 children, depart every 10-15 minutes), and canoe or kayak rentals ($20/hour, $75/day) can be arranged through **Jenny Lake Boating** (307/734-9227, www.jennylakeboating.com).

Hiking and Biking

Jenny Lake is at the heart of the park's largest concentration of popular hiking trails. In addition to the **Hidden Falls, Inspiration Point,** and **Leigh Lake** trailheads, there are a number of excellent trails in the region. The mostly level **Jenny Lake Loop Trail** circumnavigates the lake with a 6.6-mile round-trip hike. The **Lupine Meadows Trailhead** offers hikers a number of ways to get up into the Teton Range.

The multiuse pathway from South Jenny Lake to Taggart Lake Trailhead offers bikers (and all nonmotorized travelers) 16 miles round-trip of smooth, level pavement. Bike racks are available at Taggart Lake Trailhead and in Moose. Bicycles can be rented from **Dornan's** (12170 Dornan Rd. in Moose, 307/733-2415, www.dornans.com). In addition to adult mountain bikes ($15/hour, $34 half-day, $40/day or 24 hours, $210/week),

Jenny Lake rests up against the Tetons.

Dornan's rents kids' bikes, Trail-a-Bikes, bike racks, and Burley carriers for toddlers.

FOOD

The **Jenny Lake Lodge Dining Room** (307/543-3352, www.gtlc.com, 7:30am-10:30am, 11:30am-1:30pm, and 6pm-10pm, last seating at 9pm, daily early June-early Oct.) offers a fine dining experience in an original log cabin. Reservations are required for all three meals and should be booked well in advance. Men are required to wear dinner jackets. The food is incredibly creative and incorporates local flavors. Signal Mountain pancakes with huckleberries and buffalo hash appear on the prix fixe breakfast menu ($28), and lunch ($14-16) consists mostly of upscale sandwiches and salads. The main event at the restaurant is the prix fixe five-course dinner (price varies but does not include gratuity or alcohol). There are options for each course that rotate every night. Depending on the day, you may be dining on wild mushroom tempura, local Wyoming buffalo carpaccio,

Relax on the porch of Jenny Lake Lodge.

offers beautiful vistas in all directions. The rooms are pricey, but guests get a lot for their dime. A gourmet breakfast, five-course dinner, horseback riding, and access to bicycles are all included in the rates. If you are looking for a romantic getaway, consider booking one of the suites, which come with wood-burning stoves.

A much more affordable, and truly rustic, option is the **American Alpine Club Climbers Ranch** (307/733-7271, www.americanalpineclub.org, $16 AAC members, $25 nonmembers), located just three miles south of Jenny Lake. The ranch has small log cabins that serve as dormitories for 4-8 people. Guests must bring their own sleeping bags and pads, towels, cooking equipment, and food. Cooking and dishwashing facilities, toilets, and showers with hot water are available. No camping is allowed. There is also a general store on the grounds where you can stock up on groceries as well as hiking and camping supplies.

juniper-scented venison loin, wild-caught king salmon, or roasted squab—no matter what's on the menu, it is sure to be a memorable meal.

ACCOMMODATIONS

A former dude ranch for sophisticated Easterners, **Jenny Lake Lodge** (307/543-3100, www.gtlc.com, mid-May-early Oct., cabins $716-1,000/night for 2 people) is the finest lodging in the park and the only four-diamond eco-resort. The cabins have authentic log walls, renovated baths, and touches such as handmade bed quilts that add to the charm of each room. Situated among the three lakes, the lodge is comfortably secluded but

CAMPING

The **Jenny Lake Campground** (307/543-3100, mid-May-early Oct., $25/vehicle, $11 hikers and bicyclists) is the smallest in the park and is available on a first-come, first-served basis only; it is usually full by 8am. It has 49 sites that can each accommodate one vehicle, two tents, and up to six campers. Ten additional sites are set aside for hikers or bicyclists. There are no large group sites, nor are trailers, campers, or generators allowed in the area. Because of its size and popularity, the maximum stay is seven days (at the other campgrounds it is 14 days). Flush toilets are available but no shower facilities.

Moran to Moose

The stretch of road between Moran Junction and the southernmost entrance to the park at Moose is scenic and full of interesting sights, both natural and artificial. From the historic crossing at **Menors Ferry** to the architecturally inspired **Craig Thomas Discovery and Visitor Center** and the wildlife rich **Antelope Flats,** this part of the park is heavily traveled for a good reason: There is so much to see.

SIGHTS
Cunningham Cabin

A relic of hardscrabble ranching days before the turn of the 20th century—and the site of the murder of two alleged horse thieves—Cunningham Cabin is six miles south of Moran Junction. The cabin reflects the common building materials and style of 1890, the year it was built. Known as a "dogtrot," it consists of two small structures connected by a breezeway and topped with a dirt roof.

Pierce Cunningham built a modest home for his family on Flat Creek in the late 1880s or early 1890s. A neighbor introduced Cunningham to two strangers, George Spenser and Mike Burnett, asking if they could buy hay for their horses. Cunningham sold them 15 tons of hay and arranged for them to winter in his cabin near Spread Creek. The rumor among the locals was that the men were in fact horse thieves.

In April 1893, Spenser and Burnett were the target of a posse of vigilantes from Montana. Sixteen men on horseback rode up to the little cabin on Spread Creek under cover of darkness and waited in silence for dawn. Spenser and Burnett's dog barked in the early morning hours, perhaps warning the men of the ambush that awaited them. Spenser dressed, armed himself, and walked out the front door. When the posse called for him to hold his hands up, Spenser fired his revolver in the direction of the speaker and was immediately shot. He propped himself up on one elbow and continued to fire until he collapsed. Burnett came out next, armed with a revolver and a rifle. The men shot at him, but Burnett managed to shoot the hat off one of the posse members and "crease his scalp" with the bullet. Burnett was shot and killed moments later. The two men were buried in unmarked graves a few hundred yards southeast of the cabin on the south side of a draw. Some of their bones were eventually excavated by badgers.

Mormon Row and Antelope Flats

Interesting both for its wildlife and human history, the area around Mormon Row is instantly recognizable from some of the region's most popular postcards, featuring a weathered barn leaning into the jagged mountains behind it. Listed on the National Register of Historic Places, Mormon Row is a collection of six fairly dilapidated homesteads that can be explored on a self-guided tour (brochures are available near the pink house). The area was settled around the turn of the 20th century by a handful of Mormon families who built homes, a church, a school, and a swimming hole. The settlement was abandoned and left to the elements when the Rockefellers bought up much of the land and transferred it to the National Park Service. In the 1990s the historical and cultural value of the site was recognized; the area was added to the National Register of Historic Places in 1997, and steps were taken to preserve the structures.

The Antelope Flats area—excellent for walking or biking on a flat, unpaved road—offers prime habitat for pronghorn, bison, moose, coyotes, ground squirrels, northern harriers, kestrels, and sage grouse. In the winter, the first mile of Antelope Flats Road is plowed to a small parking area, giving visitors easy snowshoe or cross-country ski access to Moulton Ranch, one of the homesteads on Mormon Row.

★ Craig Thomas Discovery and Visitor Center

Opened in 2007, the **Craig Thomas Discovery and Visitor Center** (307/739-3399, 9am-5pm daily early Mar.-Apr., 8am-5pm daily May-early June and mid-Sept.-Oct., 8am-7pm daily early June-mid-Sept.) is, among other things, an architectural masterpiece, mimicking the nearby natural masterpiece of the Teton Range. The $21.6 million structure has more than 22,000 square feet and is being used as a model for other national parks—in that more than half the funds used to build the center were donated by private individuals. The state-of-the-art facility, including video rivers that flow beneath your feet, places emphasis on the connection between humans and the natural world. Fantastic interpretive displays include a large relief model of the park that uses technology to show glacier movement and animal migration; there is also a photographic tribute to mountaineering in the region. Many of the excellent ranger-led hikes and tours depart from the Craig Thomas Discovery and Visitor Center.

Menors Ferry Historic District

In 1894, William D. Menor came to Jackson Hole and built a homestead along the Snake River. He built a ferryboat on cables to carry settlers and hopeful miners across the river, which was otherwise impassable during spring runoff. Entire wagon teams crossed on the ferry, paying $0.50 per trip, while a horse and rider paid $0.25. In 1918, Menor sold the ferry operation to Maud Noble, who doubled the fares ($1 for automobiles with local plates, $2 for out-of-staters) in the hope of attracting more tourists to the region. When a bridge was built in 1927, the ferry became obsolete, and in 1929 Noble sold her land to the Snake River Land Company, the same year the park was created. She had already donated a portion of her land for the construction of the Chapel of the Transfiguration.

Today, a replica of the ferryboat and cables has been built on-site, and visitors can meander down the 0.5-mile self-guided **Menor's Ferry Trail** past Menor's cabin, which doubles as a country store.

Chapel of the Transfiguration

Built in 1925 to serve the ranchers and dudes in the Teton Valley, the **Chapel of the Transfiguration** (307/733-2603, services 8am and 10am Sun. late May-Sept.) is a humble log cabin structure with the most spectacular mountain view framed in the window behind the altar. An Episcopal church, operated by St. John's in Jackson, it was built on land donated by Maud Noble and is a favorite spot for summer weddings. A candle-lit Christmas night service and sunrise Easter service are particularly wonderful ways to experience this historic place of worship.

★ Laurance S. Rockefeller Preserve

The former JY Ranch and longtime summer home of the Rockefeller family, the **Laurance S. Rockefeller Preserve** (307/739-3654, 9am-5pm daily early June-late Sept., center closed late Sept.-early June, trails open year-round) offers eight miles of trails through forest, wetlands, and meadows on reclaimed property along Phelps Lake and Lake Creek. The preserve is 1,106 acres and was donated to the Park Service in 2007 by the Rockefeller family with the mission of giving people access to the natural world that Laurance Rockefeller found so inspiring and sustaining. Rockefeller himself committed to returning the old JY to its most natural state by removing more than 30 structures and roads.

The Laurance S. Rockefeller Preserve Center is the first platinum-level LEED-certified building constructed in a national park and was built to give visitors a sensory experience of the natural elements found on the preserve. A poem by beloved writer Terry

Tempest Williams features prominently, and visitors can learn about the preserve and Rockefeller's beliefs about land stewardship in a comfortable and environmentally sustainable building. Several ranger programs, including sunrise hikes and children's programs, are available from the center daily throughout summer.

Murie Center

The one-time STS Ranch and former residence of wilderness champions Olaus and Mardy Murie, the **Murie Center** (1 Murie Ranch Rd., Moose, 307/732-7752 or 307/739-2246, www.muriecenter.org, 9am-5pm Mon.-Fri. mid-Mar.-mid-Oct.) is dedicated to connecting people and wilderness. It is where the Wilderness Act was authored in the 1950s and early 1960s. The ranch itself is a National Historic Landmark and the site of ongoing conservation seminars and educational workshops. On-site accommodations are available to participants, and the entire facility can be rented for conservation education programs. An excellent library and bookstore is on-site, and rangers host naturalist programs throughout the summer. Free tours of the Murie home are given at 2:30pm Monday-Friday in summer.

SPORTS AND RECREATION

Like most of Grand Teton National Park, there is an abundance of excellent hiking terrain to be discovered between Moran and Moose, and many easy strolls can combine with historic sites like the Cunningham Cabin, Menor's Ferry, and Mormon Row.

For more substantial hikes, try the **Taggart Lake Trailhead,** three miles northwest of Moose. The trail is 3.2 miles round-trip with 410 feet of elevation gain. If that isn't enough, continue on to Bradley Lake (4 miles round-trip with a 650-foot elevation gain) or Beaver Creek. Three miles south of Moose is the **Death Canyon Trailhead,** not nearly as ominous as the name would imply. The road is not suitable for trailers or RVs and is very rough for vehicles in general. However, the hike to **Phelps Lake** is perfect for families, only 1.8 miles round-trip with 420 feet of elevation gain. Black bears, moose, and marmots frequent the area, so have your bear spray at the ready.

There are plenty of biking opportunities on the paved and unpaved roads in the region, including **Antelope Flats Road** all the way to Kelly, the **Shadow Mountain Road,** and the **Moose-Wilson Road** linking Moose

The Chapel of the Transfiguration was built in 1925.

and the Laurance S. Rockefeller Preserve. The **multiuse pathway** from Moose or the Taggart Lake Trailhead to South Jenny Lake is popular for good reason.

FOOD

You'll find most of your food options in this area at Dornan's ranch. ★ **Dornan's Moose Chuck Wagon** (307/733-2415, ext. 203, 7am-11am, noon-3pm, and 5pm-9pm Sun.-Thurs., 7am-11am and noon-3pm Fri.-Sat. mid-June-Labor Day, weather dependent) serves up hearty "cowboy cuisine" during the summer. Dornan's uses beef from its own butcher shop and Dutch ovens heated over wood fires. Breakfast ($10-11) offers amazing hot sourdough pancakes, and dinner ($19-32 adults, $10-13 children 5-11) is an all-you-can-eat affair with beef or chicken, ribs, or trout. Lunch ($9.50-13) is served as well. The restaurant is used for private events on weekend evenings. And Monday night is the hootenanny, an evening of acoustic delight. It's a good idea to call ahead for evening reservations and check that it's not privately booked for the evening.

Dornan's Pizza and Pasta Company (307/733-2415, ext. 204, 11:30am-5pm Tues.-Fri., 11:30am-7pm Sat.-Mon., $9-24) offers a large variety of salads, hot sandwiches, and gourmet pizzas, rich pasta dishes, and calzones. If you are looking to pick up something to eat on your hike, stop at **Dornan's Moose Trading Post & Deli** (307/733-2415, ext. 201, 8am-8pm daily) for everything from freeze-dried meals and cold drinks to gourmet groceries and any camping equipment you might need. The deli is open May-September and is a good option for a quick meal or a sweet treat. If you have the time, don't miss a visit to **Dornan's Wine Shoppe** (307/733-2415, ext. 202, 10am-6pm daily, extended hours in summer). It is an absolute find for wine connoisseurs and novices alike, with an award-winning selection of around 1,600 varieties of wines and 150 types of cheese. *Food & Wine* magazine named it one of the 50 most amazing wine experiences in the country, and *Wine Spectator* has bestowed its Wine Award on the shop for 28 consecutive years and counting.

ACCOMMODATIONS

★ **The Triangle X Ranch** (2 Triangle X Ranch Rd., 307/733-2183, www.trianglex. com, late May-Oct. 31 and Dec. 26-mid-Mar., $1,850-2,560 pp/week summer, $140 pp/night winter) has been in operation since 1926. Twenty-six miles north of Jackson and 32 miles south of Yellowstone, it is the only

Dornan's is the perfect place to eat, stay, play, and shop.

authorized guest ranch concessionaire in the entire National Park System and sits right inside Grand Teton National Park. Not surprisingly, the setting is gorgeous, and you can see the entire mountain range from this secluded getaway.

The lodge, which is the center of activity and meals, is the original main house used by two generations of the Turner family. The 20 log cabins are also originals that once housed families in different parts of Jackson Hole. The cabins come with 1-3 bedrooms; all have modern amenities and are decorated with cozy Western charm.

The ranch is also the only concession in the park that is open during winter. During the peak season (early-June-late Aug.), the minimum stay is one week (Sun.-Sun.). During the spring and fall seasons, the ranch requires a minimum four-night stay but offers reduced rates, and during the winter season, visitors can book per night. All meals, served family-style in the main lodge, are included in the price, as are the endless horseback rides, cookouts, square-dancing, and special programs for children. Winter activities include cross-country skiing, snowshoeing, and snowmobiling. Regardless of the season, there are always great opportunities for wildlife viewing.

Dornan's Spur Ranch Cabins (12170 Dornan Rd., Moose, 307/733-2522, www.dornans.com, year-round) sits idyllically on the Snake River in the middle of a wildflower meadow, and gives alpine views in all directions. This is a small, family-owned business that provides quality service with personal touches, and the location affords easy access to fly-fishing and floating adventures. There are eight one-bedroom cabins ($195-225 summer, $125-150 fall-spring) and four two-bedroom duplexes ($285 summer, $175 fall-spring) on the premises. The cabins were built in the early 1990s and are bright, airy, and furnished with lodgepole pine furniture. They each have queen beds, kitchens, living-dining areas, and covered porches with a barbecue grill nearby. Also on these 10 acres of property are a grocery and camping store, two restaurants, and an award-winning wine shop. Visitors can rent mountain bikes, canoes, and kayaks during the summer and cross-country skis and snowshoes in the winter to make the most of the surrounding area.

CAMPING

Gros Ventre (307/543-3100, www.gtlc.com, early May-early Oct., $25) is the closest park campground to Jackson and among the largest campgrounds in the park, situated at the southeast end, 11.5 miles southeast of Moose. Booked on a first-come, first-served basis, the 300-plus individual sites and five large group sites rarely fill completely. Each individual site has a fire pit and picnic table and can accommodate two tents, two vehicles, and up to six people. The campground isn't far from the river, and there are sites to be had in the cottonwoods and open sage. Nearby bathrooms include flush toilets, but no shower facilities are available. A grocery store and service station are within two miles of the campground.

Jackson Hole, Cody, and the Wind Rivers

Look for ★ to find recommended sights, activities, dining, and lodging.

Highlights

★ **Jackson Town Square:** Surrounded by archways constructed entirely out of elk antlers, this is the heart of the community for shoppers, art lovers, and diners (page 101).

★ **National Museum of Wildlife Art:** This collection is dedicated to all things wild, spanning George Catlin's bison to incredible works by Georgia O'Keeffe, Charlie Russell, and marvelous contemporary artists (page 103).

★ **National Elk Refuge:** Most magical in winter under a blanket of snow, this refuge is home to more than 11,000 elk. Tour the area by horse-drawn sleigh (page 103).

★ **Rafting on the Snake River:** The Snake winds through the valley, giving floaters unparalleled access to the area's most stunning views (page 108).

★ **Sinks Canyon State Park:** This natural wonder occurs where the Middle Fork of the Popo Agie River "sinks" into a cave and then emerges again in a great spring (page 123).

★ **Hot Springs State Park:** This park has fabulous limestone terraces as well as public baths in therapeutic waters (page 129).

★ **The Wyoming Dinosaur Center and Dig Sites:** Here, you can learn about dinosaurs, see their remains up close, and even dig for a day. There's a chance you'll find a fossil (page 131).

★ **Buffalo Bill Center of the West:** Here, five remarkable museums capture the art, natural

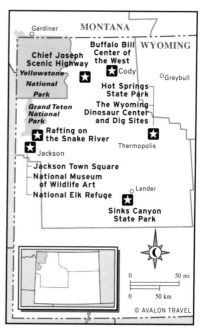

history, Native American cultures, and legends of the Old West. If you can visit only one museum in the West, this should be it (page 135).

★ **Chief Joseph Scenic Highway:** This scenic drive has high mountain plateaus speckled with wildflowers, cascading rivers, and narrow canyons teeming with wildlife (page 138).

Northwest Wyoming swings dramatically from stunning vistas and a sublime outdoor culture to the arts scene and high style of Jackson and Cody.

Some of the state's most exquisite lodgings and legendary ranches can be found in this breathtaking corner of Wyoming. The area is jam-packed with obvious destinations such as world-class museums—Cody's Buffalo Bill Center of the West and Jackson's National Wildlife Art Museum are among the best—as well as landmarks like Sinks Canyon near Lander, Hot Springs State Park near Thermopolis, the Wind River Range, and a string of scenic drives. The region provides a marvelous launching point into both Grand Teton and Yellowstone National Parks. Naturally, opportunities to explore the great outdoors here are abundant and include rafting, fishing, skiing, and hiking.

While bigger towns like Jackson and Cody are natural attractions in themselves, other towns in the region, such as Pinedale, Thermopolis, and tiny Ten Sleep, offer an authentic Wyoming experience with great museums, hot springs, historical monuments, and hole-in-the-wall cafés. Though towns like Lander and Powell lack the glitz and pomp of Jackson and Cody, they possess so much of what defines the state—rugged beauty, open space, rich history, and unrivaled wilderness access. In Wyoming, the journey from one town to the next is often the destination itself, and is by far the best way to appreciate this sparsely populated state.

HISTORY

While Wyoming had long been home to the Sioux, Crow, Cheyenne, Arapaho, Shoshone, Gros Ventre, Bannock, and Ute, a party of Frenchmen, traveling and trapping in the northwestern corner of the state as early as 1743, are thought to be the first Europeans in the area. Perhaps the most influential visitor in encouraging other trappers and mountain men to visit the region was John Colter, a member of the Lewis and Clark expedition who plied his skills as a trapper in the vicinity of what is now Jackson Hole in 1807-1808. His exploits and subsequent stories opened the area to an influx of mountain men, trappers, and traders, and by 1825 men like Jedediah

Previous: the Irma Hotel in downtown Cody; the Snake River sparkling at the foot of the Tetons. **Above:** Jackson Town Square.

Jackson Hole, Cody, and the Wind Rivers

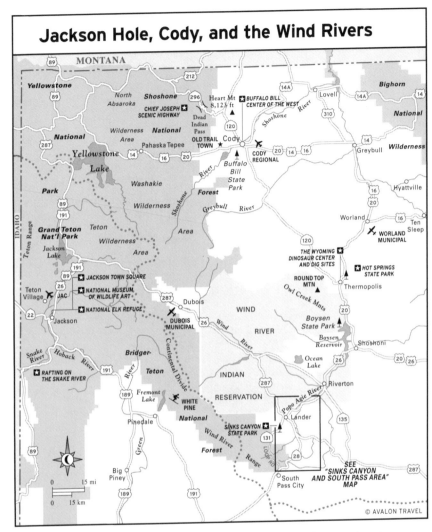

MONTANA

Yellowstone

North Absaroka
Wilderness Area

Shoshone

CHIEF JOSEPH SCENIC HIGHWAY

Heart Mt
8,123 ft

Dead Indian Pass

BUFFALO BILL CENTER OF THE WEST

Bighorn

Lovell

National

National

Yellowstone Lake

Wilderness

National

Pahaska Tepee

OLD TRAIL TOWN

Cody

CODY REGIONAL

Greybull

Wilderness

Park

Washakie

Wilderness Area

Buffalo Bill State Park

Hyattville

Grand Teton Nat'l Park

Teton

Wilderness Area

Greybull River

Shoshone

Forest

Worland

WORLAND MUNICIPAL

Ten Sleep

Jackson Lake

THE WYOMING DINOSAUR CENTER AND DIG SITES

HOT SPRINGS STATE PARK

Teton Village

JACKSON TOWN SQUARE

NATIONAL MUSEUM OF WILDLIFE ART

ROUND TOP MTN

Owl Creek Mnts

Thermopolis

Dubois

Jackson

NATIONAL ELK REFUGE

DUBOIS MUNICIPAL

WIND

RIVER

Boysen State Park

Boysen Reservoir

Shoshoni

Snake River

Hoback River

Bridger-

Teton

Continental Divide

Wind River

Ocean Lake

Snake River

RAFTING ON THE SNAKE RIVER

River

INDIAN

Riverton

Fremont Lake

WHITE PINE

RESERVATION

Popo Agie River

Lander

Pinedale

National

SINKS CANYON STATE PARK

Green River

Wind River

Forest

Range

Lodge Rd

Big Piney

South Pass City

SEE "SINKS CANYON AND SOUTH PASS AREA" MAP

0   15 mi

0   15 km

© AVALON TRAVEL

Smith, David Jackson, and Bill Sublette had made names for themselves as fearless explorers and shrewd businessmen.

By 1840, the demand for beaver pelts had bottomed out, leaving little incentive for mountain men in the region. The population temporarily swelled with pioneers headed west on the Oregon Trail, including the Applegate Wagon Train, the largest ever assembled, which brought more than 875 people and 5,000 animals through the state in 1843. Conflicts with Native Americans were inevitable as white settlers encroached on traditional hunting grounds and, more importantly, nearly wiped out the bison altogether. There were great battles that always ended tragically, most often for the Native Americans, and a series of treaties that reduced the size of their lands until there was virtually none left. Today Wyoming is home to two recognized tribes—the Shoshone and Arapaho—once

Chief Washakie and the Shoshone

The Shoshone Indians have inhabited the United States for thousands of years. Their language is one of the Uto-Aztecan languages spoken by indigenous people throughout the western United States, extending through Mexico and into South America. Also known as the Snake Indians by early European traders and explorers, they were one of the first tribes to acquire horses from the Spanish. On horseback they spread out to cover much of Wyoming, Utah, Montana, and Colorado. The tribe that occupied most of western Wyoming was known as the Eastern Shoshone, and their most famous leader was Chief Washakie.

Born around the turn of the 19th century to a Flathead (Salish) father and a Shoshone (Lemhi) mother, Washakie lived through the most tumultuous century for Native Americans. At an early age his father was killed during a Blackfeet raid, and he and his mother left to live with the Lemhi people in Idaho. During his adolescence, Washakie joined a nomadic band of Bannocks, and eventually settled with the Shoshone who called the Green River Basin in southwest Wyoming their home. During the early 1820s Washakie met and befriended a young Jim Bridger, who would later become a celebrated explorer and mountain man. Together they hunted, trapped, and traded. Their friendship was so great that one of Washakie's daughters became Bridger's third wife. Although trading and trapping ingratiated him with the white settlers and explorers, Washakie also earned the respect of his fellow Indians as a skilled warrior by participating in numerous raids.

By the mid-1800s, before Washakie became a chief, he was already an influential leader, having forged a much-needed alliance between the Shoshone and the Europeans. During the 1840s, the Shoshone actively traded with travelers and settlers. There are even stories of the Eastern Shoshone helping pioneers traverse difficult streams and round up stray cattle as they crossed through Wyoming.

The skills Washakie acquired through his friendship with Bridger and other traders and trappers served him well as a leader. He was able to negotiate ardently for the best interests of his people, getting them much-needed supplies, tools, and food. At one point, younger warriors questioned his leadership. In response, Washakie left camp and headed east, only to return a week later with seven Sioux scalps, challenging anyone who questioned him to match the feat.

Washakie was also considered to be forward-thinking. When it became clear in the early 1850s that their land was threatened by the influx of migrants and settlers, he suggested to leaders, including Brigham Young, that land be set aside for the Shoshone Indians. By the end of the decade, he was negotiating directly with the U.S. government to acquire this land. In 1863 the Treaty of Fort Bridger designated land for the tribe.

On the reservation, Washakie continued to lead. He maintained a fine balance between the new reservation life and their traditions. Living in a log cabin rather than a tipi, Washakie sent his children to the agency schools and even farmed a small piece of land. But he also made sure his children joined him on buffalo hunts. He defended Native American practices and led his fellow Shoshone warriors in the U.S. Army battles against the Sioux and Cheyenne. Washakie never stopped advocating for the needs of his people.

Toward the end of his life, Washakie was baptized twice, first as a Mormon in 1880 and later as an Episcopalian in 1899, a few months before his death in 1900. Chief Washakie was buried with full military honors, and his funeral procession stretched for miles. A warrior and peacemaker, a diplomat and an advocate for change, Chief Washakie is considered the last of the great Shoshone leaders. Wyoming has paid tribute to the influential man by naming various public places in his honor.

enemies and now neighbors sharing the Wind River Reservation.

By the 1880s, cattle ranching had taken hold, and sheep ranchers moved in just over a decade later. Both Jackson and Cody were settled much later, closer to the turn of the 20th century, because of the harsh snowy winters in Jackson and the desertlike conditions around Cody. What irrigation did for Cody by increasing the population, the creation of

Grand Teton National Park did for Jackson in 1929 by attracting tourists and jump-starting dude ranching in the area.

Wyoming's biggest boom, however, came in the form of energy—oil, gas, and coal, the production of which still dominates the state's economy despite plummeting prices and subsequent layoffs. Oil was discovered outside Cody in 1904. The largest coal deposits in the country are being mined in the Powder River Basin, and much of the western portion of the state produces natural gas. After energy, the state's second-largest source of income is tourism, which brought in $3.4 billion and supported 32,000 jobs in 2015, and among Jackson, Cody, and the national parks, the northwestern corner of the state attracts visitors in great numbers.

Wyoming's motto—"Equal Rights"—attests to the fact that Wyoming was the first territory to grant voting rights to women, in 1869, more than 20 years before its statehood was established. It was also the first state to elect a woman as governor, Nellie Tayloe Ross, who served 1923-1925.

A darker time in Wyoming's history includes the creation of the Heart Mountain Relocation Camp, located between Powell and Cody, where more than 10,000 Japanese Americans were held during World War II. Amid tremendous fear and racism across the country, politicians opposed the camp but citizens welcomed it, seeing it as a relief to 15 years of economic recession. With 2,000 laborers needed to build the camp and then 11,000 inmates who could work in the area, the Cody and Powell economies rebounded virtually overnight. Detainees arrived in August 1942, and the last ones left when the camp closed in November 1945. White homesteaders and farmers moved into the area immediately, taking advantage of the impressive irrigation system the inmates had built.

PLANNING YOUR TIME

Jackson Hole and Cody are obvious destinations, with easy (but pricey) air access; each could easily occupy visitors for 2-3 full days, and both are excellent launching pads for day trips into Yellowstone and Grand Teton National Parks. Both have their own distinctive cultures that include art and entertainment, the great outdoors, and elegant accommodations and eateries. The dude ranches outside both Jackson and Cody offer tremendous opportunities to experience the state's vast open spaces in close proximity to the hustle and bustle of town. For many people, this is the ideal way to spend a week enjoying the best of Wyoming's offerings.

The charm of Jackson is that it is pretty much anything you want it to be. Boutique shopping? Check. Gallery strolls? Check. Kitschy bars with saddle-topped stools? Check. Gourmet dining? Hard-core outdoor pursuits? Quiet afternoons in the museum? Check. Check. Check. Jackson is a great destination because it is geared to visitors who want to be entertained, pampered, challenged, and wined and dined. A few hours in the **National Museum of Wildlife Art** is time well spent. And you will want to allow an afternoon to stroll around town, browsing the shops and galleries—but don't let Jackson's shopping sirens lure you away from the majestic wilderness in every direction. In winter, try skiing at Jackson's original ski hill, **Snow King,** right in town, or at **Jackson Hole Mountain Resort** in nearby Teton Village. In summer you'll find trails to hike and dirt roads to bike, and two of the world's most incredible national parks are just up the road. Make sure to book a raft trip on the Snake River, and consider a wagon or sleigh ride on the sprawling **National Elk Refuge.**

Decidedly less glitzy than Jackson and more for the working cowboy than the urban variety (except during Rendezvous Royale), Cody is a rugged Western town with a rich history and just enough refinement to appeal to sophisticated travelers. The **Buffalo Bill Center of the West** is far and away the heart of Cody and should not be missed. A quick tour at a breakneck pace could probably be accomplished in two hours, but history buffs and Western art lovers could spend several days in the museum and not see the same exhibit twice. Cody's **nightly rodeos** in summer are a treat for the entire family, and a trip to Buffalo Bill's town would not be complete without a visit to the beautiful old hotel he built and named for his daughter, the **Irma Hotel.** The restaurant and saloon are open to nonguests, and if you go in the evening, watch the old **Cody Gunfighters** hash it out right outside the hotel Monday-Saturday at 6pm.

While disparate in philosophy, perhaps, the energy boomtown of Pinedale and the outdoor mecca of Lander both offer excellent access to the spectacular Wind River Mountains. The region is absolutely worth exploring as a destination for outdoor and nature lovers, and as a beautiful setting for travelers en route from one place to the next.

Jackson Hole

Visitors love Jackson (population 10,135, elevation 5,672 feet) because it encompasses the best of the West in a charming town with a spectacular setting. Western indeed, Jackson boasts a classic boardwalk around town, saloons with swinging doors and saddles for bar stools, and architecture built on elk antlers. At the same time, Jackson is clearly mountain chic, with a number of high-end boutiques and art galleries, a phenomenal performing arts center, gourmet dining, and ritzy accommodations.

The valley itself, known as Jackson Hole because it is entirely surrounded by mountains, is 48 miles long and up to 8 miles wide in places. With the Tetons as the most significant landmark, Jackson Hole gives rise to the headwaters of the Snake River, fed abundantly by numerous mountain streams. Because of its remarkable setting, Jackson Hole is a natural playground with offerings for just about anyone. In winter, outdoor enthusiasts can ski downhill at two well-known ski areas, Snow King and Jackson Hole Mountain Resort, or go the cross-country route just about anywhere, including nearby Grand Teton National Park. For those less interested in working up a sweat, a sleigh ride in the National Elk Refuge is a memorable experience. When the snow melts, there is no end to the amount of adventurous options this valley offers, with fly-fishing and wildlife-watching among the less exhausting. From hiking and mountain biking to rafting and rock climbing, Jacksonians do it all.

SIGHTS
★ Town Square
Almost European in its layout with a central square, Jackson's **Town Square** is uniquely distinguished by four dramatic archways constructed in 1932 entirely from naturally shed and sun-bleached elk antlers. It is the focal point of town and a good meeting spot, with shady trees and the occasional musician. In the summer, late May-early September, Town Square is the site of the free **Jackson Hole Shootout,** a spirited reenactment of frontier justice, which plays for crowds Monday-Saturday at 6pm. In winter, the arches are illuminated by strings of lights, creating a magical setting.

Within easy walking distance of the square are more than 70 eateries—from mouthwatering pizza joints with ski-bum prices to the very tony—and a number of fine art galleries and shops that sell everything from high-end furs to T-shirts and knickknacks. There are also plentiful espresso and ice cream shops for those in need of instant energy.

Jackson Hole Historical Society and Museum
Just down Cache Street from Town Square, the **Jackson Hole Historical Society and Museum** (225 N. Cache St., 307/733-2414,

Downtown Jackson

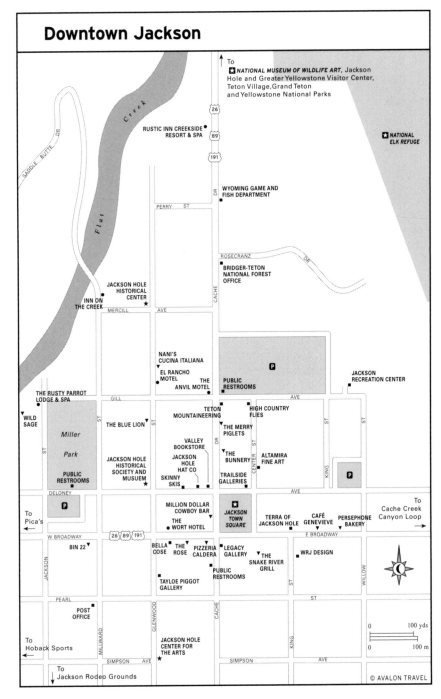

To ★ NATIONAL MUSEUM OF WILDLIFE ART, Jackson
Hole and Greater Yellowstone Visitor Center,
Teton Village, Grand Teton
and Yellowstone National Parks

★ NATIONAL ELK REFUGE

RUSTIC INN CREEKSIDE RESORT & SPA

WYOMING GAME AND FISH DEPARTMENT

PERRY ST

ROSECRANZ DR

BRIDGER-TETON NATIONAL FOREST OFFICE

JACKSON HOLE HISTORICAL CENTER ★

INN ON THE CREEK

MERCILL AVE

NANI'S CUCINA ITALIANA

EL RANCHO MOTEL

THE ANVIL MOTEL

PUBLIC RESTROOMS

JACKSON RECREATION CENTER

THE RUSTY PARROT LODGE & SPA

GILL

AVE

WILD SAGE

Miller Park

THE BLUE LION

TETON MOUNTAINEERING

HIGH COUNTRY FLIES

THE MERRY PIGLETS

VALLEY BOOKSTORE

JACKSON HOLE HAT CO

THE BUNNERY

ALTAMIRA FINE ART

PUBLIC RESTROOMS

JACKSON HOLE HISTORICAL SOCIETY AND MUSEUM ★

SKINNY SKIS

TRAILSIDE GALLERIES

KING ST

DELONEY

P

To Pica's

MILLION DOLLAR COWBOY BAR

THE WORT HOTEL

★ JACKSON TOWN SQUARE

TERRA OF JACKSON HOLE

CAFÉ GENEVIEVE

PERSEPHONE BAKERY

To Cache Creek Canyon Loop

W BROADWAY

26 89 191

E BROADWAY

BIN 22

JACKSON

BELLA COSE

THE ROSE

PIZZERIA CALDERA

LEGACY GALLERY

THE SNAKE RIVER GRILL

WRJ DESIGN

WILLOW

PUBLIC RESTROOMS

TAYLOE PIGGOT GALLERY

PEARL

POST OFFICE

CACHE

KING ST

To Hoback Sports

MILLWARD

GLENWOOD

JACKSON HOLE CENTER FOR THE ARTS ★

0   100 yds
0   100 m

SIMPSON AVE

SIMPSON

AVE

To ↓ Jackson Rodeo Grounds

© AVALON TRAVEL

www.jacksonholehistory.org, 10am-5pm Mon.-Sat., $5 adults, $4 seniors over 60 and students, free for children 12 and under) is actually two museums within easy walking distance of one another. One is dedicated to the history of homesteading and dude ranches in the area, and the other to Indians of the Greater Yellowstone (the latter is open only in summer). The collections include historical photos of the region, Indian artifacts, fur trade-era tools, and firearms. Admission is good for both museums. The society also operates the hands-on Mercill Archaeology Center, which is only open to school groups by appointment at the time of this writing in 2016. In summer, the historical society offers free walking tours of Jackson (10:30am Tues.-Thurs.). Tours depart from the center of Town Square. For a historical perspective on the town and valley, this is the best place to begin.

★ National Museum of Wildlife Art

Just three miles north of Town Square overlooking the National Elk Refuge, the **National Museum of Wildlife Art** (2820 Rungius Rd., 307/733-5771, www.wildlifeart.org, 9am-5pm daily summer, 9am-5pm Mon.-Sat., 11am-5pm Sun. winter, $14 adults, $12 seniors 60 and over, $6 for one child 5-18, $2 each additional child, free for children under 5) is an absolute find. In existence in various forms since 1984, the museum's 14 galleries represent the lifetime study and collection of wildlife art by Bill and Joffa Kerr. More than 5,000 objects reside in the permanent collection, primarily paintings and sculpture by artists that range from early Native American artists to masters both past and present, including Pablo Picasso, Carl Rungius, John James Audubon, Robert Bateman, and Kent Ullberg. A three-quarter-mile sculpture trail, which is free and open to the public, was added in 2013. The trail combines marvelous art with the stunning landscape around Jackson, and often plays host to live music, theatre, yoga, and other programs. Audio guides to the museum are included with paid

admission, and coupons for discounts on admission are offered on the museum's website.

The museum itself is a work of art: Inspired by the ruins of a Scottish castle, the red Arizona sandstone building emerges from the hillside like a natural outcropping of rock and often reminds visitors of Anasazi ruins.

★ National Elk Refuge

During the winter months, more than 5,000 elk, generally 6,000-7,000, descend from their mountain habitat to the **National Elk Refuge** (532 N. Cache St., 307/733-9212, www.fws.gov) located in Jackson Hole. The large number of elk make the refuge a popular wintertime attraction (in the summer, birds and other wildlife populate the range). Horse-drawn sleigh rides through the refuge are offered mid-December-first Saturday in April. The elk are accustomed to the vehicles, allowing visitors to travel easily through the herds. Reservations (307/733-0277 or 800/772-5386) are strongly suggested. Tickets can be purchased from the **Jackson Hole and Greater Yellowstone Visitor Center** (532 N. Cache St., 307/733-3316, $21 adults, $15 children 5-12, free for children under 5, $375/private sleigh), and a free shuttle will take visitors three miles north of Jackson to the departure point. Tours run 10am-4pm daily and last about an hour. Dress warmly as the wind can be quite biting during the tour.

Jackson Hole and Greater Yellowstone Visitor Center

A terrific place to start any type of exploration of the area, including the National Elk Refuge, which operates out of the same building, the **Jackson Hole and Greater Yellowstone Visitor Center** (532 N. Cache St., 307/733-3316, www.fws.gov, 8am-7pm daily Memorial Day-Sept. 30, 9am-5pm daily Oct. 1-Memorial Day) is a phenomenal resource with seven agencies represented, including the local chamber of commerce, the National Park Service, and the Bridger-Teton National Forest. Visitors can obtain annual park passes and hunting and fishing licenses as well as get trip planning assistance, directions, and maps aplenty. Talk about convenient one-stop shopping. The wildlife exhibits inside are matched by sweeping wildlife observation decks outside that overlook the National Elk Refuge. The real treasure here, though, is the staff, all of whom are friendly, knowledgeable, and more than willing to roll up their sleeves for whatever help you need. Short interpretive talks are offered throughout the season, and naturalists are often on hand at the upper viewing deck with spotting scopes, binoculars, and field guides.

Teton Village

Twelve miles northwest of Jackson is **Teton Village,** an Alps-like enclave nestled around the state's largest and most popular ski hill. The area pulses with energy and activity as soon as the snow flies, and although it quiets down in the shoulder seasons, it is an enormously popular destination in summer as well. Even so, these days it's quite a bit quieter than the center of Jackson. In addition to the abundant lodging, shopping, and dining options, the area is a hub for outdoor activities such as hot-air ballooning, paragliding, horseback riding, and, of course, a myriad of mountain-oriented sports. Plenty of concerts and special events are also held year-round.

National Bighorn Sheep Interpretive Center

Set in Dubois, 85 miles east of Jackson on U.S. Highway 287/26, the **National Bighorn Sheep Interpretive Center** (10 Bighorn Ln., 307/455-3429 or 888/209-2795, www.bighorn. org, 9am-6pm daily summer, 10am-4pm Mon.-Sat. winter, $4 adults, $2 children 8-17, free for children under 8) is dedicated to educating the public about these remarkable, majestic creatures and their habitats. Visitors are welcomed by a stunning bronze of a ram and led inside to several hands-on exhibits that will delight little ones and fascinate animal lovers, 16 mounts of wild sheep from around the world, and a great little gift shop with everything from T-shirts to children's toys and wares by local artists. November-March, the center offers tours to the winter range of the **Whiskey Mountain Habitat Area,** providing an excellent opportunity to see the bighorn sheep in their natural, windswept habitat. Reservations for the 3-5-hour tours should be made at least 48 hours in advance by calling the center. The cost is $100 per person.

Elk are plentiful in winter at the National Elk Refuge.

The Elk Conundrum

Established in 1912, the National Elk Refuge was the first Wyoming state-run feeding ground for elk. In the 1930s and 1940s, more feeding grounds were created to help the animals survive the harsh winters, and in part to keep them from entering areas reserved for cattle grazing. The thriving herd in Jackson ultimately was used to replenish other herds of elk and aid the reintroduction of elk throughout the country. However, as a result of the large number of elk concentrated in these feeding grounds, the animals are much more susceptible to contagious diseases including brucellosis and, more recently, chronic wasting disease. Wyoming lost its federal brucellosis-free status in 2004 when cattle acquired the disease after coming into contact with elk from the refuge.

In 2005 the U.S. Department of Agriculture's Animal Plant Health Inspection Service reported that there was a 50-80 percent rate of brucellosis infection among elk on feedlots, and though that number has dropped to 30 percent in more recent reports, it is still substantially higher than the 1-3 percent infection rate in wild free-ranging elk. Before the National Elk Refuge was created, the elk from southern Yellowstone would migrate and spread past the area of the refuge into southwestern Wyoming. As the winter came to a close, they moved back to their summer habitat. Today it's believed that the 11,000 elk in the Jackson herd alone migrate to and from the refuge at the risk of spreading both brucellosis and chronic wasting disease. As of 2015, the National Elk Refuge is one of 21 feeding grounds for elk in the western part of the state. A study published in 2016 showed that four of the five strains of brucellosis are found on Wyoming feeding grounds, a discovery that pinned the blame for the spread of brucellosis outside Yellowstone on the elk, as opposed to the bison that have long been treated as the culprits.

The question now is, what can be done? The argument has been made that the elk should return to their historic migration routes and original winter ranges rather than being concentrated in the feedlots. Today, however, many of those routes and ranges have been developed for housing, ranches, or other businesses. Furthermore, the idea of elk and cattle competing for food on the open range is worrisome to many Wyoming ranchers. So, although the scientific consensus is that it would be best for the elk to return to their natural migration patterns, the challenge is finding places in the wild that can sustain them throughout the year.

ENTERTAINMENT AND EVENTS
The Arts

Among the most impressive facilities in the state is the relatively new **Jackson Hole Center for the Arts** (265 S. Cache St., 307/734-8956 or 307/733-4900, www.jhcenterforthearts.org), a truly inspired art campus in the heart of downtown that offers educational programs and facilities along with professional theater, dance, and music as well as a remarkable space for major community events. Check out the schedule online—there is always something happening. Of particular note at the Center for the Arts is the **Off Square Theatre Company** (240 S. Glenwood St., 307/733-3021, www.offsquare.org), which produces excellent and

wildly diverse shows ranging from classic American musicals (*Mary Poppins*) and dramatic masterpieces (*The Taming of the Shrew*) to side-splitting comedies (*Vanya and Sonia and Masha and Spike*). Regardless of the offerings, a night at the theater in Jackson is a night well spent.

ART GALLERIES

The art scene in Jackson is both rarefied and approachable, and it is an increasingly important part of both the community and the local economy. There are more than 30 galleries in town. Among the favorites are **Trailside Galleries** (130 E. Broadway, 307/733-3186, www.trailsidegalleries.com, 10am-5:30pm Mon.-Sat., noon-5pm Sun. June-Oct., 10am-5:30pm Mon.-Sat. Nov.-May) and **Legacy**

Gallery (75 N. Cache St., 307/733-2353, www.legacygallery.com, 10am-5pm Mon.-Sat.), both with classic examples of Western art in its traditional and contemporary forms. **Altamira Fine Art** (172 Center St., 307/739-4700, www.altamiraart.com, 10am-5pm daily or by appointment) has a more loftlike urban feel and represents groundbreaking contemporary artists, including Rocky Hawkins, Duke Beardsley, Ed Mell, Marshall Noice, John Felsing, Amy Ringholz, and John Nieto. The **Tayloe Piggot Gallery** (62 S. Glenwood St., 307/733-0555, www.jhmusegallery.com, 10am-6pm Mon.-Wed., 10am-8pm Thurs.-Sat., 11am-5pm Sun.) is cutting-edge cool with both emerging and mid-career artists in a variety of media. For more information on all the galleries in Jackson, visit the **Jackson Hole Gallery Association** (www.jackson-holegalleryassociation.com).

Festivals and Events

Weekly events in Jackson during the summer season (Memorial Day-Labor Day) include the **Jackson Rodeo** (447 Snow King Ave., 307/733-7927, www.jhrodeo.com, 8pm Wed. and Sat. June, 8pm Wed., Fri., and Sat. July-Labor Day, $15-35), a fun family event with bull riding, team roping, barrel racing, bareback broncs, and plenty of other action. Food and refreshments are sold at the chuck wagon.

For one of Jackson's favorite regular events, check out the **Town Square Shootout** (6pm Mon.-Sat.) on the Town Square. It's free and a lot of fun for visitors.

An annual event built around the well-known Boy Scout Elk Antler Auction, where the boys sell the shed antlers they collect from the National Elk Refuge, **Elk Fest** (307/733-3316, www.elkfest.org) takes place the weekend before Memorial Day and includes plenty of food, community concerts, children's activities, and many opportunities to learn about elk.

Happening each year over Memorial Day weekend all around town is Jackson's long-running **Old West Days** (307/733-3316, www.jacksonholechamber.com), which features a

horse-drawn parade, old-town entertainment, a rodeo, a mountain man rendezvous, and a host of other events that celebrate Jackson's rough-and-tumble origins.

Happening in late July-early August, the nearly weeklong **Teton County Fair** (Teton County Fairgrounds, 307/733-5289, www.tetoncountyfair.com) includes family-friendly events like pig wrestling, a rodeo, a demolition derby, concerts, a carnival, and plenty of agricultural and animal exhibits.

The equivalent of Cody's Rendezvous Royale, Jackson's **Fall Arts Festival** (307/733-3316, www.jacksonholechamber.com) is a 10-day event in mid-September that unites the community and attracts a crowd of art lovers with a phenomenal range of art-related events, including the prestigious **Jackson Hole Art Auction** (www.jacksonholeartauction.com) and **Western Design Conference** (www.westerndesignconference.com), gallery walks, open-air art fairs, historic ranch tours, and culinary coups.

The **Grand Teton Music Festival** (McCollister Dr., Teton Village, 307/733-1128, www.gtmf.org, $10-100) takes place annually during July-August. It is held in the all-wooden Walk Festival Hall, which recently underwent a $4.85 million renovation to improve the intimate setting and provide top-notch acoustics. Known as one of the top classical music festivals in the country, it showcases an impressive list of musicians and singers. Running annually since 1962, past performers include Sarah Chang, Itzhak Perlman, the New York Philharmonic, and the Mormon Tabernacle Choir. In addition to the summer festival, the organization hosts concerts during the winter. Family concerts are free, as are students, and open rehearsals can be attended for as little at $10.

One of the most renowned bluegrass festivals in the country takes place on the western slopes of the Grand Tetons in Targhee during mid-August. The **Grand Targhee Bluegrass Festival** (www.grandtarghee.com, 3-day pass from $149, day passes also available, camping $35-115) draws a large number of the best bluegrass musicians in the country, including Brother Mule, Danny Barnes, and Sarah Jarosz, along with a large number of fans. Held at the Grand Targhee Resort (800/827-4433), tent and RV camping is allowed in the national forest during the festival weekend. In addition to performances all day long, there is also plenty of food, arts, and crafts available.

Also taking place at Grand Targhee Resort, in mid-July, the decade-old **Targhee Fest** (www.grandtarghee.com, 3-day pass from $149, day passes also available, camping $35-115) is a lively three-day music festival with an eclectic mix of artists such as Los Lobos and John Hiatt. Camping is also allowed in the national forest during this event.

The **Jackson Hole Film Festival** (www.jacksonholefilmfestival.org) is a biennial event dedicated to nature conservation, held in late September-early October. The six-day festival attracts leaders in science, conservation, and media as numerous films are screened and related social events and activities are organized throughout the week. The festival is held at the Jackson Lake Lodge, except for the final event, which screens selected finalists at the Center for the Arts in downtown Jackson. The festival is slated to run in 2017, 2019, and 2021.

Winter Fest (307/733-3316, www.jacksonholechamber.com) gives residents and visitors alike one more reason to celebrate the snow. Happening over two weeks in February, the celebration includes events like snow sculpting, skiing, ice skating, and wine tasting.

Another winter event everyone looks forward to is the **Eukanuba Stage Stop Dog Race** (307/734-1163, www.wyomingstagestop.org). It takes place from the last weekend in January through the first week of February. Begun in 1996, it is the largest U.S. dogsled race outside Alaska. The race begins in Jackson and runs 500 miles to Park City, Utah. It is unusual in that the participants stop for the night in towns along the way, including Lander, Pinedale, Big Piney-Marbleton, Alpine, Kemmerer, Lyman, Evanston, and Uinta County. Each town along the route celebrates with different festivities as they greet and cheer on the racers.

SHOPPING

For those with time and money, shopping can practically be an athletic pursuit in Jackson, particularly in the streets and alleyways around **Town Square.** In the early 1990s, Jackson was populated with a number of outlet stores, but today most of those have been pushed out by more sophisticated boutiques. There are so many fascinating little shops to pop into, from gorgeous high-end art galleries to the few remaining tacky but fun T-shirt and tchotchke shops.

For an independent bookstore, **Valley Bookstore** (125 N. Cache St., 307/733-4533, www.valleybookstore.com, 9am-9pm daily June-Aug., 9am-7pm Mon.-Sat., 10am-6pm Sun. Sept.-May) is pretty great and has been providing local readers with fabulous books and stellar recommendations for nearly 50 years. The owners grew up in Jackson and have a superb local and regional section.

For top-of-the-line women's and children's clothes in a spacious, almost Zen-like setting, visit **Terra of Jackson Hole** (105 E. Broadway, 307/734-0067, 11am-6pm Mon.-Sat., noon-5pm Sun.), which would not be out of place in Manhattan or San Francisco. Another glorious place filled with beautiful things is **Bella Cose** (48 E. Broadway, 888/733-3338, www.bellacose.com, 10am-6pm Mon.-Sat., noon-5pm Sun.), which offers elegant home decor as well as kitchen and dining items; it clearly caters to the second-home crowd. For a handmade cowboy hat to take home, visit **Jackson Hole Hat Company** (45 W. Deloney, 307/733-7687, 10am-6pm Mon.-Sat., noon-5pm Sun.). It crafts custom cowboy hats in materials ranging from straw to 100 percent beaver fur, as well as carries lines by Bailey and Stetson and accessories including tooled and beaded hatbands, belts, and hat racks.

One of the most exquisite design studios anywhere, **WRJ Design** (30 S. King St.,

307/200-4881 or 307/733-2357, www.wrjdesign.com, 10am-6pm Mon.-Fri., weekends by appointment) has a Jackson showroom filled with furnishings, unique objects, fine art, and curated lines from around the world. Owned by renowned designers Klaus Baer and Rush Jenkins, WRJ's style is elegant, earthy, and contemporary.

SPORTS AND RECREATION
Fishing

Surrounded by abundant rivers and streams, including the Snake River and its myriad mountain tributaries, plus Grand Teton and Yellowstone National Parks, Jackson has become something of a fly-fishing mecca.

The best-known trout stream in the region is the Snake River, which winds more than 60 miles on lazy flats and then blasts through the Snake River Canyon, which offers more white-knuckle rafting than graceful casting. The Upper Snake, much of which is in Grand Teton National Park, is characterized by braided channels with cutbanks and log jams, and the water holds native cutthroats. Drift boating is popular as a way to maximize the water covered (and scenery enjoyed), but there are ample opportunities to get out and wade-fish. The section of the river that goes through the canyon is almost exclusively fished by boat (self-bailers come in handy in the Class II-III rapids), and despite the action of the waves, the fish are more plentiful in the canyon, though not always easy to catch.

Jackson has no shortage of fly-fishing guides or fly shops. Among the best is a small outfit, **Teton Fly Fishing** (544 Clark St., 307/413-1215, www.tetonflyfishing.com), run by Nate Bennett, who loves teaching his clients about the art of fishing as much as he loves hooking a fish. He books only one trip daily so that the pace can be less breakneck and far more enjoyable. Bennett gets his clients on a variety of types of water and, like a good fish whisperer, somehow gets the fish to bite. An artist by training, Bennett ties all his own flies and loves to share. His trips ($450 half-day, $525 full-day for up to 2 anglers) on the Snake, Salt, and Green Rivers include all equipment, flies, transportation, streamside lunch, and full access to his unlimited knowledge and expertise.

A great resource for fishing are the friendly folks at **JD High Country Outfitters** (50 E. Broadway, 307/733-7210 or 866/733-7210, www.highcountryflies.com, 9am-8pm daily summer, reduced hours in winter). The staff are experts on waters all over the region, and in addition to guiding services, the shop has a great selection of flies, equipment, and clothing.

★ Rafting on the Snake River

One of the greatest attractions for summertime visitors to Jackson is rafting the Snake River. There are close to two dozen rafting companies to choose from in the area, and most are open mid-May-September. Below are a few options for those who are interested in experiencing the river, whether it be a tranquil day float through Grand Teton National Park or white-water adventure a little farther south in the canyon. Most adult fares average $70-80 for an eight-mile trip. Increasingly popular are combination trips, which include a scenic float or white-water raft trip with other activities ranging from wildlife tours to horseback rides to gourmet Dutch-oven meals.

Barker-Ewing (800/448-4202, www.barker-ewing.com, $74-81 adults, $64-76 children) is a family-operated business that has been running small trips for more than 50 years.

Dave Hansen Whitewater (800/732-6295, www.davehansenwhitewater.com, $75 adults, $60 children) has been in the business since the late 1960s. Dave actually named two of the largest waves on the river, the Lunch Box and the Big Kahuna.

Another option with a variety of trips down the Snake River is **Mad River Boat Trips** (800/458-7328, www.mad-river.com, $68 adults, $48 children).

For experienced floaters who want to tackle the Snake unguided, **Rent-a-Raft** (U.S.

89, Hoback Jct., 13 miles south of Jackson, 307/733-2728, www.rentaraft.net) offers 11-foot ($65), 12.5-foot ($90), 13-foot ($105), and 14-foot rafts ($125) as well as sit-on-top kayaks ($40) and shuttle service from its headquarters.

Hiking and Mountain Biking

Although plenty of hikers choose to hit the phenomenal trails in Grand Teton and Yellowstone National Parks, with so many mountains in every direction around Jackson, there is no shortage of amazing hikes outside the parks. Many of the trails outside the parks are open to mountain bikers as well.

One trail with immediate proximity to town that skirts the Gros Ventre Wilderness Area is the **Cache Creek Canyon Loop,** which is part of the Greater Snow King Trail Network. It is a popular trail for hikers, mountain bikers, and in winter, cross-country skiers. To get to the trailhead, drive east on Broadway to Redmond Street, across from the hospital; turn right and go 0.4 mile to Cache Creek Road. Turn left and continue just over 1 mile to the parking lot at road's end. Hikers can amble along both sides of the creek on this 4-mile loop, gaining only 350 vertical feet. Connecting trails lead to Game Creek and Granite Falls, or back to Snow King in Jackson.

Ten miles west of town near Teton Pass is **Phillips Pass,** an incredible and somewhat strenuous day hike at the edge of the Tetons and the Jedediah Smith Wilderness Area. The trail is open to hikers and mountain bikers. To get to the trailhead, head west to Teton Pass on Highway 22. Two miles east of the summit is Phillips Canyon Road (Forest Rd. 30972). There is no parking at the trailhead, which is 0.5 mile down this road, so park safely across the highway in a small pullout or on Phillips Canyon Road close to the highway. The 8-mile out-and-back trail starts at 8,000 feet in elevation and is spectacularly beautiful, particularly in late summer, as it winds through flower-drenched meadows and forest to the alpine country above the tree line. As always

in this part of the country, be prepared for significant weather changes and encounters with wild animals.

For excellent guided hiking in the Tetons and around the valley, contact **The Hole Hiking Experience** (307/690-4453 or 866/733-4453, www.holehike.com, half-day from $235 for up to 2 hikers, $88 pp for 3 or more, full-day $440 for up to 2 hikers, $175 pp for 3 or more), which offers a wide variety of trips from half-day naturalist-guided trips geared to families to strenuous all-day hikes and even yoga-hiking combinations. For guided mountain bike trips for the whole family (including kids on Trail-a-Bikes and in trailers) or more extreme riders, contact **Teton Mountain Bike Tours** (545 N. Cache St., 307/733-0712, www.tetonmtbike.com) for half-day (from $70 pp), full-day (from $125-175 pp plus $10 box lunch), multiple-day, and specialty trip offerings. It also rent bikes.

Hoback Sports (520 W. Broadway Ave., 307/733-5335, www.hobacksports.com, 9am-7pm daily) has all kinds of rental bikes for adults and kids, from road bikes and hybrids to full-suspension mountain bikes, and can point bikers in the direction of any kind of ride they seek.

Horseback Riding

Another popular way to experience the great outdoors in Jackson is on horseback. Several options, including hourly rentals, half-day trail rides, or overnight pack trips, are available from the many local outfitters in and around town. For half-day trail rides, expect to pay around $115 per person.

Located 35 miles south of Jackson, **Jackson Hole Outfitters** (307/654-7008, www.jacksonholetrailrides.com, early June-Labor Day) starts its trail rides in the secluded Greys River camp and follows trails through the Bridger-Teton National Forest. It offers half-day rides ($115), full-day rides ($165), extreme rides ($195), and overnight stays ($95) in comfortable canvas tents and real beds.

Spring Creek Ranch (307/733-8833 or 800/443-6139, www.springcreekranch.com)

offers one-hour rides ($49), two-hour rides ($69), and half-day rides ($159) along the East Gros Ventre Butte. It also offers dinner rides ($90 adults, $75 children 12 and under). Age restrictions vary for the different rides.

Mill Iron Ranch (307/773-6390 or 888/808-6390, www.millironranch.net) is located 10.5 miles south of Jackson on U.S. Highway 89/191 and offers two-hour ($65), four-hour ($110), or full-day trips ($160-185) that can be combined with breakfast, lunch, or a steak dinner for an additional charge.

Golf

Golf is becoming increasingly popular in Jackson Hole (maybe because the ball seems to fly so much farther at altitude), and there are a couple of world-class public courses. The **Jackson Hole Golf & Tennis Club** (5000 Spring Gulch Rd., 307/733-3111, www.jhgtc.com, $65-185) offers an award-winning 18-hole course designed by Bob Baldock and renovated twice by Robert Trent Jones II, most recently in 2004. Local conservation hero Laurance Rockefeller once owned the course, which says a lot about its natural beauty. The 18-hole course at **Teton Pines Country Club** (3450 Clubhouse Dr., 307/733-1005 or 800/238-2223, www.tetonpines.com, $140-160 for 18 holes, $40-95 for 9 holes) in Teton Village was designed by Arnold Palmer and has been highly ranked by *Condé Nast Traveler, Audubon International,* and *Golf Digest,* among others.

Skiing

Jackson's reputation among the West's premier ski towns is not hard to explain. There are three developed downhill ski resorts, the closet one to town being right in town.

Snow King Mountain (400 E. Snow King Ave., 800/522-5464, www.snowking-mountain.com, full-day $55 adults, $35 high schoolers 15-18 and seniors 65 and over, free for children 5 and under, half-day $45 adults, $30 high schoolers and seniors 65 and over; night skiing 4pm-7pm $30 adults, $25 high schoolers and seniors) soars skyward just six

Snow King Mountain

blocks from Town Square, making Jackson a ski town in the most literal sense. The mountain was developed for skiing in 1939, making it the first in the Jackson area and one of the first in the country. The area boasts 1,571 feet of vertical drop over 400 acres with two double chairlifts, one triple lift, a surface tow, and the ever-popular **Snow Tubing Park.** The area is open for day and night skiing. Discounts are available for lodging guests. Nonskiers can pay to ride the lift just to enjoy the breathtaking views of town and the valley from the summit. In the summer, the trails and lifts are open for hiking, mountain biking, and paragliding, plus a cowboy roller-coaster, an alpine slide, and a ropes course.

In nearby Teton Village, the ski area at **Jackson Hole Mountain Resort** (307/733-2292, www.jacksonhole.com, $81-139 adults, $61-112 seniors, $51-73 children 14 and under, free for children 5 and under, prices rise as the season progresses, especially around the holidays, discounts available by purchasing online) is in fact two mountains, Apres Vous and

Rendezvous, which together offer skiers 2,500 skiable acres, a vertical drop of 4,139 feet, and open access to another 3,000-plus acres of backcountry terrain. There are 133 trails, of which a whopping 50 percent are geared to experts, 40 percent for intermediate skiers, and 10 percent for beginners. The ski hill averages 459 inches of snow annually. In Jackson, this is the mountain to ski and be seen.

The **aerial tram** (307/733-2292, 9am-5pm daily late May-mid-June, 9am-6pm daily mid-June-early Sept., single ride $27-42 adults, $21-34 seniors 65 and older, $16-25 children 6-17, $75-95 family, free for children under 6) known as Big Red takes hikers, bikers, paragliders, backcountry skiers, and lookie-loos up to the summit of Rendezvous Peak (4,139 feet in 12 minutes). At the top, a fabulous little waffle hut, **Corbet's Cabin** (307/739-2688, 9am-5pm late May-early Oct.), makes you wish you had hiked the whole way.

Although you need to go through Idaho to get there, **Grand Targhee Resort** (3300 Ski Hill Rd., 307/353-2300, www.grandtarghee. com, full-day $80-85 adults, $57-62 seniors 65 and over, $36-41 juniors 6-12, free for children under 6) in Alta, Wyoming, is a destination in itself. The skiing in winter is out of this world, with huge dumps of powder and expansive terrain. The resort also offers Nordic skiing, tubing, guided snowcat tours, sleigh-ride dinners, snowmobile tours, and ice climbing. In summer, the mountain stays awake for hiking, mountain biking, horseback riding, and a couple of renowned musical events, including **Targhee Fest** and the **Grand Targhee Bluegrass Festival.**

For avid Nordic skiers, the blanket of snow transforms many favorite local hiking trails into first-rate ski trails. From hitting the groomers at local golf courses, including **Teton Pines** (3450 N. Clubhouse Dr., 307/733-1005 or 800/238-2223, www.teton-pines.com, $15 adults, $10 seniors, $5 children) to hoofing into the backcountry in Grand Teton National Park, there is terrain for everyone. The **Jackson Hole Nordic Center** (3395 Village Dr., 307/739-2629, www.jhnordic.com) at Teton Village offers 11 miles of groomed trails for classic and skate skiers. Rentals are available on-site. In town, gear can be purchased or rented from **Skinny Skis** (65 W. Deloney Ave., 307/733-6094 or 888/733-7205, www.skinnyskis.com) or **Teton Mountaineering** (170 N. Cache St., 307/733-3595, www.tetonmtn.com).

FOOD

For every opportunity this region provides to exert energy by skiing, hiking, biking, or other pursuits, Jackson offers many more ways to replenish your supply. The number of outstanding restaurants in this town puts just about every other town in Wyoming—and many western states—to shame.

As a rule, every day in Jackson should start with a trip to **The Bunnery** (130 N. Cache Dr., 307/733-5474, www.bunnery.com, 7am-3pm daily, $10-16). The food is entirely made from scratch and utterly scrumptious. The baked goods—including its trademark OSM (oats, sunflower, millet) bread and homemade granola—are beyond compare, and the enormous and diverse menu offers plenty of healthy options as well as a few decadent ones. The "Get Your Buns in Here" bumper stickers are also good for a laugh. Be prepared to wait, however; The Bunnery is beloved by visitors and locals alike.

Just as the best days in Jackson should start at The Bunnery, so too should they finish at the **Million Dollar Cowboy Bar** (25 N. Cache Dr., 307/733-2207, www.milliondollarcowboybar.com, 11am-2am daily summer, noon-2am daily winter, Fri.-Sat. 9pm-1:30am off-season, $8-15), right on Town Square. The bar has been a centerpiece of Jackson since 1937 when the first liquor license was issued in the state. The saddle bar stools should absolutely be sat upon and visitors are encouraged to check out the impressive collection of Western memorabilia adorning the bar. There is live music regularly, and patrons who don't want to go too far can enjoy a hearty meal next door in the **Million Dollar Cowboy Steakhouse** (307/733-4790, www.

jhcowboysteakhouse.com, 5:30-10pm daily, $17-33), featuring specialties like bone marrow and cheddar fondue, Cajun duck poppers, bison carpaccio, and any kind of steak you can imagine. Reservations are recommended.

Inspired by New York's EATALY, but every bit Jackson Hole, **Bin 22** (200 W. Broadway, 307/739-9463, www.bin22jackson.com, wine bar 11:30am-10pm Mon.-Sat., 3pm-10pm Sun., $6-29) is a great spot for a light bite or to pick up a bottle of wine to go. It has all sorts of salamis and cheeses, plus appetizers and tapas-style plates.

New on the Jackson scene, and often with a line out front, **Persephone Bakery** (145 E. Broadway, 307/200-6708, www.persephonebakery.com, 7am-6pm Mon.-Sat. and 7am-5pm Sun. summer, call ahead for winter hours, breakfast $8-10, lunch $8-14) is an artisanal bakery and café, known for rustic and elegant breads and pastries, and excellent salads and sandwiches for lunch. It also offers afternoon high tea service (reservations required) and a nice wine list and cocktail menu. How's that for a Jackson Hole bakery?

One of the newest and most interesting places for craft cocktails, excellent wine, and a gourmet meal is **The Rose** (50 W. Broadway, 307/733-1500, www.therosejh.

com, 5:30pm-2am daily, $12-25, $70 7-course tasting menu), founded by the same team who created the insanely hip Death & Co. in New York City. There is free live music four nights a week, and a phenomenal chef's dinner on Wednesdays. Everything here is artisanal and local, from the food and cocktails to the dinner plates and art.

Set in a 1910 log cabin, one of the oldest residential structures in town, **Café Genevieve** (135 E. Broadway, 307/732-1910, www.genevievejh.com, 8am-9pm daily, breakfast and lunch $9-15, dinner $14-39) serves inspired home cooking with dishes like fried green tomatoes, sweet and spicy candied bacon (known as pig candy), fried chicken, and jambalaya. It serves a killer breakfast until 3pm with specialties like Cajun Benedict and fried chicken and waffles.

A fresh and delicious arrival on Jackson's culinary scene is **Pica's Mexican Taqueria** (1160 Alpine Ln., 307/734-4457, www.picastaqueria.com, 11am-10pm daily summer, 11am-10pm Mon.-Sat. winter, $8.25-15), which offers the freshest take on tacos, burritos, great salads, and authentic Mexican dishes. Another terrific Mexican restaurant right in town is **The Merry Piglets** (160 N. Cache St., 307/733-2966, www.merrypiglets.com,

Café Genevieve is set in a 1910 log cabin.

11:30am-9pm daily, $11-26), which serves classic taco, burrito, chimichanga, and enchilada plates with fresh salsas, sauces, and tortilla chips, all made in-house daily. As are the fabulous margaritas! The fish is wild, the meat is pasture-raised, and no partially hydrogenated oils are used. The portions are big, and the flavors are very satisfying.

Known for its rack of lamb, but accomplished at everything on the menu, **The Blue Lion** (160 N. Millward St., 307/733-3912, www.bluelionrestaurant.com, 5:30pm-9pm daily, $19-43) has been a staple of the Jackson food scene for more than two decades, with menu items ranging from elk and buffalo tenderloin and Idaho trout to rack of lamb and hazelnut-crusted chicken. There's also a children's menu. Reservations are recommended.

For carb loaders, the best spot in town is undoubtedly **Nani's Cucina Italiana** (242 N. Glenwood St., 307/733-3888, www.nanis.com, 5pm-9pm daily, $18-34), a gem of a place. The menu changes monthly—each one features a different region of Italy—and the restaurant serves up authentic dishes with farmers market-fresh ingredients. Everything is made from scratch, and the flavors cannot be overpraised. The ambience is quiet and comfortable, and the outside decks are a treat in good weather.

Every ski town worth its salt needs a good hometown pizza joint. **Pizzeria Caldera** (20 W. Broadway, 307/201-1472, www.pizzeriacaldera.com, 11am-9:30pm daily, $11-17) serves up thin-crust Napoletana-style pizza baked over stone-hearth fires. Options range from classic Italian margherita to pure Jackson Hole, like the Bisonte, with bison sausage and fresh sage. There is also a great beer and wine list, plus yummy salads, pastas, and tapas.

Although it is every inch a Four Seasons, this is still Wyoming, and there is a casualness that puts visitors at ease here. The hotel has some exquisite restaurants, **Westbank Grill** (serving breakfast, lunch, and dinner) among them, but a great little spot is the **Ascent Lounge** (7680 Granite Loop Rd., Teton Village, 307/732-5000, www.fourseasons.

com/jacksonhole, 4pm-11pm daily, $10-39), which feels like an oversize living room and serves casual but still elegant light fare that ranges from flatbread to burgers. It's smaller than the resort's other restaurants, with seating for 38. As it's quite popular with the locals, the overflow spills out onto the gorgeous heated mountainside patio.

Also in Teton Village, a longtime favorite is the **Mangy Moose Restaurant and Saloon** (3295 Village Dr., 307/733-4913, www.mangymoose.com, 9am-2pm and 5pm-10pm daily summer and ski season, $15-32). The menu is packed with upscale pub fare including a bison burger with truffle fries, prime rib, baby back ribs, and grilled rainbow trout. The saloon is open daily at 11am-2am in the summer and ski season.

Right on the Town Square is one of Jackson's most celebrated eating establishments, the **Snake River Grill** (84 E. Broadway, 307/733-0557, www.snakerivergrill.com, 5:30pm-9:30pm daily summer, from 6pm daily winter, $23-41). A visual feast in addition to being a gastronomical delight, the Snake River Grill has largely defined Jackson Hole cuisine with offerings like cast-iron roasted elk chop, lamp chop "Lollipops" and wild game Korean hot bowl. The menu is diverse, constantly changing, and completely mouthwatering. It's worth noting that although children are welcome in the restaurant, no high chairs or children's menus are available.

Another elegant option for an unforgettable meal is at the Rusty Parrot's **Wild Sage** (175 N. Jackson St., 307/733-2000, www.rustyparrot.com, 5:30pm-9:30pm daily, $30-57). With only eight tables, the service is as notable as the food. From Wagyu tenderloin to dry-aged buffalo rib eye, Wild Sage has made quite a name for itself in the Intermountain West culinary scene. Reservations are strongly recommended.

ACCOMMODATIONS

While there are plenty of places to hang your hat in Jackson, during the prime seasons those places will not come cheap. The best deal in town is still the **Anvil Motel** (215 N. Cache St., 800/234-4507, www.anvilmotel.com, $86-235), just a block off Town Square. The rooms are cute and comfortable with microwaves, mini refrigerators, and air-conditioning. The $5 per day amenity fee includes Wi-Fi, parking, and continental breakfast. Tucked right behind the Anvil is the bargain-friendly **El Rancho Motel** (240 S. Glenwood St., 307/733-3668, $117-220), which is slightly more spartan and does not have air-conditioning. Both properties were undergoing a major renovation as of fall 2016, and prices are expected to rise significantly. Even if these two properties are no longer budget-friendly, they are comfortable and ideally located.

Although independent hotels and inns tend to reflect more of Jackson's charm, there are plenty of nice chain hotels, some of which can offer good deals, particularly in the off-seasons. Among them are **Hampton Inn** (350 S. Hwy. 89, 307/733-0033, www.hamptoninn3.hilton.com, $148-452); **Jackson Hole Super 8** (750 S. Hwy. 89, 307/733-6833, www.jacksonholesuper8.com, $102-287), which is steps away from the free bus service in town; and **Motel 6** (600 S. Hwy. 89, 307/733-1620, www.motel6.com, $52-196).

An adorable and comfortable bed and breakfast with easy access to both town and country is **Inn on the Creek** (295 N. Millward, 307/739-1565, www.innonthecreek.com, $139-668), which offers balconies, fireplaces, king beds, and private Jacuzzis in some of its rooms. Another very peaceful place to stay with a babbling creek to help lull you to sleep is the **Wildflower Lodge at Jackson Hole** (3725 Shooting Star Ln., Wilson, 307/733-4710, www.jhwildflowerlodge.com, $400-500), which boasts cozy handcrafted log beds, fluffy comforters, and delicious food. There's even a kids' bunkroom with eight beds for families traveling together.

Almost as close to Town Square but quite a bit higher on the luxury scale is **The Wort Hotel** (50 N. Glenwood St., 800/322-2727, www.worthotel.com, $159-799), built in 1941 and a landmark in town, complete with the legendary Silver Dollar Bar & Grill, which has more than 2,000 inlaid silver dollars as time capsule-type decorations. The rooms are plush, and the location is great. Just down the street, the **Rusty Parrot Lodge & Spa** (175 N. Jackson St., 307/733-2000 or 888/739-1749, www.rustyparrot.com, $235-1,200) is like a little oasis at the edge of town. From the on-site spa to the world-class dining at Wild Sage Restaurant, every little detail is well considered. The 31 rooms and suites are luxurious; some even have fireplaces and jetted tubs.

Just four blocks from Town Square, **Rustic Inn Creekside Resort & Spa** (475 N. Cache, 800/323-9279 or 307/733-2357, www.rusticinnatjh.com, double queen rooms $129-349, double queen cabins $139-889, creekside king cabins $229-569, 2-bedroom spa suites from $999) is an oasis of calm. The creekside cabins are farther from the road and quieter, but the whole property is lovely on 12 beautifully landscaped acres. The log cabins are cozy and elegantly appointed. The spa is excellent, as are on-site dining options.

For unparalleled luxury in the heart of this mountain village, Jackson has plenty of options. **Amangani** (1535 NE Butte Rd., 307/734-7333, www.amanresorts.com, from $875 off-season) is perched on the edge of a butte with stunning views from every window of meadows and mountains. In addition to deluxe suites and first-class service, Amangani rents spectacular homes. In Teton Village at the base of the ski hill, the 5-star **Four Seasons Resort** (7680 Granite Loop Rd., 307/732-5000, www.fourseasons.com, $389-2,500) offers ski-in/ski-out access with exquisite amenities including glorious dining, a spa, and flawless service.

Away from the hustle and bustle of town, perched on a ridge overlooking the entire valley is the **Spring Creek Ranch** (1800 Spirit Dance Rd., 307/733-8833 or 800/443-6139, www.springcreekranch.com, from $180 spring and fall, $285 early summer, $360 summer, $215 winter), which boasts a variety of accommodations, including hotel rooms, cabins, condos, and exclusive mountain villas. The property is entirely self-contained with two restaurants on-site, a spa, and a slew of activities. The views from here trump just about everything else in the region, and the quiet gives Spring Creek Ranch tremendous appeal.

At Teton Village, **Hotel Terra** (3335 W. Village Dr., 307/739-4000 or 800/631-6281, www.hotelterrajacksonhole.com, $159-1,115) is a hip choice, at once luxurious and sustainable. The ecofriendly rooms have clean lines, retro-funky appointments, and lots of gadgets for techies, including iPod docking stations, flat-screen high-definition TVs, and Bose surround sound. The 132 guest rooms and suites range in size and style from urban studios and Terra guest rooms to 1-3-bedroom suites. There are two restaurants on-site, a lively bar, a rooftop swimming pool and hot tub, a day spa, and a fitness center.

GUEST RANCHES

For many visitors, the best way to enjoy Jackson Hole is to while away the days at a scenery-soaked dude ranch somewhere in the valley. After all, it was the dude ranches that jump-started Jackson's economy in the 1920s and 1930s. A multitude of wonderful choices are available, ranging from the historic and rustic, like the **Flat Creek Ranch** (15 bumpy miles from Jackson in isolated splendor, 307/733-0603 or 866/522-3344, www.flatcreekranch.com, 3-night stays from $2,400 for 2 people, all-inclusive), and the extravagant, like **Lost Creek Ranch & Spa** (U.S. 89, Moose, 30 minutes north of Jackson, 307/733-3435, www.lostcreek.com, cabins $5,600-14,500/week), to the family-oriented, like the **Heart Six Guest Ranch** (Moran, 35 miles north of Jackson, 307/543-2477, www. heartsix.com, 1-3-bedroom cabins $199-249 nightly). There are options for every preference: proximity to town, emphasis on riding, this century or last, weekend or weeklong stays, and more.

For a comprehensive listing of the dude ranches in the vicinity of Jackson Hole, contact the **Dude Ranchers' Association** (866/399-2339, www.duderanch.org). Another full-service operation that can help you find nearly any type of lodging, transportation, and activities in and around Jackson Hole is **Mountain Resort Services** (877/791-0211, www.mtnresortservices.com).

CAMPING

Camping is by far the most economical way to stay in and around Jackson, and there are 14 campgrounds within a 15-mile radius of downtown. Among the closest to town is the **Curtis Canyon Campground** (Flat Creek Rd., 7 miles northeast of Jackson, 307/739-5400, www.fs.usda.gov/btnf, late May-late Sept., $12), which offers phenomenal views of the Tetons, immediate access to the National Elk Refuge, and terrific mountain hiking trails.

For more information on specific public campgrounds, contact the **Bridger-Teton National Forest** (340 N. Cache Dr., Jackson, 307/739-5500, www.fs.usda.gov).

For RV parks in Jackson, try the large and conveniently located **Virginian Lodge** (750 W. Broadway, 307/733-2792 or 800/262-4999, May 1-Oct. 15, www.virginianlodge.com, full hookups $85-95), which has both motel rooms and 103 RV sites in addition to all the amenities you could want, including laundry, a pool, a hot tub, a salon, a restaurant, and a saloon.

INFORMATION AND SERVICES

The most comprehensive spot to get information on the area is the **Jackson Hole and Greater Yellowstone Visitor Center** (532 N. Cache St., 307/733-3316, www.fws. gov, 8am-7pm daily Memorial Day-Sept. 30, 9am-5pm daily Oct. 1-Memorial Day), which has representatives from the Jackson Hole Chamber of Commerce (307/733-3316), the National Park Service, the Bridger-Teton National Forest, and four other agencies all under the same sod roof.

TRANSPORTATION
Getting There

Nine miles north of town off U.S. Highway 89, entirely within the borders of Grand Teton National Park, is the **Jackson Hole Airport** (JAC, 1250 E. Airport Rd., 307/733-7682, www.jacksonholeairport.com), which offers daily flights on **American** (800/433-7300, www.aa.com), **Delta/SkyWest** (307/732-0364 or 800/221-1212, www.delta.com), and **United/United Express** (800/241-6522, www.united.com). Depending on the season, nonstop flights can be found to and from Denver, Salt Lake City, Dallas/Ft. Worth, Minneapolis, Chicago, Atlanta, San Francisco, Houston, New York, Seattle, Washington DC, and Los Angeles.

The only buses that serve Jackson Hole are with **Alltrans** (307/733-3135 or 800/443-6133, www.jacksonholealltrans.com), which offers service to and from Salt Lake City, plus private transportation, shuttle service, and even guided tours of the area.

The major routes into Jackson Hole—including U.S. Highway 89/191/287 from Yellowstone and Grand Teton National Parks, U.S. Highway 26/287 from the east, Highway 22 from the west over Teton Pass, and U.S. Highway 189/191/89 from the south—can all experience weather closures in the winter, particularly over Teton Pass. There is no car traffic in the southern portion of Yellowstone during the winter. For Wyoming road reports, call 800/WYO-ROAD (800/996-7623, www.wyoroad.info).

Jackson is roughly 240 miles south of Bozeman, 177 miles southwest of Cody through Yellowstone National Park, and 275 miles northeast of Salt Lake City. Keep in mind that while distances through the national parks may be shorter in actual mileage, the time is often extended by lower speed limits, traffic congestion, and animal jams. In addition, most of the park roads are closed in winter, and car travel is not possible between Bozeman and Jackson or between Cody and Jackson. Driving distances around the parks increase significantly.

Getting Around

Car-rental agencies operating at the Jackson Hole Airport include **Avis, Hertz,** and **Enterprise.** Off-airport rental agencies in downtown Jackson include **Dollar, Thrifty, National, Alamo,** and **Leisure Sports** (307/733-3040, www.leisuresportsadvenutre.com).

In town, **Alltrans** (307/733-3135, www.jacksonholealltrans.com) provides airport shuttles and a variety of tours. Shuttles can also be arranged through **Jackson Hole Shuttle** (307/200-1400, www.jhshuttle.com). There are 30 taxi companies in Jackson, all of which can be found on the Jackson Hole Airport website (www.jacksonholeairport.com). Among them are **Broncs Car Service** (307/413-9863, www.jackson-hole-taxi.com), **Canyon Taxi** (307/200-8858, www.canyontaxiservice.com), **Jackson Hole Taxi** (307/699-3369, www.jacksonholetaxi.us), and **Village Taxi** (307/690-0463, www.villagetaxijacksonhole.com). Taxi rates from the airport into town are generally $35 for 1-2 people. Service to Teton Village is usually around $60 for 1-2 people.

Pinedale

Like so many small communities that dot the West, Pinedale (population 1,837, elevation 7,201 feet) started as a ranch that doubled as a post office. Organized in 1904 and incorporated in 1912, the small community has an interesting mix of people and, thanks to the state's energy boom and extraction of natural gas nearby, some unavoidable growing pains. However, the population has been on the decline since 2013, with the drop in oil prices and slowdown in production.

Nestled between the western flank of the staggeringly beautiful Wind River Mountains and the 11-mile-long Fremont Lake, Pinedale is a natural playground for hiking, climbing, sailing, and fishing. The other great pastime in these parts is history, and the town has done an excellent job of preserving it with the Museum of the Mountain Man and annual events like the Green River Rendezvous in July. Not necessarily a well-known destination, Pinedale, which is the county seat for Sublette County, is a natural stopping point between Jackson (78 miles north) and Rock Springs (100 miles south), with great access to some of Wyoming's most extraordinary mountains and lakes.

SIGHTS
Museum of the Mountain Man

The **Museum of the Mountain Man** (700 E. Hennick St., 307/367-4101 or 877/686-6266, www.museumofthemountainman.com, 9am-5pm daily May-Oct., $10 ages 13 and over, $8 seniors, free for children 12 and under) is dedicated to preserving the history of the fur trapping and trading era. Its exhibits are full of interesting artifacts and interpretive materials related to the Western fur trade and the life of Native Americans in the region during this period. Visitors can view Jim Bridger's rifle, learn about beaver trapping and the processing of fur, and see a full-size buffalo hide tipi (there are not many of these remaining in the United States) that has been extensively and authentically furnished. The museum also houses exhibits related to local history, including the settling of Sublette County and the development of Pinedale over the last 100 years.

Granite Hot Springs

En route from Jackson to Pinedale, some 12 miles south of Hoback Junction on U.S. Highway 189/191, is the turnoff for **Granite Hot Springs** (307/690-6323, 10am-8pm daily summer, 10am-6pm daily winter, $6 adults, $4 children). The 10-mile-long scenic drive is on a gravel road that ends at the parking lot for the hot springs. Camping is allowed along the road but not within the last 1.5 miles before the springs. In the winter the road is groomed to allow access on skis, snowshoes, snowmobiles, or dogsleds. The pool is situated below the Gros Ventre mountain range and was built by the Civilian Conservation Corps in 1933. The water is usually about 93°F in the summer and 112°F in winter. There is a nice deck for lounging, and changing rooms are available. There is also a nearby campground (late May-Sept., $15), run by the same people who manage the hot springs.

If you are visiting during the winter, a popular way to access the hot springs is by dogsled. **Jackson Hole Iditarod Sled Dog Tours** (307/733-7388 or 800/554-7388, www.jhsleddog.com) offers full-day trips to the hot springs and include a hearty lunch and a steak or trout dinner (prepared on-site while you are enjoying a dip in the springs).

ENTERTAINMENT AND EVENTS

The **Green River Rendezvous** (307/367-4101 or 877/686-6266, www.meetmeonthegreen.com) is a huge community event that takes place the second full weekend of July. The city prides itself on the fact that 6 of the 15 Rocky Mountain Rendezvous were held here in the Green River Valley at Horse Creek. The first rendezvous was held in 1825 and continued each summer until 1840. For about three weeks trappers, traders, and Native Americans would come together to trade and resupply their outfits, exchange stories, catch up with old friends, get incredibly drunk, and participate in all sorts of boisterous behavior.

Today the Green River Rendezvous is more family-friendly while still bringing the era of the mountain man to life. There are plenty of games, crafts, living istory demonstrations, guest speakers, a mountain man encampment, programs for children, and a rodeo. The pageant, which is usually held on Sunday, should not be missed. It is an entertaining re-enactment of an 1830s rendezvous. The participants, in original costumes, are lively characters who barter, trade, and duel.

A newer addition to the summer lineup is the **Wind River Mountain Festival** (307/367-2440, www.greatoutdoorshop.com), put on by the Great Outdoor Shop and held in late July. In addition to concerts, you'll find music, yoga, hiking, camping, gear demos and workshops, a craft beer fest, and other adventures. The events are held in Pinedale at the American Legion Park.

SPORTS AND RECREATION
Fremont Lake

The second-largest natural lake in the state, **Fremont Lake** (3.2 miles north of Pinedale, www.pinedale.com) was formed glacially and is more than 600 feet deep in places. The lake was named for John C. Fremont, who mapped the area in 1842 in advance of the Oregon Trail. The lake is a natural recreation site with opportunities for boating, sailing, water-skiing, fishing, and camping. Though there are no designated hiking trails around the lake, most of the shoreline is undeveloped and can be walked on. Renovated in 2013,the 54 RV and tent campsites at **Fremont Lake Campground** ($12), operated by the U.S. Forest Service at the lower end of the lake, are

generally open late-June-early September and can be reserved through www.recreation.gov (877/444-6777). Also at the lower end of the lake, the **Sandy Beach** picnic area is for day use only.

For an incredibly scenic drive or bike ride, **Skyline Drive** is a 16-mile paved road along the lake's eastern shore that leads to a campground and hiking trails at the edge of the Bridger Wilderness.

The only commercial facility at Fremont Lake is the idyllic **Lakeside Lodge Resort & Marina** (99 Forest Service Rd., 307/367-2221 or 877/755-5253, www.lakesidelodge.com, year-round), which offers 12 beautiful cabins ($75-169), a full-service restaurant (307/367-3555, lunch and dinner daily summer, dinner daily winter), and fishing boat rentals ($30 for 2 hours, $60 half-day, $95 full-day), pontoon boats ($40/hour, $160 half-day, $325 full-day), and ski boats ($120 for 2 hours, $250 half-day, $425 full-day), plus stand-up paddleboards, kayaks, and canoes.

Fishing and Boating

There are literally hundreds of lakes in the vicinity of Pinedale that contain several species of trout and a few Montana grayling, as well as an assortment of freestone waterways that include the world-class Green, Hoback, and New Fork Rivers. Wild trout abound in smaller streams too, including Faler Creek, Fish Creek, and North Cottonwood Creek in the Wyoming Range, some of which are private-lease streams.

The best place to start any fishing expedition is at **Two Rivers Emporium** (211 W. Pine St., 307/367-4131 or 800/329-4353, www.2rivers.net), which can outfit you from rod to leader to fly and offers a range of guided trips (from $480/day float fishing for 1-2 people), including wading on private waters, and can include lodging and gourmet meals.

With so many lakes in the region, canoeing is a wonderful and quiet way to navigate the myriad waterways. Lake-use canoe and kayak rentals ($35/day) and stand-up paddleboards ($45/day) are available in town from

An angler casts a line near Pinedale.

the **Great Outdoor Shop** (332 W. Pine St., 307/367-2440, www.greatoutdoorshop.com, 7am-9pm Mon.-Sat., 8am-8pm Sun. summer, 8am-8pm daily winter). It also offers an amazing range of services, including guided fishing trips and gear rental, shuttles to the best trailheads and the airport in Jackson, backpacking, and gear rentals for rock or ice climbing.

Motorized and nonmotorized boats are available for rent on both Fremont and Half Moon Lakes at **Lakeside Lodge Resort & Marina** (877/755-5253, www.lakesidelodge. com, $15-60/hour with 2-hour minimum) and **Half Moon Lake Lodge** (307/367-6373, www.halfmoonlakelodge.com, $50/hour pontoon, $20/hour fishing boat, $10/hour kayak and canoe, with 2-hour minimum for all).

Hiking and Rock Climbing

The Wind River and Wyoming Ranges, which include the Jim Bridger and Gros Ventre Wilderness Areas, offer some of the best hiking and climbing in the state. Hundreds of miles of trails crisscross the area and give hikers and backpackers access to hundreds of thousands of acres of gorgeous alpine and subalpine terrain. Many of the trailheads are at 9,000 feet and higher, so be prepared for significant and immediate changes in the weather. Prime hiking season this high is short—mid-July-mid-September—and it can snow any day of the year. Average daytime summer temperatures peak in the 70s and 80s, with nighttime lows dropping into the 30s. Afternoons often bring rainstorms with lightning, so be prepared to get lower in a hurry. Always be aware that this is black bear and grizzly bear country, so plan ahead to bring pepper spray.

Among the favorites in the area is the easily accessible **Elkhart Park Trail,** the only one accessed by a paved road, just 15 miles northeast of Pinedale. The heavily hiked trail departs from the **Trails End Campground** at 9,100 feet in elevation. Great day hikes will lead you into the Wind River Mountains and places like **Photographer's Point** and **Miller Lake.** A staffed Forest Service visitors center at the Elkhart Park trailhead can provide information about trails and trail conditions.

Another excellent series of trails is in the **Green River Lakes,** 52 miles north of Pinedale (31 paved miles and 21 miles of good gravel). The **Hiline Trail,** among others, starts at a 39-site campground at 8,000 feet in elevation and runs almost the length of the Winds, 80 miles south over jaw-droppingly beautiful terrain. There are several fishable lakes in the area and an abundance of ways to enjoy a day hike.

For more information on specific trails, conditions, and maps, contact the **Bridger-Teton National Forest office** (29 E. Fremont Lake Rd., Pinedale, 307/367-4326, www.fs.usda.gov).

Mountain Biking

The 2,700-mile **Great Divide Mountain Bike Route** from Banff, Alberta, to the U.S.-Mexican border, along the spine of the Rockies, passes directly through Pinedale.

There is plenty of good rugged terrain to be explored by mountain bike. Due to the weather, however, most trails are only good for biking 3-5 months of the year. **Sweeny Creek** and **Grouse Mountain Trails** have some good short rides, or for the more adventurous (and fit), try the ride up **Half Mountain.** From the top you can bike almost the entire length of the ridge and take in some spectacular views.

During the summer, **White Pine Ski Resort** (74 White Pine Rd., 10 miles northeast of Pinedale, 307/367-6606, www.whitepineski.com) is open to mountain bikers. The chairs on the ski lift can accommodate riders and their bikes; bikes are available for rent at the resort as well. Special biking trails for all levels of experience have been groomed for the ride downhill. For a more tranquil and scenic ride, opt for one of the flatter cross-country trails.

For more trail ideas in the Pinedale area, visit www.singletracks.com.

Skiing

The state's oldest ski area, **White Pine Ski Resort** (74 White Pine Rd., 10 miles northeast of Pinedale, 307/367-6606, www.whitepineski.com, all-day $48 adults, $35 youth and seniors, $6 children 5 and under) is tucked in the Bridger-Teton National Forest above Fremont Lake. Though relatively small when compared to others in the Jackson area, the resort is a wonderful family-oriented ski hill with lodging, two restaurants, rentals, and free cross-country skiing in winter.

In summer, the mountain is open for mountain biking, scenic chairlift rides, hiking, horseback riding, and, because of its proximity to the lake, fishing.

Horseback Riding

The Bridger-Teton National Forest is a wonderful experience on horseback. The **White Pine Ski Resort** (74 White Pine Rd., 10 miles northeast of Pinedale, 307/367-6606, www.whitepineski.com) offers single and multinight pack trips. One amazing option is the overnight pack trip to Sweeney Lake (from

$450 pp), during which anglers can fish for prized golden trout. **Half Moon Lake Resort** (208 Forest Service Rd., 9 miles northeast of Pinedale, 307/367-6373, www.halfmoonlakelodge.com, $40/hour, $70 for 2 hours, $90 half-day, $125 full-day, $225 full-day with fishing) also offers trail rides and pack trips with horses suited for all levels of experience.

Golf

At the west end of town, **Rendezvous Meadows Golf Course** (Club House Rd., 307/367-4252, www.golfpinedale.com, $20 for 9 holes, $27 for 18 holes) is a nice nine-hole public course.

FOOD

Among Pinedale's oldest and most favorite restaurants is the **Patio Grill and Dining Room** (35 W. Pine St., 307/367-4611, 11am-9pm daily, $9-16), known for home-cooked, authentic Mexican food.

For a fun evening with excellent beer, try the **Wind River Brewing Company** (402 W. Pine St., 307/367-2337, www.windriverbrewingco.com, 11am-11pm Sun.-Thurs., 11am-midnight Fri.-Sat., $8-32) for great salads, appetizers, sandwiches, burgers, and steaks. Its award-winning hand-crafted ales are the icing on the cake.

A good place for a filling meal for the whole family is **Old Stones Smokehouse & Country Pizza** (4 Country Club Ln., 307/367-6760, www.windriverpizza.com, 11am-9pm Mon.-Sat., 11am-8pm Sun., $7-27), which serves barbecue and gourmet stone-hearth pizza, plus calzones, pasta, salads, and all variety of bar-type appetizers. There's also a salad, soup, and pizza buffet ($4.50 kids 3-8, $8.95 adults lunch, $9.95 adults dinner).

A unique dinner option that reflects the people and culture of Pinedale is the family-run ★ **Pitchfork Fondue** (9888 U.S. 191, 307/367-3607, www.pitchforkfondue.com, 5pm-8:30pm Thurs.-Sat., $10.95-29.95), an ingenious Western outdoor cookout at the fairgrounds south of town. Tender steaks are seared in large cast-iron cauldrons of oil (yes, on pitchforks) and served with fondue sauces, hot homemade potato chips, fruit salad, green salad, beverages, and homemade brownies. The picnic tables can accommodate 240 people, but call ahead for reservations and current pricing.

ACCOMMODATIONS

Because of a population boom driven by the energy industry, there are quite a few accommodations in and around Pinedale, particularly given the size of the town. **The Log Cabin Motel** (49 E. Magnolia St., 307/367-4579, www.thelogcabinmotel.com, $74-169) is as charming as it is conveniently located. Built in 1929, the motel lives up to its name by remaining true to Pinedale's architectural style. The cabins vary in size, but most are quite spacious with partial or full kitchens, covered porches, satellite TV, and Wi-Fi.

The **Half Moon Lake Resort** (9 miles northeast of Pinedale, 307/367-6373, www.halfmoonlakelodge.com, $110-145) has eight cabins tucked into the trees in addition to a lodge restaurant and bar overlooking the lake. Activities on-site include fishing, hiking, boating, and horseback riding. Another great lakeside resort is the **Lakeside Lodge Resort and Marina** (3.5 miles northeast of Pinedale, 877/755-5253, www.lakesidelodge.com, year-round), with 12 beautiful and modern cabins ($75-169), all with immediate waterfront access and splendid views.

CAMPING

Sublette County is 80 percent public land, making camping in the region a viable option. The closest (and happily, the most scenic) RV and tent campsites can be found at **Fremont Lake Campground** (5 miles northeast of Pinedale, www.recreation.gov, late-June-early Sept., $12) and the **Half Moon Lake Campground** (10 miles northeast of Pinedale, June-Sept., 877/444-6777, www.recreation.gov, $7). There is no potable water at Half Moon Lake, and 11 of its spots can be reserved.

For more information on U.S. Forest Service campgrounds and backcountry camping, contact the **Bridger-Teton National Forest office** (29 E. Fremont Lake Rd., Pinedale, 307/367-4326, www.fs.usda.gov).

INFORMATION AND SERVICES

The **Sublette County Visitor Center** (19 E. Pine St., 307/367-2242 or 888/285-7282, www.sublettechamber.com, 9am-6pm daily summer, 9am-5pm Mon.-Fri. winter) can provide information about the local area and the region for everything from hiking trails to fishing guides and up-to-date event calendars.

Two comprehensive websites for activities and businesses in the area are www.pinedaleonline.com and www.visitpinedale.org.

The **Sublette County Library** (155 S. Tyler Ave., 307/367-4114, www.sublettecountylibrary.org, 10am-8pm Mon.-Fri., 10am-5pm Sat.) offers plenty of interesting events in addition to its sizable collection. Free Wi-Fi is provided, and public computers with free Internet access are available for 30 minutes at a time.

Though the nearest hospital is 78 miles north in Jackson, Pinedale is served by the **Pinedale Medical Clinic** (625 E. Hennick St., 307/367-4133, 8am-5pm Mon.-Fri., 8am-noon Sat.).

TRANSPORTATION
Getting There

The nearest commercial airports are in Jackson (78 miles), Rock Springs (100 miles), Idaho Falls, Idaho (190 miles), and Salt Lake City (250 miles). Private jets can be accommodated at **Pinedale Wenz Field** (307/367-4136 or 307/367-6425).

Rental cars are available in Jackson and Rock Springs. The closest Greyhound bus service is also in Rock Springs.

Getting Around

For shuttle service in Pinedale, the **Great Outdoor Transportation Company** (322 W. Pine St., www.gotcoshuttle.com, 307/367-1764) offers taxi service, gear drops, and fishing shuttles.

Lander

Tucked in the foothills of the Wind River Mountains on the banks of the Popo Agie (po-PO-zhuh) River and adjacent to the Wind River Indian Reservation, Lander (population 7,732, elevation 5,357 feet) is an outdoor lover's town and a vibrant, growing community. The area was first visited by white fur trappers as early as 1811, and oil was discovered in 1824 but not developed until the mid-1880s. The area was the home ground of Chief Washakie and his Shoshone people. In 1869 a small military post was established here to protect the Shoshone from enemies that included the Sioux and Arapaho. The valley, once known by Native Americans as Pushroot for its fertile soil, was farmed early on to great success thanks to the soil, relatively mild winters, and little wind.

Not a large town by any stretch, Lander is a welcoming place with friendly people, a decidedly outdoor-oriented culture, and immediate access to some of the most stunningly rugged wilderness in the country.

SIGHTS
Wind River Reservation

The **Wind River Reservation** sits on 2.2 million acres and is home to more than 8,600 Northern Arapaho Indians (www.northernarapahoe.com) and 3,900 Eastern Shoshone (www.easternshoshone.org) tribal members. It surrounds the city of Riverton, with the towns of Lander, Shoshoni, and Thermopolis close to its borders. There is not a lot of intermingling between the native and nonnative communities, or between the Arapaho and Shoshone themselves, for that matter; the arrangement to leave both tribes on the same reservation was decided by the U.S. government without their consent. The western part of the reservation, including the towns of Fort Washakie, Burris, and Crowheart, is occupied by the Shoshone, and the eastern part, including the towns of Ethete and Arapaho,

are occupied by the Arapaho. Although the reservation struggles with problems of poverty and unemployment, it is also home to an incredibly rich history, important traditions, and pristine wilderness.

A drive through the reservation affords visitors magnificent views of Wyoming's undeveloped natural beauty and the majestic Wind River Mountains. The reservation is easily accessible by car, and its roads are open to visitors. If you'd like to hike, fish, camp, or boat, however, access is restricted to certain parts of the reservation, and a recreation fee or fishing permit is required. Hunting by nonnatives is not allowed. The **Tribal Fish and Game Office** (307/332-7207), located in Fort Washakie, can provide more information about fees and permits, as can the chambers of commerce in Lander, Riverton, and Dubois. Fort Washakie is also the location of the **Shoshone Tribal Cultural Center** (90 Ethete Rd., 307/332-9106, 9am-4pm Mon.-Fri.) and the gravesites of the two most prominent Shoshone Indians, Chief Washakie (it was his hometown) and Lewis and Clark's fearless guide, Sacagawea.

The biggest draw to the reservation are the powwows held throughout the summer season. These large cultural celebrations usually take place over a three-day weekend and include dancing, singing, parades, and traditional games. Competitors come from across the country, and both tribes host their own powwows. The largest Shoshone powwow is the **Eastern Shoshone Indian Days Powwow and Rodeo** (307/332-9106)**,** an all-Indian rodeo usually held the fourth weekend in June. The event hosts more than 700 dancers and 15 professional drumming groups. The largest Arapaho powwow is the **Ethete Celebration** (307/332-2992) in late July. For additional information about the powwows and weekly events, contact the **Wind River Heritage Center** (307/856-0706) or the

Peaceful Coexistence: The Shoshone and the Arapaho

The Treaty of Fort Bridger, signed in 1863, designated 44 million acres as "Shoshone Country." This large parcel of land not only included territory in Wyoming but also crossed into Colorado, Utah, and Idaho. However, there was no formal demarcation, and settlers and migrants continued to settle the land in the south, up into the Green River Valley, forcing the Shoshone into Arapaho territory in order to hunt. Furthermore, gold was discovered near South Pass, and coal near Rock Springs, and both mining towns and farms were popping up along the Wind River drainage.

In 1868, another treaty was signed, establishing the much smaller 2.2-million-acre Wind River Reservation. For a variety of reasons, land continued to be ceded to the government, including the Popo Agie Valley and the present-day towns of Shoshoni and Thermopolis. Shoshone Chief Washakie bartered determinedly to improve life on the reservation for his people. He asked for specific physical improvements, goods, and protection from their Indian enemies. (Fort Brown, renamed Fort Washakie in 1878, resulted from this bargaining.) Today the reservation stretches 70 miles west-east and 55 miles north-south and is home to about 3,900 Eastern Shoshone and 8,600 Northern Arapaho Indians.

Understanding why two tribes, historically great enemies, would share the same reservation requires a history lesson and some imagination. By 1877, most Native Americans had been relocated to reservations, yet the Northern Arapaho remained landless. With winter rapidly approaching, the U.S. government turned to Chief Washakie, requesting that the Shoshone share their reservation with the Arapaho just for the winter. Washakie conceded, but made it clear that by spring the visitors must be relocated. Spring came and went with Washakie repeatedly demanding that the Arapaho be removed from the reservation. His pleas fell on deaf ears, and the former archenemies were forced to make the best of the situation.

They each established their own governments and mostly occupied separate parts of the reservation. The Arapaho settled the eastern part of the land, with the towns of Ethete and Arapaho as their hubs; the Shoshone developed the western portion, which includes the towns of Fort Washakie, Burris, and Crowheart. Although there have been few major conflicts, the two cultures tend to keep to their own with little interest in intermixing.

Today the reservation has some incredibly beautiful vistas of the Wind River Valley and its craggy mountains. Standing in the middle of its pristine wilderness, it's not evident that oil and gas fields are the primary source of revenue for the reservation. Although plagued by unemployment and poverty, the two tribes possess a great sense of cultural pride, explicitly expressed each May-September through a series of powwows and other cultural celebrations.

For more information on the Wind River Reservation, or to plan a visit, contact the **Wind River Heritage Center** (1075 S. Federal Blvd., Riverton, 307/856-0706, www.windriver.org).

Wind River Visitor's Council (800/645-6233, www.windriver.org).

★ Sinks Canyon State Park

A place that is as beautiful as it is fascinating, **Sinks Canyon State Park** (3079 Sinks Canyon Rd., 6 miles south of Lander, 307/332-6333 or 307/332-3077, www.sinkscanyonstatepark.org, sunrise-10pm daily, visitors center 9am-6pm daily Memorial Day-Labor Day, free) is filled with recreational opportunities and one of the state's geological wonders. Here in the canyon is where the Middle Fork of the Popo Agie River plunges into a cave, only to emerge 0.5 mile away in an area known as the Rise. What makes it so interesting is that geologists have determined that it takes more than two hours for the water to make the journey. In addition, there is plenty of water emerging at the Rise that did not enter at the Sinks. Adding yet another layer of mystery is that the water is a couple of degrees warmer when it emerges than when it disappeared.

Aside from its geological and scenic

attributes, Sinks Canyon is a fantastic place for hiking, rock climbing, fishing (but not in the trout-laden waters at the Rise, where vending machines dole out food for these lunkers), and wildlife-watching. Keep your eyes peeled for transplanted bighorn sheep, moose, and any number of bird species.

Loop Road

Among the most scenic drives in the region, and perhaps the state, is a roughly 70-mile seasonal route known locally as the **Loop Road.** From Lander, follow the signs to Sinks Canyon State Park via Highway 131. Just beyond Bruce's Camp parking area, the 32-mile Loop Road climbs past Frye Lake, Fiddler's Lake, and Louis Lake to a junction that leads south to South Pass City Historic Site or north to Atlantic City and Highway 28, which brings travelers 35 miles back to Lander. Along the way, the Wind River Range unfolds in all its majesty, and hikers will have no shortage of trailheads to amble down. Because of its extreme altitude, the road is often not open until July due to snow, and it closes as early as September again because of snow.

South Pass City Historic Site

One of the region's few gold mines, **South Pass City Historic Site** (125 S. Pass Main St., 35 miles south of Lander, 2 miles off Hwy. 28, 307/332-3684, www.southpasscity.com, early May-Sept., $4 nonresidents, $2 residents) is a beautifully restored site with 20 original log, frame, and stone structures including the jail, a livery, a stable, a school, saloons, and homes. The city was founded in 1867 and, in addition to its mining legacy, is well remembered for its pivotal role in women's suffrage. A territorial representative from South Pass City, William Bright, introduced the bill that made Wyoming the first territory to grant women the right to vote in 1869; South Pass City's justice of the peace, Esther Hobart Morris, was the first woman to hold political office in the United States.

The South Pass Hotel has been refurbished to give visitors a sense of 1880s Wyoming.

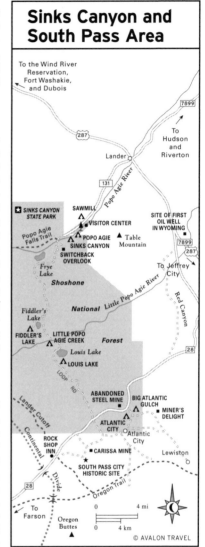

The Smith-Sherlock General Store is open for shopping, and the Miner's Exchange Saloon offers visitors a chance to shoot pool on an 1840s billiards table.

Every year in mid-July, **Gold Rush Days** celebrates the town's heritage with a vintage baseball tournament, food, entertainment, and interpretive programs. The town's

Sinks Canyon State Park

than 80 different types of beer while enjoying family-friendly music, food, and games.

The **International Climber's Festival** (307/349-1561, www.climbersfestival.org) is held each July and attracts outdoor enthusiasts from around the world. The festival features lectures, activities, social events, and a trade show. Visit the website to check which events require tickets.

Lander is also a stop on the **Eukanuba Stage Stop Dog Race** (307/734-1163, www.wyomingstagestop.org), which takes place late January-early February.

Stop by the **Lander Area Chamber of Commerce** (160 N. 1st St., 307/332-3892 or 800/433-0662, www.landerchamber.org, 8am-5pm Mon.-Fri. year-round, 9am-2pm Sat. summer only) to get more information or to buy tickets for any of the events in town.

SPORTS AND RECREATION
Hiking and Rock Climbing

Known as the roof of Wyoming and the spine of the Rockies, the Wind River Range offers phenomenal hiking and climbing from Lander. Among the trails accessible from the Loop Road between Sinks Canyon State Park and South Pass City are the easy 7-mile **Christina Lake Tail,** the easy-to-moderate 6.5-mile **Louis Lake Trail,** and the difficult 17-mile multiuse **Shoshone Lake Trail.**

For hiking that is somewhat closer to Lander, with scenery no less dramatic, **Sinks Canyon State Park** (www.sinkscanyonstatepark.org) offers six miles of easy-to-moderate trails in a figure-eight layout.

For expert guidance and equipment related to rock climbing, the best resource in town is **Wild Iris Mountain Sports** (166 Main St., 307/332-4541 or 888/824-5968, www.wildirisclimbing.com, 9am-7pm Mon.-Fri., 9am-6:30pm Sat., 10am-5pm Sun.), named for one of the region's best-known climbing areas. Another renowned spot for climbers is Sinks Canyon State Park.

For more information on trails and conditions, contact the Shoshone National Forest's

Carissa Mine was purchased by the state, overhauled significantly for safety, and can now be toured. There's also a nice 1.6-mile trail, the **Flood & Hindle Mining Trail,** which winds along the creek through willows and pine forest. Guided walks are offered at 11am every Saturday in July and August.

ENTERTAINMENT AND EVENTS

The most popular event in Lander is its **Pioneer Days** (www.lotra.org) festival. It takes place around the Fourth of July and includes a parade, Indian dancing, a buffalo barbecue, fireworks, and a nightly rodeo ($10 adults, $5 children 6-12). The rodeo celebrates 125 years in 2019, making it the oldest paid rodeo in the world.

A much younger but also entertaining event is the **Lander Brew Fest** (307/332-3892 or 800/433-0662, www.landerbrewfest.com), which takes place in mid-June. More than 18 breweries from the Rocky Mountain region participate, allowing visitors to sample more

NOLS and the Wind River Range

In 1965, one year after the Wilderness Act had passed, an Outward Bound instructor named Paul Petzoldt founded the **National Outdoor Leadership School** (NOLS) in Sinks Canyon. Having spent much of his youth in the Tetons and the Wind River Range, much of which was not even mapped, Petzoldt created a school specifically to train outdoor leaders, educators, and conservationists. That year, a small group of male NOLS students spent a full month in the Wind River Range.

Within a year, female students were admitted to NOLS for the 30-day outdoor leadership training in the Winds, and in 1970, more than 750 students enrolled in summer courses. NOLS started branching out in the 1970s with programs (and eventually bases) in Alaska, East Africa, Mexico, Idaho, and Washington's Northern Cascades. Still, the school never lost touch with Wyoming and the Winds, and in 2002 an impressive **world headquarters** (284 Lincoln St., Lander, 307/332-5300 or 800/710-6657, www.nols.edu) was completed in Lander.

So what are these mountains that gave rise to one of the world's most esteemed wilderness education programs?

The Wind River Range cuts through Wyoming with 100 miles of jagged peaks, crystalline lakes, boulder-strewn meadows, two national forests, and three pristine wilderness areas. The range has 48 summits topping 12,000 feet, 8 summits above 13,500 feet, and seven of the largest glaciers in the Lower 48. At 13,804 feet, Gannett Peak is the crown of this magnificent range and the highest peak in the state. The Cirque of the Towers, 10 miles into the Bridger Wilderness at the southern end of the range, offers some of the most dramatically scenic hiking in the Lower 48, and plenty of technical rock climbing. The Winds are bisected by the Continental Divide to form three major drainages for the Columbia River, the Colorado River, and the Missouri River.

The area has long been a favorite backpacking destination for the adventurous, and access is possible from both the east and west sides. In addition to the Continental Divide Trail, which traverses the range from South Pass to Union Pass on its way between Canada and Mexico, there are hundreds of miles of hiking trails crisscrossing the Winds. Among the more popular trailheads are Big Sandy, Boulder Creek, Elkhart Park, and Green River Lakes. For more solitude, try some of the low-use trailheads like Burnt Lake, Half Moon Lake, and Meadow Lake.

For information on trails and backcountry regulations, contact the **Bridger-Teton National Forest office** (29 E. Fremont Lake Rd., Pinedale, 307/367-4326, www.fs.usda.gov).

Washakie Ranger Office (333 Hwy. 789 S., 307/332-5460, www.fs.usda.gov, 8am-4:30pm Mon.-Fri.).

Fishing

With the Wind River Range as an impressive backdrop to Lander, the fishing in this part of the state varies from crystalline alpine lakes to small but productive rivers, including the **Wind River, Bull Lake Creek,** the **Sweetwater River,** and various forks of the **Popo Agie River.** Unlike most of the state, the fishing around Lander is exclusively wade-fishing.

Daily guided fishing trips can be arranged through **Sweetwater Fishing Expeditions** (2939 Sinks Canyon Rd., 307/332-3986, www.

sweetwaterfishing.com), which offer a variety of adventures that include day trips ($440-495 for 1-2 anglers), 5-10-day expeditions ($1,865-2,625 pp), and horseback ($1,000-1,500 pp) trips.

Golf

The **Lander Golf Club** (1 Golf Course Dr., 307/332-4653, $16-33) is an 18-hole, par-71 course.

FOOD

With so many ways to burn energy, it's surprising that there aren't more eateries to refuel. Still, you won't starve in Lander. **The Breadboard** (1350 W. Main St., 307/332-6090, 11am-7pm Mon.-Fri., 11am-4pm

Gannett Grill/Lander Bar

at the Gannett Grill operates in the summer, serving delicious ice cream and thick shakes. For drinks, **Coalter Loft** (5pm-10pm Thurs.-Fri.) is an elegant bar with a 2nd-story deck overlooking Main Street; its trivia night (7pm-10pm Thurs.) is good fun.

ACCOMMODATIONS

Since it's a great launching point into the Winds, Lander's number of accommodations is growing. Chain hotels include the shiny new and extremely comfortable **Holiday Inn Express & Suites** (1002 11th St., 307/332-4005 or 800/465-4329, www.hiexpress.com, $137-183), plus the **Inn at Lander** (260 Grand View Dr., 307/332-2847 or 866/452-6337, www.book.bestwestern.com, $81-150), which has 101 guest rooms as well as an on-site restaurant, guest laundry, and a year-round hot tub. The **Rodeway Inn Pronghorn Lodge** (150 E. Main St., 307/332-3940 or 866/452-6337, www.choicehotels.com, $98-104) is another good bet in town.

For a more historical and completely unique option, the **Miner's Delight Inn Bed & Breakfast** (290 Atlantic City Rd., Atlantic City, 307/332-0248, www.minersdelightinn.com, 2-night minimum in summer, $100-130) offers both rooms and cabins, which share a bathroom in the inn. The inn was for sale as of 2016, so keep an eye on the website.

Five miles outside of town, at the foot of the Winds, are the **Outlaw Cabins** (2411 Squaw Creek Rd., 307/332-9655 or 877/732-9655, www.outlawcabins.com, $125-153), two cozy, handcrafted log cabins set on the Wunder Ranch. Each cabin is private and comes with a kitchenette and loft area. A stream runs through the property, and there is plenty of wildlife to be watched. The hosts are warm and friendly and will gladly tell you stories of the four outlaws who were supposedly buried on the property.

CAMPING

As evidence of the community's commitment to the outdoor experience, free overnight camping is permitted in Lander's **City Park**

Sat.-Sun.) has been serving up soup and subs for more than 30 years. A hub of the community in more ways than one, The Breadboard donates proceeds from refills ($0.25) to local charities.

Foodies in Lander need look no farther than four wonderful establishments, owned by the same folks and sharing one historic block downtown. ★ **Cowfish** (148 Main St., 307/332-8227, www.cowfishlander.com, 5pm-10pm daily summer, 5pm-9pm Mon.-Sat. fall-spring, $13-33) offers an assortment of fresh seafood, salads, steaks, pasta, and homemade desserts impressive enough to make you forget you are in Wyoming; it's impossible to leave hungry. Right next door, the **Gannett Grill/Lander Bar** (126 Main St., 307/332-8228, www.landerbar.com, 11am-9pm daily, $7-29) is a local favorite with hand-tossed pizzas, juicy burgers made from local beef, gorgeous salads from the on-site organic garden, and locally brewed beer. The outdoor dining option is insanely popular when the weather is good. **Scream Shack** (noon-9pm daily summer)

(405 Fremont St.). RVs are invited to park in the parking lot.

The best public camping is found in **Sinks Canyon State Park** (3079 Sinks Canyon Rd., 6 miles south of Lander, 307/332-6333 or 307/332-3077, www.sinks-canyonstatepark.org, $11 nonresidents, $6 residents), which has two primitive state park campgrounds: **Sawmill** and **Popo Agie.** There is also one campground on the national forest, **Sinks Campground** ($15). Several national forest campgrounds are located along the Loop Road, including sites at **Louis Lake** ($10), **Fiddlers Lake** ($15), and **Worthen Meadow** ($15). No advanced reservations are available. **Showers** are available in town at the community swimming pool (450 S. 9th St.) and the NOLS campus (284 Lincoln St.).

Sleeping Bear RV Park and Campground (715 E. Main St., 307/332-5159 or 888/757-2327, www.sleepingbear-rvpark.com) offers 4 tent sites ($23), 40 full RV hookup sites ($39-42), 6 water and electric hookup sites ($30.50), cabins with shared bath ($48), and cabins with private bath ($58). Amenities include Wi-Fi, picnic tables, and fire rings, plus access to clean bathrooms with showers.

INFORMATION AND SERVICES

The **Lander Area Chamber of Commerce** (160 N. 1st St., 307/332-3892 or 800/433-0662, www.landerchamber.org, 8am-5pm Mon.-Fri., 9am-2pm Sat. summer, 8am-5pm Mon.-Fri. fall-spring) acts as a visitors center.

For information and maps related to backcountry hiking and camping, contact the Shoshone National Forest's **Washakie Ranger Office** (333 Hwy. 789 S., 307/332-5460, www.fs.usda.gov, 8am-4:30pm Mon.-Fri.).

The **Fremont County Library** (307/332-5194, 10am-9pm Mon.-Thurs., 10am-4pm Fri.-Sat.) is located at 451 North 2nd Street.

The largest medical facility in the area is the **Lander Regional Hospital** (1320 Bishop Randall Dr., 307/332-4420, www.lsagewes-thealthcare.com), which has a 24-hour emergency department. The **Lander Medical Clinic Urgent Care** (307/332-2941, www.landermedicalclinic.com, 7am-5pm Mon.-Fri., 9am-1pm Sat.) is at 745 Buena Vista Drive.

TRANSPORTATION
Getting There

The closest commercial airport to Lander is 26 miles away, the **Riverton Regional Airport** (RIW, 4830 Airport Rd, Riverton, 307/856-7063, www.flyriverton.com). **Denver Air Connection** (866/373-8513, www.denverai-rconnection.com, 30-seat jets) and **Great Lakes** (800/554-5111, www.flygreatlakes.com, 9-seat propeller planes) operate daily flights to and from Denver. Private air travel is available at **Hunt Field Airport-Lander** (KLND, 307/332-2870).

Shuttles to and from nearby airports can be arranged through **Share-a-Ride Wyoming** (307/240-9010, www.sharearidewyoming.com) in Riverton ($35 pp one-way), Jackson ($210 pp one-way), and Casper ($170 pp one-way). Reductions apply for more than one passenger, and additional fees apply for late night arrivals.

By road, Lander is 163 miles south of Cody, 160 miles southeast of Jackson, 157 miles southeast of Yellowstone National Park, 136 miles east of Pinedale, and 79 miles southwest of Thermopolis.

Getting Around

The **Wind River Transportation Authority** (307/856-7118, www.wrtabuslines.com) offers fixed-route bus service around town.

Thermopolis

At the south end of the Bighorn Basin, Thermopolis (population 3,038, elevation 4,504 feet) is a notably sunny town with 321 sunny days on average each year; it also has natural hot water forming the world's largest mineral hot spring.

The town was originally called Old Town Thermopolis, one of two Wyoming settlements built around mineral hot springs; the other is Saratoga. Around the turn of the 20th century, when an analysis of the water suggested potential health benefits, the town's name was shortened to Thermopolis in a calculated marketing move. Local mineral deposits—including coal, copper, and oil—plus the arrival of the railroad bolstered the Thermopolis economy, but for the most part tourism was and continues to be the major economic force. Teddy Roosevelt and Butch Cassidy and his gang were among the most famous frequent visitors to Thermopolis.

A surprising number of fantastic attractions can be found in this small, friendly town surrounded by the Owl Creek Mountains. At **Hot Springs State Park,** mineral terraces create a stunning background for herds of grazing bison. The **Wyoming Dinosaur Center** is among the best paleontology sites in the state. And the **Legend Rock Petroglyphs** (which can only be opened in the off-season with a key from the Hot Springs State Park headquarters or the Thermopolis-Hot Springs Chamber of Commerce!) is one of the most compelling examples of prehistoric rock art in the state. From fishing and rafting on the Bighorn to horseback riding in the Owl Creek Mountains, there are a variety of ways to enjoy the natural beauty surrounding town. This is small-town Wyoming in its truest and best form.

SIGHTS
★ Hot Springs State Park
Hot Springs State Park (538 N. Park St., 307/864-2176, http://wyoparks.state.wy.us) is a natural phenomenon featuring terrain with brilliant hues, unique rock formations, and, of course, hot springs. The mineral deposits and various life forms paint the park different shades of red, orange, green, brown, and yellow. In summer the park explodes with vibrant flower gardens. Because the two national parks in the state's northwest corner draw the large crowds, if you make it to this park, you're guaranteed a more leisurely, chaos-free visit.

Originally part of the Wind River Reservation, the hot springs were believed by the Shoshone to be a gift from the Great Spirit. The U.S. government bought Big Springs and the surrounding territory from the Arapaho and Shoshone in 1896. Chief Washakie, who signed the agreement, had one stipulation: The waters should be freely available to all so that anyone could receive the great health and healing benefits. As a result, Wyoming's first state park was created along with the State Bath House, which is free and open to the public to this day. Although one might argue that the 20 minutes that come free with entry to the pool is not exactly what Chief Washakie had in mind, it's still a great place that reflects his deep respect for these medicinal waters.

Big Springs, considered the largest hot spring in the world, is the main attraction in the park. The water's temperature is 135°F, and more than 8,000 gallons per day trickle and gush freely over large mineral-painted terraces into the Bighorn River. Boardwalks allow visitors to walk along the terraces, springs, and cooling pools; they lead to a long suspension bridge that crosses the Bighorn and provides great views of this remarkable area.

The **State Bath House** (538 N. Park St., 307/864-3765, 8am-5:30pm Mon.-Sat., noon-5:30pm Sun.) has the only free thermal pools in the park. There is an indoor and outdoor soaking pool, although the outdoor pool is closed in the winter, along with smaller private tubs in the locker rooms. The water from the hot springs is piped to these mineral pools and is kept at 104°F. Open year-round, the pools are small but clean and well maintained. Lockers, towels, and even swimsuits (if you dare) can be rented for a nominal charge. If you are looking for more elaborate swimming facilities (including slides, steam rooms, and hot tubs), there are several commercial facilities inside the park, including **Hellie's Tepee Spa** (144 Tepee St., 307/864-9250, www.tepeepools.com, 9am-9pm daily, $12.50 ages 5-62, $10.50 seniors 63 and over, $6.25 children 4 and under) and **Star Plunge** (115 Big Springs Dr., 307/864-3771, www.starplunge.com, 9am-9pm daily, $12.50 ages 5-64, $10 seniors 65 and over, $6 children 4 and under,), the latter of which has indoor and outdoor pools and slides. Part of being in this community is feeling like you have stepped back into the 1980s. You'll rock out to Journey and Whitesnake while you soak, but if you go with it, you will love this place. Most of the pools do not take credit cards, so come prepared with cash or a checkbook, and bring coins for the lockers too.

Hot Springs County Museum and Cultural Center

This small town has done an impressive job of collecting and displaying artifacts from its lively past. **Hot Springs County Museum and Cultural Center** (700 Broadway, 307/864-5183, www.hschistory.org, 9am-5pm Mon.-Sat. May 1-Sept. 30, 9am-4pm Tues.-Sat. Oct. 1-Apr. 30, $5 adults, $3 seniors 60 and over and children 16 and under, mention of website gets you $1 off) consists of the two-story main museum building and five additional structures in the vicinity. The museum building was, in various incarnations, a Ford garage, a Coke bottling plant, and a technical college before opening as the county museum in 1980.

One of the museum's more interesting exhibits is dedicated to the outlaws of Wyoming. Thermopolis was frequented by outlaws such as Butch Cassidy and the Sundance Kid. The museum has the cherrywood bar from the Hole in the Wall Saloon and the stained-glass windows from Hack Hollywood's Saloon, two of their favorite watering holes in town. There are also exhibits highlighting the town's varied sources of revenue, including coal mining, oil drilling, and petroleum extraction. The 1st floor of the main museum re-creates

Boardwalks keep visitors safe from the geothermal features in Hot Springs State Park.

The Wyoming Dinosaur Center arranges digs.

is its proximity to the **Warm Springs Dig Site.** Excavations still take place here each summer.

During the summer, visitors can take a tour of the site, or participate in the **Dig for a Day Program** (307/864-2997 for reservations, $150 adults, $100 children with paying adult), which allows you to work at the actual dig site, learning about the process and the science involved. Advanced registration is required, and digs happen daily late spring-early fall. Specific days throughout the summer also are set aside for the **Kids' Dig Program,** which caters to budding archaeologists.

Admission to the museum is $10 adults and $8 children 4-12 and seniors 60 and over. The dig site tour is $12 adults and $10.50 children 4-12 and seniors 60 and over. The best option is to purchase the combination package, which includes entrance to the museum and the tour, for $18.50 adults and $14.50 children and seniors. Families of four can pay a flat rate of $60, which includes both the museum and the tour.

Legend Rock Petroglyph Site

Although it may seem like a small adventure just to find the prehistoric drawings at **Legend Rock Petroglyph Site,** 21 miles outside Thermopolis, the sheer number and variety make it a worthwhile visit. The easiest way to visit the petroglyphs is first to stop at the Hot Springs State Park office (located at the corner of Park St. and Hwy. 789, 307/864-2176, www.wyoparks. state.wy.us), where you can pick up a map to the site (the unmarked route can be difficult to locate) and a gate key in non-summer months. Once at the parking lot for Legend Rock, you can choose to hike the 0.5 mile to the petroglyphs or drive down the hill (in non-summer months when there is no host at the site, you will need the key to unlock the gate). A host is on-site 8am-6pm daily in summer. Etched along the sandstone cliffs are numerous animal and human figures that have been linked to different time periods throughout history, some dating back

businesses from an early 1900s Main Street, including a dentist's office, a post office, a general store, and a jail. They have been designed mostly using artifacts from the time period and even from the original stores. The Cultural Center has rotating exhibits by local artists.

★ The Wyoming Dinosaur Center and Dig Sites

Located at the Warm Springs Ranch, where dinosaur fossils from the Jurassic period have been unearthed, the **Wyoming Dinosaur Center** (110 Carter Ranch Rd., 307/864-2997 or 800/455-3466, www.wyodino.org, 8am-6pm daily mid-May-mid-Sept., 10am-5pm daily mid-Sept.-mid-May) is a 16,000-square-foot complex that houses more than 200 displays. In addition to 20-some full-size dinosaur skeletons and casts from the local site and from around the world, there is also a preparation lab on-site. Visitors can watch technicians cleaning recently discovered fossils. One of the special features of the museum

2,000 years. There are more than 92 prehistoric petroglyph panels and upwards of 300 petroglyph figures. Unfortunately, not all visitors to the site have treated the paintings respectfully, and it's important not to touch or try to remove the petroglyphs.

ENTERTAINMENT AND EVENTS

The **Gift of the Waters Pageant** is held during the first weekend in August and re-creates the selling of the hot springs by the Shoshone and Arapaho Indians to the U.S. government, based on a play written in 1925. The pageant suggests it was a fair transaction between equal partners, which wasn't exactly the case. However, Native Americans from the Wind River Reservation do participate in the event, which is followed by a powwow. The event is a one-hour performance on both Friday and Saturday nights, starting at 6pm. Contact the Thermopolis-Hot Springs Chamber of Commerce (220 Park St., 307/864-3192 or 877/864-3192, www.thermopolis.com) for more information.

The **Thermopolis Cowboy Rendezvous** (www.thermopoliscowboyrendezvous.com) is a rodeo held the weekend after Father's Day and includes a pancake breakfast, street dance, parade, and more, in addition to riding events.

SPORTS AND RECREATION
Hiking

Although there is no national forest in immediate proximity to Thermopolis, the locals like to hike around their landmark **Round Top Mountain.** In Hot Springs State Park, there are 6.2 miles of accessible walking and hiking trails, the most popular being **Spirit Trail,** which meanders through the park.

Boating and Fishing

Both white-water and scenic river trips are offered on the Wind and Bighorn Rivers and can be arranged exclusively through the Indian-owned **Wind River Canyon Whitewater and Fly Fishing** (210 Hwy. 20 S., Ste. 5, 307/864-9343 or 888/246-9343, www.windrivercanyon.com). Roughly two-hour white-water trips on the dramatic upper or lower canyon sections start at $59 per person, and all-day trips covering the whole canyon are $109 per person. Scenic two-hour trips are $39 per person. Trips run Memorial Day-Labor Day. As the only outfitters on the Wind River, the company also offers a variety

The Wind River Canyon is popular for outdoor recreation.

of guided fishing trips. All-day float-fishing trips on the upper or lower canyon are $795 for 1-2 people with lunch included. Full-day trips on the Bighorn are $525 and half-days are $400.

Golf

There is a nine-hole public course at **Legion Town and Country Club** (141 Airport Rd., 307/864-5294, $11-18).

FOOD

Widely considered the best restaurant in town, **Stones Throw Restaurant** (143 Airport Rd., 307/864-9494, www.stonesthrowthermopolis. com, 4pm-close daily, $9-30) offers everything from homemade soups and salads to burgers, steaks, and seafood. Its specialty dish is Jäger-schnitzel.

For a speedy and delicious meal almost any time of day, **Thermopolis Café** (109 S. 6th St., 307/864-3686, 6am-2pm Tues.-Wed., 6am-2pm and 5pm-8pm Thurs.-Sat., $6-14) is a great bet. It offers breakfast all day, super speedy service, a salad bar, and hearty and delicious items ranging from sandwiches to burgers.

Serving bistro-style sandwiches, paninis, and mouthwatering burgers along with homemade kettle chips, soups, and salads, the **Front Porch Deli and Grill** (536 Arapahoe St., 307/864-3494, www.fpdeli.com, 11am-2:30pm Mon and Sat., 11am-2:30pm and 5pm-8pm Tues.-Fri., $9-11) serves delicious meals made to order, plus offers a great kids' menu.

Another place for a satisfying meal is the **Black Bear Café** (111 N. 5th St., 307/864-3221, 6:30am-3pm Mon.-Fri., 7am-3pm Sat.-Sun., $4-11). It serves up the biggest cinnamon rolls you can imagine, plus a delicious buffalo breakfast plate, homemade chili, and milk shakes you'll dream about.

No matter where you fill your belly in Thermopolis, always save room for an ice-cold treat from **Dairyland** (510 Park St., 307/864-2757, 11am-10pm daily Apr.-Sept.), which serves delicious frozen yogurt and ice cream the old-fashioned way. It offers burgers

and fries too, but it is the ice cream that brings people back again and again.

ACCOMMODATIONS

With its history of attracting visitors to its medicinal waters, Thermopolis has quite a large, if not necessarily diverse, number of accommodations.

The snazziest hotel by far is the ★ **Best Western Plaza Hotel** (116 E. Park St., 307/864-2939, www.bestwesternwyoming. com, $127-212), a historic hotel in Hot Springs State Park. It's the only hotel in town where pets are not permitted, but it is by far the nicest hotel.

Right across the street in this beautiful parklike setting is the pet-friendly **Days Inn Thermopolis** (115 E. Park St., 307/864-3131, www.daysinn.com, $91-199). Hunters will flip for the vast number and types of taxidermied mounts throughout the property, and the hunting photos that line the walls. Vegetarians, however, may want to reconsider a meal at the hotel's **Safari Club Restaurant & Lounge.** The hotel is slightly rundown (perhaps just the pet-friendly rooms), but the location is ideal.

Some of the more budget-friendly options in town include the recently remodeled **Paintbrush Inn** (605 S. 6th St., 307/864-3155, www.paintbrushinn.com, $85), which features basic air-conditioned ground-floor rooms with Wi-Fi and kitchenettes; and the very comfortable and homey **Elk Antler Inn** (501 Hwy. 20, 307/864-2325, www.elkantlerinn. com, $65-113), with two- and three-bed suites and two-bedroom suites. There is also a nice **Quality Inn** (166 S. Hwy. 20, 307/864-5515, www.choicehotels.com, $100-235) in town.

CAMPING

While there is no camping permitted in the most desirable of spots—Hot Springs State Park—there are a few RV parks in Thermopolis that allow tent camping as well. The **Fountain of Youth RV Park** (250 U.S. 20 N., 307/864-3265, www.fountainofyouth-rvpark.com) is open year-round and offers

RV sites (from $35), tent sites (from $25), a cabin and a guest house ($135 for up to 4 people), and a bunkhouse (from $45 for 2 people). There is also a large hot springs pool on-site, laundry facilities, and free Wi-Fi.

The **Eagle RV Park** (204 U.S. 20 S., 307/864-5262 or 888/865-5707, www.eaglervpark.com) features a shady campground with RV sites (from $37.15), tent sites (from $20.50), and air-conditioned camping cabins (from $44-78 for 2 people). Amenities include free Wi-Fi, a game room and playground, and laundry facilities.

The nearest public campgrounds to Thermopolis are 17 miles south of town in **Boysen State Park** (15 Ash St., Shoshoni, 307/876-2796, www.wyoparks.state.wy.us, $17 for nonresidents) in the Wind River Canyon. Though barren by every definition, the reservoir is beautiful and offers great swimming and colorful rock hounding.

INFORMATION AND SERVICES

The **Thermopolis-Hot Springs Chamber of Commerce** (220 Park St., 307/864-3192 or 877/864-3192, www.thermopolis.com, 8am-5pm Mon.-Fri. summer, 9am-5pm Mon.-Fri.

winter) is the very best place to get interesting and accurate information on the area. You will walk away with 100 ideas of cool things to do.

The **Hot Springs County Library** (307/864-3104, www.hotspringscountylibrary.wordpress.com, 9am-6pm Mon.-Fri., 10am-2pm Sat., closed holidays) is at 344 Arapahoe Street.

There is a 24-hour emergency room at **Hot Springs County Memorial Hospital** (150 E. Arapahoe St., 307/864-3121, www.hscmh.org).

TRANSPORTATION

The closest commercial airports to Thermopolis are in Worland (30 miles) and Riverton (65 miles). **Great Lakes** (800/554-5111, www.flygreatlakes.com) operates flights to Denver out of both airports. **Denver Air Connection** (866/373-8513, www.denverairconnection.com, 30-seat jets) offers daily service between Riverton and Denver.

No bus service is available to or from Thermopolis.

By road, Thermopolis is 82 miles southeast of Cody, 150 miles southeast of the east entrance to Yellowstone National Park, and 190 miles south of Billings.

Cody

It seems somehow fitting that this western town was the brainchild of one of the West's most colorful and dynamic showmen. Indeed, Cody (population 9,833, elevation 5,088 feet), named for Buffalo Bill Cody, is a small town that packs a lot of punch. Set as it is in the arid Bighorn Basin, you might expect Cody to be all dust and tumbleweeds. But that couldn't be further from reality, although there are plenty of both when the Wyoming wind kicks up. Cody is high style with shiny boots and fringe on almost everything. Cody is Molesworth furniture, a little gaudy sometimes but an absolute classic. Cody is a nightly rodeo and old-time gunslingers. In many ways, Cody is the

old West, the *real* West, that visitors want to see and experience.

An obvious destination in and of itself, Cody is home to what is arguably the best Western art and history museum in the world. The Buffalo Bill Center of the West is beyond compare. Visitors could spend a week in the complex's five separate museums and never see the same exhibit twice. The compact downtown is scenic and historic, with world-class art galleries, fun tourist shops, and great eateries. There are plenty of Western entertainment options as well across the valley.

Just outside town, the landscape shifts into the lush South Fork, and into the high country

SIGHTS
★ Buffalo Bill Center of the West

The West's version of the Smithsonian, the **Buffalo Bill Center of the West** (720 Sheridan Ave., 307/587-4771, www.bbhc.org, 10am-5pm Thurs.-Sun. Dec.-Feb., 10am-5pm daily Mar.-Apr., 8am-6pm daily May-Sept. 15, 8am-5pm daily Sept.16-Oct., 10am-5pm daily Nov., $19 adults, $18 seniors 65 and over, $16 students over 18 with ID, $12 children 6-17, free for children under 6, $1 discount available by purchasing tickets online) is a collection of five extraordinary museums plus a research library. The **Buffalo Bill Museum** celebrates the private and public life of town father W. F. "Buffalo Bill" Cody. The **Whitney Gallery of Western Art** reflects the diverse history of art of the American West from the early 19th century to today with original paintings, sculpture, and prints by some of the best-known deceased masters and contemporary geniuses. The **Plains Indian Museum** examines the culture and history of the Arapaho, Crow, Cheyenne, Blackfeet, Sioux, Shoshone, and others through an impressive collection of Native American art and artifacts. The **Cody Firearms Museum** is home to the world's largest assemblage of American arms along with some European arms dating back to the 1500s. The **Draper Museum of Natural History** offers exhibits that interpret the Greater Yellowstone Ecosystem from human and natural science perspectives. Finally, the **Harold McCracken Research Library** is an extraordinary resource for studies of the American West.

This complex is indeed the grand dame of Western history and art. In addition to its own unrivaled permanent collections, the museums feature a constantly shifting assortment of compelling traveling exhibits and special events. Check the website for events before you arrive. If you only see one museum on your journey out West, this one is it.

The BBCW also has two restaurants, the Eatery and the Coffee Bar, for quick bites and caffeine fixes.

Cody Trolley Tours

Early June-late September, one of the best ways to get an overview of Cody, its founding father, and the natural environment that rolls out in every direction is the **Cody Trolley Tours** (307/527-7043, www.codytrolleytours.com, $27 adults, $25 seniors 65 and over, $15 children 6-17, free for children under 6, call for tour schedules), which offers hour-long narrated tours and covers 100 years of history in 22 miles. Highlights include stories about Buffalo Bill, Annie Oakley, the Crow Indians, and a 1904 bank robbery in Cody by the Hole-in-the-Wall gang. The tour includes a "Best of Cody" souvenir guide and can be arranged to include admission to the Buffalo Bill Center of the West. Reservations can be made and tickets purchased on the front porch of the Irma Hotel (1192 Sheridan Ave.), which is also where the tours depart. As an added service, free transportation can be provided to and from your hotel. Call to make reservations.

Old Trail Town

Located on the site of the original Cody City (about 2 miles west of Cody), **Old Trail Town** (307/587-5302, www.oldtrailtown.org, 8am-7pm daily mid-May-Sept., $9 adults, $8 seniors over 65, $5 children 6-12, free for children under 6) is a fascinating collection of historic buildings from the Wyoming frontier. The re-created town is the result of local historian and archaeologist Bob Edgar's hard work and dedication, with more than 26 buildings dating 1879-1901 and at least 100 wagons, maintained in nearly original condition, helping create an authentic feel of the bygone pioneer era. Among the highlights is the old Rivers Saloon, its walls still marked by bullet holes (it was a favorite meeting place of Butch Cassidy and the Sundance Kid) and a cabin from Hole-in-the-Wall country. A

Cody and Vicinity

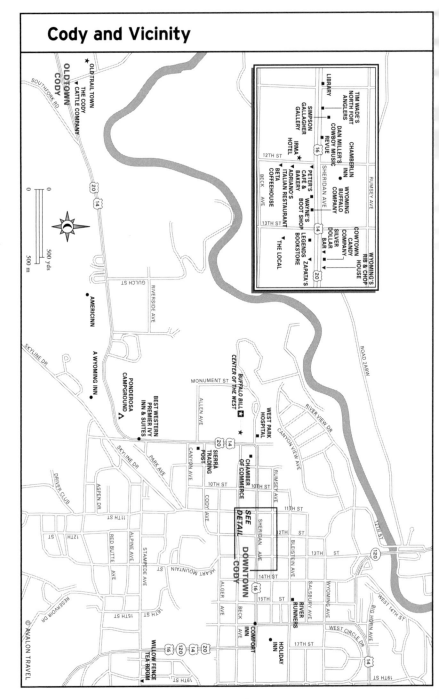

graveyard in the Old Trail Town complex has the reinterred bodies of many infamous characters of the Old West, including that of John "Liver Eating" Johnston (frequently spelled Johnson). The reburial of his body in Old Trail Town was attended by more than 2,000 people including the actor Robert Redford, who played the famous mountain man in the 1972 movie *Jeremiah Johnson*.

Irma Hotel

Naming it after his beloved youngest daughter and calling it "just the sweetest hotel that ever was," Buffalo Bill built the stately **Irma Hotel** (1192 Sheridan Ave., 307/587-4221 or 800/745-4762, www.irmahotel.com, $82-182) in 1902 with the idea that tourists from around the world could stay here en route to Yellowstone National Park. The hotel was designed by a well-known church architect from Nebraska, and some exterior walls are made of local river rock. The cherrywood bar, one of the most photographed features in town, was built in 1902 as well. Additions were added in 1929 and 1976-1977. Still the heart of downtown, the Irma is starting to show her age a little bit. The rooms are basic but still charming, and it's fun to stay in Buffalo Bill's original suite or imagine the royalty that stayed in many of the other rooms. You don't need to spend a night, though, to get a real sense of the history. Visitors can enjoy a drink at the bar or a full meal at **The Irma restaurant,** which serves breakfast, lunch, and dinner and is known for prime rib and delicious steaks. The atmosphere alone is worth the price of the meal.

Heart Mountain

Heart Mountain lies halfway between Cody and Powell and takes its name from the twin summits atop the mountain range that resemble a heart. Driving east on U.S. Highway 14A, the mountains become clearly visible. The range is a puzzle for many geologists and has inspired heated debate. It seems to be part of rock formations found in Yellowstone National Park, 60 miles away, but how they ended up in their present location is unclear. Furthermore, it is an "upside down" mountain, with strata of limestone appearing at the top with younger strata below.

Heart Mountain was the site of a Japanese American internment camp during World War II. Between 1942 and 1945, more than 14,000 people of Japanese descent (at least two-thirds of whom were American citizens) were relocated to this isolated terrain. Confined by barbed-wire fences and armed

The Buffalo Bill Center of the West is the premier museum complex in the Rocky Mountains.

The Legend of Buffalo Bill

When it comes to Buffalo Bill Cody, born William F. Cody, it can be difficult to discern fact from fiction. The man was legendary in every sense of the word, and for the most part he earned the reputation that still follows his name. Born in Iowa in 1846, Cody made his way out west in 1857 with his father. Cody's father died en route, leaving the boy to fend for himself, finding work as a cowboy and Pony Express rider. He became an Army scout at the end of the Civil War and even earned the Congressional Medal of Honor in 1872 for valor in action during the Indian Wars. He reportedly earned his nickname after the Civil War when he shot 4,280 bison in the span of 18 months on behalf of the Kansas Pacific Railroad.

Cody was a natural hunter and was frequently asked by the Army to guide visiting dignitaries. The hunts were greatly publicized, and an eager public greedily consumed tales of Cody's adventuresome pursuits. In 1873, with a string of dime-store novels glorifying him, Cody agreed to perform a melodramatic stage show highlighting his exploits alongside other legendary figures Wild Bill Hickok and Texas Jack Omohundro. In July 1876, just weeks after Custer's defeat at the Little Bighorn, Cody and the Fifth Regiment for whom he was scouting at the time met a band of Cheyenne warriors. Cody killed and scalped a warrior named Yellow Hair, avenging Custer's death and securing his place among the country's military heroes of the day.

In 1883, Cody produced his well-known Wild West Show, which would travel the world for more than three decades, earning him both fame and fortune. Cody became a shrewd businessman, investing in an Arizona mine, hotels in Sheridan and his namesake Cody, ranching, coal and oil development, filmmaking, publishing, and tourism. He used his wealth and reputation to espouse such causes as women's suffrage and, eventually, the just treatment of Native Americans.

As a symbol of the burgeoning West, Cody's expertise was relied on by every U.S. president from Ulysses S. Grant to Woodrow Wilson. He mingled with world-famous artists and dined with kings. Indeed, Buffalo Bill lived a life quite worthy of the legends that continue to define the man.

---

prison guards, they did their best to create a sense of community and normalcy under difficult living conditions. Of the 120,000 people detained in the 10 internment camps across the country, not one was ever found guilty of espionage or conspiring with the enemy. The camps were a result of heightened wartime hysteria, the fear-mongering of politicians, and acute racism.

Opened in 2011, the **Heart Mountain Interpretive Center** (1539 Road 19, Powell, 307/754-8000, www.heartmountain.org, 10am-5pm daily May 15-Oct. 1, 10am-5pm Wed.-Sat. Oct. 2-May 14, $7 adults, $5 seniors/students, free for children under 12) is dedicated to preserving the memory of this dark period in American history and telling the stories of those it affected.

Today, in addition to the interpretive center and a short, paved walking trail, there are three buildings in various stages of decay and different plaques noting the memories of the victims, including one honoring the more than 600 internees who left the camp to fight in the U.S. Army during the war.

Also in this region is the **Heart Mountain Ranch** (307/754-8446, www.nature.org), a 13,000-acre plot of land managed by The Nature Conservancy. It has a large number of rare plants, numerous species of birds, and large mammals such as elk and mule deer. A seven-mile easy-to-moderate hiking trail takes hikers to the mountain's summit. An **interpretive cabin** (8am-5pm Thurs.-Sun. May-Sept.) offers information about the geology, cultural significance, and ecology of Heart Mountain and the surrounding land.

★ Chief Joseph Scenic Highway

Linking Cody with the northeast entrance to Yellowstone National Park is the seasonally open 47-mile **Chief Joseph Scenic Highway.** It is a winding and at times hair-raising drive that cuts through mountainous country, providing views of spectacular waterfalls and mountain vistas of the Absarokas, Cathedral Cliffs, and the mouth of Sunlight Basin, and occasionally a glimpse of wildlife. Interpretive signs along the way tell the story of the Nez Perce's 1877 flight from the U.S. Army under the leadership of Chief Joseph, for whom the highway is named. For adventurers, the highway gives unparalleled access to some incredible hiking trails.

From Cody, drive north 17 miles on Highway 120, turning left (west) onto Highway 296, known as the Chief Joseph Scenic Highway. The road climbs over Dead Indian Summit, above 8,000 feet, and then drops into the magnificent Clark's Fork Valley. The road ends at Crandall, Wyoming, the only place on the highway to buy provisions or find lodging. Ten miles west of Crandall on the Beartooth All American Road (known locally as the Beartooth Highway) is Cooke City and the northeast entrance to Yellowstone National Park. Plan on spending at least two hours to drive the full 74 miles or so from Cody to Cooke City.

Buffalo Bill Scenic Byway

The shorter of two routes to Yellowstone, this one to the east entrance, the 52-mile **Buffalo Bill Scenic Byway** winds through the rugged North Fork Canyon along the Shoshone River. President Theodore Roosevelt was among its admirers, calling the road the most beautiful 50 miles in the United States.

From Cody, head west on U.S. Highway 20/14/16. The road ends at the east entrance to Yellowstone.

ENTERTAINMENT AND EVENTS
Nightlife

Although drinking while driving was only outlawed in Wyoming in 2002, drive-through liquor stores are still a surprise to many visitors. People often take their parties to go. For traditionalists who like to have a drink in a more stationary location, Cody offers plenty of great bars. Among them are the historic **Irma** (1192 Sheridan Ave., 800/745-4762, 11am-2am daily) and the **Silver Dollar Bar** (1313 Sheridan Ave., 307/527-766, kitchen 11am-9pm daily, bar until 2am if there are customers), which often has live country music and serves good bar food.

For family-oriented nightlife, try **Dan Miller's Cowboy Music Revue** (1171 Sheridan Ave., 307/272-7855, www.

Heart Mountain stands sentinel near Cody.

Heart Mountain Relocation Center

Situated between the towns of Cody and Powell, in the midst of some overgrown barley fields, stand a few dilapidated buildings. Utterly abandoned, they strike an odd picture in the high desert. These shells are remnants of a dark period in U.S. history.

With the bombing of Pearl Harbor in December 1941, war hysteria and anti-Japanese fervor reached new heights in the United States. There had been anti-Asian sentiment along the West Coast for decades, primarily directed at hard-working Chinese laborers who would work anywhere, doing anything, for nearly nothing. When the government virtually stopped Chinese immigration, Japanese immigrants quickly became the targets of racism. For many Americans, the attack on Pearl Harbor somehow justified this racial prejudice. President Roosevelt signed Executive Order 9066 in February 1942, authorizing the roundup and removal of all people of Japanese ancestry, regardless of their U.S. citizenship status.

By the early spring, Japanese immigrants and Japanese Americans were given 10 days to gather their families, packing only what they could carry, and report to makeshift assembly centers where they would be deported to camps. Wyoming was home to a relocation center called Heart Mountain. It was isolated, had means for a steady water supply, and was an easy place to transport individuals and supplies. These new dwellings were concentration camps, surrounded by barbed wire, guard towers, searchlights, and guards with machine guns.

The camp covered more than 4,600 acres and housed 468 barracks. These poorly assembled, tar-papered buildings were divided into sections. The average room was 20 by 20 feet and was shared by one family, equipped only with cots, one unadorned hanging light, and a potbellied stove, which didn't always work. The shelters provided little relief from Wyoming's searing summers and frigid winters. Also constructed on the site were mess halls, communal bathrooms and showers, laundry rooms, a hospital, a sewage plant, two places of worship, and even a high school. The camp at Heart Mountain became Wyoming's third-largest city.

Construction began in June 1942, and by August 11, 1942, the first trainload of internees arrived. More than 14,000 internees entered the camp during 1942-1945. Its largest population was nearly 11,000. Despite the dire circumstances and human rights violations, life at Heart Mountain proved to be a testament to the human spirit. The internees demonstrated a deep resilience and determination to create and maintain a community within its ragged confines. There were general stores, two movie theaters, barbershops, high school athletic teams, a weekly newspaper, and a democratically elected camp government. They also made the most of their barren surroundings, extending the irrigation system, planting 27 different types of fruits and vegetables, and raising profitable hog and poultry farms. The cities of Powell and Cody, although never entirely welcoming to these outsiders, benefited economically from the camp and its internees by purchasing inexpensive but necessary goods, like meat and produce, and by hiring the internees as cheap labor to pick their crops. During the three years the camp was open, 552 births and 185 deaths were registered.

Internees were allowed to leave beginning January 1945. Each internee was granted $25 and a bus ticket to his or her destination, though many internees no longer had any other place to call home. The last internees left the camp on November 10, 1945.

In 1990, all survivors of Heart Mountain were issued a check for $20,000 and a signed apology from President George H. W. Bush.

cowboymusicrevue.com, 4pm-5:15pm Mon.-Sat. May, 6:30pm-7:45pm Mon.-Sat. June-Sept., $16 pp for music only, $40 pp includes buffet dinner at 5:30pm prior to 6:30pm show), which features a night of music, comedy, and poetry. Combination tickets include admission to the Buffalo Bill Center of the West.

Festivals and Events

Making this Western town one of the best places in the state to see rodeo, the **Cody Nite**

Rodeo (421 W. Yellowstone Ave., 307/527-9453, www.codystampederodeo.com, June-Aug., $10-20) is held nightly in summer at the rodeo grounds except July 1-5 during the Cody Stampede. Running every summer since 1939, the rodeo is two hours filled with daring cowboys and cowgirls looking to make a name for themselves on the circuit. Kids are invited to join in on the calf scramble. Gates open at 7pm, and the action begins at 8pm.

The town's rodeo fever hits its high over the Fourth of July during the annual **Cody Stampede Rodeo** (519 Yellowstone Ave., 307/587-5155, www.codystampederodeo.com, grandstand seats $20-25 adults, $10 children 12 and under). The stampede has been running for nearly 100 years and was inspired by Buffalo Bill's own Wild West Show. This is one of the biggies for pro rodeo cowboys and cowgirls, with the bull-ride purse alone bringing the winner $50,000. For world-class rodeo action, it's hard to beat.

One of the few towns to stage nightly gunfights in summer (Jackson is another), Cody enchants visitors with Old West characters that stage a hilarious, silly, and at times gripping street performance and gunfight known as the **Cody Gunfighters** (307/202-1113, www.codygunfighters.com, 6pm Mon.-Sat. June-Sept.). The shows are free and are performed adjacent to the Irma Hotel (1192 Sheridan Ave.).

By far the biggest arts-related event of the year in Cody is the **Rendezvous Royale** (307/587-5002 or 888/598-8119, www.rendezvousroyale.com), which happens in mid-September and ushers in the last hurrah of Cody's almost manic summer season. The week is packed with events that include **Cody High Style,** which celebrates Western design in its myriad forms, and the **Buffalo Bill Art Show and Sale,** which boasts its own impressive line of events, with a quick draw in the park and studio tours. The town is full of style icons, design gurus, and blissed-out art collectors, and the energy pulses nearly around the clock. Several galleries and shops host concurrent events. Some of the best

shows by contemporary Western masters open at **Simpson Gallagher Gallery** (1161 Sheridan Ave., 307/587-4022, www.simpsongallaghergallery.com).

SHOPPING

Cody is a great town for shopping, particularly if fine art or Western fashion is your thing. A stroll up and down **Sheridan Avenue** can be very productive, and expensive.

Start at **Wayne's Boot Shop** (1250 Sheridan Ave., 307/587-5234, www.waynesbootshop.com, 9am-6pm daily June-mid-Sept., shortened hours fall-spring) for the right pair of kicks. Wayne's has been selling the best-quality cowboy, hiking, and hunting boots since 1955. Now owned by Wayne's son, the store also sells casual and comfort shoes, as well as hats.

For outdoor gear and casual wear at great prices, visit **Sierra Trading Post** (1402 8th St., 307/578-5802, www.sierratradingpost.com, 9am-8pm Mon.-Sat., 10am-7pm Sun.), which sells everything from clothing and footwear to outdoor gear, luggage, and home goods at deep discounts. Quilters will delight in an afternoon at **Friends and Co. Quilt Shop** (402 E. Warren, 307/527-7217, www.friendsandco.net, 10am-5pm Mon.-Fri., 10am-4pm Sat.), which offers classes, private lessons, and more fabric than you can imagine. Book lovers will want more time at **Legends Bookstore** (1350 Sheridan Ave., 307/586-2320, www.legendsbooks.com, 10am-8pm Mon.-Sat., noon-7pm Sun.), an outstanding independent bookstore with plenty of events featuring local and regional authors, plus gifts, cards, and great toys.

Cody has an impressive number of fine art galleries, and you should wander Sheridan Avenue to see many of them. But be sure not to miss **Simpson Gallagher Gallery** (1161 Sheridan Ave., 307/587-4022, www.simpsongallaghergallery.com, 10am-5:30pm Mon.-Sat.), which carries the work of contemporary Western masters including Clyde Aspevig, Carol Guzman, T. D. Kelsey, T. Allen Lawson, William Matthews, Julie Oriet, and

Kathy Wipfler. The gallery has marvelous rotating shows and features both painting and sculpture.

If shopping wears you out, fuel up on made-in-Wyoming smoked elk and bison jerky or summer sausage, barbecue sauces, jams, spices, and other local specialties at **Wyoming Buffalo Company** (1270 Sheridan Ave., 307/587-8708, www.wyobuffalo.com, 9am-8pm Mon.-Sat.). Or appease your sweet tooth at **Cowtown Candy Company** (1323 Sheridan Ave., 307/587-8212, www.cowtowncandy.com, 10am-7pm Mon.-Sat., shortened hours fall-spring), which specializes in turtles, fresh cream and butter truffles, and homemade fudge.

SPORTS AND RECREATION
Hiking

Even though Cody itself is in something of a desertlike bowl, there is abundant hiking in the beautiful forests and mountains to the north, south, and west of town. There are several districts of the Shoshone National Forest within relatively close proximity to town. Trails worth pursuing include the **Bald Ridge Trail** (County Rd. 7RP, off Hwy. 120, 18 miles north of Cody). The five-mile trail climbs nearly 4,000 vertical feet through Bureau of Land Management land to the summit of Bald Ridge. The views, naturally, are breathtaking. The area is closed December-April to protect critical winter habitat for elk and mule deer. And remember, this is grizzly bear territory, so you should take all necessary precautions.

For more information on trails and conditions, contact the **Shoshone National Forest** (808 Meadow Lane Ave., 307/527-6241, www.fs.usda.gov) or the **Bureau of Land Management** (1002 Blackburn Ave., 307/578-5900, www.blm.gov).

For less vigorous hiking, visit the **Cody Country Chamber of Commerce** (836 Sheridan Ave., 307/587-2777 or 800/393-2639, www.codychamber.org, 8am-7pm daily summer, 8am-5pm Mon.-Fri. fall-spring) and pick up the "Cody Pathways" brochure and map of nonmotorized trails in the region.

Fishing and Rafting

The Shoshone River runs right through the heart of Cody, offering both white-water rafting opportunities and plenty of excellent fishing. Among the rafting companies in town that offer everything from two-hour white-water floats to half-day scenic tours and weeklong trips are **River Runners** (1491 Sheridan Ave., 800/535-7238, www.riverrunnersofwyoming.com, $33 adults, $29 children 12 and under for 2 hours, $78 adults, $68 children half-day), **Wyoming River Trips** (233 Yellowstone Ave., 307/587-6661 or 800/586-6661, www.wyomingrivertrips.com, $34 adults, $32 children 12 and under for 2 hours, $65-72 half-day), and **Red Canyon River Trips** (1119 12th St., 307/587-6988 or 800/293-0148, www.codywyomingadventures.com, $33 adults, $31 children for 2 hours, discounts for families, $65-75 half-day, $140 full-day).

There is an abundance of prime fishing waters within an easy drive from Cody, including the Shoshone River, the Clarks Fork of the Yellowstone River, and hundreds of lakes. For fishing gear or advice on local hatches and water conditions, head to **Tim Wade's North Fork Anglers** (1107 Sheridan Ave., 307/527-7274, www.northforkanglers.com, 9am-6pm Mon.-Sat.). In addition to all the gear, the shop offers guided wading trips or float trips. Hours here can change according to the weather, so call first.

Mountain Biking

If you are looking to do some exploring on bikes, **Absaroka Bikes** (2201 17th St., 307/527-5566, 10am-6pm Mon.-Thurs., 10am-4pm Fri., 10am-2pm Sat. Memorial Day-Labor Day, 10am-5pm Tues.-Thurs., 10am-4pm Fri., 10am-2pm Sat. Labor Day-Memorial Day) offers bike rentals, guided bike tours, and maps of bike trails around the area.

Horseback Riding

Head out one mile past the rodeo grounds on

the left to **Cedar Mountain Trail Rides** (12 Spirit Mountain Rd., 307/527-4966, $35 for 1 hour, $50 for 2 hours), where you will be attended by knowledgeable and friendly guides who are especially good with beginners. The trails wind up Cedar Mountain and provide great views of the town below. If you are interested in a full-day ride, guides take the horses and riders by trailer 35 minutes north to Elk's Fork; lunch is provided.

Golf

Golfers can hit the links at the 18-hole semi-private **Olive Glenn Golf & Country Club** (802 Meadow Lane Ave., 307/587-5551, www.golfoliveglenn.com, $68 for 18 holes with cart) or at the **Powell Golf Club** (600 WYO Hwy. 114, 7 miles east of Powell, 307/754-7259, www.powellgolfclub.com, $35-59 for 18 holes).

There is also a great miniature course for the whole family at **Cody Miniature Golf** (Cody's City Park, 307/587-3685, $5 pp).

FOOD

Although much of the state can be classified as meat and potatoes only, Cody leans toward slightly more variety. For a great cup of coffee and a light breakfast of homemade pastries and bagels (admittedly the homemade cinnamon rolls may not count as light), stop into the **Beta Coffeehouse** (1450 Sheridan Ave., 307/587-7707, 6:30am-6pm Mon.-Fri., 8am-6pm Sat., 9am-2pm Sun.). A favorite community gathering spot, the Beta often hosts live music and open-mike nights. In the winter, the homemade soups are beyond compare. **Peter's Café & Bakery** (1219 Sheridan Ave., 307/527-5040, www.peters-cafe.com, 6:45am-7pm Mon.-Sat., $4-12) is another great place for a quick bite, whether breakfast, burgers, espresso, or ice cream. Daily soups, specials, and desserts should not be missed.

A wonderful spot for lunch during the week is the **Willow Fence Tea Room** (1913 Stampede Ave., 307/587-0888, 11am-2pm Mon.-Fri., $6-14), which has wonderful teas, homemade soups, sandwiches, salads, and

sweets. It's like eating in your grandmother's living room.

Known for its "spaghetti Western cuisine," **Adriano's Italian Restaurant** (1244 Sheridan Ave., 307/527-7320, www.adrianositalianrestaurant.com, 4pm-10pm daily, $15-26) combines classic cowboy cuisine and Italian in fantastic ways. Try a carbonara burger or flatiron steak with linguine and alfredo sauce.

For Mexican food, nothing beats **Zapata's** (1362 Sheridan Ave., 307/527-7181, www.zapatascody.com, 11am-2pm and 5pm-8pm Mon. and Wed.-Thurs., 11am-2pm and 5pm-9pm Fri., 11am-9pm Sat., noon-8pm Sun., $7-17), which serves outstanding New Mexico-style Mexican food including fish tacos, snow crab enchiladas, and homemade salsas and sauces.

Open only in summer, **The Cody Cattle Company** (1910 Demaris St., 307/272-5770, www.thecodycattlecompany.com, doors open at 5:15 daily June-late-Sept., dinner and show $26 adults, $21 children 3-12) serves up a bountiful all-you-can-eat chuck-wagon dinner—including brisket, steak, potato, beans, and more—and a live country music show starting nightly at 6:30pm. You can pair your dinner and a show with tickets to the nightly rodeo, which is within walking distance, for the cowboy trifecta.

Among the best places for steak, ribs, and chops in town is **Wyoming's Rib & Chop House** (1367 Sheridan Ave., 307/527-7731, 11am-10pm daily summer, 11am-9pm Sun.-Thurs., 11am-10pm Fri.-Sat. winter, $12-34), an excellent (and expanding) regional chain. From its buffalo rib eye to the cedar plank salmon, the food is always great. Reservations are strongly suggested.

Cody's best-kept culinary secret is likely ★ **The Local** (1134 13th Ave., 307/586-4262, 8:30am-2pm and 5pm-9pm Tues.-Sat., $11-33), an American bistro with inventive creations relying on ingredients sourced from local producers. This is farm-to-table cuisine in its best Wyoming iteration. The salads are phenomenal, as are the lamb gyros, the Ishawooa Mesa beef burgers, and the yam chips.

An absolute must for at least one meal (if you are not staying at the hotel) is **The Irma** (1192 Sheridan Ave., 307/587-4221, www.irmahotel.com, 7am-9pm daily year-round, breakfast $6.50-11, lunch $8.50-17, dinner $9.50-33). The prime rib dinner buffet is famous (5pm-8:30pm daily May-June 15, 5pm-9pm daily mid-June-Aug., 5:30pm-8pm Fri.-Sat. Sept.-Apr., $25.99 adults, $9.99 children 7-10, free for children 6 and under), but it's really the history and ambience of the place that make it a must. The Irma also serves a breakfast buffet (7am-11am daily June-Sept., 7am-11am Sat.-Sun. Oct.-May, $10.95 adults, $4.95 children 7-10, free for children under 6) and lunch buffet (11:30am-2pm Mon.-Sat. summer, $10.99 adults, $5.99 children 7-10, free for children 6 and under, 11:30am-2pm Sun. year-round $14.99 adults, $6.99 children 7-10, free for children 6 and under).

It doesn't get more local or more traditional than **Cassie's Supper Club** (214 Yellowstone Ave., 307/527-5500, www.cassies.com, 11am-10pm daily, lunch $8-13, dinner $12-36), named for its original proprietor, Cody's most beloved madam. When the city asked her to close her brothel in the early 1930s, Cassie complied, sort of: She opened her supper club at the west end of town, where it stands today. The atmosphere is dark, the mood light, the food hearty, and the history rich. It is Cody's hot spot for two-stepping and has three bars to help lubricate the dancers. It should be stated that Cassie's brothel business died with her in 1952.

ACCOMMODATIONS

Geared as it is toward the flocks of visitors headed to Yellowstone, Cody has an abundance of accommodations, many of them newer. Among the best deals in town is the basic but appealing and independently owned **A Wyoming Inn** (720 Yellowstone Ave., 307/587-4208, www.hotelcody.com, May-Oct., $73-150). Among the chain hotels in town are **AmericInn** (508 Yellowstone Ave., 307/587-7716, $127-289), **Comfort Inn** (1601 Sheridan Ave., 307/587-5556, www.comfortinn.com,

$122-245), **Holiday Inn** (1701 Sheridan Ave., 800/315-2621, www.holidayinn.com, $138-246), and the very upscale **Best Western Premier Ivy Inn & Suites** (1800 8th St., 307/587-2572, www.bestwesternwyoming.com, $170-293).

For significantly more charm, the ★ **Chamberlin Inn** (1032 12th St., 307/587-0202 or 888/587-0202, www.chamberlininn. com, $125-325) is a stately complex built in 1904 and beautifully restored in 2007. There are 21 individual rooms, including several suites, all of which are unique. Ernest Hemingway spent the night in one of them in 1932—his signature is still in the guest register.

Buffalo Bill's beloved **Irma Hotel** (1192 Sheridan Ave., 307/587-4221 or 800/745-4762, www.irmahotel.com, $79-197) is another classic in Cody. Showing a few more signs of wear than the Chamberlin, but with its own marvelous history and central location, the Irma is an important landmark and central to this community.

Just outside Yellowstone's east entrance, **Pahaska Tepee** (183 North Fork Hwy., 307/527-7701 or 800/628-7791, www.pahaska. com, $108-983) is another of Buffalo Bill's historic lodges. The complex is vast, with the old 1904 lodge, newer housekeeping cabins, and deluxe modern condos and a seven-bedroom family reunion lodge, but so are the recreational opportunities. From horseback riding to cross-country skiing, Pahaska Tepee is like a giant playground with immediate proximity to Yellowstone.

GUEST RANCHES

Since Cody is cowboy country, after all, it's fitting that there are a number of guest ranches in the area. Most are geared heavily toward horseback riding and provide lodging in individual and often charmingly rustic cabins. Other activities such as fishing and hiking are regularly available. Things like cell phone coverage, satellite TV, and Wi-Fi are simply not on the menu. These ranches provide true opportunities to get away from life as you know it in some of the most spectacular country on the planet.

Forty miles west of Cody, the **Absaroka Mountain Lodge** (1231 North Fork Hwy., 307/587-3963, www.absarokamtlodge.com, $115-225 cabins, $45-60 twin cabin with no plumbing) dates back to 1917 and is one of the largest and best-known. Unlike many guest ranches in the area, the Absaroka Mountain Lodge is not all-inclusive; guests select and pay for activities, including fishing and horseback riding, and eat meals in a restaurant.

Founded by the grandson of Buffalo Bill, the **Bill Cody Ranch Resort** (2604 North Fork Hwy., 26 miles west of Cody, 307/587-2097 or 800/615-2934, www.billcodyranch.com) is exactly halfway between Cody and Yellowstone in the magnificent North Fork Valley. Cabins rent for $120-270, and meals and activities are paid separately. Packages are also available.

The **7D Ranch** (774 Sunlight Rd., 307/587-9885, www.7dranch.com, from $2,072/week for 1 person in a cabin) is a small, remote ranch in the Sunlight Basin, 50 miles northwest of Cody, offering cozy, rustic accommodations, horseback riding and fishing, pack trips, and hunting trips.

For more guest ranches in the Cody area, contact the **Wyoming Dude Ranchers' Association** (1122 12th St., Cody, 307/587-2339, www.wyomingdra.com).

CAMPING

Buffalo Bill State Park (47 Lakeside Rd., 307/587-9227, www.wyoparks.state.wy.us, May-Sept., $17 nonresidents), 11 miles west of Cody, offers the closest public campgrounds. Situated below the Absaroka Mountains, the park has two campgrounds: North Shore Bay Campground has 37 sites, and North Fork Campground has 62 sites.

A good, fully equipped private facility in town is the **Ponderosa Campground** (1815 8th St., 307/587-9203, www.codyponderosa.com, mid-Apr.-mid-Oct., $30 tents, $35-49 RVs, $31 tipis, $60 cabins for 2 people). There is a cowboy cappuccino bar, a convenience store, a playground, clean restrooms and showers, and many other amenities in this large complex.

INFORMATION AND SERVICES

The **Cody Country Chamber of Commerce** (836 Sheridan Ave., 307/587-2777 or 800/393-2639, www.codychamber.org, 8am-7pm daily summer, 8am-5pm Mon.-Fri. fall-spring) acts as a visitors center and a ticket outlet for events around town, and avid walkers can pick up a map of trails. Excellent planning tools are also available online at www.yellowstonecountry.org.

For information on recreational trails and public camping in the region, contact the **Shoshone National Forest** (808 Meadow Lane Ave., 307/527-6241, www.fs.usda.gov) or the **Bureau of Land Management** (1002 Blackburn Ave., 307/578-5900, www.blm.gov).

The main **post office** (307/527-7161, 8am-4:30pm Mon.-Fri., 9am-noon Sat.) is located at 1301 Stampede Avenue.

The airy and bright **Park County Library** (307/527-1880, www.parkcountylibrary.org, 9am-8pm Mon.-Thurs., 9am-5:30pm Fri., 9am-5pm Sat., 1pm-4pm Sun.) is located at 1500 Heart Mountain Street.

Cody's **West Park Hospital** (707 Sheridan Ave., 307/527-7501 or 800/654-9447, www.westparkhospital.org) has a 24-hour emergency room. The hospital also runs an **Urgent Care Clinic** (424 Yellowstone Ave., 307/578-2903, 8am-6:30pm Mon.-Fri., 9am-5:30pm Sat., 9am-3:30pm Sun.) for illnesses and injuries that do not require hospital care.

Visitors can do laundry at **Cody's Laundromat** (1728 Beck Ave., 307/587-8500, www.codylaundromat.weebly.com, 24 hours daily) or **Eastgate Laundry** (1813 17th St., 307/587-5355, 6am-10pm Mon.-Fri.).

TRANSPORTATION
Getting There

The Cody area is served commercially by the **Yellowstone Regional Airport** (COD, 2101 Roger Sedam Dr., 307/587-5096, www.flyyra.com), just a two-minute drive from downtown, which has daily flights by **Delta/SkyWest** (307/586-1890 or 800/221-2121, www.delta.com, www.skywest.com), **United** (800/864-8331, www.united.com), and **United Express/SkyWest** (307/586-1890 or 800/864-8331, www.ual.com). The airport is 52 miles from the east entrance to Yellowstone National Park. Air and shuttle services are also available from Billings (107 miles). Long-term and short-term outdoor vehicle parking at the airport is free.

By road, Cody is 177 miles northeast of Jackson, 163 miles north of Lander, 84 miles northwest of Thermopolis, and 52 miles east of Yellowstone National Park.

Getting Around

Car-rental companies operating at the Yellowstone Regional Airport include **Avis, Budget, Dollar, Hertz,** and **Thrifty.**

For service between Cody and Billings, local taxi service in town, and tours to Yellowstone, contact **Phidippides Shuttle Service** (307/527-6789 or 866/527-6789, www.codyshuttle.com).

For regular taxi service, contact **Cody Cab** (307/272-8364). Tours of Yellowstone and Grand Teton National Parks can also be arranged.

Sheridan, Devils Tower, and Northeast Wyoming

Look for ★ to find recommended
sights, activities, dining, and lodging.

Highlights

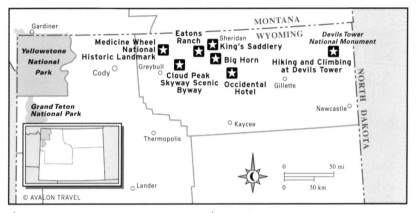

© AVALON TRAVEL

★ **King's Saddlery:** Part museum, part Western tack store, this is the hub of Sheridan (page 153).

★ **Medicine Wheel National Historic Landmark:** High in the Big Horns on a narrow ridge is this mysterious, Stonehenge-esque feature thought to be 500-800 years old (page 154).

★ **Eatons Ranch:** The oldest dude ranch in the world is certainly one of the most traditional (page 160).

★ **Big Horn:** This tiny little town is full of character, with a gem of an art museum, plenty of polo, and wonderful Western celebrations (page 162).

★ **Occidental Hotel:** Catch a glimpse of what the good life looked like in the Old West (page 164).

★ **Cloud Peak Skyway Scenic Byway:** This stunning road climbs over and cuts through the Big Horn Mountains, passing by beautiful spots and providing access to historic sites (page 165).

★ **Hiking and Climbing at Devils Tower:** Rising more than 1,200 feet above the Belle Fourche River, the nation's first national monument is a magnet for hikers and climbers (page 178).

N ortheast Wyoming encompasses rocky peaks, meadows full of wildflowers, river-carved canyons, and wide-open spaces, as well as classic Western town Sheridan and the Powder River Basin towns of Gillette and Buffalo.

Long a prime buffalo hunting territory for Native Americans, the area has seen great conflict between Indians and encroaching settlers. Today that relationship is dynamic and evident throughout much of the region, even at Devils Tower, where climbers are making strides toward working in cooperation with the Native Americans who consider the feature sacred.

The economy here is based almost entirely on natural resources: coal and coal-bed methane, livestock production, and tourism in these vast and beautiful places. There are tiny museums in towns like Sheridan and Big Horn, among many others, that celebrate a way of life that seems in no danger of disappearing, with the relative vastness and remote feel of the region. Although towns like Gillette are growing as quickly as trains can haul coal—then shrinking just as fast when production slows—plenty of places exist where time stands still in northeast Wyoming. From

horseback riding and fishing to hiking and rock climbing, the region has no shortage of recreational opportunities.

HISTORY

Stretching from the eastern flank of the Big Horn Mountains east to the Black Hills and bordered on the south by the North Platte River, the Powder River Basin was prime hunting territory for a number of different Native American groups. Among the early inhabitants were the Crow Indians, who were ultimately driven north by the Sioux, likely in the mid-1800s. Arapaho and Cheyenne moved in and allied with the Sioux against miners heading hurriedly to the gold fields in Montana and the military who had come to protect them. One of the first recorded conflicts with whites included an incident near modern-day Kaycee (named for the KC Ranch) when Lutheran missionaries set up a mission to convert Crows. When the

---

Previous: Devils Tower; polo match in Big Horn. **Above:** horse and rider at Eatons Ranch.

Sheridan, Devils Tower, and Northeast Wyoming

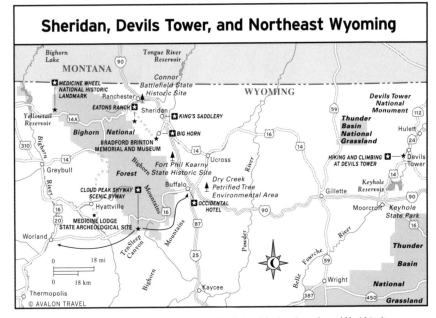

missionaries arrived and set up camp in 1860, the Crow were no longer in the area, and the Sioux and Cheyenne did not want the missionaries around. One of the missionaries quickly deserted the mission, another was killed by the Indians, and the others fled for their lives. The Indians felt justified running the missionaries off and burning the mission because the Treaty of 1851, signed at Fort Laramie, had declared everything east of the Big Horns to the Black Hills and north of the North Platte River to be Indian territory.

In order to bypass inevitable conflict, most miners traveling through the region to Montana's gold fields traveled south of the Powder River Basin on the Oregon Trail. In 1864, however, as mining towns were booming overnight in Montana, John Jacobs and John Bozeman built the first trail through the area, saving prospectors weeks of travel time. The Bozeman Trail became known as the "Bloody Bozeman" for the numerous mortal conflicts. Jacobs and Bozeman dealt with their fair share of Indian encounters during the completion of the trail, including one in which Jacob's daughter, herself half-Indian, was beaten for traveling with white men.

The area was essentially a war zone as early as 1854, during the first of three Sioux wars. Only after the 1876-1877 Great Sioux War, which included Crazy Horse's surrender, and the Ghost Dance War, which ended with the Massacre at Wounded Knee in 1890, did the Sioux commit to living on the reservation. During those decades numerous battles flared between significant leaders on both sides, including Sioux chief Red Cloud, Dull Knife, and Col. H. B. Carrington. The 1876 Dull Knife Battle robbed the Cheyenne of all their winter supplies, including lodge poles, canvases, and clothes, and even their winter food storage. Part military tactic, part revenge for the recent death of Custer and his men at the Battle of the Little Bighorn in June of that year, the U.S. Army destroyed everything the Cheyenne had gathered for winter, and the surviving Indians, women and children included, fled on foot in temperatures that fell below -30°F. The Cheyenne surrendered a few weeks later.

The reservation spread into the Black Hills, much of which was thought to be gold-rich and was purchased by the government from the Sioux in 1876. Although the Indian Peace Commission had originally offered $6 million, and the Sioux, understanding the value the white men saw in the soil, had asked for $70 million, a final sale price of $4.5 million eliminated Indian ownership of the land.

With the Indian Wars winding down, a new type of conflict arose between the moneyed cattlemen and the hardscrabble homesteaders across the Powder River Basin. Texas cattle had come into the region between 1875 and 1884. They were grazed on the open range until homesteaders started fencing off pastureland and watering holes. The cattle herds continued to increase while the open rangeland decreased. With drought followed by freezing temperatures, cattle numbers sustained cataclysmic losses over the winter of 1886-1887, later referred to as the "Great Die-up." Cattlemen became even more resolved to make their outfits profitable.

While the cattlemen were trying to rid themselves of pesky rustlers and homesteaders, a hired group called the Regulators pursued a "dead list" of ambitious and outspoken homesteaders and people believed to be rustlers. Known as the Johnson County Wars, there were major conflicts between cattlemen and townspeople who supported the outspoken homesteaders.

The last Indian battle in Wyoming took place on October 30, 1903, southwest of Newcastle, when Sioux returning to their reservation from Montana ran into lawmen from Newcastle. At stake was the issue of whether or not the Indians were violating game laws by hunting off the reservation. Three lawmen were killed, and the Indians eventually surrendered, were put on trial, and were ultimately acquitted.

Throughout the 20th century, the story of this corner of Wyoming centered on cattle and sheep production and, more recently (and far more lucratively), coal and coal-bed methane production. With wide-open ranch country and Devils Tower as the country's first national monument, it's not a stretch to see why

tourism, too, continues to play an important role in the region.

PLANNING YOUR TIME

Travelers heading east or west on I-90 will have easy access to much of the region. **Sheridan** is a wonderful town to visit and a terrific hub for many of Wyoming's **dude ranches.** Although most ranches are busiest in summer, a few open in May, and some stay open into fall for hunters. Just down the road from Sheridan, the tiny town of **Big Horn** is home to the **Bradford Brinton Memorial and Museum,** on a gentleman's ranch where you could easily while away an afternoon. Nearby **Buffalo,** the starting point for the 47-mile **Cloud Peak Skyway Scenic Byway,** has a historic downtown with a great little museum and easy access to a number of sites that feature prominently in Wyoming history, including **Fort Phil Kearny** and the infamous **Hole in the Wall** region where Butch Cassidy and the Sundance Kid were known to hide out. Though not exactly a touristy destination, **Gillette** offers nice parks, a terrific public pool and waterslide, and one of the region's best culinary experiences, **The Chophouse Restaurant.** Summer, late spring, and early fall are the best times to hit this corner of the state because of the blue skies and easy opportunities to be outdoors. They're still here in the winter, of course, but one gets the feeling that everyone is hunkered down, waiting for spring.

Though **Devils Tower** is not exactly on the way to anywhere, it is for many the highlight of a trip to Wyoming as an obvious recreation spot for climbers, hikers, and campers. The trip can be made fairly easily in a day from just about anywhere in northeast Wyoming. It's wise to plan your visit to Devils Tower sometime other than June, when the voluntary ban on hiking and climbing is in place, or the first and second weeks in August, when bikers headed to or from the huge Sturgis Motorcycle Rally in South Dakota's Black Hills can descend on the tower in crowds of hundreds and even thousands.

Sheridan and Vicinity

Although Sheridan (population 17,828, elevation 3,745 feet) continuously touts itself as the midpoint between Yellowstone National Park and the Black Hills, it sells itself short. It's true that it is conveniently located, but this authentic Western town has much more to offer than proximity to other places.

Rich with history, Sheridan is the town where Martha Jane Canary transformed herself into Calamity Jane. In an 1872 battle, she heroically rescued Captain Egan, who dubbed her "Calamity Jane, the heroine of the plains." The town's first building was erected in 1878 by trapper Jim Mason. In 1881 the tiny cabin was converted into a post office and store named Mandel. The town was eventually platted by J. D. Loucks, who named it for his Civil War commander, General Philip H. Sheridan, and with the coming of the railroad in 1892, Sheridan quickly became a cattle town. The iconic Sheridan Inn was opened in 1893 and was the town's unofficial center, with Buffalo Bill as its operator for two years; he used the inn as a place to audition acts for his Wild West Show.

One of the most charming towns in the state, with an extensive historic downtown, Sheridan has the feel of the Old West, although that is slowly beginning to change as traditional Main Street businesses are gradually being replaced by high-end art galleries and gourmet eateries. Still, Wyoming's best-known saddlery is here and in no danger of leaving, as are some classic watering holes like the Mint Bar, along with numerous historic sites. Surrounded by dusty but beautiful countryside and the pastoral and magnificent Big Horn Mountains, Sheridan claims to be the lowest town in Wyoming at 3,745 feet.

The tiny (and unincorporated) town of Big Horn (population 490) is on the eastern slopes of the Big Horn Mountains, with Little Goose Creek running through. The town was settled in the late 1880s by such well-known sheep and cattle ranchers as the Moncreiffe brothers, the Wallop family, the Gallatin family, and Bradford Brinton, whose home is a gem of a museum and one of the best reasons to visit Big Horn. The other reason to visit is to check out a polo match, a favorite pastime of the town.

SIGHTS
Trail End State Historic Site

The **Trail End State Historic Site** (400 Clarendon Ave., 307/674-4589, www.trailend. org, 1pm-4pm daily Apr.-May, 9am-6pm daily June-Aug., 1pm-4pm daily Sept.-mid-Dec., 10am-5pm Memorial Day and Labor Day weekends, $4 nonresidents, $2 residents, children 17 and under free if accompanied by an adult) is situated high on a bluff overlooking town. The four-acre grounds are impeccably manicured and have retained much of their original landscaping, designed nearly a century ago. The museum is the former home of John B. Kendrick, one of Wyoming's most famous sons. Kendrick was orphaned early in life and got his start at age 15 as a ranch hand. Originally from Texas, he followed cattle into Wyoming and, taken with its beauty, decided to stay. He went on to become a successful rancher and businessman, accumulating more than 200,000 acres of land. Kendrick would become Wyoming's first governor and later a U.S. senator. Kendrick referred to the house, begun in 1908 and completed in 1913, as the "end-of-the-trail mansion," and it's where he would spend the last 20 years of his life when he wasn't in Washington DC.

The house is built in the Flemish revival style, with rich mahogany walls, exposed-beam ceilings, and 18 beautifully decorated rooms. What is unique to this historic house is that almost everything on display (furniture, rugs, magazines, books, and photographs) is the original property of the Kendrick family. Self-guided tours are available; for groups larger than eight, reservations for guided tours can be made two weeks in advance.

Sheridan Inn

When the **Sheridan Inn** (856 Broadway, 307/674-2178, www.sheridaninn.com) opened in 1893, it was considered the finest hotel between Chicago and San Francisco. Designed after a Scottish inn and with a bar imported from England, the inn was the only hotel in Sheridan to have electric lights (200 of them, to be exact). The porch runs the full 130-foot length of the hotel, and there are 62 dormer windows.

Buffalo Bill Cody helped inaugurate the hotel—chilled champagne was served—and

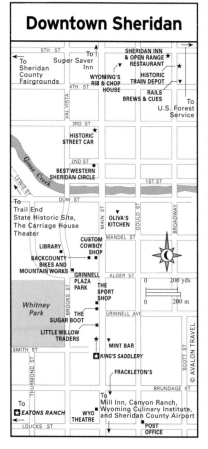

went on to become a co-owner. He would hold auditions for his Wild West Show on the hotel's veranda, and the Sheridan Inn quickly became the social center for Sheridan's affluent residents.

The hotel has hosted famous guests, including presidents Theodore Roosevelt, Howard Taft, and Herbert Hoover. Its longest resident, however, is said to still reside in the hotel: Catherine B. Arnold worked and lived at the inn for 64 years, from her arrival in 1901 until she left, only when the hotel closed, in 1965. She had worked as a desk clerk, seamstress, housekeeper, and hostess, and her dying request was to be buried in the hotel. When she died three years later, her ashes were placed in the wall of the 3rd-floor room she often occupied. According to local lore, the presence of "Miss Kate" is still felt. From the sound of footsteps and lights turning on and off to doors being opened and shut, the rumor is that she still likes to manage the inn.

The hotel reopened in 1967 and continued to operate for another 20 years before closing its doors again. In 1991 a restaurant opened in the inn and tours of the building were available, but it no longer functioned as a hotel. In the fall of 2012, the property was completely shuttered until Bob and Dana Townsend of Oklahoma purchased it, continued the restoration, and reopened the hotel and restaurant, Open Range, in 2015. Today the hotel is, once again, at the center of the Sheridan community.

★ King's Saddlery

In a town full of Western stores, **King's Saddlery** (184 N. Main St., 307/672-2702 or 800/443-8919, www.kingssaddlery.com, 8am-5pm Mon.-Sat.) is indeed aptly named. A legendary tack store founded by the King family in the late 1940s, founder Don King is a local hero and was a renowned saddle maker. Many of his saddles are on display in the store's **Don King Museum** (8am-5pm Mon.-Sat., donation requested) as well as at the National Cowboy Hall of Fame and the PRCA Rodeo

Hall of Fame. For six years, Don handcrafted the PRCA World Championship saddles.

In addition to the store's dizzying selection of rope, hats, and Western tack, the museum houses hundreds of saddles, wagons, coaches, Indian artifacts, cowboy memorabilia from around the world, and original art. Don't leave without a King Ropes baseball cap, which promotes the saddlery's most famous product; it will connect you with other cowboy aficionados the world over.

Ucross Foundation

Twenty-seven miles east of Sheridan, nestled in the midst of a 20,000-acre working cattle ranch (half of the land is protected by The Nature Conservancy), is the artists haven known as **Ucross** (30 Big Red Ln., 307/737-2291, www.ucrossfoundation.org). About 100 artists from around the globe are invited to take up residence at the foundation each year, since 1981, for a few weeks at a time. The foundation's mission is simply to provide a workplace where writers, composers, painters, and other artists can live and work uninterrupted for an extended period of time. There are usually 10 residents on the grounds at the same time. Pulitzer Prize-winning author Annie Proulx has been a significant supporter of Ucross, and Elizabeth Gilbert wrote part of her novel *Eat, Pray, Love* while in residence.

Big Red was the main house of the original ranch and now serves as an important part of the complex. It is decorated with antique furniture and houses a gallery (8:30am-4pm Mon.-Fri., 10am-4pm Sat. July-Labor Day) that hosts four annual exhibitions, which are open to the public. The gallery is closed between exhibitions, so call ahead or check online before you go.

Bighorn Scenic Byway

One stretch of stunning road between Yellowstone to the west and Mount Rushmore and the Black Hills to the east is the **Bighorn Scenic Byway,** a 57-mile stretch of road that starts at Shell, Wyoming, in the dramatic Shell Canyon. Winding up through the Bighorn

National Forest past Shell Falls, the byway slips through narrow canyons past red chimney rocks and towering cliffs. The highest point on the drive is Granite Pass, just above the Antelope Butte Ski Area. North of the pass, the byway intersects with U.S. Highway 14A, known as the Medicine Wheel Passage for its access to Medicine Wheel National Historic Landmark. In addition to a diversity of landscapes—rangeland, forest, subalpine, and alpine—there is an abundance of wildlife in the region; travelers can watch for elk, moose, and deer. The access to public campgrounds and hiking trails is better on this byway than just about anywhere in the Bighorn National Forest. The byway's eastern end (although U.S. Hwy. 14 continues on) is just west of Ranchester.

★ Medicine Wheel National Historic Landmark

High atop a bluff in the Big Horn Mountains, some 70 miles (about a 90-minute drive) west of Sheridan on U.S. Highway 14A, **Medicine Wheel National Historic Landmark** is a 74-foot-wide stone circle with 28 interior spokes connecting the exterior with an interior circular mound. Made of limestone slabs and boulders, the Medicine Wheel is a mysterious landmark that has spiritual but unexplained significance to many Native American groups. First seen by white explorers in the late 1800s, thoughts on its origins are vast and varied: Some link it back to the worship of the Aztecs; others attribute it to early French or Russian explorers. The most common viewpoint, however, is that it was built by one of the tribes in the region: Crow, Arapaho, Shoshone, Sheep Eater, or Cheyenne. The star alignments suggest the medicine wheel could have been constructed as early as the 13th century, and the solstice alignments are accurate even today. The only carbon dating from the site, done on a piece of wood, suggests a minimum age of 1760. There are tipi rings around the site and worn travois trails to the site, suggesting heavy usage. Stone markers in the shape of arrows point

The Mint Bar is "where good friends meet."

good reason, is the **Mint Bar** (151 N. Main St., 307/674-9696, www.mintbarwyo.com, 10am-2am Mon.-Sat.), which boasts hundreds of artifacts and mounts, furniture made in the tradition of Thomas Molesworth, hundreds of local cattle brands on the wall, and ambience that cannot be beat. Don't leave without a pair of satin underpants that touts the Mint as a place "where good friends meet." Another classic old spot for a cold one, a game of pool, or just an interesting local history lesson is **Rails Brews and Cues** (841 Broadway St., 307/672-5617, www.sheridanrails.com, noon-2am Mon.-Sat., noon-10pm Sun.), located in the old depot.

The Arts

Sheridan is home to two theaters, the **Carriage House Theater** (419 Delphi Ave., 307/672-9886) and the **WYO Theater** (42 N. Main St., 307/672-9084), the oldest vaudeville theater in the state.

Festivals and Events

Sheridan is a strong community of locals and regular yearly visitors that supports a multitude of weekly events, including the Thursday **Sheridan Farmers Market** (307/672-8881, www.downtownsheridan.org, 5pm-7pm Thurs. mid-July-mid-Sept.) at Grinnell Plaza Park (W. Algers St. and N. Brooks St.) and Tuesday evening **Concerts in the Park** (www.sheridanwyoming.org) at Kendrick Park. The third Thursday of each month is the **Third Thursday Street Festival** (www.downtownsheridan.org), with music and food vendors in the heart of downtown. For much bigger name entertainment over a weekend in mid-June, **Big Horn Country USA** (www.bighorncountry.us) is a popular camping and music festival.

Since 1930, the **Sheridan WYO Rodeo** (www.sheridanwyorodeo.com) has been one of the most celebrated events in the state, and its renowned posters hang as graphic art all across the West. The mid-July event entails four nights of PRCA rodeo, multiple concerts, the Chris LeDoux Spurs and Spikes Memorial

to a number of nearby medicine wheels, including those in Meeteetse and Steamboat Mountain in southwest Wyoming near Rock Springs.

Although the site was designated a National Historic Landmark in 1970, little was done to protect the artifacts from the elements, livestock, and, rather unfortunately, disrespectful visitors. Today the U.S. Forest Service (2013 Eastside 2nd St., Sheridan, 307/674-2600, www.fs.usda.gov) is responsible for protecting and preserving the area, and Native American guides have been hired to interpret the site for visitors. Driving to the site itself is restricted, so plan to park at the ranger station and walk about 1.5 miles on a gravel road.

ENTERTAINMENT AND EVENTS
Nightlife

Whether you are cruising in a beat-up pickup truck or on foot, you don't have to leave Main Street for a taste of Sheridan's nightlife. The most famous of all the watering holes, and for

Golf Tournament, a traditional Indian Relay with a $25,000 payout, a parade, and a foot race. The **First People's Pow Wow and Dance** (www.sheridanwyoming.org) is a celebration with traditional dancers and drum teams held over the course of several days during the Sheridan WYO Rodeo on the lawn at the Sheridan Inn.

Held annually the last week of July, the **Sheridan County Fair** (1650 W. 5th St., Sheridan, 307/672-2079, www.sherfair.com, free) offers games, contests, and events to entertain the whole family, including a pancake breakfast, horse and livestock shows, community exhibits, inflatable games and slides, and the usual 4-H and FFA events.

Later in the summer, typically in early to mid-August, the **Sheridan County Rodeo** (www.sherfair.com) is held at the local fairgrounds. Less flashy than the Sheridan WYO Rodeo, this old-school small-town rodeo showcases the abundant local talent the region is known for. Events are open to adults and kids in more than two dozen events, including roping, racing, pole bending, goat tying, and steer wrestling.

The **Suds n' Spurs Brew Fest** (307/672-2485) is an end-of-summer event with live music, food vendors, and, of course, plenty of beer. Held in Whitney Commons Park (200 W. Alger St.) in late August, a $30 ticket buys unlimited samples from more than 20 breweries. Transportation is available from the Sheridan Trolley.

SHOPPING

After a requisite stop at **King's Saddlery** (184 N. Main St., 307/672-2702 or 800/443-8919, www.kingssaddlery.com, 8am-5pm Mon.-Sat.), shoppers can stroll up and down historic **Main Street** with its abundance of art galleries, boutiques, and classic Western stores.

For appropriate cowboy and cowgirl duds, stop into the **Custom Cowboy Shop** (1286 Sheridan Ave., 800/487-2692, www.customcowboyshop.com, 9am-6pm Mon.-Sat. Oct.-May, 9am-8pm Mon.-Sat., 10am-7pm Sun. June-Sept.), which was founded by cattle

rancher and saddle maker Don Butler in 1976 as a way to make ends meet. Today this store, as well as another location in Cody, carries everything from saddles and tack to hats, buckles, scarves, clothing, jewelry, and housewares.

A couple of great Main Street shops worth visiting are **Little Willow Traders** (166 N. Main St., 307/672-0200, www.littlewillowtraders.com, 10am-5:30pm Mon.-Sat.), which sells rustic home furnishings, gifts, clothing, and more, and **Over the Moon Boutique** (176 N. Main St., 307/673-4821, 10am-5:30pm Mon.-Thurs., 10am-5pm Fri.-Sat.), which sells women's clothing, jewelry, bath and body products, handmade jewelry, baby clothing, and gifts.

The Sugar Boot (198 N. Main St., 307/675-1825, 10am-5pm Mon.-Sat.) is an old-timey candy shop with hand-dipped ice cream and retro toys, too.

For sporting goods, try **The Sport Shop** (208 N. Main St., 307/672-5356, 9am-5:30pm Mon.-Fri., 9am-5pm Sat.) and **Back Country Bikes & Mountain Works** (330 N. Main St., 307/672-2453, www.backcountrybikes.com, 9am-5:30pm Mon.-Fri., 9am-4pm Sat.).

SPORTS AND RECREATION
Hiking

With the Big Horn Mountains looming so close to town, there is plenty of country to get lost in within an easy drive from Sheridan. To plan a good hike or backpacking trip, visit the **U.S. Forest Service** (2013 Eastside 2nd St., Sheridan, 307/674-2600, www.fs.usda.gov) for maps and advice. Right downtown, **The Sport Shop** (208 N. Main St., 307/672-5356) and **Back Country Bikes & Mountain Works** (330 N. Main St., 307/672-2453, www.backcountrybikes.com, 9am-5:30pm Mon.-Fri., 9am-4pm Sat.) can outfit hikers and backpackers or just offer friendly advice.

For adventurous types keen to head out, there are hundreds of trails in the **Bighorn National Forest,** many of which can be accessed from the Bighorn Scenic Byway on U.S.

Highway 14. One such trail is the **Tongue River,** an 18.2-mile out-and-back hike that leaves from a trailhead roughly 9 miles west of Ranchester on County Road 92 in the Tongue River Canyon. Though the trail climbs more than 3,000 vertical feet over 9 miles, hikers looking for a shorter route will be delighted with the 2-mile round-trip hike along the gushing river and up a set of switchbacks to a rather large limestone cave that can be explored if you have the right equipment (headlamps are essential). Be on the look-out, however, for livestock, poison ivy, and rattlesnakes; even with them, this is a beautiful spot.

An interactive map of the trails and campgrounds in the area is available online (www. sheridanwyoming.org).

Fishing

There is no shortage of fantastic fishing spots around Sheridan. Anglers have long flocked to the region to wet a line on the **Tongue River, Little Goose Creek,** and **Big Goose Creek** as well as any of the dozens of pristine alpine lakes in the region, including **Sibley Lake** and **Lake DeSmet.**

For up-to-date information and all the gear you could possibly need, stop into **Fly Shop of the Bighorns** (334 N. Main St., 307/672-5866, www.sheridanflyfishing.com, 7am-6pm Mon.-Sat., 7am-3pm Sun., shortened hours off-season). It offers guided walks and wades as well as float trips to blue-ribbon trout waters on both public and private lands as **Rock Creek Anglers.** Half-day wade fishing trips start at $250 for one angler, $390 for two, and $540 for three. All-day wade fishing trips are $400 for one angler, $500 for two, and $675 for three. All-day float trips are $475 for one angler and $525 for two. Private water leases can add fees of $100-150 per rod to the cost.

Horseback Riding

While Sheridan is surrounded by some of the best guest ranches in the country that focus on riding, there aren't many options for visitors to town who are looking for a riding

opportunity without the full-on ranch experience. About 20 minutes from Sheridan is **Rangeland Enterprises** (394 Beaver Creek Rd., 307/672-6717, www.rangelandhunting-adventures.com, $40/hour, minimum age 6, reservations required). Day trips, overnight adventures, and hunting expeditions are also offered. Outside of Buffalo on U.S. Highway 16 West, **South Fork Mountain Lodge & Outfitters** (307/267-2609, www.southfork-lodge.com) offers a range of activities and amenities, included horseback riding options ($80-250), May-November.

Golf

One semiprivate and one public golf course are in the vicinity of Sheridan. The **Hidden Bridge Golf Club** (550 Mydland Rd., 307/752-6625, www.hiddenbridgegolf.com, $30 for 9 holes including cart, $45 for 18 holes including cart, $35 all-day play with cart Mon.-Thurs.) is close to downtown. The municipal **Kendrick Golf Course** (65 Golf Course Rd., 307/674-8148, $30 for 9 holes with cart, $46 for 18 holes with cart) offers 18 holes with discounts for families and twilight play.

FOOD

Unlike much of rural Wyoming, Sheridan is quite cosmopolitan when it comes to dining options. There is plenty of variety—think Chinese, Korean, and Mexican—plus some sophisticated gourmet eateries. Even so, it's never hard to find a juicy burger or steak in this cattle country.

Relatively new on the culinary scene is **Open Range** (856 Broadway, 307/675-1152, www.sheridaninn.com, 11am-9pm daily, $11-32) inside the legendary Sheridan Inn. A classic steak house with Western flair—think buffalo sliders and Rocky Mountain oysters—Open Range is formal without being stuffy. From sandwiches and burgers to seafood and steak, meals are prepared from scratch and served artfully in good-sized portions for high-altitude appetites. Another high-end restaurant in the Sheridan community since 2013 is the comfort-gourmet cuisine at

The Mustangs of the Pryor Mountains

One of the most unforgettable experiences you can have in the West is to witness the wild mustangs of the Pryor Mountains that straddle Montana and Wyoming. The majority of these horses share the hereditary line of those brought by Spanish explorers to the Americas more than five centuries ago. The mustangs are small horses with narrow but deep chests and strong, short backs. They are often distinguished by a solid stripe running down their backs or the unique "zebra" stripes across their legs.

Although initially wary of the animals that the conquistadores rode, Native Americans quickly learned to prize them. Through the years they were traded and often stolen in raids. Horses used by the Indians or white settlers were known to stray, and by the mid-1800s enough free stallions and mares had mated that there were more than two million wild horses living west of the Mississippi. At the same time, however, homesteaders were staking out their land and settling in the area. The mustangs' land was needed for houses, farms, and cattle grazing. Seen as an impediment to progress, the wild horses quickly began to disappear, hunted for sport or captured alive, where they were sent to slaughter and used by pet food companies. By the 1950s, only a handful of herds were left.

In response to the work of grassroots organizations and public outcry, the U.S. government sanctioned the **Wild Horse Range** in 1968. Some 31,000 acres were set aside to protect these majestic animals in the Pryor Mountains. Three years later, the Wild Free Roaming Horse and Burro Act stipulated that these horses were "an integral part of the natural system of the public land" and were to be protected from future harassment.

Today around 150 mustangs live on a now 38,000-acre range, which is maintained by the Bureau of Land Management (BLM). The mustangs live in small social units known as harems, which consist of a dominant stallion, a head mare, other mares, and colts. There are currently estimated to be about 30 harems, which produce 20-30 foals each year. In order to balance the well-being of the horses with the well-being of the public land, the BLM has overseen a wild horse adoption program since 1973.

The best place to launch a visit to the Pryor Range is the **Pryor Mountain Wild Mustang Center** (U.S. 14A, Lovell, Wyoming, 307/548-9453, www.pryormustangs.org, 9am-5pm Mon.-Sat. summer, 10am-3pm Mon.-Fri. winter), where staff can tell you about current sightings and locations.

If you drive north along Highway 37 from U.S. Highway 14A east of Lovell into the Bighorn Canyon Recreation Area, you may get lucky and see some mustangs. Sightings are more frequent on East Pryor Mountain, but travel is much more difficult and requires four-wheel drive. There are outfitters willing to take you into the backcountry for a better chance of seeing these wild and beautiful creatures. It is critical that your presence does not impact or change their behavior in any way. The standard distance to keep from the mustangs is 100 feet.

Frackleton's (55 N. Main St., 307/675-6055, 10am-2pm and 4pm-10pm Mon.-Sat., 10am-2pm Sun., lunch $7-16, dinner $10-33). The restaurant serves American bistro cuisine featuring familiar, mouthwatering burgers, salads, pastas, and juicy steaks. Among the local favorites are penne pasta with gorgonzola sauce, pan-roasted beef tenderloin, and the Original Bar & Grill Burger.

A tried-and-true favorite in town (and across the state) is **Wyoming's Rib & Chop House** (847 N. Main St., 307/673-4700, www.ribandchophouse.com, 11am-9pm Sun.-Thurs., 11am-10pm Fri.-Sat., $12-40), which is known for its steaks, seafood, and baby back ribs.

A good local place for a quick breakfast or lunch with Mexican flair is **Oliva's Kitchen** (437 N. Main St., 307/673-0986, 6am-9pm Mon.-Sat., $10-23). Locals line up for enchiladas and Oliva's famous *alambre*, grilled beef topped with chopped bacon, peppers, onions, cheese, salsa, and avocado.

For another gourmet, and rather

unexpected treat for weekday lunches, try the **Wyoming Culinary Institute** (1841 S. Sheridan Ave., 307/764-3388, www.sheridan. edu, 11:30am-2pm and 5pm-8pm Thurs.-Fri., $9-18) at Sheridan College. Specialties include risotto croquettes, starburst grapefruit salad, shrimp sliders, and lobster thermidor penne. There's even a kids' menu.

ACCOMMODATIONS

Sheridan has a broad assortment of roadside hotels and motels. One of the most interesting is the ★ **Mill Inn** (2161 Coffeen Ave., 307/672-6401 or 888/357-6455, www. sheridanmillinn.com, $65-140), cleverly built in an 1890s flour mill and listed on the National Register of Historic Places. The modern rooms are standard and comfortable. For historic charm though, nothing beats the **Sheridan Inn** (856 Broadway, 307/674-2178, www.sheridaninn.com, $139-349). Built in 1893 and reopened as a hotel in 2015, the hotel has long been a hub of the community. Buffalo Bill even auditioned performers for his Wild West Show on the rambling front porch. The 22 rooms and suites are named for important people in Buffalo Bill's storied life.

Among the best budget-friendly options in town is the **Super Saver Inn** (1789 N. Main St., 307/672-0471, www.supersaverinn. com, $59-77), near the VA Medical Center; it is clean and very basic, offering microwaves, coffeemakers, refrigerators, free Wi-Fi, and a laundromat on-site. The 37 guest rooms are pet-friendly (for $8 additional), and the inn's rates are the lowest in town.

At the other end of the spectrum, the **Comfort Inn** (1950 E. 5th St., 307/675-1101, www.choicehotels.com, $99-199) is geared to business travelers and has spacious oversize rooms with nice amenities, including a complimentary continental breakfast buffet, a fitness room, free Wi-Fi, a pool, and a self-service business center. Every room offers either a view of the Big Horn Mountains or the prairie. Located on a hilltop east of I-90, the Comfort Inn is quiet with easy access to town.

Among the other chain hotels in town

are **Motel 6** (911 Sibley Circle, 307/673-9500, $49-119), **Days Inn** (1104 E. Brundage Ln., 307/672-2888, $70-144), **Best Western Sheridan Center** (612 N. Main St., 307/674-7421, $93-140), and **Holiday Inn** (1809 Sugarland Dr., 307/672-8931 or 800/315-2621, $95-169).

For a unique experience just 15 miles south of Sheridan (take Hwy. 335 to County Rd. 77 to Canyon Ranch Rd.), the 3,000-acre **Canyon Ranch** (59 Canyon Ranch Rd., Big Horn, 307/751-6785 or 307/751-3580, www. canyonranchbighorn.com) has been run by the Wallop family for more than a century and offers ranch-type accommodations and vacation rentals as well as activities like fly-fishing, polo, and wildflower viewing. From historic cabins ($265-335/night, $1,500-2,350/week) upgraded with all the modern amenities—flat-screen TVs, Wi-Fi, modern kitchens, and laundry rooms—to the Canyon Ranch Lodge ($2,350/week), this is ranch living at its most beautiful.

GUEST RANCHES

One beloved dude ranch in the area, operating for more than a century, is the **H F Bar** (307/684-2487, www.hfbar.com, $300/day ages 13 and over, $240/day children 5-12, all-inclusive, 7-day minimum June-Sept.), located about 35 miles from Sheridan or 20 miles northwest of Buffalo. The cabins are at once rustic and comfortable, and activities include horseback riding, fishing, hiking, and sporting clays, among others.

Another option is the **Wyoming High Country Lodge** (Forest Rd. 13, 307/529-0914, www.wyhighcountry.com, from $90 pp mid-Sept.-May, $85-125 June-mid-Sept.), which is about 30 miles outside of Lovell in the Bighorn National Forest. This year-round ranch offers rustic rooms and cute cabins, and any number of activities (except horseback riding!) including fishing, hiking, mountain biking, ATV trips, hunting, snow-kiting, cross-country skiing, and snowmobiling.

For a comprehensive list of dude ranches across the region, contact the **Dude**

The Nation's First Dude Ranch

In 1868, a trio of brothers left Pittsburgh in pursuit of more adventure than their father's dry goods store promised. Howard Eaton settled in the Badlands of North Dakota; his brothers Alden and Willis joined him a few years later, and together the three established a small ranch near what would become the town of Medora, North Dakota. On the Custer Trail Ranch, the brothers made their living by supplying wild game to railroad workers and hay to the nearby U.S. Army fort, while establishing their own herds of horses and cattle.

Stories of their adventures trickled east, and before long the much-loved brothers hosted an endless string of friends. In 1882, realizing the financial strain he and others were placing on the hospitable Eatons, Bert Rumsey insisted on paying for the privilege of staying on the ranch. In so doing, Rumsey became the world's first "dude," a term coined by Howard Eaton. Modest as it was—guests slept several to a bed or on the floor, paying $25 per month for the right to do chores—the dude ranching industry was born.

The brutal winter of 1886-1887 changed dude ranching from a practicality to a necessity: The Eatons lost all but 150 of their 1,500 cattle to the cold and snow. The paying guests kept the Eatons afloat.

In 1904, the Eaton brothers bought 7,000 acres of land on the northeastern slope of the Big Horn Mountains. They announced to their friends that they'd be taking a year off to build structures on the ranch: cabins, barns, and a dining hall. Some 70 dudes showed up anyway and for about $100 apiece built many of the cabins that stand today. Although Howard and Willis remained lifelong bachelors, Alden married and set into motion the family that would run the ranch for more than a century. His great-great-grandson, Jeff Way, is the ranch general manager today, and like his family before him, he and his own family welcome guests every summer.

Not much has changed since 1903. Days start early with the thunder of horses being brought down from night pasture. The clanging of an old locomotive wheel signals the start of hearty meals served family-style in the old dining hall. There are still Saturday-night cookouts and West-

Ranchers' Association (307/587-2339, www.duderanch.org), which represents more than 100 of the West's most respected ranches. Another excellent resource for finding the ideal dude ranch vacation is **Gene Kilgore's Ranchweb** (www.ranchweb.com).

★ Eatons Ranch

A half-hour's drive from Sheridan, nestled along Wolf Creek in the Big Horn Mountains, is **Eatons Ranch** (270 Eaton Ranch Rd., 307/655-9552, www.eatonsranch.com, $240-300/day pp early June-mid-Aug., $220-260/day pp late May-early June and mid-Aug.-Sept., all-inclusive), the oldest dude ranch in the world and the cream of the crop. The cabins are old and charming, and the wonder of Eatons is that it rarely changes through the decades. The founding family is still running the ranch, which can accommodate up

to 125 guests, and many of the dudes' families have been coming for generations as well. The riding is excellent, and Eatons is among the only ranches where riders can take to the mountains or prairies without a wrangler (although one is always available). The setting is magnificent and diverse—with mountains, canyons, and prairies to ride—and the traditions here are time-tested. In the winter, bed-and-breakfast packages are available for single night or longer stays.

CAMPING

There are numerous public campgrounds in the Bighorn National Forest, many of which are easily accessed from the Bighorn Scenic Byway. For information about specific sites and, in some cases, to make reservations, contact the **U.S. Forest Service** (2013 Eastside 2nd St., Sheridan, 307/674-2600, www.fs.usda.

The Eatons brand is prominently displayed on the barn.

ern dances, picnics, softball games, rodeos, and more riding than the horsiest Easterner could ever dream of.

The dude season at **Eatons Ranch** (307/655-9285, www.eatonsranch.com) runs late May-September, and the ranch can accommodate 125 guests in 47 cabins and three suites in the main ranch house. Depending on the dates and cabin selected, adult nightly rates for a six-night stay range $220-300, children 6-17 are $200-220 per night, and children under 6 are not charged. Rates include transportation to and from Sheridan, accommodations, all meals, and riding.

gov). Reservations can be booked at some sites through www.recreation.gov.

A handful of RV parks are scattered around town. The **Sheridan KOA** (63 Decker Rd., 307/674-8766 or 800/652-7621, www.koa.com, $35-80) offers tent and RV sites, 1-2-room cabins, bike rentals, fishing, miniature golf, a swimming pool, and free Wi-Fi.

INFORMATION AND SERVICES

The office of **Sheridan Travel and Tourism** (1517 E. 5th St., 307/673-7120, www.sheridanwyoming.org, 8am-5pm daily summer, 8am-5pm Mon.-Fri. fall-spring) is conveniently located at the **State of Wyoming Information Center** (just east of I-90 at exit 23) and can offer very helpful advice in person or over the phone.

For information on hiking, camping, and

other recreation in the Bighorn National Forest, contact the **U.S. Forest Service** (2013 Eastside 2nd St., Sheridan, 307/674-2600, www.fs.usda.gov). Information on fishing and hunting is available through the **Wyoming Game and Fish Department** (700 Valley View Dr., 307/672-7418, www.wgfd.gov).

The **main post office** (307/672-0714, 7:30am-5:30pm Mon.-Fri., 8am-noon Sat.) in Sheridan is located at 101 East Loucks Street.

The **Sheridan County Fulmer Public Library** (335 W. Alger St., 307/674-8585, www.sheridanwyolibrary.org, 9am-9pm Mon.-Thurs., 9am-5pm Fri.-Sat.) has both Internet-connected computers and free Wi-Fi available.

Sheridan Memorial Hospital (1401 W. 5th St., 307/672-1000, www.sheridanhospital. org) has a 24-hour emergency room. There are also two urgent care facilities in town:

Big Horn Urgent Care (813 Highland Ave., 307/673-5501, 10am-8pm Mon.-Sat.) and **Urgent Care Clinic of Sheridan** (1842 Sugarland Dr., Ste. 103, 307/673-5586, 8:30am-5:30pm Mon.-Wed. and Fri., 8:30am-4:30pm Thurs., 9am-4pm Sat., 10am-3:30pm Sun.).

Do laundry at **Wash Yer Wooleys Laundry** (2220 Coffeen Ave., Unit D, 307/752-0389, 24 hours daily).

TRANSPORTATION
Getting There

The tiny **Sheridan County Airport** (SHR, 908 W. Brundage Ln., 307/674-4222) offers daily flights to and from Denver on **Denver Air Connection** (866/373-8513, www.fly-sheridan.com). The nearest larger airports are about 135 miles away (2 hours by car) in Billings (BIL) and Casper (CPR).

Bus service in the region is provided by **Jefferson Bus Lines** (307/674-6188 or 800/451-5333, www.jeffersonlines.com). The non-ticketing bus stop in Sheridan is located at Good 2 Go Food Store (1229 Brundage Ln., 307/672-6802). The nearest ticketing stop is in Buffalo, Wyoming.

By car, Sheridan is 103 miles northwest of Gillette, 147 miles east of Cody, 199 miles east of Yellowstone National Park, and 324 miles northeast of Jackson.

Getting Around

Rental cars are available from **Avis, Budget,** or **Enterprise.** Local taxi service is available by calling **Sheridan Taxi** (307/674-6814) or **CJ Taxi** (307/655-5756).

★ BIG HORN

Located on the eastern flank of the Big Horns, the tiny town of Big Horn (population 490, elevation 4,081 feet) packs a lot of punch. The town was initially settled by upper-class ranchers and European aristocrats; among them was the Moncreiffe family, who raised prize sheep in the region. Although the town never officially incorporated, at one time the population purportedly passed 1,000 but rapidly dwindled in 1893 when the railroad came to Sheridan, nine miles northeast. Still, with its heritage of gentleman ranchers and a significant population boom since 2000, Big Horn has an assortment of fascinating sites and a unique culture that makes a stop in town worthwhile.

Sights

For starters, **The Brinton Museum** (239 Brinton Rd., 307/672-3173, www.bbmandm.org, 10am-5pm Mon.-Sat., noon-5pm Sun., $10 adults, $8 seniors 62 and over and students 13 and over with ID, free for children under 13) is an exquisite museum housed on the grounds of a genteel 1920s and 1930s working ranch. Bradford Brinton was a wealthy businessman from Chicago when he bought the ranch in 1923. He turned it into an elaborate estate to showcase his ever-growing collection of art, which he left to his sister when he died. She meticulously maintained the home and collection and left both to the Northern Trust Company of Chicago. Tours through the 20-room Brinton home are available. And inside the 24,000-square-foot, eco-conscious rammed-earth museum is one of the most important collections of Native American and Western art in the Rocky Mountains. It showcases the largest collection of works by Hans Kleiber in the world, in addition to a surprising number of works by Charlie Russell and Frederic Remington. In addition to four galleries on three floors, the museum has a gift store and farm-to-table bistro, which utilizes fresh produce grown on-site and, in good weather, opens onto a lovely patio with views to the mountains.

Another surprising museum in this tiny little town is the **Bozeman Trail Museum** (335 Johnson St., 307/674-6363 or 307/674-8050, 11am-4pm Sat.-Sun. Memorial Day-Labor Day, free). Built in what was a log blacksmith shop to serve travelers along the trail, the museum includes Indian artifacts, photos, pioneer clothing, books, tools, and other artifacts.

Sports and Recreation

Big Horn is also the **polo** hotbed of Wyoming,

The Bozeman Trail

Although the Bozeman Trail was not given a name until John Jacobs and John Bozeman plowed through the region to give optimistic miners and settlers access to the quickest route through the Powder River Basin, the trail was an ancient migratory route long used by animals and Paleo-Indians. Today this modern transportation corridor is rich with evidence from the past: pictographs, petroglyphs, and ledger art. There are oral histories of trappers and traders in the area that date back to the mid-1700s; written records from Lewis and Clark, who zigzagged across the trail; and evidence that mountain men, missionaries, and the U.S. military all used the trail that, until the first gold rush in southwest Montana in 1862, probably resembled a well-used, age-old game trail.

Enter Jacobs and Bozeman in 1863. Leading a wagon train toward the gold fields in Montana, the men were just 140 miles beyond Deer Creek when they met a large party of Northern Cheyenne and Sioux warriors. Although the bulk of the wagon train turned back toward the Oregon Trail crossing southern and central Wyoming, Bozeman and a few of the men continued on horseback through the region. The following year, Bozeman again led a wagon train through the region, this time with help from Allen Hurlbut and mountain man Jim Bridger. Although nonnative traffic through the area was illegal under the Fort Laramie Treaty of 1851, military support for the Bozeman Trail was evident in various campaigns throughout the region. The treaties signed at Fort Sully in 1865 gave the military unchecked authority to build roads and forts along the Bozeman Trail, and in 1866 alone, more than 2,000 people traveled on it to Montana, with Fort Reno and Fort Phil Kearny established to protect civilians. On December 21, with tensions high between Native Americans and the military, an entire command of 81 men, under Capt. William J. Fetterman, was demolished by Sioux warriors.

In 1868, after several more battles, the Bozeman Trail and the forts along it were abandoned as indefensible by the U.S. Army. Still, the trail saw traffic from expeditions sent to scout the Yellowstone area and the Black Hills. When the Cheyenne were ultimately defeated by General Crook in November 1876 and forced to live on a reservation, the Bozeman Trail once again opened the region to significant settler traffic. Gradually, it became the preferred route for telegraph lines, stagecoaches, and eventually, an interstate highway.

with practice games on Wednesday and Friday at 1pm and 3pm, and tournament games on Sunday at 2pm in June and at 1pm and 3pm in July and August, at the noteworthy **Big Horn Equestrian Center** (932 Bird Farm Rd., 307/673-0454, www.thebhec. org). Admission to the announced matches is free, and concessions are available. Every year on Labor Day Sunday-Monday, the center closes out the season with **Don King Days,** a classic Western celebration with polo, championship steer roping, bronco riding, and wild-cow milking. The center is also one of the local favorite places to spend the **Fourth of July,** with a phenomenal fireworks display.

Buffalo and Vicinity

A neat little Western town with a lot of history and a surprising Basque influence, Buffalo (population 4,638, elevation 4,645 feet) was settled in 1879. Historically it is among Wyoming's biggest sheep towns, which was true as recently as the 1980s, until a late-spring storm after shearing in 1984 caused major losses and reminded locals of the Great Die-up of 1886-1887. Political and environmental conditions never allowed ranchers to recover. Instead, Buffalo makes the most of its beautiful location in the foothills of the Big Horn Mountains, its easy access to scenic drives and outdoor adventures, and its historic buildings and museums.

SIGHTS
Jim Gatchell Memorial Museum

The origins of the **Jim Gatchell Memorial Museum** (100 Fort St., 307/684-9331, www.jimgatchell.com, 8am-4pm Mon.-Fri., 9am-5pm Sat. June-Sept., 8am-4pm Mon.-Fri. Oct.-May, $5 adults, $4 seniors, $3 children 6-17, free for children under 6) can be traced back to the opening of the Buffalo Pharmacy in 1900, the first of its kind in town. People from all walks of life—cattle barons, outlaws, and homesteaders—frequented Jim Gatchell's drugstore, and many would give him small mementos that he kept. Over time, they began entrusting him with pieces of Johnson County history. He also befriended the local Indians, and they too would bestow on him different cultural and personal artifacts.

After Gatchell passed away in 1954, his family donated his collection to Johnson County with the condition it would be shared with the public. The museum was established three years later. Its focus is on Johnson County's frontier-era history, and more than 15,000 pieces are on display. There is a large array of Native American artifacts and many pieces that can be traced back to the U.S. Cavalry, plus a variety of wagons, historical photos, a model of Fort Phil Kearny, artifacts from the fateful Fetterman Fight, and many interpretative materials related to the Bozeman Trail.

★ Occidental Hotel

Entering the **Occidental Hotel** (10 N. Main St., 307/684-0451, www.occidentalwyoming.com, $75-285), many visitors feel as if they've stepped back in time. The hotel has been painstakingly restored to its original 1880s splendor, which includes many of its original furnishings such as light fixtures, the back bar, tin ceilings, a piano, and stained glass. Even the bullet holes throughout the bar are mementos of rowdier days. The place is said to be part museum, part hotel, part bar and restaurant. Visitors can follow a brochure for a self-guided tour or take a free 15-minute guided tour. Hotel guests have a variety of individual suites to choose from, each uniquely decorated with different antiques and features to match the original era. On Thursday nights, the saloon hosts a jam session featuring high-caliber bluegrass, Western, and folk musicians.

Dry Creek Petrified Tree Environmental Area

To find the unusual Dry Creek Petrified Forest, drive east from Buffalo seven miles on I-90, take the Red Hills Road exit (exit 65), and drive north on Tipperary Road for five miles to the Petrified Tree Area access road. In the midst of this sagebrush country, you can follow a 0.8-mile loop that winds through the remnants of petrified trees that date back 60 million years to when the area was swampland covered by metasequoia trees. Some of the stumps are larger than four feet in diameter, and the numerous rings can be identified. The loop that takes visitors through the area is also an eight-station ecological trail with information about the process of petrifaction and the unique history of the land.

Fort Phil Kearny State Historic Site

Located between Sheridan and Buffalo off I-90, the **Fort Phil Kearny State Historic Site** (528 Wagon Box Rd., Banner, 307/684-7629, www.fortphilkearny.com, grounds dawn-dusk daily, $4 nonresidents, $2 residents, free for children under 18) commemorates the fort that stood on the site 1866-1868.

The fort was commissioned at the height of the Indian Wars when the Sioux stood by their vow to fight for their traditional hunting grounds against anyone who dared cross into the Powder River Basin. Although Col. H. B. Carrington attempted to get permission for the fort's construction from Sioux chief Red Cloud, it was never given. The soldiers lived with nearly constant attacks by the Sioux. In the first six months, some 154 people were killed by Indians, and 700 horses, mules, and cattle were stolen.

At 17 acres, the fort was a complete settlement, with a stockade, variety of living quarters, social club, guard house, hospital, even a laundress row. But the structures alone were little help in keeping the soldiers safe. The battles that took place in close proximity to the fort include the Fetterman Fight and the Wagon Box Fight. By 1868 the railroad had made the Bozeman Trail obsolete, and the military abandoned the fort as indefensible. It was burned to the ground, likely by the Cheyenne, in 1868.

At the site of the fort today are an **interpretive center and museum** (8am-6pm daily May-Sept., noon-4pm Wed.-Sun. Oct.-Dec. 21) that provide information for self-guided tours of the grounds and outlying sites. A cabin built by the Civilian Conservation Corps was crafted to resemble officers' quarters. Several of the battlefields are accessible within five miles of the fort.

★ Cloud Peak Skyway Scenic Byway

Traveling from Buffalo on U.S. Highway 16 over the southern portion of the Big Horn Mountains toward Ten Sleep and Worland, the 47-mile paved Cloud Peak Skyway Scenic Byway offers breathtaking scenery of the Cloud Peak Wilderness and the only view of Cloud Peak itself, the highest mountain in the Big Horns. This remarkable stretch of road is the southern-most route across the Big Horns. The summit is at 9,666 feet, and the road also winds through the spectacular Tensleep Canyon. Multiple turnouts are along the way for travelers to stretch their legs and enjoy the view; the road also passes **Fort McKinney** and runs just 20 miles south of **Medicine Lodge State Archeological Site,** known for its ancient petroglyphs, pictographs, and idyllic campgrounds. There is also ample access to hiking trails in the Bighorn National Forest.

ENTERTAINMENT AND EVENTS

The biggest event in Buffalo is the week-long annual **Johnson County Fair and Rodeo** (307/684-7357, www.johnsoncounty-fairgrounds.webs.com), held at the Johnson County Fairgrounds during the end of July and first week of August; it culminates with a three-day rodeo. There are also two rodeos weekly in the region: The **Cowgirl Rodeo** (www.johnsoncountycowgirls.webs.com), featuring women, girls, and boys under 16, is held each Tuesday night at the Johnson County Fairgrounds June-August, and the **Kaycee Lion's Club Rodeo** is held every Friday night at Harold Jarrard Park in nearby Kaycee (7pm, $5 admission); call the **Buffalo Chamber of Commerce** (307/684-5544) or **Kaycee Chamber of Commerce** (307/738-2444), respectively, for more information. Also in the area, the tiny town of Ten Sleep has been hosting regular rodeos since 1908, when audience members circled their covered wagons to form a makeshift arena. The Ten Sleep **Beauty and the Beast Rodeo**

The Fetterman Fight of 1866

During the 1860s onslaught of eager gold seekers looking for a quick route to riches in Montana, John Bozeman led many travelers along the trail that would eventually bear his name, taking them from southeast Wyoming across the Powder River Basin into Montana. The Sioux who inhabited the region had fought and removed the Crows and were determined to prevent white settlers from moving in as well. Travelers were warned not to venture past the Northern Platte River, and the military felt that in order to protect the Bozeman Trail, new forts would need to be established.

In June 1866 the military met with the Sioux chief Red Cloud, to attain permission to build forts in the area. Though he refused, and despite a warning by the Sioux, the commander of the area, Col. H. B. Carrington, gave orders to build a fort at the fork of Big Piney and Little Piney Creeks. The fort was named after Civil War general Phil Kearny. Both the Cheyenne and Jim Bridger had warned Carrington that it was a death wish to build the fort in the middle of the Sioux's hunting ground. But the warnings went unheeded.

1866 Fetterman Fight memorial

True to their word, the Sioux made numerous attacks on the fort. Within the first five months, there were many civilian and military losses as well as the theft of horses, mules, and cattle. The fort's construction required timber and logs to be shipped in from the nearby Big Horn Mountains, and the trains were easy targets for the Sioux.

In mid-December 1866, Capt. William J. Fetterman and his 18th Cavalry were stationed at the fort. Fetterman did not think highly of the Sioux's fighting skills and was convinced that if given the opportunity, his 80 men "could ride through the whole Sioux nation." In response, Jim Bridger reminded Fetterman and his men that although they had fought in the South during the Civil War, "they don't know anything about fighting Indians."

On December 21, 1866, the Sioux attacked a lumber train heading toward the fort. Fetterman and his men responded to the cries for help, intending to ward off the attackers. The 18th Cavalry pursued the attackers, chasing the Indians who dared to taunt them, and rode right into a well-designed ambush about five miles from the fort. The 81 men were dead within 30 minutes. No one would see such an obliteration of U.S. troops until Custer's last stand at the Battle of the Little Bighorn 10 years later.

For this brief period, the Sioux had successfully defended their territory. The Bozeman Trail was no longer used, and by 1868 Fort Kearny was abandoned.

Today the site of the fight, which is two miles from the fort along Old Highway 87, is marked by a stone monument. The site of **Fort Phil Kearny** (528 Wagon Box Rd., Banner, 307/684-7629, www.fortphilkearny.com, grounds dawn-dusk daily, $4 nonresidents, $2 residents, free for children under 18) has been designated a National Historic Landmark. Although the original fort was burned to the ground, most likely by Indians, it was partially reconstructed in 2000. There is also a small **museum** (8am-6pm daily May-Sept., noon-4pm Wed.-Sun. Oct.-Dec. 21).

(307/366-2311, www.tensleeprodeo.com) is held over Memorial Day, and the **Fourth of July Rodeo** (307/366-2311, www.tensleeprodeo.com) happens over two days.

Since 2012, **Longmire Days** (307/684-5544, www.buffalowyo.com) has become the biggest event of Buffalo's summer season. A celebration of all things Longmire—the books by local author Craig Johnson and popular TV adaptation on Netflix—this event includes a 5K race, autograph sessions with the author and actors, an arts and crafts show, food vendors, and plenty of other entertainment. It's like an Old West version of Comic-Con, if such a thing is possible.

SPORTS AND RECREATION
Hiking

In addition to the wealth of trails in the nearby **Bighorn National Forest** (www.fs.usda.gov), Buffalo has an excellent 12-mile trail system in town. Known as the **Clear Creek Trail System,** the well-marked trails can be accessed around town at various spots, including the historic shopping district on Main Street, the motel circle near the intersection of I-25 and U.S. Highway 16, the city park, and the Mosier Gulch picnic area. Mountain bikes are welcome on the trail, and maps are available through the Buffalo Chamber of Commerce (307/684-5544 or 800/227-5122, www.buffalowyo.com).

Swimming

Buffalo has a wonderful free public outdoor swimming pool, the largest in the state, attracting locals and visitors alike on warm summer days. The enormous pool at **Washington Memorial Park** (S. Burritt Ave. and W. Angus St., free) is surrounded by trees, walking trails, and prime picnic spots. There is also a water park for kids and a snack shack. The pool is open mid-morning-sunset June-August.

Fishing

For fishing gear and current conditions on such varied water as **Clear Creek, Rock Creek,** the **Powder River,** and a variety of mountain and prairie lakes, stop in to **The Sports Lure** (66 S. Main St., 307/684-7682, www.sportslure.com, 8am-6pm Mon.-Sat., 10am-4pm Sun.).

Buffalo offers an excellent way to pair two of the state's favorite pastimes. For guided fishing trips on horseback to any of 200 mountain lakes and streams in the Big Horns, contact **South Fork Mountain Lodge & Outfitters** (U.S. 16 W., 16 miles west of Buffalo, 307/267-2609, www.southfork-lodge.com, $250 full-day). Its guides know how to find the rainbows, brookies, native cutthroats, browns, and golden trout.

To leave the horse behind and just focus on the fish, **Rock Creek Anglers** (1301 Rock Creek Rd., Saddlestring, 888/945-3876, www.rockcreekanglers.com, half-day wading trip for 1 angler $250, all-day wading trip for 1 angler $400, all-day drift boat trip for 1 angler $475) can get you onto any number of rivers, plus private waters, for a chance at hauling in some trout. It can also arrange accommodations.

Horseback Riding

Outside of Buffalo on U.S. Highway 16 West, the **South Fork Mountain Lodge & Outfitters** (307/267-2609, www.southfork-lodge.com) offers the full range of activities and amenities, including two-hour rides ($80), four-hour rides with lunch ($150), and full-day wilderness rides including lunch ($250), May-November. It also offers pack trips, drop camps, fishing and hunting trips, plus overnight accommodations in streamside log cabins.

Golf

Golfers can hit the links at the 18-hole **Buffalo Golf Course** (500 W. Hart St., 307/684-5266, www.buffalowygolf.com, $37 for 18 holes, $15 cart/rider). In 2009, this course was voted the best municipal golf club in Wyoming by *Golf Digest*.

FOOD

Known for its hearty breakfasts and great burgers, **Main Street Diner** (41 N. Main St., 307/684-5627, 7am-2pm Tues.-Fri., 7am-noon Sat., 8am-noon Sun., $6-12) has a full menu and a homey small-town feel.

Up in Smoke (94 S. Main St., 307/217-2290, www.upinsmokebuffalowy.com, 4pm-11pm Fri.-Sat., serving until 10pm, $13-30) offers a unique approach to barbecue. It incorporates organic produce, dairy, and chicken whenever possible; all dishes are made from scratch; and take-out containers, made from cornstarch, are biodegradable. In other words, if there is such a thing as healthy and green barbecue, this is it. Sit outside on warm summer evenings and savor the delicious food with a regional microbrew or a premium Scotch. And there's live music on Friday and Saturday nights. Up in Smoke accepts cash and local checks only.

For family dining and three square meals a day, this western states chain restaurant, **Bozeman Trail Steakhouse** (675 E. Hart, 307/684-5555 or 888/351-6732, www.thebozemantrailsteakhouse.com, 11am-9pm daily, $9-29), is a safe bet for everyone. Little ones will love the kids' menu, and adults will appreciate the variety from steaks and game to Mexican specialties, huge salads, and good old-fashioned favorites like chicken-fried steak.

By far the most upscale dining experience in town is **The Virginian** (10 N. Main St., 307/684-5976, www.occidentalwyoming.com, from 5pm Tues.-Sat., $22-40), named for Owen Wister's iconic novel and located in the historic Occidental Hotel. The ambience is 1890s chic, and the food is globally gourmet, with offerings including bison rib eye, elk tenderloin, and filet mignon Occidental. The beer and wine list is impressive too. For an unforgettable meal in a one-of-a-kind setting, this is a marvelous place for dinner. Also in the Occidental, a wonderful spot for breakfast, lunch, dinner, or an ice cream treat anytime is the **Busy Bee Café** (7am-8pm daily summer, 7am-4pm off-season, hours may be shortened depending on patronage, $7-12), which serves hearty Western fare

including biscuits and gravy, bison burgers, and world-class root beer floats.

ACCOMMODATIONS

For such a small town, Buffalo has a surprising number of chain hotels and motels, which indicates its popularity with travelers. A great mom-and-pop option with the best rates in town is the **Big Horn Motel** (209 N. Main St., 307/684-7822, www.bighorn-motel.com, $62-132). Rooms are clean and comfortable. There's a little art gallery on-site, and the personal touches—including baked goods made with eggs from the owners' chickens—make this a wonderful place to stay. Among the chain hotels are the 62-room **Comfort Inn** (65 U.S Hwy. 16 E., 307/684-9564, www.comfortinn.com, $80-153), the pet-friendly **Days Inn** (333 E. Hart St., 307/684-2219, www.daysinn.com, $64-99), and **Holiday Inn Express Hotel & Suites** (106 U.S. Hwy. 16 E., 307/684-9900, www.hiexpress.com, $96-185).

The ★ **Occidental Hotel** (10 N. Main St., 307/684-0451, www.occidentalwyoming.com, $75-285) is an upscale historic gem that is worth every penny. From its historical ties to such figures as Owen Wister and Teddy Roosevelt, among others, to its fantastic restaurant, this is a uniquely Wyoming getaway.

GUEST RANCHES

For an authentic cowboy and cowgirl experience at a working ranch, try the **TA Guest Ranch** (28623 Old Hwy. 87, 307/684-5833, www.taranch.com), south of Buffalo off I-25 on Crazy Woman Creek. Established as a working ranch in 1883, this 8,000-acre working cattle ranch offers beautifully restored Victorian accommodations, gourmet meals, riding twice daily, fly-fishing, and a variety of other dude-ranch activities. The ranch focuses on local history and takes guests to tipi rings and Bozeman Trail sites on the property as well as important battlefields nearby. Since guests get to work, ride, and even share meals with the ranch crew, there is a real sense of camaraderie. The T-A Ranch is one of the few in the area that does not require a weeklong stay, so visitors can enjoy the ranch's activities and amenities for as little as one night. All-inclusive rates start at $350 per day for adults (25 percent discounts are available for stays of longer than four days); bed-and-breakfast rates that don't include riding or meals range $100-150 based on double occupancy.

Another wonderful family-oriented ranch in the area is the **HF Bar Ranch** (1301 Rock Creek Rd., Saddlestring, 307/684-2487, www.hfbar.com, from $300/day ages 13 and up, $240/day children 5-12, all-inclusive), which offers wonderful riding and an assortment of fun activities for kids. The HF Bar is the second-oldest dude ranch in the country after Eatons Ranch in Wolf.

CAMPING

Thirty-two inexpensive public campgrounds ($10-16) can be found nearby in the **Bighorn National Forest** (877/444-6777, www.recreation.gov), about 15 miles west of Buffalo on U.S. Highway 16. Closer to town is the **Big Horn Mountains Campground** (8935 Hwy. 16 W., 307/684-2307, www.buffalocamping.com, $19 tents, $28 RVs), owned and run by Paul and Bev Chaffee. Tent sites are available with or without electricity, the restrooms are always clean, there is a 24-hour laundry room, and discounted weekly rates are available.

INFORMATION AND SERVICES

The **Buffalo Chamber of Commerce** (307/684-5544 or 800/227-5122, www.

buffalowyo.com, 8am-6pm Mon.-Fri., 10am-4pm Sat.-Sun. Memorial Day-Labor Day, 8am-5pm Mon-Fri. Labor Day-Memorial Day) is located at 55 North Main Street. The **Summer Info Center** (187 U.S. Hwy. 16 E., 9am-6pm daily June-Oct.) is a great place for local information.

For information on hiking, camping, and other recreation in the Bighorn National Forest, contact the **U.S. Forest Service** (2013 Eastside 2nd St., Sheridan, 307/674-2600, www.fs.usda.gov).

The **Johnson County Library** (307/684-5546, www.jclwyo.org, 10am-8pm Mon.-Thurs., 10am-5pm Fri.-Sat. year-round, 1pm-4pm Sun. Sept.-May) is located at 171 North Adams Avenue.

The **Johnson County Healthcare Center** (497 W. Lott St., 307/684-5521, www.jchealthcare.com) has a 24-hour emergency room.

TRANSPORTATION

Although Buffalo does have a small airport, the nearest commercial and charter air service is available in Sheridan (33 miles north) and Gillette (72 miles east).

Bus service throughout the region is provided by **Jefferson Bus Lines** (307/674-6188 or 800/451-5333, www.jeffersonlines.com).

By car, Buffalo is 123 miles northeast of Thermopolis, 182 miles east of Cody, 234 miles east of Yellowstone National Park, and 341 miles northeast of Jackson.

Gillette

Founded as a livestock center and transformed into a minerals hub with one of the largest and most easily accessible coal seams in the world, Gillette (population 31,797, elevation 4,550 feet) was organized in 1869 and named for a railroad engineer, Edward Gillette. After a significant oil boom in the late 1960s, coal extraction in the area was boosted by the 1970 Clean Air Act, which mandated cleaner-burning low-sulfur coal, most of which is produced in the West. The Thunder Basin mine opened in 1978, producing 6 million tons of coal that year, and by 1993 was producing upwards of 34 million tons annually, the largest amount from any mine in the world at that time. Because the seams are closer to the surface, mines in the Powder River Basin quickly outproduced mines in the southern part of the state. After a coal-bed methane boom in the 2000s led to a population increase, with modern-day prospectors working as miners and drillers, another bust—in the form of diminishing oil, gas, and coal prices—is shaping the area as some of the largest coal producers go bankrupt, leading to reduced wages for workers and growing unemployment. While unemployment at the end of 2015 hovered around 4.3 percent—less than half the 9 percent figure from 2009—the community is poised to see how hard this bust will hit.

This is a working town with all sorts of growing pains related to coal, oil, and gas extraction. While it certainly has the infrastructure for people traveling through, Gillette is not typically on the top of the vacation radar. Still, it does make an excellent launching point to some of northeast Wyoming's wide-open spaces, and with its enormous tax base, it has managed to develop some phenomenal recreational facilities, many of which are free. The Avenue of Arts on 4J Road, for example, is a walking path lined with ever-changing sculptures. Visitors learn quickly that community means everything here—and Gillette residents are quick to point out that people came for the job, stayed for the money, then never left because of the community.

SIGHTS
Campbell County Rockpile Museum

The exhibits at the **Rockpile Museum** (900 W. 2nd St., 307/682-5723, www.ccgov.net, 9am-5pm Mon.-Sat., free) are focused on the local history of Campbell County. The museum has accrued a wide array of artifacts and displays them creatively. Visitors can see the inside of a general store, the tools and trade of an early medical clinic, and a large rifle collection. An actual homestead cabin and tiny one-room schoolhouse have been moved to the grounds, and there is an impressive collection of wagons, carriages, and even an old horse-drawn hearse. Hands-on activities for children are available, including a fun dress-up area with old-time garb. Since this is the heart of coal country, watch the short film about coal excavation and distribution; the large-scale explosions are sure to catch any viewers' attention.

CCSD Science Center

The **Campbell County School District's Science Center** (525 W. Lakeway Rd., 307/686-3821, www.campbellcountyschools. net, 9:30am-3:30pm Tues.-Fri. summer, 9:30am-3:30pm Mon.-Fri. fall-spring, closed late May-mid-June, free) is open to the public. Located in the Lakeway Learning Center, the science center occupies almost 10,000 square feet and offers young visitors numerous opportunities to discover, inquire, experiment, and learn. There are live animal displays (children can visit with an African pygmy hedgehog, an African bullfrog, ferrets, exotic birds, and even a python) and more than 60 interactive exhibits.

Wright Centennial Museum

Located 35 miles south of Gillette in the small town of Wright, the **Wright Centennial Museum** (104 Ranch Ct., 307/464-1222, www.wrightcentennialmuseum.org, 10am-5pm Mon.-Fri., 10am-2pm Sat. mid-May-early Oct., free) houses a small collection of artifacts from the surrounding area. The museum's collection has been largely amassed from the donations of residents. On display are vintage clothes, kitchen and bathroom furnishings from old homesteads, tools, saddles, and even a prostitute's "dresser box" with her personal items (including a gun). The town was established by the Atlantic Richfield mining company, and so there are many exhibits and interpretive materials dedicated to the mining industry.

ENTERTAINMENT AND EVENTS

Most of Gillette's large-scale events take place in the massive facility known as **Cam-Plex** (1635 Reata Dr., 307/682-0552, www.camplex.com), which hosts concerts, theater productions, conventions, expos, sporting events, public ice skating, and good ol' Wyoming rodeos. Visit the website to see what events are scheduled when you're in town.

Rodeos are held almost every weekend during the summer at Cam-Plex. The **PRCA Rodeo,** which takes place in late July or early August, is quite popular, and the **National High School Rodeo Finals** in July are also a huge draw. Almost 6,000 people descend on Gillette for this annual weekend event.

Head out to the **Gillette Thunder Speedway** (7999 Hwy. 51, 307/682-8866 or 307/660-1717, www.gillettespeedway.com) for stock-car races almost every Saturday night during the summer; check the website for the current schedule.

In the winter, the **Powder River Symphony Orchestra** (307/363-0041, www.prsymphony.org) performs concerts at Cam-Plex, including family-friendly events.

SPORTS AND RECREATION
Swimming

With a soaring tax base in the 2000s, it's no surprise Gillette built up a wealth of terrific public facilities, including the outdoor **Gillette City Pool** (909 S. Gillette Ave., 307/682-1962, www.ccgov.net, 10am-8pm Mon.-Fri., 10am-4:30pm Sat., 1pm-4:30pm Sun., June-early Sept. weather-dependent, free). Admission is free to the massive outdoor pool and all of its facilities, which includes a deep-diving well, zero-depth entry for toddlers, waterslides, a bathhouse, a concession area, a sand playground, climbing structures, and a sunbathing area. The **Campbell County Recreation Center** (250 W. Shoshone Ave., 307/682-8527, www.ccgov.net, 5am-10pm Mon.-Thurs., 5am-9pm Fri., 8am-5pm Sat., 1pm-5pm Sun., $5 adults, $3.50 junior and senior high school students, $3 children, $11 family) is a phenomenal facility that has a climbing wall, a kids' zone, an aerobics room, a gymnasium, a lap pool, a leisure pool, and a sports complex. Call for swim session hours, which include open swim and lap swim.

Kids will be deliriously happy at the **Caribbean Cove Indoor Water Park** (2577 S. Douglas Hwy., 307/682-1717, 8am-10pm daily, though hours can vary seasonally, $6 pp hotel guests, $8 pp non-hotel guests), an 11,000-square-foot indoor water park with a lazy river, waterslides galore, a kiddie pool, and an activity pool. The water park is located inside the Fairfield Inn & Suites.

Golf

Golfers do not lack options in Gillette. The nine-hole **Gillette Golf Club** (1800 Country Club Rd., 307/682-4774, $16 for 9 holes, $26 for 18 holes) and the 18-hole **Bell Nob Golf Club** (4600 Overdale Dr., 307/686-7069, $50 for 18 holes with cart, $35 for 9 holes with cart), which underwent a vast remodel in 2013 with added putting greens and a clubhouse, are both open to the public. The Bell

Gillette

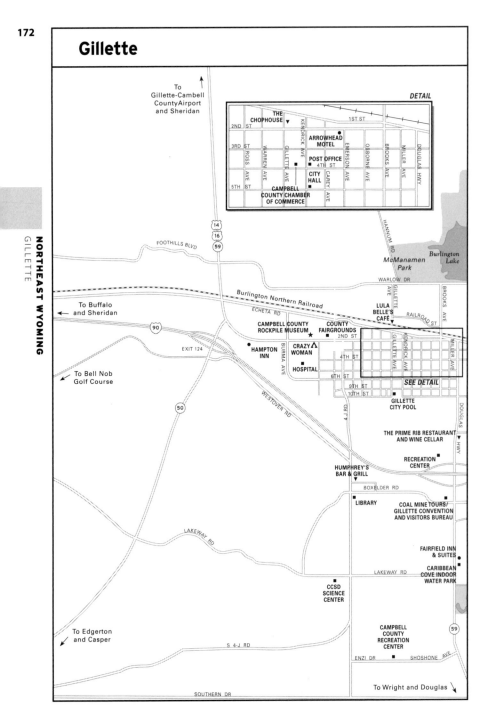

To Gillette-Cambell County Airport and Sheridan

DETAIL

2ND ST

THE CHOPHOUSE ▼

KENDRICK AVE

1ST ST

3RD ST

ROSS AVE
WARREN AVE
GILLETTE AVE

ARROWHEAD MOTEL

EMERSON AVE
OSBORNE AVE
BROOKS AVE
MILLER AVE
DOUGLAS HWY

POST OFFICE
4TH ST

CITY HALL

CAREY AVE

5TH ST

CAMPBELL COUNTY CHAMBER OF COMMERCE

FOOTHILLS BLVD

14
16
59

HANNUM RD

McManamen Park

Burlington Lake

WARLOW DR

Burlington Northern Railroad

GILLETTE AVE

BROOKS AVE

ECHETA RD

LULA BELLE'S CAFÉ ▼

RAILROAD ST

To Buffalo and Sheridan

90

CAMPBELL COUNTY ROCKPILE MUSEUM ★

COUNTY FAIRGROUNDS

2ND ST

GILLETTE AVE
KENDRICK AVE
MILLER AVE

EXIT 124

HAMPTON INN

BURMA AVE

CRAZY WOMAN

4TH ST

SEE DETAIL

To Bell Nob Golf Course

HOSPITAL

6TH ST

50

9TH ST
10TH ST

WESTOVER RD

3RD ST

GILLETTE CITY POOL

DOUGLAS HWY

THE PRIME RIB RESTAURANT AND WINE CELLAR ▼

RECREATION CENTER

HUMPHREY'S BAR & GRILL ▼

BOXELDER RD

LIBRARY

COAL MINE TOURS/ GILLETTE CONVENTION AND VISITORS BUREAU

LAKEWAY RD

FAIRFIELD INN & SUITES ▼

CARIBBEAN COVE INDOOR WATER PARK

LAKEWAY RD

CCSD SCIENCE CENTER

CAMPBELL COUNTY RECREATION CENTER

59

To Edgerton and Casper

ENZI DR
SHOSHONE AVE

S 4-J RD

To Wright and Douglas ↘

SOUTHERN DR

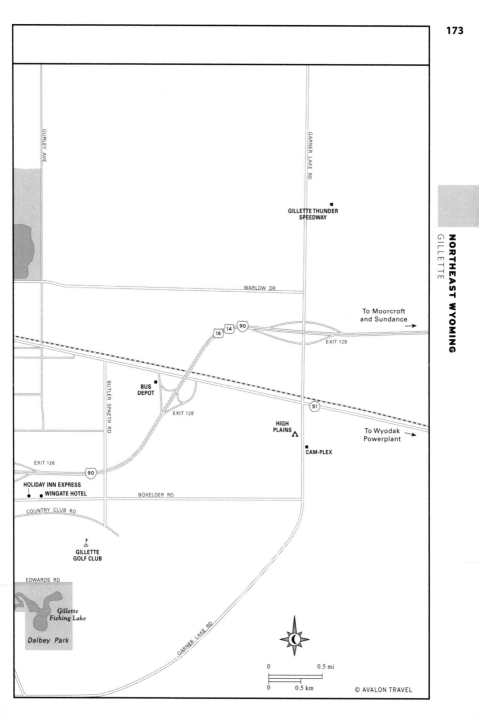

The Johnson County War

With lush grasslands and rich river valleys ideal for grazing animals, Powder River country was long a popular area for both Native Americans and early homesteaders. The battles between the Indians and settlers for this territory are well documented. But the confrontations among white settlers were equally contentious, none more so than the Johnson County War.

Between 1875 and 1884, hundreds of thousands of cattle were brought to or through the Powder River Basin. Cattle barons were quick to realize that the rich, wide-open grasslands were perfect to sustain their herds. By the late 1870s and early 1880s, homesteaders were competing with the cattle barons for the land. Numerous settlers moved in and began putting up fences, plowing land, and raising their livestock. Also during this time, there was further competition from smaller cattlemen known as rustlers, who also appropriated land, and at times stray cattle, for their herds.

In 1892, the Wyoming Stock Growers Association, made up of influential ranchers, planned to rid themselves of this ever-increasing problem in Johnson County. The plan was simple: Hire men who would terminate anyone infringing on their territory—meaning the settlers and the rustlers. They gathered a group of about 50 gunmen, with an offer of $5 per day and a $50 bonus for each man killed. The Regulators, as the gunmen were called, were provided a "dead list" that named about 70 men as their targets.

The men arrived in Casper on April 5 and planned to sweep the area from Casper to Buffalo. On arrival they cut the telegraph lines so news of what they were about to do would not reach other towns. They heard that over a dozen men on their list were at the KC Ranch. When they arrived, there were in fact only four men, two of whom were not on the list and were left unharmed. The two other men, Nate Champion and Nick Ray, were believed to have stolen a few stray calves during their time as rustlers. The Regulators set upon the house with their guns, killing Ray but unable to hit Champion, who remained holed up in the house. He wrote poignant notes about the attack, predicting he would never make it out alive. By early evening the gunmen had set fire to the house and fired on Champion, killing him as he ran from the flames. Two fellow rustlers had passed the house during the shootout, and word soon spread of the imminent onslaught.

The Regulators saw these initial kills as a success and set their sights on Buffalo. They pulled into the T-A Ranch, just 14 miles outside town, to rest briefly. Unbeknownst to them, however, their journey had ended.

The people of Buffalo and settlers outside town had heard about the shootout at the KC Ranch and made a call to arms. The townsmen were committed to defending themselves and exacting revenge. The 200 "Home Defenders" rode out of town and surrounded the Regulators at the T-A Ranch. The Regulators believed their death was imminent. However, one man escaped, and word reached Wyoming governor Amos W. Barber, who supported the cattle barons in their miscalculated efforts to rid the state of rustlers. In turn, Barber contacted two state senators, who were also supporters of the Wyoming Stock Growers Association, the bastion of the cattle barons, and they called on the president for help. President Harrison ordered the troops from Fort McKinney to calm the riot and arrest the invaders being held inside.

Ultimately, justice was never served to the Wyoming Stock Growers Association for their harebrained plan, nor to those who attempted to carry it out. The troops who arrested the Regulators did not turn them over to Johnson County, fearing retaliation by the townspeople. Instead they took them to Cheyenne to await trial. The prisoners were held in Cheyenne at the expense of Johnson County, and when Johnson County could no longer manage the expense of keeping them locked up, they were released on their own recognizance. The gunmen quickly fled or slipped under the radar. Due to the difficulty and expense involved, the court eventually threw the case out. The tensions between the ranchers and the rustlers would not dissipate for years.

Nob course also has a par 3 9-hole course ($8 adults, $2 children, $1 children with an adult).

FOOD

A great but tiny spot for breakfast, lunch, and sensational homemade pies, among other specialties, is **Lula Belle's Café** (101 N. Gillette Ave., 307/682-9798, 5am-3pm Mon.-Sat., 6am-2pm Sun., $5-12). Another popular spot for lunch and dinner is **Humphrey's Bar & Grill** (408 W. Juniper Ln., 307/682-0100, www. humphard.net, 11am-10pm Mon.-Thurs., 11am-11pm Fri.-Sat., 10am-9pm Sun., $9-23), which has an enormous menu and more than 50 beers on tap. After a significant expansion, **The Prime Rib Restaurant and Wine Cellar** (1205 S. Douglas Hwy., 307/682-2944, www. primeribgillette.com, 11am-10pm Mon.-Thurs., 11am-10:30pm Fri., 4pm-10:30pm Sat., 4pm-9:30pm Sun., $10-50) is a nice place for lunch or dinner, and a perfect choice for wine lovers.

For a hearty and sure-to-please meal, try the **Rib & Chop House** (2721 S. Douglas Hwy., 307/685-9200, www.ribandchophouse. com, 11am-9:30pm daily winter, expanded hours in summer, $13-38), which opened in late 2016. The restaurant has several large-screen TVs and an impressive variety of craft beers on tap. A custom broiler cooks the Montana-founded chain's renowned steaks at 1,800 degrees, but the menu is hefty, offering everything from seafood pasta and cedar plank salmon to ahi, pulled pork, and pot roast. A patio with five outdoor fire pits is open when weather permits.

The best and by far the best-known restaurant in Gillette is **The Chophouse** (113 S. Gillette Ave., 307/682-6805, www.gillette-chophouse.com, 11am-3pm and 5pm-10pm Mon.-Fri., 5pm-10pm Sat., $11-38). Open for lunch and dinner, it offers an excellent selection of steaks, seafood, pasta, and Italian specialties. This restaurant has a serious following for good reason.

ACCOMMODATIONS

Because of the influx of workers in the mining industry, Gillette has an abundance of accommodations, most of which are chain hotels. One notable exception is the friendly **Arrowhead Motel** (202 S. Emerson Ave., 307/686-0909, www.magnusonhotels.com, $44-79), which offers clean, basic rooms with microwaves, refrigerators, and a daily continental breakfast.

Among the most popular upscale chain hotels, appealing to business travelers and families alike, are the **Holiday Inn Express** (1908 Cliff Davis Dr., 307/686-9576, www.holidayinnexpress.com, $113-228), **Hampton Inn** (211 Decker Court, 307/686-2000, www.hamptoninn.com, $101-258), and the **Wingate Hotel** (1801 Cliff Davis Dr., 307/685-2700, www.wingatehotels.com, $79-249), all of which offer a multitude of plush amenities for road-weary travelers. The **Fairfield Inn & Suites Gillette** (2577 S. Douglas Hwy., 307/682-1717, www.marriott.com, $126-219) is the perfect place to stay if you want to spend time in the indoor water park.

CAMPING

If you are attending an event at Cam-Plex, campgrounds are available on-site. Otherwise, the interestingly named **Green Tree's Crazy Woman Campground** (1001 W. 2nd St., 307/682-3665, www.crazywoman-campground.com, year-round, $16-42), has 85 RV sites, tent sites, clean restrooms, and, especially important in the summer, shaded sites. The campground doesn't accept credit cards.

INFORMATION AND SERVICES

The **Gillette Convention and Visitors Center** (1810 S. Douglas Hwy., Bldg. A, 307/686-0040 or 800/544-6136, www.visit-gillettewright.com, 8am-7pm daily late May-early Oct., 9am-4pm Mon.-Fri. early Oct.-late May) is an excellent resource for the region, located in a log-sided building in the parking lot of the Flying J travel plaza.

Another source for business and relocation information for the Gillette area is the

Campbell County Chamber of Commerce (314 S. Gillette Ave., 307/682-3673, www.gillettechamber.com, 8am-5pm Mon.-Fri.).

The main branch of the **post office** (307/682-3727, 7am-5:30pm Mon.-Fri, 9am-1pm Sat.) in Gillette is located at 311 South Kendrick Avenue.

The wonderful **Campbell County Public Library** (307/682-3223, www.ccgov.net, 9am-9pm Mon.-Thurs., 9am-5pm Fri.-Sat. year-round, 1pm-5pm Sun. Sept.-May) is located at 2101 South 4J Road.

Campbell County Memorial Hospital (501 S. Burma Ave., 307/688-1000, www.ccmh.net) has a 24-hour emergency room. There is also a walk-in clinic on hospital grounds (8am-7pm Mon.-Fri., 8am-6pm Sat.-Sun. Last patients are taken one-half hour before closing.

Wash clothes at **Eastside Laundry** (1080 E. U.S. Hwy. 14/16, 307/685-2722, 7am-9pm daily). Another laundry with free Wi-Fi is **Surf'n Suds** (203 S. Richards Ave., 307/686-9266, 7am-9pm daily).

TRANSPORTATION
Getting There
The **Gillette-Campbell County Airport** (GCC, 2000 Airport Rd., 307/686-1042, www.iflygillette.com) offers daily flights to and from Denver and Salt Lake City. Carriers include **United** (800/864-8331, www.united.com) and **Delta** (800/221-1212, www.delta.com).

Bus service in the region is provided by **Powder River Transportation** (307/682-0960), **Trailways** (www.trailways.com), and **Greyhound.**

By car, Gillette is 70 miles east of Buffalo, 136 miles north of Casper, 250 miles east of Cody, 301 miles east of Yellowstone National Park, and 411 miles northeast of Jackson.

Getting Around
Car rentals are available in town from **Enterprise** (603 E. 2nd St.), **Avis** (2000 Airport Rd.), and **Rent-A-Wreck** (513 E. 2nd St., 307/363-4388, www.rentawreck.com).

Taxis are available through **City Cab** (307/685-1000), but note that only cash is accepted.

Devils Tower National Monument

Rising 1,267 feet above the Belle Fourche River, Devils Tower is an iconic rocky sentinel that was formed some 50-60 million years ago and has fascinated people for generations. The tower was instantly recognizable in the 1977 film *Close Encounters of the Third Kind,* where it bridged human and alien life forms. Composed of phonolite porphyry, which is a volcanic rock created by magma and similar to granite without the quartz, the massive columnar feature looks like an otherworldly cat-scratching post. Scientists refer to it as a laccolith, or igneous intrusion, meaning that magma welled up into a pocket of sedimentary rock, where it cooled and hardened. Over millions of years, the sedimentary rock was eroded away by natural forces, leaving the phenomenal tower.

The country's first national monument, Devils Tower is both a sacred site to many Native Americans and a climbing mecca for rock hounds from around the globe. The two groups have managed a hard-won, if somewhat delicate, respect for each other through a voluntary climbing closure in June every year, the month traditionally known for the greatest number of Native American ceremonies. Climbers are strongly encouraged to refrain from climbing or hiking around the tower during the closure.

Still, Devils Tower is a recreational hot spot with several climbing routes for beginners and experts alike, plus some eight miles of hiking trails that circle the tower and wind through the nearby forests and meadows. Although it's not exactly conveniently located, 33 miles north of I-90, Devils Tower is the type of destination—like Mount Rushmore—that visitors are happy to go out of their way to see. Especially for those with an interest in hiking or climbing, it's easy to make a day of Devils Tower.

HISTORY

According to the National Park Service, more than 20 Native American tribes have historically attached cultural and spiritual significance to Devils Tower. Many of the tribes have sacred stories related to the tower, which often determined their name for the feature. The Arapaho, for example, called the tower Bear's Tipi. Similarly, the Cheyenne referred to it as Bear's Lodge, Bear's House, and Bear Peak. The Crow are known to refer to it as Bear's Lair, and the Lakota, who often had winter camps at the tower, called it a variety of names that include Bear Lodge, Grizzly Bear's Lodge, Ghost Mountain, and funnily enough, Penis Mountain. The Kiowa called the feature Tree Rock or Aloft on a Rock, and their origin story for the rock is among the best known. The story goes that the tribe was camped along the river, and seven sisters and their brother were playing when the brother turned into a bear, forcing the sisters to flee in search of safety. They climbed onto a rock and prayed for divine intervention. The rock began to grow skyward as the bear clawed at it to get to the sisters. Eventually, the girls were so high that they became the stars in the Big Dipper, and the tower still bears the scars of the bear's ferocious claws.

Many tribes conducted their most sacred events—including sun dances, sweat lodges, vision quests, and funerals—in the shadow of the tower, and they still do. In 2014, formal requests were made by both the Lakota and Oglala Sioux tribes to officially change the name of the monument from Devils Tower to Bear Lodge. Politicians in Wyoming rejected the request, but it could be changed by an Act of Congress or a Presidential Proclamation as early as April 2017.

First studied in 1875 by scientists H. Newton and Walter P. Jenney, who were commissioned to complete a geological survey of the area, the land surrounding the tower was wisely pulled from homestead acreage in 1892, and the government created Devils Tower Reserve the following year. President Theodore Roosevelt dedicated Devils Tower as the country's first national monument in 1906.

Although it is constantly overrun by

Devils Tower rises from the rolling hills like an otherworldly spire.

people, the area around and on top of the tower is ecologically significant. A colony of threatened black-tailed prairie dogs, who today occupy only 2 percent of their former habitat, make their home in the soft soils around the tower. Prairie falcons are known to nest in the cracks of the tower, requiring temporary closures to protect their young. Even on the grassy top of the tower, which is about the size of a football field, many wildlife species have been recorded, including chipmunks, mice, pack rats, and snakes.

Playing into the "because it's there" mentality, adventurers have long looked at ways to climb the soaring monolith. The first recorded ascent involved an oak peg ladder on July 4, 1893, by local ranchers Bill Rogers and W. A. Ripley, much to the delight of local revelers. Rogers's wife, Linnie, was the first woman to climb it (using the ladder) two years later on July 4, 1895. Both spectacles included crazy patriotic costumes, some 2,000 spectators, and live music. Although the ladder was no longer used after 1927, portions of it are still visible on the southwest side of the tower.

Technical rock climbers made the first ascent in 1937 in just four hours and 46 minutes, opening the tower to scores of climbers and dozens of firsts, including George Hopkins, who parachuted onto the summit in 1941 without an exit plan. Hopkins was stranded on the summit for six days before he was rescued. Since then, numerous routes have been established up the rock, and the fastest free climb of Devils Tower was in the 1980s by Todd Skinner, who made the climb without ropes or protection in an astonishing 18 minutes. Today's average climb for two people requires 4-6 hours up and 2 hours for the rappel down.

ENTERTAINMENT AND EVENTS

A tradition since the early 1880s, when settlers would descend on the area for a few days at a time to camp, picnic, and enjoy one another's company, the **Old Settler's Picnic**

was formalized as an annual event in 1932 on Father's Day weekend. The tradition continues today, after a 40-year lapse starting in the 1960s, with a large gathering of locals and visitors who come to enjoy food, Western music, cowboy poetry, kids' activities, and nondenominational church.

The annual **Cultural Program Series** changes from year to year but consistently offers fascinating lectures, entertainment, and living history displays over the course of the summer season (May 31-Aug. 31). For information on current happenings, contact the visitors center at the base of the tower (307/467-5283) or look online at the *Park News* newsletter (www.nps.gov).

The National Park Service hosts a fantastic spectrum of ranger-guided programs throughout the summer season. Offerings include a 1.3-mile guided **Tower Walk,** a variety of 20-minute **Interpretive Talks,** hour-long **Evening Programs,** and fantastic 90-minute **Full Moon Walks** that leave from the Joyner Ridge Trail parking lot. For information on any of the regularly scheduled events, contact the visitors center at the base of the tower (307/467-5283, www.nps.gov).

SPORTS AND RECREATION
★ Hiking and Climbing

Non-climbers interested in hiking will delight in the 1.3-mile trail around the base of the tower, plus the additional 7 miles of trails that meander through the nearby forest and meadows. Trail maps are available at the visitors center (307/467-5283, www.nps.gov). The 2.8-mile **Red Beds** trail winds through meadows and ponderosa pines, with a significant elevation gain, to the Joyner Ridge. Plan on two hours for the Red Beds hike.

Each year the tower is climbed by some 5,000 people who come to slip their fingers and toes into the hundreds of parallel cracks that divide the hexagonal columns of Devils Tower. Although the entire tower offers more than 200 routes with technical difficulties ranging 5.7-5.13, the **Durrance Route,** first pioneered in 1938, is the most common. A few bolted face climbs were established in the 1980s and 1990s, but new bolts and fixed pitons are prohibited. Only a handful of fatalities have occurred over the years, most of which happened on the descent.

All climbers must register at the **climber registration office** next to the visitors center; registration is free.

Climbing is strongly discouraged during the **June voluntary climbing closure,** advocated by the National Park Service out of respect for the many Native American cultures that recognize the tower as a sacred place.

CLIMBING GUIDES

For inexperienced climbers, hiring a licensed guide is the best way to approach the monolith. About seven companies are licensed to guide climbers on Devils Tower, a list that can change from year to year. Among them is **Above All Climbing School & Guides** (307/467-5267 or 888/314-5267, www.devilstowerclimbing.com, $400 for 1 climber, discounts for additional climbers). The school offers excellent instruction and guiding through play days, instruction days, and summit days. Combination specials that include lodging are available. Other guiding companies licensed to work in the monument include **Above Ouray Ice and Tower Rock Climbing Guides** (307/756-3516 or 888/345-9061, www.towerguides.com, $305 for 1 climber, $199 pp for 4 climbers, no credit cards) and **Sylvan Rocks Climbing School and Guide Service** (605/484-7585, www.sylvanrocks.com), which requires two-day courses ($685 for 1 climber, $490 pp for 3 climbers) to attempt the summit.

FOOD

No food is sold inside the monument, so you will have to bring your own supplies or eat before you arrive at Devils Tower. Restaurants and grocery-convenience stores are in Moorcroft (33 miles), Sundance (28 miles), and Hulett (9 miles).

ACCOMMODATIONS

Other than the Belle Fourche Campground, there are no accommodations inside the monument. The **Devils Tower Lodge Bed & Breakfast** (just north of the monument, 307/467-5267 or 888/314-5267, www.devilstowerlodge.com, $150-225) is owned by climbing guide Frank Sanders and offers comfortable rooms with unparalleled access to the tower.

CAMPING

The only campground in the monument proper is the 50-site **Belle Fourche Campground** (307/467-5283 ext. 635, $12), open in the summer season for tent campers and RVs on a first-come, first-served basis. Running water is available, but no RV hookups.

Just outside the monument, the **Devils Tower KOA** (60 Hwy. 110, 307/467-5395 or 800/562-5785, www.devilstowerkoa.com) has RV hookups ($48-57), cabins ($70-115), and tent sites ($29-37), plus an on-site heated swimming pool, snack bar, nightly hay rides, and free Wi-Fi. With the tower looming in the background, the nightly outdoor showing of *Close Encounters of the Third Kind,* filmed largely at the campground, is an unforgettable experience.

INFORMATION AND SERVICES

Vehicular **entrance fees** for seven days are $10. Pedestrians, bicyclists, and motorcyclists can enter for seven days for $5.

The National Park Service operates a great **visitors center** (307/467-5283, www.nps.gov, 8am-7pm daily Memorial Day-Labor Day, 9am-5pm daily Labor Day-Sept., 9am-4pm daily Oct.-Memorial Day) in the parking lot beneath the tower. Housed in a classic 1938 Park Service log cabin constructed by the Civilian Conservation Corps, the visitors center is staffed and has a number of interesting geological, natural, and cultural history exhibits.

While the number of visitors to the

monument continues to grow, it is generally not overcrowded. That changes in August, and be prepared to wait in long entrance lines in the weeks surrounding the Sturgis Motorcycle Rally in nearby Sturgis, South Dakota, each summer. If you don't like crowds, this is not the time to go to Devils Tower. To check on dates for the rally, visit www.sturgismotorcyclerally.com.

The nearest health care facilities are the **Hulett Medical Clinic** (122 Main St., Hulett, 307/467-5281), seven miles north of Devils Tower, and the **Moorcroft Clinic** (101 W. Crook St., Moorcroft, 307/756-3414), 33 miles south of Devils Tower. The nearest hospital to treat trauma is **Campbell County Memorial Hospital** (501 S. Burma Ave., Gillette, 307/688-1000, www.ccmh.net), 61 miles away in Gillette.

The speed limit in the monument is 25 mph. Each year, dozens of wild animals are hit and killed by cars, and reduced speed can positively impact the number of fatalities.

Do not feed the wildlife. Prairie dogs are especially sensitive and can die from eating any human food.

TRANSPORTATION

By car, **Devils Tower National Monument** (Hwy. 110, 307/467-5283, www.nps.gov, $10 1-7-day vehicle pass, $5 motorcycle and individual hiker or bicyclist pass) is 33 miles northeast of the I-90 exit at Moorcroft and 27 miles northwest of Sundance. The monument is 61 miles northeast of Gillette, 131 miles northeast of Buffalo, 309 miles east of Cody, and 363 miles east of Yellowstone National Park.

The nearest commercial airports are located in Gillette (61 miles southwest) and Rapid City, South Dakota (120 miles east).

Southern Wyoming

Look for ★ to find recommended sights, activities, dining, and lodging.

Highlights

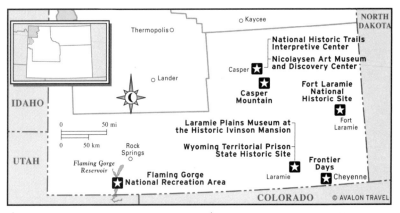

★ **Nicolaysen Art Museum and Discovery Center:** With an impressive collection of more than 6,000 works by contemporary artists, The Nic is a phenomenal tribute to the current art scene in the West (page 189).

★ **National Historic Trails Interpretive Center:** Among the best museums in the state, this place gives visitors a sense of pioneer life on many of the historic trails that crisscross the state (page 189).

★ **Casper Mountain:** The skiing, hiking, camping, and fascinating local folklore give this area its own magical identity (page 190).

★ **Laramie Plains Museum at the Historic Ivinson Mansion:** This museum is a labor of love for the people who operate it and a gift to visitors (page 199).

★ **Wyoming Territorial Prison State Historic Site:** Part agriculture exhibit, part broom factory, and part Old West town, this is also the best old prison in the West (page 199).

★ **Fort Laramie National Historic Site:** This was a fur trading fort, a military outpost, and an important witness to the dramatic conflicts and sweeping change of the 19th century in the American West (page 209).

★ **Frontier Days:** The big daddy of Wyoming rodeos draws thousands of eager spectators to its big-name country music concerts, carnival, parades, and world-class professional rodeo (page 210).

★ **Flaming Gorge National Recreation Area:** Fed by the Green River, this natural playground composed of cliffs and Technicolor desert rock formations surrounds a 91-mile-long reservoir (page 219).

An enormous expanse of diverse terrain that includes everything from vast prairie and rugged mountain peaks to red desert and windblown dunes, southern Wyoming in many ways defines the state.

It has celebrated events, an important intellectual culture, and a wealth of historic sites. This region is also at the heart and soul of Wyoming's agricultural tradition, both past and present. But interestingly, the lower half of the state is less traveled *to* and more often traveled *through*.

With I-80 in the far south and a series of smaller roads bisecting the landscape east-west and north-south, it seems this section of Wyoming is thick with travelers on their way someplace else, which has been true for more than a century. Most of the West's great travel routes—the Oregon Trail, the Overland Trail, the Bozeman Trail, and eventually the Northern Pacific Railway—cut through this dramatically shifting landscape, exposing travelers, if only briefly, to the diversity of terrain.

In the southeast corner around Cheyenne—the state's capital, known for its festive, even rowdy, rodeo, called Frontier Days—the landscape shifts, greens, and begins to look more like Colorado. Just north and west of Cheyenne, Laramie presents an interesting blend of university counterculture and age-old Western tradition in a literary-meets-cowboy dance. Beyond town, three impressive mountain ranges offer prime climbing opportunities, then give way to the plains and prairies where sheep and cattle rather than trees dot the horizon. Farther north on I-25, the frontier town of Casper is experiencing a renaissance as a fishing and outdoor-loving town.

Heading west on I-80, the landscape is loaded with minerals, and the entire area is rich with mining history, dinosaur fossils, and the stark beauty of the Flaming Gorge National Recreation Area. There are wildlife refuges, endless spots to wet a line, and little ranching communities and outposts that give southern Wyoming its flavor.

Previous: Sweetwater County; Wyoming State Capitol in Cheyenne. **Above:** windmills and cattle.

Southern Wyoming

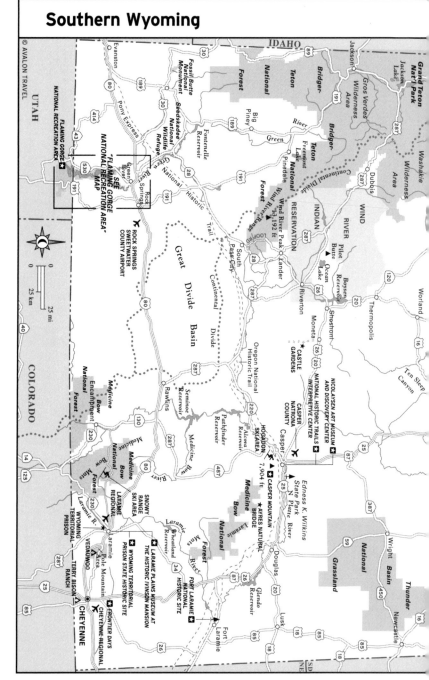

© AVALON TRAVEL

HISTORY

Southern Wyoming is a land of corridors, home to the Oregon, Mormon, California, Cherokee, and Overland Trails. The Pony Express crossed through here, as did the nation's first transcontinental railroad and the first transcontinental automobile route. It makes sense that early Wyoming was defined not by settlers so much as by travelers.

What initially attracted Native Americans to this region also attracted traders, trappers, and immigrants. The North Platte and Sweetwater Rivers created natural passageways across the land. They provided water and food for both men and livestock and kept the grasslands well irrigated. Buffalo grazed across the grassy plains with Indians always in close pursuit. The Shoshone, Arapaho, Cheyenne, and Sioux Indians all hunted in the region.

Fur trappers, known as the Astorians, were the first nonnatives to see South Pass. They stumbled on this crossing of the Continental Divide during their return trip east to St. Louis. It was later found again by Thomas Fitzpatrick in 1824 and subsequently used by many trappers, traders, and mountain men on their journeys west. By the 1840s there were marked trails that followed rivers through South Pass. But the movement into Wyoming really picked up after 1843, when a large wagon train left Missouri and arrived in Washington six months later. Hundreds of thousands of immigrants, following their "manifest destiny" and in search of gold, religious freedom, or just a better life—passed through Wyoming over the Oregon Trail. Today Wyoming is home to the longest unchanged portion of the Oregon Trail.

Fort Laramie in the east and Fort Bridger in the west became important way stations, allowing travelers to stock up on food and supplies, repair wagons, trade goods, and even swap their tired livestock for fresh animals. Troops were stationed in the forts to provide protection from Native Americans.

Initially, the Indians did little to prevent the travelers from crossing the land they used.

Realizing that the wagons were just moving through with no intention of staying, the migrants were not viewed as a threat. But it soon became evident that the migration was taking a toll on the land as well as their way of life. The grass that sustained the buffalo was being destroyed by wagons and consumed by livestock. The buffalo themselves were being killed to make way for cattle grazing land and railroad tracks. The Indians were not ready to give up their traditional way of life; confrontations ensued, and by the 1860s military stations were established along the trail. By the time the transcontinental railroad entered Wyoming, it was evident that the land no longer belonged to the Indians.

In the early 1860s, stagecoaches, freight, and mail wagons ran along the Overland Trail, which loosely followed the Cherokee Trail of 1848. When the railroad arrived in Wyoming in 1867, it also followed this route. The railroad changed Americans' perception of Wyoming—rather than a passageway, it had become a destination. It no longer took months, only days to arrive in Wyoming. It was easier to export goods from the territory and target destinations that were farther away. With its prime grazing land and natural resources, Wyoming began to attract settlers.

Beginning in 1867, tent cities sprang up overnight wherever railroad crews laid tracks. These small "hell on wheels" towns consisted of ramshackle houses, brothels, saloons, and gambling tents. Cheyenne, Laramie, Carbon, and Rock Springs were all initially settled in this manner. As the tracks moved west, the makeshift towns would often close up and follow suit. However, the more innovative entrepreneurs found other ways to remain relevant or linked to the railroad business, and they prospered. The southern part of the state housed the first five original counties of the Wyoming Territory, which extended all the way from Colorado to Montana.

The first makeshift railroad town to be settled was Cheyenne in July 1867. Initially a boisterous, mayhem-filled tent city, it soon began to blossom. By November it had 4,000 residents and was dubbed the "magic city" for its large population boom. Fort D. A. Russell was established nearby, and the military presence helped to settle things down. Cheyenne became an important shipping center, exporting cattle and supplies to the East and importing the latest fashions and desirables. Thanks to the cattle barons, by the 1880s Cheyenne was considered one of the wealthiest cities per capita in the world.

Laramie became a permanent town when the Union Pacific Railroad decided to locate its division headquarters there. Like Cheyenne, it had wild and rowdy days, but by 1887 Wyoming University was established, opening its enrollment to both women and men. Laramie went on to hold the distinct honor of having the first women voters in the country.

Like most of these towns in southern Wyoming, Laramie's future was intrinsically tied to the railroad, and when the Union Pacific established a rolling mill in town, it immediately brought with it new improvements. Union Pacific was awarded mineral rights to tracts of land along the railroad, and this also shaped the character of southern Wyoming. When coal was discovered at Carbon, miners from England and Finland came to work the mines, as well as those in Rock Springs and Evanston. Since Union Pacific coal sold at cheaper prices (and the company could ship it at almost no cost), it eventually monopolized the industry, and Rock Springs became the biggest coal producer in the West.

A mixture of railroad and natural resources also led to the establishment of Casper. Originally it was set up as a station for the Fremont, Elkhorn and Missouri Valley Railroad, with its first residents creating a town site in 1888. After a relatively common and lawless beginning, Casper prospered with the discovery of oil. When the first oil well was drilled in 1887, an onslaught of land speculators and other investors arrived, looking to get rich. When the Salt Creek Oil Field was established 40 miles north of Casper, the town

responded by building a refinery and went on to become a booming town. Casper's wealth peaked in the 1920s and crashed heavily with the rest of the country in 1929. Like cities all across the West, Casper seemed destined to repeat this boom-and-bust cycle through the rest of the 20th century. The 21st century has brought another natural resource boom in the form of rehabbed rivers and hungry trout that appeal to avid anglers and lovers of the outdoors.

Coal, oil, and natural gas are still important sources of income for Wyoming. But Casper, like many of Wyoming's towns, has realized the need to diversify in order to protect its economy. The tourism industry has grown in this part of the state, and if you can take the time to veer off I-80, which runs parallel to the Union Pacific transcontinental route, you will find yourself crossing century-old trails, exploring abandoned trading posts, and experiencing traditions that bring southern Wyoming's unique history to life.

PLANNING YOUR TIME

Cheyenne, Casper, and Laramie are all sizable cities for Wyoming and could occupy visitors for at least a full day each. In Cheyenne, a number of museums are worth seeing, including the **Wyoming State Museum** and the **Frontier Days Old West Museum,** among others. In this part of the state, summer is the most popular time to travel thanks to sunny, warm days and easy road conditions. Bear in mind, however, that Cheyenne's population explodes during **Frontier Days,** the second half of July, and accommodations can be tough to find.

In Laramie, there are more museums including the outstanding **Wyoming Territorial Prison,** plenty of opportunities to get out and experience some of Wyoming's most beautiful landscapes, and a fascinating university culture that brings with it abundant entertainment and a lively downtown with some darn good eateries. Laramie can be a bit windy and bleak, even frigid, in winter, but the university culture keeps things lively with concerts, lectures, sporting events, and other happenings. In Casper, the state's second-largest city after Cheyenne, there is a growing interest in the region's fishing on the **North Platte River** and plenty of year-round recreational opportunities in the nearby **Laramie Mountains, Medicine Bow National Forest,** and **Casper Mountain.**

Southwest Wyoming, by contrast, is a series of small towns experiencing the boom-and-bust of energy extraction and a vast swath of starkly beautiful land primed for recreation. There are indeed a number of museums in the areas of Green River and Rock Springs, but the vast majority of people who come to spend any time in this region come for the outdoors, which can be pleasant mid-spring-late fall. Summer can be hot, but the **Flaming Gorge National Recreation Area** is a gateway to the dramatic Green River country and offers plenty of places and ways to cool down.

Casper

A sprawling town near the center of the state, in many ways Casper (population 59,628, elevation 5,123 feet) has long been a hub for people traveling the region, first the Native Americans and later the settlers making use of the multiple pioneer trails in the region. Casper's booms and busts came with the trails, the railroad, and eventually oil and gas exploration. Its reputation as a rough-and-tumble town is well earned, and one can't help but chuckle to think of Butte, Montana's minor league baseball team, the Copper Kings, ditching one of the roughest towns in the West to become the Casper Ghosts (the team left Casper in 2011 for Colorado, where members now play as the Grand Junction Rockies, an affiliate of the Denver Rockies.)

Although Casper is indeed industrial, rather large, and perhaps overly spread across the landscape, the town is experiencing something of a renaissance and solid population growth in recent years. In addition to a world-class contemporary art museum, the beautiful North Platte River, once hopelessly polluted, has been cleaned up and is earning a reputation as one of the best fisheries in the West. The river boasts more than 4,000 fish per mile on most stretches, including the renowned 5.5-mile "Miracle Mile" and the blue-ribbon tailwaters of the "Grey Reef." There is a wealth of incredible outdoor opportunities just outside town at the city's unofficial year-round playground, Casper Mountain. In the heart of town, the Platte River Trails offer nearly 10 miles of walking and biking trails alongside the river, an ideal spot to stretch your legs or take your pooch for a stroll and a dip. Casper is indeed worth a visit; you may well be surprised by all that is here.

SIGHTS

History lovers will delight in the opportunity to walk around Casper at night with **Casper Theater Company Tours** (307/267-7243, www.caspertheatercompany.net, $25 pp, summer-fall). Visitors are shown around town by costume-clad actors playing the roles of long-gone citizens who lived during Casper's 1890-1920 heyday. Over the course of about an hour, you'll learn about murders, hangings, and love triangles. You could also opt for a guided ghost tour of Casper's most haunted buildings, or the Casper Sand Bar, site of a former tent city known as the center of Casper's debauchery and gruesome crime. In the fall, a tour of the cemetery brings to light fascinating stories about the characters who shaped Casper. Under the leadership of artistic director Donna Fisher, the talented Casper Theater actors give visitors an entertaining way to get a feeling for the town's wild and woolly past.

Casper

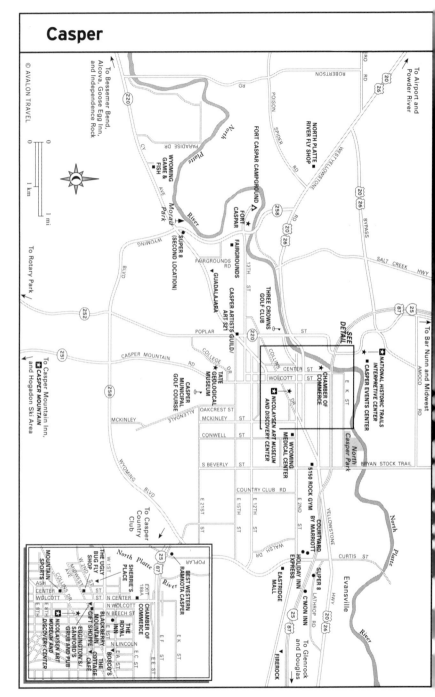

© AVALON TRAVEL

0 — 1 km
0 — 1 mi

To Bessemer Bend,
Alcova, Goose Egg Inn,
and Independence Rock

To Airport and
Powder River

ROBERTSON

POISON

SPIDER RD

WEST YELLOWSTONE RD

20 26

20 26

BYPASS

SALT CREEK HWY

NORTH PLATTE
RIVER FLY SHOP ■

FORT CASPAR CAMPGROUND △

FORT
CASPAR ★

258

20 26

North Platte River

PARADISE DR

WYOMING
GAME &
FISH ■

Morad Park

220

CY

WYOMING BLVD

To Rotary Park

252

251

To Casper Mountain Inn,
and Hogadon Ski Area

CASPER MOUNTAIN RD

WYOMING BLVD

McKINLEY

258

SUPER 8
(SECOND LOCATION) ■

FAIRGROUNDS ■

FAIRGROUNDS RD

13TH

CASPER ARTISTS GUILD/
ART 321

GUADALAJARA ▼

POPLAR

220

COLLEGE DR

ALLENDALE

TATE
GEOLOGICAL
MUSEUM ★

CASPER
MUNICIPAL
GOLF COURSE

OAKCREST ST

McKINLEY ST

CONWELL ST

S BEVERLY ST

E 21ST ST

To Casper
Country
Club

THREE
CROWNS
GOLF CLUB

COLLINS ST

CENTER ST

WOLCOTT

CHAMBER OF
COMMERCE ★

★ NICOLAYSEN ART MUSEUM
AND DISCOVERY CENTER

WYOMING
MEDICAL CENTER ■

COUNTRY CLUB RD

E 15TH ST

E 12TH ST

WALSH DR

BRYAN STOCK TRAIL

E 2ND ST

■ 5150 ROCK GYM

COURTYARD
BY MARRIOTT ●

HOLIDAY INN
EXPRESS ●

SUPER 8 ●

C'MON INN ●

25
87

20 26

EASTRIDGE
MALL

LATHROP RD

YELLOWSTONE

CURTIS ST

Evansville

North Platte River

To Glenrock
and Douglas

FIREROCK

SEE
DETAIL

★ NATIONAL HISTORIC TRAILS
INTERPRETIVE CENTER

■ CASPER EVENTS CENTER

North Casper Park

E K ST

AMOCO RD

25

87

To Bar Nunn and Midwest

DETAIL (inset):

MOUNTAIN
SPORTS ■

THE UGLY
BUG FLY
SHOP ■

SHERRIE'S PLACE ●

North Platte River

W 1ST

COLLINS DR

W 2ND

MIDWEST AVE

ASH

CENTER
WOLCOTT

E 8TH

N CENTER ST

N WOLCOTT ST

N BEECH ST

E 1ST ST

E 2ND ST

POPLAR

25
87

EXIT
188A

BEST WESTERN
RAMKOTA CASPER

CHAMBER OF
COMMERCE ★

★ NICOLAYSEN ART
MUSEUM AND
DISCOVERY CENTER

BLACKBERRY
MOUNTAIN
GIFT SHOP ●

EGGINGTON'S ●

SANFORD'S
GRUB AND PUB ●

THE
ROYAL
INN ●

BOSCO'S ●

THE
COTTAGE
CAFE ●

N LINCOLN

N DURBIN

E C ST

E D ST

E E ST

E F ST

E K ST

★ Nicolaysen Art Museum and Discovery Center

The museum around which Casper revolves is the impressive **Nicolaysen Art Museum and Discovery Center** (400 E. Collins Dr., 307/235-5247, www.thenic.org, 10am-5pm Tues.-Sat., noon-4pm Sun., $5 adults, $3 children 5-17, free on Sun.). Focusing solely on work by contemporary artists in the Rocky Mountains, The Nic, as it is known locally, has a permanent collection of more than 6,000 works that includes paintings, sculpture, textiles, drawings, photos, and prints; it features the region's most important traveling exhibitions related to their mission. The Discovery Center offers hands-on art activities for visitors of all ages along with a lineup of classes and special programs. The museum is very invested in the Casper community and often serves as host to some favorite local events. In summer the **Casper Downtown Farmers Market** (5pm-7:30pm Tues. mid-July-mid-Sept.) is held on the museum grounds, and on Wednesday evenings during summer the museum hosts **Wednesday Night Live,** a series of musical, visual, and edible outdoor events. There's also a wonderful art show and sale in early November.

Tate Geological Museum

A great little free museum associated with Casper College since 1980 is the **Tate Geological Museum** (125 College Dr., 307/268-2447, www.caspercollege.edu/tate, 9am-5pm Mon.-Fri., 10am-4pm Sat., free), which houses nearly 3,000 fossil and mineral specimens. The museum is also home to "Dee," an 11,600-year-old Columbian mammoth (the oldest and largest mounted specimen in the world) who was likely 65 or 70 years old when he died. The collection includes dinosaur bones and fossilized footprints found in Wyoming. A fossil prep lab allows visitors to watch and ask questions of working paleontologists, and an interactive "Dino Den" will delight kids.

Fort Caspar

Positioned at a critical river crossing for the

Oregon, Mormon, Pioneer, California, and Pony Express Trails, **Fort Caspar** (4001 Ft. Caspar Rd., 307/235-8462, www.fortcaspar-wyoming.com, museum 8am-5pm and fort buildings 8:30am-4:30pm daily May-Sept., museum 8am-5pm Tues.-Sat. Oct.-Apr., $3 adults, $2 children 13-18 May-Sept., $1.50 adults, $1 children Oct.-Apr., always free for children under 13) was built in 1862 to protect travelers through the area and was occupied by the military until 1867. When the Army decommissioned the site and took as many of the materials as they could with them to build Fort Fetterman in 1867, Native Americans burned what remained to the ground. In 1936, a Works Progress Administration crew rebuilt several of the buildings on the original site. The fort and museum are operated by the City of Casper.

Exhibits at the fort include reconstructions of the Mormon Ferry, Guinard Bridge, and Richard Bridge that predated the fort, as well as fort history, pioneer trail history, and other agricultural, oil, and gas exhibits related to the region. The museum also hosts interesting traveling exhibitions.

★ National Historic Trails Interpretive Center

Among the state's most renowned museums, the **National Historic Trails Interpretive Center** (1501 N. Poplar St., 307/261-7700, www.blm.gov, 8am-5pm Tues.-Sun. late May-early Sept., 9am-4:30pm Tues.-Sat. early Sept.-late May, $6 adults, $5 seniors 62 and over, $4 students, free for 15 and under) tells the gritty story of Manifest Destiny and westward expansion on the historic pioneer trails through interactive exhibits and multimedia presentations. The museum's exhibits are both indoors and out, and they succeed in giving visitors a real sense of what day-to-day life was like for the early pioneers. The museum's seven distinct galleries are dedicated to four of the trails that cut through the region, as well as Native Americans, mountain men, explorers, and the trails today. There's even a virtual river crossing experience. Wyoming's BLM manages more than 340 miles (60 percent) of the Oregon, California, Mormon, Pioneer, and Pony Express Trails in the state, and this museum celebrates both the heritage of those trails and the remarkable ability to still see and experience them in much the same way. For information on all of Wyoming's trails, their rich history, and ways to experience them, visit www.wyoshpo.state.wy.us/trailsdemo.

Ayres Natural Bridge

Some 50 miles southeast of Casper and 10 miles west of Douglas is one of Wyoming's earliest tourist attractions, **Ayres Natural Bridge** (208 Natural Bridge Rd., 307/358-3532, 8am-8pm daily Apr.-Oct., free), a natural arch where LaPrele Creek worked its way through a 100-foot-long, 50-foot-high solid rock wall over the centuries. It is set in a lovely 22-acre park. The Native Americans of the region thought of the natural bridge as a sinister place because of a tale about a young brave being struck by lightning in the canyon. The legend developed until it was widely believed among the Indians that an evil spirit lived beneath the bridge. Travelers on the Mormon Trail, which crossed the creek two miles north of the site, discovered the bridge and the legend, and often visited the area to escape the Native Americans.

There are 12 beautiful campsites within the park boundaries; pets are not allowed in the park.

★ Casper Mountain

When Casper residents are eager to flee the city, particularly in the heat of summer, they head to **Casper Mountain,** an alpine oasis just minutes from town. In addition to the popular **Hogadon Ski Area,** several campgrounds and parks, and miles of beautiful, forested hiking and biking trails, Casper Mountain is also rich with history and culture.

An early settler from Missouri, Elizabeth "Neal" Forsling, fled a horrible marriage with her two young daughters to homestead on the top of Casper Mountain in the 1920s. An artist and writer, Forsling was strong, independent, and loved the mountain with all of her being. She fell in love with and married a local rancher, Jim, who joined her in her happy life on the mountaintop, but when he froze to death at the age of 38 while skiing home from town with supplies, Neal dedicated herself even more to the land on which she lived. She painted and

Casper Mountain provides a bird's-eye view of the city.

wrote stories about the spirits, trolls, fairies, and other beings that lived on Casper Mountain. She hosted a summer solstice party in 1930 that would become the Mid-Summer's Eve Celebration that continues today. Singlehandedly, Neal Forsling created a mythical culture on the mountain that persists today.

Forsling donated her land and cabin to Natrona County in 1973. She died a few years later, and the county turned her home into a wonderful museum named for the book of stories she created about the mountain: The **Crimson Dawn Museum** (1620 Crimson Dawn Rd., 307/235-1303, museum 10am-7pm Sat.-Sun. June-Sept., park 8am-8pm daily June-Sept.) is at the center of the Mid-Summer's Eve Celebration.

ENTERTAINMENT AND EVENTS
Theater

Performing in an intimate theater-in-the-round, Casper's **Stage III Community Theatre** (900 N. Center St., 307/234-0946, www.stageiiitheatre.org) is an entirely volunteer organization that produces six productions annually between September and June. The company has been entertaining Casper since 1980, with evening and matinee offerings ranging from classic dramas to mysteries and comedies.

Founded in 2014, **Casper Theater Company** (735 Cy Ave., 307/267-7243, www.caspertheatercompany.net) is a semi-professional theater company offering four productions each season, plus a marvelous variety of living-history tours throughout summer and fall focusing on Casper's wild and ignominious heyday.

Rodeos

Rodeo is serious business in this part of the state—or anywhere in Wyoming, for that matter. One of the biggest is the **College National Finals Rodeo** (509/529-4402, www.cnfr.com), held annually at the Casper Events Center (800/442-2256) in mid-June.

More than 400 cowboys and cowgirls from 100 universities and colleges compete for champion status in saddle bronc riding, bareback riding, bull riding, tie-down roping, steer wrestling, team roping, barrel racing, breakaway roping, and goat tying.

Another big rodeo in Casper is the **PRCA Rodeo** held annually in conjunction with the **Central Wyoming Fair** (1700 Fairgrounds Rd., 307/235-5775 or 888/225-2600, www.centralwyomingfair.com) in mid-July. The fair has been in operation since 1904 and comes with all the hoopla and community spirit you'd expect.

Mid-Summer's Eve Celebration

Held each year on June 21, the summer solstice, the **Mid-Summer's Eve Celebration** (Crimson Dawn Park, 1620 Crimson Dawn Rd., 307/235-9311) is a unique event that showcases the history and spirit of Casper. The stories around this event, started in 1930 by Casper Mountain resident, artist, and author Neal Forsling, are considered by some to be Wyoming's only folklore. The event starts with a storytelling walk through the forest, amid a network of rock shrines, and culminates with a bonfire that everyone is invited to throw red dirt into, in hopes of seeing their fondest wish granted. It is a charming celebration of the witches, spirits, and trolls said to inhabit the mountain.

Beartrap Summer Festival

Undoubtedly one of the best outdoor music festivals in the region, the **Beartrap Summer Festival** (307/266-5252, www.beartrapsummerfestival.com) brings Casper Mountain to life with bluegrass music the first weekend in August. The event hosts big-name bands and musicians for two days mid-morning-dusk. Rounding out the festival are musical workshops, an arts and crafts marketplace, an open-air food court, and supervised children's activities. Pets are welcome on a leash. Discounted tickets can be purchased in advance by phone.

SHOPPING

A central shopping locale for much of the region, Casper has every sort of shopping imaginable, from big malls and shopping centers to box stores and downtown boutiques. The largest facility in the region by far is the **Eastridge Mall** (601 SE Wyoming Blvd., 307/265-9392, www.shopeastridge.com), anchored by Target, Best Buy, Macy's, Bed Bath and Beyond, Sears, Dick's Sporting Goods, and J. C. Penney.

There are some smaller stores too that should not be missed. **Blackberry Mountain Gift Shop** (251 S. Center St., 307/234-6605, www.bbmgs.com, 10am-5pm Tues.-Fri., 10am-2pm Sat.) is a quirky little place with everything from home decor and seasonal decorations to candles, jewelry, and incredible china. A terrific place to find work by local artists is the **Casper Artists Guild/ Art 321** (321 W. Midwest Ave., 307/265-2655, www.casperartguild.com, 10am-4pm Tues.-Sat.), which hosts regular shows in a variety of media as well as active workshops for artists (including regular Sunday afternoon painting sessions). The gift shop is an excellent place to find one-of-a-kind works by local artists.

For a sweet tooth or an espresso with a side of chocolate, the best spot in Casper is **Donells Candies** (201 E. 2nd St., 307/234-6283, www.donellschocolates.com, 9am-5:30pm Mon.-Fri., 9am-5pm Sat., 11am-4pm Sun.), which has been churning out delectable handmade chocolates, savory nuts, and all flavors of popcorn since 1956. The store is still owned and operated by the founding family, and with brisk Internet sales it has found admirers the world over. The Donells expanded the downtown store and added an espresso bar where candy lovers can also order hand-dipped ice cream.

SPORTS AND RECREATION
Hiking and Biking

In addition to the abundance of hiking and biking trails just outside the city in places like Casper Mountain, there are a number of green trails within city limits. The **Platte River Trails** (www.platterivertrails.com) wind nearly 10 miles along the river's edge and can be accessed in a number of parks, including **Morad Park** and **Casper Whitewater Park,** as well as at the Holiday Inn on the River. **Rotary Park,** just south of town at the base of Casper Mountain, is home to the beloved Garden Creek Falls and 4.5-mile **Bridle Trail,** which climbs 1,200 feet and offers views of the falls and the city below.

Just six miles east of town on Highway 252, **Edness K. Wilkins State Park** (S. Poplar St., 307/577-5150, http://wyoparks.state.wy.us, $6 nonresidents) is a serene spot with giant cottonwoods, swimmable river access, ideal picnic spots, fishing, boat access, and a playground. There are also 2.8 miles of paved trails for walkers, and birders will delight in the more than 40 species that can be counted in a single day in the park.

Casper Mountain is the best place for serious hiking and biking. Among the many popular trails in the area is the unique **Lee McCune Braille Trail** for both sighted and visually impaired hikers.

Avid bikers without wheels can rent great mountain bikes from **Mountain Sports** (543 S. Center St., 307/266-1136, www.caspermtnsports.com, 9am-6pm Mon.-Sat., 11am-4pm Sun.).

Skiing

Casper's easy access to the mountains makes this town an ideal winter getaway. Just 15 minutes from town is **Hogadon Ski Area** (2500 W. Hogadon Rd., Casper Mountain, 307/235-8499, www.hogadon.net, 9am-4pm Wed.-Sun., full-day $42 adults, $37 youth, half-day $34 adults and youth, free for seniors 70 and over), a small, family-friendly mountain that offers 20 percent beginner terrain and 40 percent each intermediate and advanced. There are 27 trails and two lifts, and a snowboard terrain park for more adventurous riders. Group and private lessons are available, as are rentals.

For Nordic skiers, the **Casper Mountain**

Trails Center (9301 S. Circle Dr. on Casper Mountain, 307/237-5014 or 307/259-0958, www.natronacounty-wy.gov, sunrise-10pm daily, $10 day pass) offers 42 kilometers of groomed trails for both classical and skate skiers, in addition to a 1.2-kilometer lighted loop. There are an additional 30 miles of backcountry and snowshoe trails in the area as well.

For equipment rentals for just about any sport in any season, head to **Mountain Sports** (543 S. Center St., 307/266-1136, www. caspermtnsports.com, 9am-6pm Mon.-Sat., 11am-4pm Sun.).

Rock Climbing

As Casper's status among outdoor junkies continues to climb, rock climbing is another of the region's well-known offerings. **Fremont Canyon** (www.fremontcanyon. com) has world-class granite climbing for people of all ability levels (5.6-5.13d in difficulty), with cliffs ranging 40-400-plus feet. The area is known for its steep crack climbs but does offer some sport climbing and bouldering problems. To get to the canyon, which overlooks Alcova Reservoir, head south from Casper on Highway 220 to the town of Alcova; the canyon is 10 miles farther south, accessed by the Fremont Canyon Bridge.

To practice or get information on other area climbs, visit Casper's in-town climbing gym, **5150 Rock Gym** (408 N. Beverly St., 307/337-2166, www.5150rockgym.com, 2pm-9pm Mon.-Sat., $8 day use, $2 gear rental).

Fishing

Fishing in the cold waters of the North Platte River is something of a comeback story. Around the turn of the 20th century, the North Platte was known as one of the great trout fisheries of the West; as an example, a celebration in Saratoga in 1907, known as the Railroad Days Celebration and Fish Fry, required more than 3,000 fish to be caught in two days to feed visitors. The river was thick with trout, and anglers flocked to the area to catch them. As industrialization spread across the country, feedlots and oil refineries increasingly dotted the landscape and polluted the North Platte until it was nearly uninhabitable. Only since 1997 have sweeping measures been taken to restore the river, an effort that has, by all accounts, been enormously successful. In fact, *American Angler* magazine voted the Grey Reef section of the North Platte River the number one big fishery in the world in 2005. The area is widely considered the best rainbow trout tailwater in the Lower 48. The largest trout caught in the North Platte, in the fabled Grey Reef section, was a 22-pound brown trout. Average rainbows in this river weigh upwards of five pounds and measure 16 to 20 inches.

Today, in part because of its shallow depth and slow current, the river can be fished for hundreds of miles, and anglers can expect to see the noses of rainbows, browns, Snake River cutthroats, walleye, and the occasional cutbow, a rainbow-cutthroat hybrid.

Casper offers an abundance of fly shops and guides. A good place to start for a license and regulations is **Wyoming Game and Fish** (3030 Energy Ln., Ste. 100, 307/473-3400, www.wgfd.wyo.gov). For gear or guided trips, contact the **Ugly Bug Fly Shop** (240 S. Center St., 307/234-6905, www.crazyrainbow. net, 9am-5:30pm Mon.-Fri., 8am-4pm Sat.), which has full-day ($425/boat) and half-day ($325/boat) guided fly-fishing trips. A full-day guided float trip on the Miracle Mile is $475 per boat. Discounts are available in the off-season (Nov.-Mar.), when the weather can be lousy but the fishing great. The **North Platte River Fly Shop** (7400 Hwy. 220, 307/237-5997 or 307/277-6282, www.wyomingflyfishing.com, 9am-4pm Mon.-Fri., 9am-2pm Sat.) offers all-day guided trips in boats ($425 for 2 anglers) or wade fishing ($425 for 2 anglers). Single anglers and off-season trips are discounted.

Golf

Casper has 90 holes for avid golfers, including a world-class course designed by Robert Trent Jones Jr. built on an old remediated oil refinery: The **Three Crowns Golf Club** (1601 King Blvd., 307/472-7696, www.threecrowns-golfclub.com, $70 for 18 holes, $40 for 9 holes Mon.-Thurs., $75 for 18 holes, $50 for 9 holes Fri.-Sun.) is a par-72 course that opened in 2005 and has a resort-like feel.

Another course worth playing is the **Casper Municipal Golf Course** (2120 Allendale Blvd., 307/223-6620, www.casperwy.gov, $32 for 18 holes, $20 for 9 holes Mon.-Fri., $34 for 18 holes, $22 for 9 holes Sat.-Sun.), which has 27 holes on three distinct nines. Opened in 1929, the course is consistently ranked among the best municipal courses in the state.

For some of the most unique golfing in the state, try the **Salt Creek Country Club & Golf Course** (Hwy. 387, Midwest), which offers nine holes of mowed prairie grass fairways and sand greens at only $2 per round. Golfers share the course with pronghorn, deer, and prairie dogs.

FOOD

Casper is a breakfast lover's town: You'll find a number of great places to start the day right. **Eggington's** (229 E. 2nd St., 307/265-8700, 6am-2pm Mon.-Sat., 7am-2pm Sun., $4-14) serves breakfast and lunch to a bustling crowd. It offers everything from omelets and pastries to burgers and salads. A somewhat hidden but marvelous spot for lunch is ★ **The Cottage Café** (116 S. Lincoln St., 307/234-1157, 11am-1:30pm Mon.-Fri., $10-12), which is tucked into a residential neighborhood and serves delicious homemade soups, paninis, pastas, and more. Another weekday-only place that serves up great, classic breakfasts and lunches is **Sherrie's Place** (310 W. Yellowstone Hwy., 307/235-3513, 6:30am-2pm Mon.-Fri., $4-11). From cinnamon rolls and stuffed French toast to fried chicken and good old-fashioned malts, this place is the real deal.

For good Mexican food, which southern Wyoming seems to have no shortage of, try **Guadalajara** (3350 CY Ave., 307/234-4699, 11am-9pm Sun.-Thurs., 11am-10pm Fri.-Sat.,

$12-17). **Bosco's** (847 E. A St., 307/265-9658, 11am-1:30pm and 5pm-close Tues.-Fri., 5pm-close Sat., $10-20) serves wonderful Italian meals (including gluten-free options) in an intimate setting. Another favorite in town is the Wyoming/Dakotas chain **Sanford's Grub & Pub** (61 SE Wyoming Blvd., 307/315-6040, www.thegrubandpub.com, 11am-10pm daily, $8-24), which has an outrageously big menu featuring Cajun twists on American food, and plenty of beer; its $1 pints are well known among beer lovers. Kids will delight in the fact that every square inch of wall is covered with memorabilia and garage-sale findings. For a high-end steak, chops, and seafood place, try the **FireRock Steakhouse** (6100 E. 2nd St., 307/234-2333, 11am-10pm Mon.-Thurs., 11am-11pm Fri.-Sat., 11am-9pm Sun., $11-30), serving aged steaks cooked over a wood-fired grill, rack of lamb, pork chops, and all sorts of toppings and sides including shrimp and lobster. FireRock Steakhouse also has a full-service bar.

Part Asian bistro and part sushi bar, **Dsasumo** (320 W. First St., 307/237-7874, www.dsasumo.com, 11am-2:30pm and 4:30pm-9pm Mon.-Fri., 11am-9pm Sat., lunch $11-14, dinner $14-21) is a new and great find in Casper. Most of the food is Thai but there are plenty of fusion choices and a great sushi menu. Don't miss the specialty cocktails.

Starting in 1942, cowboys would ride up to the bar known as **The Wonderbar** (256 S. Center St., 307/234-4110, www.thewonderbar.com, 11am-midnight Mon.-Sat., $8-16) for a beer for themselves and their mount. Then they would ride through the bar and out the back alley. Joe Lowndes, a member of the famed "Wild Bunch," was a regular. Today you don't see horses and riders in the bar, but the place is still a popular watering hole for locals. And the restaurant serves big burgers, sandwiches, salads, excellent homemade potato chips, and anything you could want to wet your whistle. Its informal slogan is, "It's more fun to eat in a bar than drink in a restaurant." How true.

ACCOMMODATIONS

Casper has no shortage of places to stay, and many chain hotel options are available. The **Best Western Ramkota Casper** (800 N. Poplar St., 307/266-6000 or 800/528-1234, www.casper.ramkota.com, $81-146) is a large facility that caters both to business travelers (in-room desks, free Wi-Fi, and a business center) and to families with the Castaway Bay Indoor Water Playground, geared to young children. Among the other chain hotels in Casper are **C'Mon Inn** (301 E. Lathrop Rd., 307/472-6300 or 866/782-2690, www.cmoninn.com/casper, $119-152) with king Jacuzzi suites, the newer 100-room **Courtyard by Marriott** (4260 Hospitality Ln., 307/473-2600, www.marriott.com/cprcy, $102-173), **Holiday Inn Express** (4250 Legion Ln., exit 185 on I-25, 307/237-4200, www.hiexpress.com, $120-217), and two pet-friendly **Super 8** motels (269 Miracle Rd. or 3838 CY Ave., 800/800-8000, www.super8.com, $74-101).

A more budget-friendly option downtown is **The Royal Inn** (440 E. A St., 307/234-3501, www.caspermotel.com, $39-50), which offers clean, basic rooms with microwaves and refrigerators, free Wi-Fi, and on-site laundry machines. The inn also provides gas barbecue grills and a briquette for guests who want to cook out.

For an unforgettable wilderness B&B experience just out of town, ★ **Sunburst Lodge** (2700 Micro Rd., 307/235-9086, www.sunburst-lodge.com, $135-165) is located on Casper Mountain next to Hogadon Ski Area and just 20 minutes from town. There is much exploring to be done year-round just outside the lodge along with cozy accommodations and sumptuous meals inside.

CAMPING

The closest public camping in the vicinity of Casper is 10 miles south of town on **Casper Mountain,** a breezy, forested all-season playground for locals. There are four campgrounds on the mountain; **Beartrap Meadow** (Casper Mountain Rd., 307/235-9311, $10) is the only one with water and is also the nicest of the four. Various campsites maintained by the Bureau of Land Management (307/261-7500, www.wy.blm.gov, $7) include the **Rim** and **Lodgepole Campgrounds** in the Muddy Mountain Environmental Education Area, which can be accessed from gravel roads off Casper Mountain Road. Both have vault toilets, and the campgrounds are connected by a two-mile interpretive nature trail.

For a scenic lakeside campground 28 miles west of Casper on County Road 407, off Highway 220, **Alcova Reservoir** has numerous **campgrounds** (County Rd. 407/Kortes Rd., 307/235-9311, www.natronacounty-wy.gov, $35 full hookups, $10 unserviced), including **Westside Campground, Black Beach,** and **Cottonwood.** Unserviced sites are first-come, first-served, and sites with hookups are by reservation only.

A few private campgrounds and RV parks are also available right in town. Set along a bend in the North Platte River, the **Fort Caspar Campground** (4205 Fort Caspar Rd., 307/234-3260 or 888/243-7709, www.ft-casparcamp.org, $24-43) offers basic tent and RV sites on gravel, a lodge, ponds, and several walking trails; it also provides free Wi-Fi.

INFORMATION AND SERVICES

The **Natrona County Travel and Tourism Council** (139 W. 2nd St., Ste. 1B, 307/234-5362 or 800/852-1889, www.visitcasper.com, 8am-5pm Mon.-Fri.) has a wealth of information for visitors. The **Casper Area Chamber of Commerce** (500 N. Center St., 307/234-5311 or 866/234-5311, www.casperwyoming.org, 8am-6pm Mon.-Fri, 9am-5pm Sat., 1pm-4pm Sun. Memorial Day-Labor Day, 8am-5pm Mon.-Fri. Labor Day-Memorial Day) is an excellent resource for local businesses and relocation information.

Post offices are located at 411 North Forest Drive (307/237-8556, 8:30am-5pm Mon.-Fri., 9am-noon Sat.) and at 150 East B Street (9am-5:30pm Mon.-Fri., 9am-noon Sat.).

The **Natrona County Public Library** (307/577-7323, www.natronacountylibrary. org, 9am-8pm Mon.-Thurs., 9am-5pm Fri.- Sat., 1pm-5pm Sun.) is located at 307 East 2nd Street.

Wyoming Medical Center (1233 E. 2nd St., 307/577-7201 or 800/822-7201, www.wmc-net.org) is the largest health care facility in the state and offers everything from 24-hour emergency medicine to highly specialized care.

Laundry facilities are available at **Hilltop Laundromat** (2513 E. 3rd St., 307/234-7331, 7:30am-5:30pm Mon.-Fri., 9am-5:30pm Sat.- Sun.) and **CY Laundromat** (2300 CY Ave., 307/265-2151, 7am-9pm Mon.-Fri.).

TRANSPORTATION
Getting There
The **Casper/Natrona County International Airport** (CPR, 8500 Airport Pkwy., 307/472-6688, www.iflycasper.com) is located on U.S. Highway 20/26 approximately nine miles west of downtown. Two carriers, **United** (800/864-8331, www.united.com) and **Delta** (800/221-1212, www.delta.com), provide daily flights to and from Denver and Salt Lake City.

Car-rental agencies at the airport include **Avis, Budget,** and **Hertz. Enterprise** (120 S. Forest Dr.) has an office in town.

Regular bus service to and from Casper is available on **Greyhound** (601 N. Center St.,) and **Black Hills Stage Lines** (601 N. Center St., 877/779-2999, www.blackhillsstagelines. com).

By car, Casper is 145 miles east of Lander, 148 miles north of Laramie, 178 miles northwest of Cheyenne, 240 miles northeast of Green River, 242 miles south of Gillette, 284 miles east of Jackson, and 267 miles southeast of Yellowstone National Park.

Getting Around
The easiest public transportation in Casper is **The Bus** (307/265-1313, www.catcbus.com, 6:30am-6:30pm Mon.-Fri., $1 general, $0.75 students, $0.50 reduced, free for children 5 and under), a fixed-route transit system. The Casper Area Transportation Coalition also offers **Dial-a-Ride,** which must be reserved before 3pm at least one day in advance; it's better to reserve two days early. The cost is $5, or $2 for seniors and people with special needs, $1 for children 12 and under accompanied by an adult.

Local taxi service is provided by **Casper Cabs** (307/577-7777, www.caspercabs.com), **Blue Cab** (307/337-7303, www.bluecabcasper. com), and **Eagle Cab** (307/797-3818, www. eagle-cab.net).

Laramie

Nestled in a high basin between the Laramie and Medicine Bow Mountains, Laramie (population 31,814, elevation 7,173 feet) is a charming combination of Old West frontier town and sophisticated university town, all with immediate proximity to the natural rocky playground that envelops the city.

Like so many cities in the region, Laramie can trace its roots back to a fort, Fort John Buford, built in 1866 to protect travelers on the pioneer trails, most notably the Overland Trail. In 1867, railroad workers plotting the course through the Laramie Valley rumbled into town, bringing with them numerous businesses to support their way of life. When the first passengers disembarked from the Union Pacific train in Laramie City in 1868, there were 23 saloons ready for them to wet their whistles.

Fort Buford, by then known as Fort Sanders, was abandoned in 1882, but other significant structures had been built in Laramie. The Wyoming Territorial Prison was first built in 1872 as a response to the lawlessness of the area. And in 1887, Wyoming University, now known as the University of

Wyoming, opened its doors to both men and women. It's worth pointing out that women in Laramie were the first in the United States to sit on a jury and to vote, both in 1870.

Today, Laramie continues to be among the most progressive cities in the state, although it hasn't lost any of its cowboy swagger. The 150-year-old downtown buildings are beautiful and authentic examples of the finest frontier architecture. From old-school quilt shops to herb stores, cowgirl yarn shops to outdoor stores, downtown Laramie is a charming mix of old and new West. For proof, look no further than Ivinson and First Streets, where cowboy and motorcycle bars share customers with a vegetarian café and a global cuisine bistro. The town is full of important historic sites and an arresting spectrum of museums. The university gives Laramie just enough academic culture to keep the town young and vibrant with concerts, lectures, sports, and coffeehouses, and the surrounding wilderness is well used without becoming overcrowded.

SIGHTS
American Heritage Center

Established in 1945, the **American Heritage Center** (2111 Willett Dr., 307/766-4114, www.ahc.uwyo.edu, 10am-7pm Mon., 8am-5pm Tues.-Fri., free) houses one of the most extensive nongovernmental historical collections in the country. In addition to the manuscripts collections, a rare book center has more than 55,000 items that date back to medieval times. Topics range from the American West, an obvious and natural specialty, to British and American literature, natural history, conservation, women authors, and book arts, among countless others. The center is open to the public and is utilized constantly by scholars from all over the world. The center also hosts an array of fascinating events from lectures and symposia to rare and important exhibits. The website offers viewers a meaningful look into the digital collection, audio-visual collection, and virtual exhibits.

University of Wyoming Art Museum

Located in the same architecturally stunning complex as the American Heritage Center, the **University of Wyoming Art Museum** (2111 Willett Dr., 307/766-6622, www.uwyo.edu/artmuseum, 10am-5pm Mon.-Sat. May-Aug. and Dec.-Jan., 10am-7pm Mon., 10am-5pm Tues.-Sat. Feb.-Apr. and Sept.-Nov., free) brings art from around the world to Wyoming. Its permanent collection houses more than 7,000 objects, including European and American paintings, prints, and drawings; 19th-century Japanese prints; 18th-19th-century Persian and Indian miniature paintings; 20th-century photography; and African and Native American artifacts. The museum also hosts important exhibitions focused on everything from regional art to international museum collections.

University of Wyoming Geological Museum

In a university with several compelling museums covering everything from anthropology to insects, another great one is the **University of Wyoming Geological Museum** (West Campus, near N. 9th St. and E. Lewis St., 307/766-3386, www.uwyo.edu/geomuseum, 10am-4pm Mon.-Sat., free). The museum houses some of the best fossils in the country and dedicates plenty of space to Wyoming's earliest inhabitants: the dinosaurs. In addition to the usual suspects—from *Allosaurus* to *T. rex*—the museum lays claim to one of only six *Apatosaurus* skeletons on display worldwide. This one is 145-160 million years old and was discovered in Albany County in 1901. There are also skeletons of *Diatryma gigantea,* a prehistoric carnivorous flying dinosaur more than seven feet tall, found in 1876. One of the most unique exhibits is the fossilized remains of a dinosaur that died giving birth. The bones of the baby are clearly visible. Dozens of displays tell the stories of the more than 50 species of dinosaur whose remains have been found in Wyoming soil. And when displays are missing here, they are often

Laramie

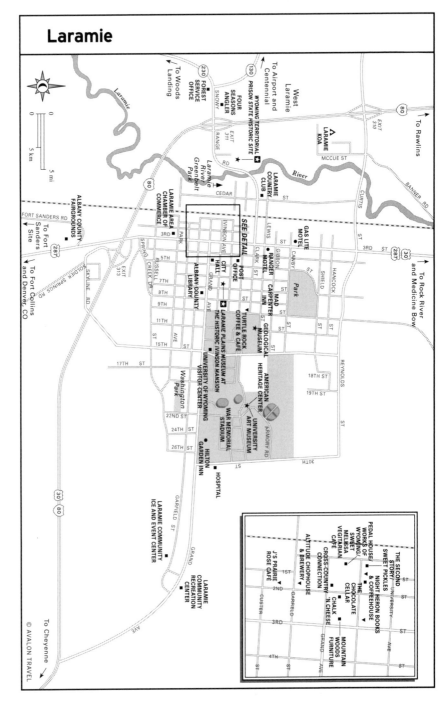

To Woods
Landing

To Airport and
Centennial

West
Laramie

To Rawlins

FOREST
SERVICE
OFFICE

WYOMING TERRITORIAL
PRISON STATE HISTORIC SITE

FOUR
SEASONS
ANGLER

SNOWY

RANGE

EXIT
311

RD

LARAMIE
KOA

MCCUE ST

EXIT
310

80

To Rawlins

Laramie

Laramie
River
Greenbelt
Park

Laramie
River Park

CEDAR

LARAMIE
COUNTRY
CLUB

River

CURTIS

BANNER RD

80

LARAMIE AREA
CHAMBER OF
COMMERCE

ALBANY COUNTY
FAIRGROUNDS

FORT SANDERS RD

To Fort
Sanders
Site

To Fort Collins
and Denver, CO

287

SOLDIER SPRINGS RD

SKYLINE RD

SPRING CREEK

EXIT
313

3RD

PARK

VINSON AVE

5TH

RUSSELL

7TH

8TH

9TH

11TH

15TH

17TH ST

LEWIS

CLARK ST

CITY
HALL

ALBANY COUNTY
LIBRARY

GRAND AVE

POST
OFFICE

CARPENTER
INN

MAD
CARPENTER
INN

TURTLE ROCK
COFFEE & CAFE

LARAMIE PLAINS MUSEUM AT
THE HISTORIC IVINSON MANSION

UNIVERSITY OF WYOMING
VISITOR CENTER

Washington
Park

22ND ST

24TH ST

26TH ST

GIBBON

CANBY

GAS LITE
MOTEL

RANGER
MOTEL

GEOLOGICAL
MUSEUM

SHIELD

HANCOCK

Park

3RD ST

30

287

To Rock River
and Medicine Bow

REYNOLDS

18TH ST

19TH ST

AMERICAN
HERITAGE
CENTER

WAR
MEMORIAL
STADIUM

UNIVERSITY
ART MUSEUM

ARMORY RD

30TH

HILTON
GARDEN INN

HOSPITAL

GARFIELD ST

GRAND AVE

LARAMIE COMMUNITY
ICE AND EVENT CENTER

LARAMIE
COMMUNITY
RECREATION
CENTER

30

80

To Cheyenne

© AVALON TRAVEL

0   5 mi
0   5 km

SEE DETAIL

SEE DETAIL

J'S PRAIRIE
ROSE CAFE

PEDAL HOUSE/
WORKS OF
WYOMING

MELISSA
SWEET
CHOCOLATE
CELLAR

SWEET
MELISSA
VEGETARIAN
CAFE

ALTITUDE CHOPHOUSE
& BREWERY

CROSS-COUNTRY
CONNECTION

CHALK
'N CHEESE

MOUNTAIN
WOODS
FURNITURE

THE SECOND
STORY

NIGHT HERON BOOKS
& COFFEEHOUSE

UNIVERSITY

SWEET PICKLES

1ST

2ND

3RD

4TH

CUSTER

GARFIELD

GRAND

on loan to the Museum of Natural History in New York City. These are serious bones in a very unassuming package.

★ Laramie Plains Museum at the Historic Ivinson Mansion

Entrepreneur and banker Edward Ivinson was a local hero in Laramie, not only for his ethical business practices and his community-minded role in the construction of the prison and the university, but also for the home that he built in 1892, the same year he lost the Wyoming gubernatorial race. Indeed, the **Ivinson Mansion** (603 E. Ivinson Ave., 307/742-4448, www.laramiemuseum.org, tours 9am-5pm Tues.-Sat., 1pm-4pm Sun. summer, 1pm-4pm Tues.-Sat. fall-spring, hours can change for private events, $10 adults, $7 seniors, $5 students, free for children under 6) is among Laramie's most impressive buildings. The house was designed by architect W. E. Ware and built for $40,000 with then-unheard-of amenities that included central heating, electricity, and running water. Jane Ivinson, Edward's wife, decorated the home with elegant appointments from around the world. After his beloved wife died, Ivinson donated their regal residence to the Episcopal Missionary District of Wyoming with the understanding that it be used as a school-home for teenage ranch girls who otherwise might not be educated. The school operated until 1958, at which point the house sat vacant at the mercy of vandals for more than a decade.

In 1972 the Episcopal Church sold the mansion to the Laramie Plains Museum Association. Under the museum's care, the home has been beautifully restored and is open to the public as the Laramie Plains Museum. The home is filled with artifacts from all over the state, including the largest collection of Wyoming Territorial Prison furnishings, gorgeous wood pieces made by Swedish prisoner Jan Hjorth, a regional gun collection spanning more than a century, period furnishings, and more. Seeing the artifacts in such a stunning home setting makes this museum absolutely worth seeing.

★ Wyoming Territorial Prison State Historic Site

Built in 1872 to deal with the ruffians in lawless Laramie, the **Wyoming Territorial Prison** (975 Snowy Range Rd., 307/745-3733, www.wyomingterritorialprison.com or http://wyoparks.state.wy.us, 8am-7pm daily May-Oct., $5 adults, $2.50 children 12-17, free for

The Wyoming Territorial Prison was built in 1872.

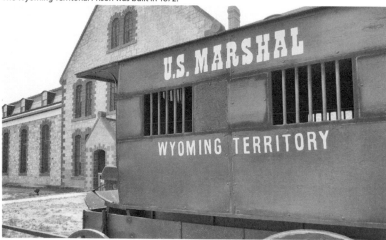

children under 12) was restored in 1989 and made into a 190-acre state historic site. The prison was in use 1872-1903, during which time more than 1,000 men and 12 women were imprisoned there. Among the most famous residents was Butch Cassidy. When Wyoming achieved statehood in 1890, work was already underway on a new state prison in Rawlins. When the Wyoming Frontier Prison opened in 1901, the transition began, and prisoners in the Territorial Prison were slowly replaced by animals from the University of Wyoming's experimental stock farm, which were housed in the prison for more than 70 years.

Rounding out the historic site are an entirely re-created frontier town; a number of buildings in various stages of restoration, including the broom factory where many of the prisoners worked on a variety of different jobs; authentic pioneer cabins; a schoolhouse; and agricultural buildings where kids can stick their arms into a simulated (and gooey!) cow's belly.

Still, the prison is the main attraction, and visitors should plan to spend at least 90 minutes touring the facility. A brochure in the gift shop provides a self-guided tour through furnished cells, the prisoner dining room, guards' quarters, women's quarters, the warden's office, and a number of other rooms and exhibit galleries. The warden's house on the grounds can also be toured.

Several things make this experience both unique and unforgettable. For starters, willing visitors are assigned the identity of a former prisoner upon entering and can find out about their prisoner throughout the facility, something that keeps kids fully involved. The prisoner ID card can be stamped at the end of the visit for a fun take-home souvenir. The museum itself is spotlessly clean and easy to explore. There are also numerous volunteers throughout the property, dressed as late 19th-century prisoners, who answer questions and tell fascinating stories. This is just a wonderful place to spend an afternoon.

ENTERTAINMENT AND EVENTS

With such a young, vibrant population, Laramie has loads of events going on year-round. From scholarly lectures on campus to concerts and meditation gatherings, offerings are plentiful and diverse. A great way to get warmed up to the history of the region is with the living history tour **Legends of Laramie** (www.visitlaramie.org), available on your smartphone or tablet. Organized by

Downtown Laramie is a wonderful place to shop and dine.

the Albany County Tourism Board, the tour includes 15 stops around Laramie highlighting everything from railroad romances and shootouts to the ghost town of Sherman 18 miles south of town.

On Wednesday nights throughout summer, the **Laramie Municipal Band,** made up primarily of students and teachers from the university, puts on free concerts in Washington Park (Sheridan St. between S. 18th St. and S. 21st St.) starting at 7:30pm. On Friday afternoon and evening July-September, the town comes downtown for the weekly and festive **farmers market** (307/742-3774, www. laramiefarmersmarket.com, 3pm-7pm). For cultural events held throughout the year at the university, including the **University of Wyoming Symphony Orchestra,** theater and dance performances, and major concerts, contact the **Fine Arts Box Office** (307/766-6666, www.uwyo.edu/finearts).

For more than 70 years, **Laramie Jubilee Days** (www.laramiejubileedays.com) has been the annual hometown celebration that draws revelers from across the region. Often scheduled in the week leading up to the anniversary of Wyoming's statehood on July 10, the event offers Fourth of July celebrations, including the biggest fireworks display in the state. Other Jubilee Days events include street dances, a classic parade, bull riding, and three nights of professional rodeo.

The **Albany County Fair** is held annually late July-early August at the fairgrounds (3520 U.S. 287, 307/742-3224, www.albanycountyfair.org) and has all the family-friendly fun visitors expect from a Western fair, including a carnival, entertainment, and 4-H activities.

SHOPPING

While the shopping options are quite varied around town, from marvelous bookstores to hippie outposts and classic Western saddleries, the experience of shopping in Laramie's historic and charming downtown cannot be beat. **The Second Story** (105 Ivinson Ave., 307/745-4423, www.personallyrecommendedbooks.com, 10am-6pm Mon.-Sat.), for example, is a gem of an independent bookstore housed in a public hall built in 1889. Since then, it has been a hotel, a bordello, a saloon, a senior center, and now a bookstore. The children's book selection is particularly good. As a bonus, with every book purchase comes a free espresso drink, made to order. Right next door, **Night Heron Books & Coffeehouse** (107 Ivinson Ave., 307/742-9028, www.nightheronbooks.com, 7am-9pm daily) offers a great selection of rare and used books. Plus, the coffee shop serves up a rotating menu of quiche, soups, sandwiches, and baked goods.

For a delectable treat, stop by **The Chocolate Cellar** (113 Ivinson Ave., 307/742-9278, 10am-5:30pm Mon.-Sat., 1pm-4pm Sun.), which has been creating handcrafted goodies since 1982. **Mountain Woods Furniture** (206 S. 3rd St., 307/745-4950 or 866/689-6637, www.mountainwoodsfurniture.com, 10am-6pm Mon.-Sat.) sells rustic log furniture handcrafted by artisans from across North America. **Chalk n' Cheese** (209 2nd St., 307/742-1800, www.chalkncheesewy.com, 10am-6pm Tues.-Fri., 10am-5pm Sat.) is a great cheese and gourmet food shop that sells kitchenware and antiques, as well as offers fun cooking classes.

Works of Wyoming (211 S. 1st St., 307/460-3304, www.worksofwyoming.org 10am-6pm Mon.-Sat.) has an excellent selection of fine art, crafts, and gifts made by Wyoming artists and artisans. **Sweet Pickles** (117 E. Ivinson St., 307/745-4114, 10am-6pm Mon.-Sat., noon-4pm Sun.) is a wonderful spot for kids, with both toys and clothes. And if the shopping wears you out, there's wonderful homemade ice cream a few doors down.

SPORTS AND RECREATION
Rock Climbing

A mecca for rock climbers and nature lovers alike, **Vedauwoo** (off I-80 exit 329, about 20 miles east of Laramie, 307/745-2300, www.vedauwoo.org) is an otherworldly jumble of enormous boulders that offer some of the best wide-crack climbing in the West. More than 500 sport climbs were documented in the first guidebook for the area, written in 1994 and no longer available. Today there are more than 900 climbs, many of which are detailed on the Vedauwoo website, and the number continues to grow. For non-climbers, the area is ideal for hiking, trail running, and even wildlife viewing. Among the animals sighted here are pronghorn, deer, moose, and even black bears and cougars. A U.S. Forest Service campground is available at the site. The elevation here is surprisingly high, at 8,000 feet above sea level.

Mountain bikers enjoy Vedauwoo.

Hiking and Biking

In addition to meandering hikes in town along the Laramie River Greenbelt and at nearby Vedauwoo, the **Pole Mountain Area** (Forest Rd. 705, off I-80 exit 323, 13 miles east of Laramie) in the Sherman Mountains offers terrific trails for hiking and biking. The **Headquarters National Recreation Trail Loop** can be a four-mile or eight-mile roundtrip loop, depending on your time and energy level. The trail winds through a number of environments, from sage and grassy meadows to pine forests, and there is plenty of opportunity for bouldering among the pink granite rocks that are reminiscent of Vedauwoo. A brochure, "Pole Mountain Summer-Use Trails," is available at the **Laramie Ranger District** (2468 W. Jackson St., 307/745-2300, 8am-5pm Mon.-Fri.).

You'll have to bring your own bike to Laramie, unless you are a student or faculty member of the University of Wyoming, in which case you can rent from the ingenious Bike Library through the **Outdoor Program** (307/766-2402), but if you need service, repairs, or just some good advice, head into the **Pedal House** (207 S. 1st St., 307/742-5533, www.pedalhouse.com).

Fishing

While Laramie isn't quite the hotbed of fishing that can be found in other parts of the state, its location makes access to varied waters relatively easy. For lake fishing, options include **Laramie Plains Lakes** (15 miles west of town off Hwy. 230) and **Lake Hattie** (20 miles southwest of Laramie off Hwy. 230). Nearby rivers filled with trout include the **Big Laramie River** and the **Upper North Platte River.** For fishing gear or guided trips, contact **Four Seasons Angler** (334 S. Fillmore St., 307/721-4047, www.fourseasonsanglers. com). Half-day wade trips for two anglers start at $380; full-day trips for two start at $430.

Golf

Golfers can hit the links in Laramie at the nine-hole **Fox Run** (489 Hwy. 230, 307/745-4161, www.foxrunlaramie.com, $37 for 18 holes, $25 for 9 holes) or the **Jacoby Park Golf Course** (3501 Willett Dr., 307/745-3111, www.jacobygc.com, $40 for 18 holes, $32 for 9 holes) on the University of Wyoming campus.

Skiing

Thirty-two miles west of town in the Medicine Bow National Forest, **Snowy**

Range Ski Area (3254 Hwy. 130, Centennial, 307/745-5750, www.snowyrangeski.com, full-day $45 adults, $39 teens 13-17, $28 children 5-12, free for kids under 5 and seniors 70 and over) has five ski lifts covering 27 trails on 250 acres: 7 beginner trails, 12 intermediate trails, and 8 expert trails. The area receives an average of 245 inches annually, with a base elevation of 8,798 feet and summit of 9,663 feet.

While Laramie is not known as a cross-country ski destination, there are miles upon miles of groomed trails just 15 minutes from town. **Tie City** and **Happy Jack Trailheads,** which give skiers access to some 30 miles of trails, are found off I-80, exit 323, then north on Happy Jack Road for a mile. A $5 parking fee is required. More information on these trails and others can be found online at www.visitlaramie.org. A terrific store for all kinds of gear, daily or weekly rentals, and first-rate advice for Nordic skiers is the **Cross-Country Connection** (222 S. 2nd St., 307/721-2851, www.crosscountryconnection. com, 10am-6pm Mon.-Fri., 9am-5pm Sat., noon-4pm Sun.).

Spectator Sports

When it comes to recreation, one cannot forget that Laramie is a college town and somewhat fanatical about its football. Attending a **Wyoming Cowboys** game at War Memorial Stadium (E. Grand Ave and N. 22nd St.) is a true Wyoming experience. It's likely the only place in Wyoming you'll ever feel crowded. For schedule and tickets, contact the **Athletic Ticket Office** (877/996-3261, www.wyomingathletics.com).

Perhaps small beans compared to the Cowboys, collegiate baseball is played at **Cowboy Field** (2623 Willet Dr., just east of War Memorial Stadium, www.laramiecolts. com). The Laramie Colts are part of the Rocky Mountain Baseball League, play upwards of 40 games per season, and still live with local families willing to take them in and feed them home-cooked meals between games.

Recreation Centers

When the wind blows in Laramie, and it will, the **Laramie Community Recreation Center** (920 Boulder Dr., 307/721-5269, www. cityoflaramie.org, 5am-9pm Mon.-Fri., 8am-8pm Sat., noon-8pm Sun., nonresidents $8 adults, $7.50 seniors 60 and over, $6.50 children 13-18, $4.50 children 3-12) offers an indoor leisure pool, an eight-lane lap pool, an outdoor pool with waterslides and a lazy river, a full-court gymnasium, weights, an indoor playground, and an abundance of classes and activities. Check the website for pool hours.

Accessed from a trailhead at West Garfield Street and South Spruce Street, the **Laramie River Greenbelt Park** offers 5.75 miles of paved walking, running, biking, and inline skating paths.

When winter comes to town, the **Laramie Community Ice and Event Center** (3510 Garfield St., 307/721-2161, www.cityoflaramie.org, 5am-9pm Mon.-Fri., 8am-8pm Sat., noon-8pm Sun., weekly schedules posted online, $5 nonresident adults, $2.50 children 3-5, drop-in figure skating $8 nonresidents, drop-in hockey $8 nonresident adults 18 and up) offers ice skating, broomball, curling, and skate rentals. When there is no ice, mid-March-September, usually, roller skating is available.

FOOD

Like all college towns worth their salt, Laramie has an abundance of good, relatively cheap places to enjoy a meal. For breakfast or lunch, a local favorite is **J's Prairie Rose Café** (410 S. 2nd St., 307/745-8140, 7am-3pm Mon.-Thurs., 7am-8pm Fri., 7am-3pm Sat., 7am-noon Sun., $6-12). The Prairie Rose, as it is known, has the best green chili in town, plus phenomenal breakfast burritos, Philly cheesesteaks, and, like all good diners, homemade pie. Its off-menu specials include everything from Italian dishes to eggs Benedict, and its Friday night dinners are most often delicious twists on juicy Wyoming steak.

For a smattering of reasonably priced global cuisine, try ★ **Jeffrey's Bistro** (123 E. Ivinson Ave., 307/742-7046, www.

jeffreysbistro.com, 11am-dinner close Mon.-Sat., $10-17), which offers hearty salads, creative daily specials like ancho-cherry barbecue chicken or hot-and-spicy Thai shrimp, and delicious entrées such as pot pie, enchiladas, Thai burritos, and Indian *dopiaza*, many of which can be made vegetarian. For serious vegetarians, **Sweet Melissa Vegetarian Café** (213 S. 1st St., 307/742-9607, 11am-9pm Mon.-Thurs., 11am-10pm Fri.-Sat., $7-11) is like green heaven in the middle of cow country. Tons of salads, pastas, and sandwiches are on the menu, as is expected, but there is also plenty of gluten-free options as well as good old-fashioned comfort food like smothered sweet potato and black bean burritos, country-fried seitan, mushroom stroganoff, and specials like spinach and artichoke manicotti with lemon cream and blueberry sauce. The fact that Sweet Melissa's adjoins a popular watering hole, **Front Street Tavern** (11am-close Mon.-Sat.), is just icing on the cake.

Serving upscale brewpub cuisine that ranges from the traditional (hickory burgers, seafood pasta, bacon-wrapped tenderloin, and cedar-plank salmon) to the unusual (Vietnamese barbecue, orange-braised pork loin, and Thai salmon burgers), **Altitude Chophouse & Brewery** (320 S. 2nd St., 307/721-4031, www.altitudechophouse.com, 11am-10pm Mon.-Sat., $9-24) perfectly pairs sensational beer with delicious and creative cuisine; don't miss the desserts.

Located in the lovely, tree-lined university area, **Turtle Rock Coffee & Café** (270 N. 9th St., 307/745-3741, www.turtlerockcoffee. com, 7am-9pm Mon.-Thurs., 7am-8pm Fri.-Sat., 8am-6pm Sun.) serves up yummy sandwiches, pastries, ice cream, and, of course, the requisite college coffee. The outdoor seating is delightful, and the Geological Museum at the University of Wyoming is just steps away.

ACCOMMODATIONS

Laramie has more than 2,000 guest rooms in town, of which several hundred are just a few years old. Accommodation options include hotels, motels, bed-and-breakfasts, and guest ranches.

For the best value in town with a convenient downtown location, the **Ranger Motel** (453 N. 3rd St., 307/742-6677, rangermotel@ wyo2u.com, $50-60) offers clean, no-frills guest rooms with air-conditioning, microwaves, and mini refrigerators.

At the other end of the spectrum, the ★ **Hilton Garden Inn** (2229 Grand Ave., 307/745-5500, www.uwconferencecenter.com, $107-195) offers all the frills you are going to find in Laramie. From Egyptian cotton sheets and ergonomic chairs to flat-screen TVs and cushy bathrobes, this hotel sets the standard for luxury.

Standard chain hotels in town include the newer **Holiday Inn Laramie** (204 S. 30th St., 307/721-9000, www.ihg.com, $112-203), the pet-friendly **Days Inn** (1368 McCue St., 800/329-7466, www.daysinn.com, $61-153), and **Super 8** (1987 Banner Rd., 307/745-8901, www.super8.com, $68-132).

A few unique lodging options are the pet-friendly and roadside **Gas Lite Motel** (960 N. 3rd St., 307/742-6616, $41-74), filled to the brim with Western knickknacks; and the fabulously quirky **Mad Carpenter Inn** (353 N. 8th St., 307/742-0870, www.madcarpenterinn.net, $95-200), a B&B near the university where the creative and delightful innkeepers have a passion for carpentry, cooking (a gourmet continental breakfast is included), and poetry. For those who want more of the rustic, backwoods-type experience, **Brooklyn Lodge** (3540 Hwy. 130, Centennial, 307/742-6916, www. brooklynlodge.com, from $199) is the ticket. Designated a National Historic Place and set in the Medicine Bow National Forest right near the ski area, the two king-bedded rooms at this bed-and-breakfast are cozy, rustic, and abundantly comfortable. Although pets are not allowed, horses can stay for $25 per night.

CAMPING

There are plenty of fantastic opportunities for camping or renting a cabin in the **Medicine Bow-Routt National Forest,** which surrounds Laramie to the east (Pole Mountain) and west (Snowy Range). The closest public campgrounds to town are the nicely forested **Yellow Pine Campground** (Forest Rd. 719, 13.2 miles west of Laramie, $10) and otherworldly **Vedauwoo Campground** (Vedauwoo Rd., 17.3 miles east of Laramie, $10). Both campgrounds have potable water.

Equidistant between Laramie and Cheyenne is **Curt Gowdy State Park** (1319 Happy Jack Rd., 307/632-7946, http://wyoparks.state.wy.us, $4 residents, $6 nonresidents, camping $10 residents, $17 nonresidents, includes day use), 24 miles east of Laramie at the edge of the Laramie Mountains. Historically, the area served as prime hunting and camping grounds for numerous Native American tribes. There are 35 RV sites that can be reserved, 15 with water hookups, none with electricity. The remaining sites are first-come, first-served. Located on three lovely reservoirs, the park offers trout and kokanee salmon fishing as well as hiking and biking trails and prime picnicking spots. Dogs are not permitted off-leash or in the water.

For information on sites in the Laramie Ranger District or other nearby areas, contact the **U.S. Forest Service** (2468 W. Jackson St., 307/745-2300, 8am-5pm Mon.-Fri.).

Just north of I-80, the **Laramie KOA** (1271 W. Baker St., 307/742-6553, www.koa.com) has tent sites ($29), RV sites ($46.50-49.50), and cabins ($60-66) in addition to free Wi-Fi, various organized activities, and a playground.

INFORMATION AND SERVICES

The **Albany County Tourism Board** (210 E. Custer St., 307/745-4195, www.visitlaramie. org, 8am-5pm Mon.-Fri., 9am-1pm Sat. June-Sept., 8am-5pm Mon.-Fri. Oct.-May) operates a convention and visitors bureau and is happy to send a visitor guide in advance of your trip. The **Laramie Area Chamber of Commerce** (800 S. 3rd St., 307/745-7339 or 866/876-1012, www.laramie.org, 8am-5pm Mon.-Fri.) can provide useful information on local businesses and relocation.

For information on recreation in the nearby **Medicine Bow-Routt National Forest** and the **Thunder Basin National Grassland,** both of which are managed by the U.S. Forest Service, visit the **headquarters** (2468 W. Jackson St., 307/745-2371, 8am-5pm Mon.-Fri.).

The **Albany County Public Library** (310 S. 8th St., 307/721-2580, www.albanycountylibrary.org, 1pm-5pm Mon. and Fri.-Sat.,

West of Laramie, the Medicine Bow-Routt National Forest offers beautiful scenery.

10am-8pm Tues.-Thurs.) has nine Internet terminals available for free.

The **post offices** are located at 152 North 5th Street (307/721-8837, 8am-5:15pm Mon.-Fri., 9am-1pm Sat.) and 1409 South 3rd Street (307/742-3055, 9am-4:30pm Mon.-Fri., 9am-3:30pm Sat.).

Ivinson Memorial Hospital (255 N. 30th St., 307/742-2141, www.ivinsonhospital.org) offers 24-hour emergency care plus specialized medicine.

This is a college town, with no shortage of laundries, including **Spic and Span Laundromat** (272 N. 4th St., 307/745-3939, 7:30am-10pm daily, last load in by 8:30pm), which offers plasma TVs, Wi-Fi, and double- and triple-load machines.

TRANSPORTATION
Getting There
The **Laramie Regional Airport** (LAR, 555 General Brees Rd., 307/742-4164, www.laramieairport.com) offers daily 40-minute flights to and from Denver on **United** (800/864-8331, www.united.com).

The only car-rental agency at the airport is **Hertz. Enterprise** (517 S. 3rd St.) has a location in town.

Greyhound serves Laramie from the Travelodge (421 Boswell).

By car, Laramie is 49 miles west of Cheyenne, 130 miles north of Denver, 148 miles southeast of Casper, 207 miles east of Rock Springs, 380 miles southeast of Yellowstone National Park, and 383 miles southeast of Jackson.

Getting Around
Laramie's taxi service is provided by **Snowy Range Taxi** (307/343-2323, www.snowyrangetaxi.com, 3pm-3am Tues.-Sat.).

Cheyenne

Just a few miles from the Colorado border is Cheyenne (population 62,448, elevation 6,062 feet), the state capital and an important historical and modern crossroads. The town was named by the Sioux, who used the word to define another tribe, which we know as the Cheyenne, that they considered alien. A settlement sprang up on July 4, 1867, in advance of the Union Pacific Railroad's arrival; the town's population thrived and culture flourished. Influential people and performers traveling across the West by train often stopped in Cheyenne, making it a rather progressive town. Today I-80 and I-25 cross in Cheyenne, bringing visitors from every direction into its historic folds.

The city's defining event, Frontier Days, was founded in 1897 and today brings nearly 200,000 people to town for 10 days in late July. Cheyenne is still a rodeo town, with one of the only visitors bureaus that lists horse-boarding stables along with hotels and motels. After all, if you're coming to Cheyenne, why not bring your horse?

High and windswept, Cheyenne is not a classic Wyoming beauty in the same way as Jackson Hole or Sheridan, but it has a compelling setting with more urban culture than in most of the state, some wonderful museums, and a smattering of ways to enjoy the great outdoors.

SIGHTS
As a wonderful prelude to this historic city, jump on the **Cheyenne Street Railway Trolley** (121 W. 15th St., 307/778-3133 or 800/426-5009, www.cheyennetrolley.com, 90-minute tours 10am, 11:30am, 1pm, 2:30pm, and 4pm Mon.-Fri., 2-hour tours 10am, noon, and 2pm Sat., noon and 2pm Sun., May-Sept., $10 adults, $5 children 2-12), departing from the beautiful old rail depot (121 W. 15th St.). The ride gives visitors a narrated overview of the city, stopping by many of the best sights,

including the Nelson Museum, Wyoming State Museum, the state capitol, Cheyenne Botanic Gardens, Old West Museum, and Historic Governors' Mansion. Visitors are welcome to hop off and hop on the next trolley, 90 minutes later on weekdays or two hours later on weekends.

Wyoming State Capitol

The cornerstone of the **Wyoming State Capitol** (200 W. 24th St. and Capitol Ave., 307/777-7220, 8am-5pm Mon.-Fri.) was laid on May 18, 1887, when Wyoming was still a territory. Modeled after the capitol in Washington DC, this National Historic Landmark went through various phases of construction, the last being the addition of the senate and house chambers, completed in 1917. The building measures 300 feet in length, and its gold dome is 146 feet high. The capitol underwent a $7.6 million renovation during the 1970s, and the dome has been gilded six times, most recently in 1988. When celebrating its centennial in 1987, the original cornerstone was removed, and the documents that had been buried inside—a map and list of territorial officers, among others—were removed and entrusted to the state archives. In December 2015, the capitol was closed to the public for what is expected to be a three-year restoration. Progress can be monitored online at www.wyomingcapitolsquare.com.

When the restoration is complete and the capitol reopened, visitors will be able to enter the rotunda on the 1st floor and gaze up three stories to the dome, created from stained glass imported from England. The governor's office is off the rotunda on the 1st floor. The 2nd floor houses the legislative chambers, decorated by four large Western murals with ceilings of Tiffany stained glass inlaid with the state seal. The balconies on the 3rd floor are always open, and visitors can view the senate and house chambers while they are in session. From the 3rd floor it is also easy to appreciate the Renaissance-revival architecture of the entire building. Don't miss the 1,000-pound Tiffany chandelier in the conference room, and look at the ornate hinges on the large cherrywood doors. '

Union Pacific Railroad Depot

At the southern end of Capitol Avenue sits the historic **Union Pacific Railroad Depot** (121 W. 15th St., 9am-6pm Mon.-Fri., 9am-5pm Sat., 11am-5pm Sun. May-Sept., 9am-5pm Mon.-Fri., 9am-3pm Sat., 11am-3pm Sun. Oct.-Apr.). Built in 1886, this was once

The Wyoming State Capitol was modeled after the nation's capitol in Washington DC.

considered the finest train depot between Omaha and Sacramento. The building occupies an entire city block and was reopened in 2004 after undergoing a major renovation. It has been restored to its original beauty, and the sandstone structure is worth a visit just to appreciate the architecture and design. During the summer, free evening concerts and other events are held in the depot plaza.

In addition to housing the Cheyenne Visitors Center and a fun restaurant, the structure is also home to the **Cheyenne Depot Museum** (121 W. 15th St., 307/632-3905, www.cheyennedepotmuseum.org, 9am-6pm Mon.-Fri., 9am-5pm Sat., 11am-5pm Sun. May-Sept., 9am-5pm Mon.-Fri., 9am-3pm Sat., 11am-3pm Sun. Oct.-Apr., $8 adults, $7 seniors and military, free for children under 12). The museum focuses on the important role the railroad played in the city's development and to the West as a whole. There are fantastic old photographs, an incredible narrow gauge model railroad that took more than 30 years to build and was opened to the public in 2012, and artifacts from the station's busiest railroad days.

Historic Governors' Mansion

The **Historic Governors' Mansion** (300 E. 21st St., 307/777-7878, 9am-5pm Mon.-Sat., 1pm-5pm Sun. June-Sept., 9am-5pm Wed.-Sat. and Tues. by appointment only Sept.-May, free, donations welcome) was home to each of Wyoming's governors 1905-1976. Although the house was never intended to be a showplace, and was intentionally built in a middle-class neighborhood just blocks from the capitol building, today the mansion is a state historic site. After a $1 million renovation project, visitors will see original decor from 1905, 1937, 1955, and the 1960s. The home was the height of modernity when it was constructed in 1905, with indoor plumbing, hot water, central heating, and electrical and gas fixtures. The most interesting tidbit about this Georgian-style building is that it housed the country's first woman governor, Nellie Tayloe Ross, 1925-1927. Visitors can view a short video about the house and its residents before beginning their self-guided tour.

Wyoming State Museum

The **Wyoming State Museum** (2301 Central Ave., 307/777-7022, http://wyomuseum.state.wy.us, 9am-4:30pm Mon.-Sat., free) is dedicated to documenting the state's history from its earliest inhabitants to the present day. In addition to the permanent collection, 3-4 traveling exhibits are showcased at a time. A 125th anniversary exhibition of Wyoming's statehood will run through the end of July 2017. Always on display are exhibits dedicated to prehistoric Wyoming and its dinosaurs, the wildlife of Wyoming, the state's mining history (including an explanation of how coal is created in nature), and a social history of the state. Other exhibits include beautiful Native American beadwork and pottery, a vast firearms collection, and a copy of the act granting women the right to vote in the Wyoming Territory. A hands-on history room for children is well equipped with vintage clothing, a child-size tipi, a chuck wagon, and dinosaur and other interactive displays. As you tour the museum, you can dial up an audio tour at 307/316-0077. The museum also holds a free Thursday Night Lecture Series.

Cheyenne Frontier Days Old West Museum

Frontier Days is such an important part of Cheyenne's local history that a museum was created to tell the story of this Western celebration. The **Old West Museum** (4610 Carey Ave., 307/778-7290, www.oldwestmuseum.org, 9am-5pm Mon.-Fri., 10am-5pm Sat.-Sun., $10 adults, $9 seniors and military, free for children under 12) is filled with memorabilia from the rodeo and focuses on frontier life in Wyoming. It has more than 150 horse-drawn carriages and wagons dating back over a century, along with large Western art exhibits and some 60,000 artifacts. There is also a fun children's history room with clever interactive displays. The museum has extended hours during the Frontier Days festival and is

Fort Laramie National Historic Site

conveniently located in Frontier Park adjacent to the rodeo. A terrific store is also on-site for gift shopping.

Nelson Museum of the West

If you are interested in viewing more cowboy and Native American memorabilia, head over to the **Nelson Museum of the West** (1714 Carey Ave., 307/635-7670, www.nelsonmuseum.com, 9am-4:30pm Mon.-Sat. June-Aug., 9am-4:30pm Mon.-Fri. May and Sept.-Oct., $5 adults, $4 seniors, free for children under 13). There are more than 20 exhibits created from the eclectic personal collection of Robert C. Nelson, including the art of the Plains Indians, firearms of the West, and furnishings from the homes of cattle barons. Look for the stuffed big-game animals scattered throughout the three floors. Audio tours are available on your phone at 307/316-0069.

Cheyenne Botanic Gardens

Should the days get hot and dusty in Cheyenne, find a stunning oasis at the

Cheyenne Botanic Gardens (710 S. Lions Park Dr., 307/637-6458, www.botanic.org, dawn-dusk daily, greenhouse 8am-4:30pm Mon.-Fri., 11am-3:30pm Sat., free). The plant diversity is stunning, and there is a unique children's village (10am-5pm Tues.-Sun., free) with drop-in activities, a pond and labyrinth, a solar conservatory, community gardens, and more.

★ Fort Laramie National Historic Site

An indelible part of Wyoming's history, **Fort Laramie** (307/837-2221, www.nps.gov, 9am-7pm daily Memorial Day-Labor Day, 8am-4:30pm daily Labor Day-Memorial Day, free) sits at the confluence of the Laramie and North Platte Rivers. It was a major trading center, a military garrison, and the site where the infamous Treaty of 1868 between the U.S. government and the Plains Indians was signed. People from all walks of life, including Indians, trappers, missionaries, and homesteaders, passed through the fort during its almost 50 years of existence.

Today there are 22 original structures on the 830 acres of this National Historic Site. The first stop at the fort should be the **visitors center,** located in the old commissary building. There is an 18-minute video that describes the fort's rich history along with exhibits with artifacts from frontier times, including weapons, uniforms, and historical photos. A free brochure is available to help visitors with a self-guided tour, or experience the audio tour ($3), which includes voices and sounds from the past.

While at the fort, visit the **cavalry barracks,** which clearly gives a sense of the cramped living quarters of the soldiers, and **Old Bedlam,** initially the fort headquarters and later used as officers' quarters. The officers were known to host wild parties in the building, hence its name. Also on the grounds is an old stone **guardhouse** where prisoners were kept, a model of the original **Fort John** building erected in 1841, and the old fort **bakery.**

The Grand Old Post

Originally built as a fur trading post in 1834, **Fort Laramie** was established as a military fort in 1849 when the U.S. government purchased the old Fort John. As was true of most of the forts across the region, its mission was to ensure the safety of pioneers traveling west on the established trails, the closest of which was the Oregon Trail. The second military fort constructed for this purpose, Fort Laramie was unique in that it was always an open fort, meaning there was no wall or fence enclosing the structures.

In 1854, three years after the Treaty of 1851, which was meant to bring peace between the Native Americans and the United States, 29 soldiers from Fort Laramie, an officer, and an interpreter were killed in the Grattan Fight. The event fueled a new ferocity in the war that raged throughout the 1860s and 1870s between Native Americans and the U.S. military. As the battles grew larger, Fort Laramie was often a staging ground and a command post.

By the late 1880s, when the Indian Wars were mostly a thing of the past, Fort Laramie became more of a village than a fort. Trees were planted on the otherwise barren landscape. Boardwalks were built in front of the officers' quarters. In March 1890, when the Union Pacific Railroad was routed south of the fort, with no enemy to fight and no trails to protect, the military decommissioned the fort and sold many of its buildings at auction.

For decades, Fort Laramie existed as a small village, attracting a few curious history buffs, but not much else. Three homesteaders secured and used some of the existing buildings for businesses or agricultural purposes, preventing them from the fate of many of the buildings, which were to be stripped and sold for valuable lumber and other materials. By the numbers, nine original buildings survived by being useful while more than 50 were demolished, moved, or stripped for lumber. In 1938, after much wrangling among federal and state officials and private landowners, including a battle over turning the fort into a golf resort, the 214 acres that had once been Fort Laramie were made a national monument. In 1960, the monument was increased to 571 acres and named a National Historic Site by Congress. A great deal of restoration took place at the fort 1950-1970.

Today, visitors can amble around the grounds and peek into several of the restored buildings. Admission is free. A very worthwhile audio tour, including readings from journals of people who lived at the fort, is available for $3 at the **visitors center** (9am-7pm daily Memorial Day-Labor Day, 8am-4:30pm daily Labor Day-Memorial Day). The fort offers a Living History Military Weekend (visit www.nps.gov for dates and details), which brings the fort to life with reenactments and various educational events. The weekend is also the time for the annual Moonlight Tour. Other events throughout the year include Haunted Prison Tours in October and Horse Barn Dinner Theater evenings in summer.

To get to the fort from Cheyenne, head north on I-80 for 80 miles to exit 92 for Guernsey and Torrington. Drive east for 27.9 miles, turn right onto Highway 160, and follow the signs. The drive is just over 113 miles and should take about an hour and 45 minutes.

ENTERTAINMENT AND EVENTS
★ Frontier Days

The biggest event in Cheyenne—the biggest in Wyoming—is **Frontier Days** (www.cfdrodeo.com), an affair that has been defining Wyoming's capital city since 1897. The largest outdoor rodeo in the country today, the celebration's origins are rather humble. Union Pacific passenger agent F. W. Angier and the editor of the local Cheyenne newspaper claimed to have dreamed up the idea based on Greeley, Colorado's "Potato Day."

The first Frontier Days was held on September 23, 1897, and drew a substantial crowd for events that ranged from a bucking horse contest to a mock stagecoach robbery and mock hanging. The troops from Fort

Russell lit cannons, and the crowd quickly followed suit by firing their own guns, sending horses and other livestock into a panic. No one was killed, and the event only reinforced Wyoming's reputation for rowdiness.

By far the most popular event at early Frontier Days was the bucking bronc contest, which allowed ranchers to pit their cowboys against each other to determine who had the best ones. Although riders could use a saddle, they had to wait until the horse came to a complete standstill before finishing their ride. They weren't allowed to hold on to any part of the saddle, but they could fan the horse with their hats, whip it, or use their spurs.

More than 120 years later, Frontier Days carries on with much the same spirit. It is now a 10-day event spanning two weekends. In recent years nearly 200,000 people have shown up to attend events that include parades, major rock and country music concerts, free pancake breakfasts, tours of an Indian village, a Western art show, a carnival, dances, and nine days of PRCA rodeo. This event has clearly earned its nickname, "the daddy of 'em all."

The event is held annually the last two weekends in July at the rodeo grounds (4610 Carey Ave.) and around town. For more information, contact the **Frontier Days office** (307/778-7222 or 800/227-6336).

Other Events

Happening over a weekend each year in mid-June, Cheyenne gathers on the beautiful Depot Plaza to celebrate beer at the **Wyoming Brewer's Festival** (www.wyobrewfest.com). The event includes a delicious Taster's Party, which pairs beer with food from Cheyenne's varied culinary scene. There is also live music both nights and plenty of festivities. The proceeds from this event benefit the Cheyenne Depot.

For 13 days in early August, the **Laramie County Fair** (3967 Archer Pkwy., 307/633-4670, www.laramiecountyfair.com), which calls itself the oldest and largest county fair in the state, offers up family entertainment with

everything from a demolition derby and dock diving for dogs to horse events and 4-H. After all the flash and sparkle of Frontier Days, the Laramie County Fair is bunny shows over bronc riding, a refreshingly traditional small-town event.

For information on regularly scheduled events such as Tuesday-night **Movies in the Park** or **symphony orchestra concerts** in the amphitheater at Lions Park, check out the Visit Cheyenne website at www.cheyenne.org.

Throughout summer, May-September, free **horse-drawn carriage rides** are offered from 15th Street and Capitol Avenue, 11am-5pm daily. Rides are dependent on weather and other downtown activities. For daily updates, call 307/778-3133.

SHOPPING

Because of its size, Cheyenne has plenty of the major superstores, but there are also some smaller and wonderful boutiques to check out. **Bohemian Metals** (314 W. 17th St., 307/778-8782, www.bohemianmetals.com, 10am-6pm Tues.-Fri., 10am-5pm Sat.) specializes in handmade jewelry, including vintage Native American pieces, gemstones and minerals, and fossils.

A wonderful place for browsing and shopping is the **Cowgirls of the West Museum & Emporium** (205 W. 17th St., 307/638-4994, www.cowgirlsofthewestmuseum.com, 11am-4pm Tues.-Fri., 11am-3pm Sat. May-Aug., extended hours during Frontier Days, free), a nonprofit museum dedicated to informing visitors about the contribution that women made to the settlement of the Old West and the contributions being made by women today. The gift shop features Wyoming-made collectibles, jewelry, Western art, antiques, and wonderful kids' items. Set in a beautiful, historic building, **Wyoming Home** (216 W. Lincolnway, 307/638-2222, www.wyoming-home.com, 9am-7pm Mon.-Fri., 9am-5pm Sat., noon-5pm Sun. summer, 10am-6pm Mon.-Fri., 10am-5pm Sat. fall-spring) has an enormous selection of Wyoming-made gifts and housewares.

The largest shopping mall in the region is **Frontier Mall** (1400 Dell Range Blvd., 307/638-2290, www.frontiermall.com, 10am-9pm Mon.-Sat., 11am-6pm Sun.), which has more than 80 stores.

SPORTS AND RECREATION

For a city known for its rodeo, Cheyenne has a vast array of recreational opportunities beyond the chutes.

Hiking and Biking

For being in the middle of a high desert, Cheyenne has a remarkable number of green parks to explore and enjoy on two feet or two wheels. The **Greater Cheyenne Greenway** links several of the parks with 10 miles of paved trails open to hikers and bikers. Sections of trail wind through Crow Creek, Dry Creek, Sun Valley, Lions Park, and Allison Draw, among other parts of town. The trails also serve as a wildlife corridor, so keep your eyes peeled.

Located halfway between Cheyenne and Laramie on the Happy Jack Road, **Curt Gowdy State Park** (1319 Happy Jack Rd., 307/632-7946, http://wyoparks.state.wy.us, $4 residents, $6 nonresidents, camping $10 residents, $17 nonresidents, includes day use) contains more than 35 miles of trails connecting three reservoirs as well as four open free-ride areas. The trails were given an Epic designation by the International Mountain Biking Association, and all are open to both hikers and bikers. Among the longer trails are **Canyon's Trail** (5.43 miles), **Stone Temple Circuit** (3.75 miles), **Lariat** (2.92 miles), and **Shoreline** (2.63 miles). The area is also open to horses. A map is available online or at the park. Pets are not permitted in the water at Gowdy, and the area is usually packed on warm weekends with campers and recreationists.

Golf

Cheyenne has a number of golf courses, including the 18-hole **Airport Golf Club** (4801 Central Ave., 307/638-3700, $25 for 18 holes, $18

Experience cowboy culture in Cheyenne.

for 9 holes, twilight and off-season discounts), **Cheyenne Country Club** (800 Stinner Rd., 307/637-2204, www.cheyennecountryclub.com, $70 for 18 holes as an unaccompanied guest), 18-hole **F. E. Warren AFB Golf Club** (6110 Golf Course Dr., 307/773-3556, www.funatwarren.com, $25 civilian guests for 18 holes, $24 civilian seniors, $18 civilian guests for 9 holes or twilight play, advance reservations required) at the air force base, 9-hole municipal **Prairie View Golf Course** (3601 Windmill Rd., 307/637-6420, $11), and 9-hole **Little America Golf Course** (2800 W. Lincolnway, 307/775-8500, $28-30 for 18 holes).

FOOD

As Wyoming's largest city by far, Cheyenne has quite a few restaurants and no shortage of chain establishments to choose from, and there are some wonderful gems worth seeking out.

One of the best local spots for breakfast or lunch is **Luxury Diner** (1401 W. Lincolnway, 307/638-8971, 6am-4pm, $5-10), a tiny railroad-themed place announced by a "Wyoming Motel" sign nearly as large as the restaurant. It's crowded but completely delightful, and the food explains the wait; try the corned beef hash and eggs or Santa Fe breakfast burrito. The **Bread Basket Bakery** (1819 Maxwell Ave., 307/432-2525, www.breadbasketbakery.com, 6am-6pm Mon.-Fri., 6am-4pm Sat., lunch $4-7) offers wonderfully fresh pastries, breads, cakes, and other goodies along with a selection of sandwiches and soups. Another great spot for a quick bite, cup of joe, or delicious frappe is **Carol's Café** (2800 W. Lincolnway, 307/775-8400, www.cheyenne.littleamerica.com, 6am-2pm daily) in the Little America Hotel & Resort.

Located just across from the historic depot on the corner of 15th and Capitol, **The Albany** (1506 Capitol Ave., 307/638-3507, www.salbanycheyenne.com, 11am-2pm and 5pm-9pm Mon.-Sat., lunch $9-13.50, dinner $10-25) has been serving locals since 1942. Owned by the same family all those years, The Albany looks more charming from the outside than it does the inside, but the food is good and hearty, from burgers, salads, sandwiches, and Mexican fare to steaks, chops, and seafood. The chicken-fried steak and Jack Daniel's bread pudding earn regular raves.

Despite the fact that **Anong's Thai** (620 Central Ave., 307/638-8597, www.anong-thai.com, 11am-3pm and 5pm-9pm Mon.-Sat., 11am-3pm and 5pm-8pm Sun., $10-18) looks like a strip club from the outside, the dishes here are authentically delicious, and the service is excellent. Anong's Thai has two other locations as well, one in Laramie and the other in Rawlins. Thai food lovers won't be disappointed by the big menu and wonderful cuisine at any of the three.

Gourmet Wyoming fare with strong Southern flair, also known as Lowcountry Southern cuisine, is the thing at **Morris House Bistro** (2114 Warren Ave., 307/369-1378, www.morrishousebistro.com, 5:15pm-9:30pm Thurs.-Sat., brunch on Sun., $19-34),

a charming little eatery set in an old house that belonged to Esther Hobart Morris, the first female justice of the peace in the United States. Although this is not an ideal spot for vegetarians, the seasonal offerings—from deep-fried delta frog legs and gumbo to quail and rib eye—are fresh and mouthwatering. The Sunday brunch (10am-12:30pm summer) is quite popular for good reason. Reservations are recommended for dinner, but are not available for brunch or patio seating in summer.

For a rustic Western dinner theater experience, try the **Bit-O-Wyo Ranch Horse Barn Dinner Show** (470 Happy Jack Rd., 307/638-6924, 6pm Sat. July-Aug., $40 pp, free for children under 7, reservations required), which includes a classic chuck wagon dinner of steak, baked beans, and applesauce, followed by a two-hour performance of cowboy music and comedy. Check the website for specific show dates.

ACCOMMODATIONS

Built in 1888 when Cheyenne was among the richest cities of its size in the world, the ★ **Nagle Warren Mansion** (222 E. 17th St., 307/637-3333 or 800/811-2610, www.naglewarrenmansion.com, $113-183) is an exquisite bed-and-breakfast boasting 12 rooms in the mansion and the adjacent carriage house. While the ambience and furnishings are a wonderful reflection of the elegant Victorian era in which the mansion was built, the amenities—including central air-conditioning, private baths, telephone, TV, and wireless Internet in each room—are decidedly 21st century. Each room is uniquely appointed and named for an important figure in the mansion's fascinating history. A sumptuous breakfast is served each morning; lunches and dinners can be arranged as well. The mansion's Murder Mystery Dinners are great fun and wildly popular, as are a variety of getaway weekends and special events. For what you pay and what you get as a guest at the mansion, this is without a doubt one of the best values in the entire state.

Undoubtedly one of the coolest signs at any motel just about anywhere is the one at the **Firebird Motel** (1905 E. Lincolnway, 307/632-5505, $49-65). The dated rooms are as basic as can be, and the motel has been hit hard by the economic downturn, but the sign is worth seeing. A good and perhaps more reliable budget-friendly choice in town is the **Fleetwood Motel** (3800 E. Lincolnway, 307/638-8908, $55-95).

An important part of the Cheyenne community since 1911, **The Historic Plains Hotel** (1600 Central Ave., 307/638-3311 or 866/275-2467, www.theplainshotel.com, $92-189) is a handsome establishment with 130 lovely rooms and suites. The hotel is decorated with art by Wyoming artists and offers a full restaurant, bar, coffee shop, and an on-site fitness center and spa. A multimillion-dollar renovation in 2003 restored the hotel to its glory, and The Historic Plains is an excellent value for your money in Cheyenne.

Cheyenne also has a number of comfortable, convenient chain hotels. Both the **Radisson Hotel Cheyenne** (204 W. Fox Farm Rd., 307/638-4466, www.radisson.com, $85-320) and **Holiday Inn Express Hotel & Suites** (1741 Fleischli Pkwy., 307/433-0751, www.ihg.com, $118-184) are good choices. **Comfort Inn & Suites** (201 W. Fox Farm Rd., 307/514-6051, www.choicehotels.com, $125-252) and **Super 8** (1900 W. Lincolnway, 307/635-8741, www.super8.com, $85-96) are a bit more budget-friendly.

The website for the **Cheyenne Convention and Visitors Bureau** (800/228-6063, www.cheyenne.org) has a handy tool where travelers can input their travel dates to see all available accommodations in the city. The tool is particularly useful the closer one gets to Frontier Days, as accommodations fill up entirely.

CAMPING

Thanks to the massive numbers of people that roll into town for Frontier Days, Cheyenne has abundant RV and tent campgrounds, not all of which are necessarily great. Among those that are really special is ★ **Curt Gowdy State Park** (1319 Happy Jack Rd., 307/632-7946, http://wyoparks.state.wy.us, $4 residents, $6 nonresidents, camping $10 residents, $17 nonresidents, includes day use), 24 miles west of Cheyenne, at the edge of the Laramie Mountains. There are 35 sites that can be reserved, 15 RV sites with water hookups, none with electricity, and the remaining sites are first-come, first-served. In addition to camping and picnicking spots, the park—located on three lovely reservoirs—offers trout and kokanee salmon fishing as well as hiking and biking trails.

Another worthwhile camping spot, particularly for families with children, is the **Terry Bison Ranch Campground** (51 E. I-25 Service Rd. E., 307/634-4171, www.terrybisonranch.com), just seven miles south of Cheyenne. There is an abundance of activities available, including horseback riding, fishing, train tours to see the ranch's population of bison, ostriches, and even camels, and even bison hunts in winter. With a restaurant on-site, the place is fully self-contained. Accommodations options include cabins ($89, or $175 during Frontier Days), bunk rooms ($59, or $62 during Frontier Days), RV sites ($23-42, or $32-64 during Frontier Days), and tent sites ($19-20).

Other options right in Cheyenne are the nicely shaded **A.B. Campground** (1503 W. College Dr., 307/634-7035, www.campcheyenne.com, $32-57 tent and RV sites), which offers nightly barbecues, and **Cheyenne KOA** (8800 Archer Frontage Rd., 307/638-8840 or 800/562-1507, www.koakampgrounds.com, $38-58 tent and RV sites, $82 cabins), which has an outdoor swimming pool in summer.

INFORMATION AND SERVICES

Cheyenne's well-organized convention and visitors bureau has a downtown **visitors center** (121 W. 15th St., Ste. 202, 307/778-3133 or 800/426-5009, www.cheyenne.org, 8am-7pm Mon.-Fri., 9am-5pm Sat., 1pm-3pm

Sun. summer, 8am-5pm Mon.-Fri., 9am-5pm Sat., 1pm-3pm Sun. fall-spring).

The **Southeast Wyoming Welcome Center** (5611 High Plains Rd., 307/777-7777 or 800/225-5996, 8am-5pm daily June-Sept., 8am-5pm Mon.-Fri., 9am-3pm Sat.-Sun. Oct.-May) is headquartered at the rest area at exit 4 on I-25 and offers abundant parking, a dump station, fresh water, clean bathrooms, picnic tables, and more information than you could possibly take in.

The main downtown **post office** (307/772-7080, 7:30am-noon Mon., 7:30am-5:30pm Tues.-Fri.) is located at 2120 Capitol Avenue.

The **Laramie County Library** (307/634-3561, www.lclsonline.org, 10am-9pm Mon.-Thurs., 10am-6pm Fri.-Sat., 1pm-5pm Sun.) is at 2200 Pioneer Avenue.

The **Cheyenne Regional Medical Center** (214 E. 23rd St., 307/634-2273, www.cheyenneregional.org) is a major medical facility with 24-hour emergency care. Another option is **College Drive Urgent Care** (4136 Laramie St., 307/637-2800, www.collegedriveurgentcare.com, 8am-8pm Mon.-Fri., 10am-4pm Sat.-Sun.).

Wash clothes at **Easy Way Laundry** (900 W. Lincolnway, 307/638-2177, 24 hours daily).

TRANSPORTATION
Getting There
Cheyenne Regional Airport (CYS, 200 E. 8th Ave., 307/634-7071, www.cheyenneairport.com) offers daily nonstop service to Denver, on **Great Lakes** (307/635-6623, www.flygreatlakes.com). Denver International Airport (DEN) is just 90 miles by car from Cheyenne. For shuttle service between Denver and Cheyenne airports, contact **Green Ride** (307/459-4433 or 888/472-6656, greenrideco.com).

Car rentals are available from **Avis, National,** and **Hertz.**

By car, Cheyenne is 49 miles east of Laramie, 100 miles north of Denver, 256 miles east of Rock Springs, 291 miles southwest of Rapid City, 393 miles southeast of Cody, 429 miles southeast of Yellowstone National Park, and 456 miles southeast of Billings.

Daily bus service in and out of Cheyenne is provided from the Rodeway Inn by **Greyhound** (5401 Walker Rd., 307/635-1327, www.greyhound.com) and **Express Arrow** (5401 Walker Rd., 877/779-2999, www.expressarrow.com).

Getting Around
Local public transportation is available in Cheyenne from **Cheyenne Transit** (307/637-6253, www.cheyennecity.org). There are also a handful of taxi companies, including **Cowboy Shuttle** (307/638-2468) and **TI Shuttle** (307/778-4066, www.tishuttle.com).

Sweetwater County

Sweetwater County in the southwest corner of Wyoming is a fascinating mix of the desert Southwest—think kaleidoscopic rock formations, mesas, and canyons—and the rugged Western appeal of Wyoming with rodeo, wild mustangs, and vast open spaces. Though not a tourist destination in the way that northwest Wyoming is—the region is shifting with the boom and bust of the energy sector—this part of the state offers constant and abundant recreational opportunities that add up to an appealing lifestyle. This is not so much cowboy country as mining country, mountain biking country, and river rafting country.

A high alpine desert, Rock Springs (population 24,138, elevation 6,271 feet) parallels Gillette in some ways—it is in the thick of an energy boom and the subsequent rapid growth—but it is located next to some pretty phenomenal country, including the unrivaled and scenic **Flaming Gorge National Recreation Area.** The city itself has a few good museums and an interesting international flavor that dates back to coal mining and railroad development around the turn of the 20th century.

Green River (population 12,752, elevation 6,109 feet) is an old railroad town that got its start as a station along the Overland and Pony Express routes. It has a rather industrial history spanning the railroads and mines in the region, but it is best known for its namesake river, which runs right through town. The Green River forms the headwaters of the Colorado River basin and was for years a prime shipping route for timber. Major John Wesley Powell launched two of his biggest expeditions from here, including his first into the unexplored Grand Canyon in 1869. Surrounded by magnificent multicolored buttes and outcroppings, the town is still very much centered around the river and is a popular launching spot for raft and kayak expeditions.

Economically speaking, Sweetwater County owes its growth to the world's largest known deposit of trona ore (a type of soda ash used in chemicals, laundry detergent, kitty litter, and glass), the production of which employs more than 2,240 people at five local mines. Soda ash produced from Wyoming's trona reserves accounts for 90 percent of all the soda ash in the United States and is Wyoming's biggest export with some 50 percent sold overseas. Though oil, natural gas, and coal extraction are dwindling in the region after a boom straddling the turn of the 21st century, mineral extraction in Sweetwater County still accounts for nearly 70 percent of the region's total revenue.

SIGHTS
Museums

There are a number of museums in this region worth a visit. The **Sweetwater County Historical Museum** (3 E. Flaming Gorge Way, Green River, 307/872-6435, www.sweetwatermuseum.org, 10am-6pm Mon.-Sat., free) will surprise visitors with its vast and thorough displays. The museum has done a good job of documenting the history of the region and exhibits many artifacts from the daily life of ranchers, miners, and the numerous immigrants who came to the region. Visitors can see everything from a dinosaur's fossilized footprint to a rifle from Butch Cassidy's gang, to an RCA Victor Victrola phonograph, and a wedding dress from 1903. There is also an engaging video and display about the horrific Chinese Massacre in Rock Springs.

In Rock Springs, the **Rock Springs Historical Museum** (201 B St., 307/362-3138, www.rswy.net, 10am-5pm Mon.-Sat., free) is situated in the stately city hall, built from sandstone in 1894 for a total cost of $28,200. The museum documents the city's diverse immigrant population, its

The Chinese Massacre

Mining was essential to the ultimate success of the Union Pacific Railroad: Closed mines threatened coal supplies, which would be disastrous because trains required a steady supply of fuel to meet their schedules. In 1875, when miners in Rock Springs and Carbon organized to demand better wages, their strike shut down Union Pacific's two largest mines. It was no surprise that the railroad looked for a quick yet cheap solution. Until this point, all the miners in Rock Springs had been white, but two weeks after the strike started, Union Pacific brought in 150 Chinese men to work the mines. By month's end, some 50 white miners had returned to work, strike organizers had been fired, and the two races were expected to work side by side. Although there was underlying resentment and racism—Chinese miners worked for less and were therefore more employable, plus this was the era when the Chinese Exclusion Act of 1882 was passed—tensions did not come to a head until a decade later.

By 1885 the number of Chinese miners at Rock Springs had increased to 331, nearly double the number of white miners. Since the miners were paid by the ton, mine assignments were important. On September 2, some white miners were upset that Chinese miners had been assigned to prime areas. They met the Chinese men outside the mine and prevented them from entering. The altercation quickly turned violent, with one Chinese miner dying from his injuries.

The mob mentality quickly picked up momentum, and soon many more white miners were vengefully hunting down Chinese miners. Many victims were scalped, mutilated, dismembered, and even burned alive. In an effort to escape the violent persecution, many Chinese miners fled into the surrounding desert.

The white miners entered Chinatown, attacking its occupants and setting fire to the buildings. The entire neighborhood burned to the ground: 79 homes were destroyed, 28 Chinese were killed, and 15 were injured. The violence shocked the nation, but it also ignited anti-Chinese violence in other small towns in the West. Reaction in Wyoming was mixed. The local newspaper supported the attacks; other papers criticized the massacre while empathizing with the plight of the white miners. The territorial governor, Francis E. Warren, requested federal help to restore peace.

Federal troops entered Rock Springs on September 5. Troops were also deployed to Evanston, where many of the Chinese had fled. Emergency troops were pulled out of the area one month later; the temporary post at Camp Pilot Butte remained occupied until 1899.

When the mines eventually did reopen, 45 men were fired by Union Pacific for their role in the violence. Sixteen men were arrested in conjunction with the riot and held in Green River. Although a grand jury was called in Green River, no indictments were handed out, and the men were released a month later to a heroes' welcome.

The only form of justice came as a response by the U.S. government to appease the Chinese government. With much finagling, President Grover Cleveland persuaded Congress to issue financial compensation to China for $149,000. During the 1920s and 1930s, the Union Pacific Coal Company paid retirement packages and purchased tickets for retired miners to return to China. Only one of the miners chose to live his final days in Rock Springs.

For more information on the Chinese Massacre or other episodes in Wyoming's storied history, visit www.wyohistory.org, an outstanding resource.

coal-mining history, and the illegal activity and outlaws it also attracted. The **Western Wyoming Community College Natural History Museum and Weidner Wildlife Museum** (2500 College Dr., 307/382-1600, 10am-1pm Mon. and Wed., 1pm-4pm Tues.-Thurs., free) houses a small collection of fossils, minerals, and Native American artifacts from the area. A large number of big-game heads from around the world are also on display. The **Community Fine Arts Center** (400 C St., 307/362-6212, www.cfacf4art.com, 10am-6pm Mon.-Thurs., noon-5pm Fri.-Sat., free) has works by Norman Rockwell, Conrad Schwiering, and Grandma Moses, among other prominent American artists.

Pilot Butte Wild Horse Scenic Tour

There are 1,100-1,600 wild horses roaming the stark landscape of the 392,000-acre **White Mountain Herd Management Area** around Rock Springs and Green River. Although they can often be spotted from I-80, a scenic road affords better opportunities for wild horse sightings. County Road 53 can be accessed either from Rock Springs or Green River; it is a 24-mile gravel road that takes about 90 minutes to drive as it winds across the White Mountains with spectacular vistas. The most likely view of the horses comes between Rock Springs and 14-Mile Hill and all the way across the top of White Mountain. Early morning and late afternoon are the best times to view wildlife. The road is only open May-October. For more information about the scenic drive, contact the Bureau of Land Management's **Rock Springs Field Office** (280 Hwy. 191 N., 307/352-0256, www.blm.gov).

Rich Nobles of **Green River Wild Horse Tour & Eco Safari** (307/875-2923 or 307/875-5711, www.greenriverwildhorsetours.com) works hard to get his customers views of the wild mustangs. For half-day tours ($75 pp), he takes passengers off the normal route in his imported all-terrain vehicle to view the wildlife up close. The trip usually covers about 70 miles and can last up to six hours.

White Mountain Petroglyphs

Some 26 miles north of Rock Springs on County Road 4-17 is one of the state's premier rock art sites, the **White Mountain Petroglyphs.** On a 300-foot cliff, hundreds of images—portraying everything from bison and elk hunts to geometric shapes and even tiny footprints—tell the stories of the Plains and Great Basin Indians who lived and traveled through the region as many as 1,000 years ago. Depictions of horses and swords suggest the natives' first contact with Europeans. The site is remote and primitive with no facilities. Pack plenty of water and food. Four-wheel drive is recommended, and you will be on foot for the last quarter mile to the site. For more information, contact the Bureau of Land Management's **Rock Springs Field Office** (280 Hwy. 191 N., 307/352-0256).

Seedskadee National Wildlife Refuge

The **Seedskadee National Wildlife Refuge** (www.fws.gov) sits along 36 miles of the Green River and encompasses over

Southwest Wyoming is an excellent place to look for wild horses.

26,000 acres of land. The Shoshone Indians first called the Green River "sisk-a-dee-agie," or "River of the Prairie Chicken." Fur traders changed the name to Seedskadee. The refuge consists of marshes, wetlands, and uplands, and more than 200 different bird species have been sighted in the area. The riparian areas have become an important nesting ground for a variety of migratory birds, including Canada geese, great blue herons, and swans. In springtime, the prairie is filled with the strange pops and whistles of the greater sage-grouse males, pining for mates. The refuge is a popular spot for fishing, wildlife viewing, and short float trips. It is 37 miles north of Green River on Highway 372. The refuge headquarters is just 2 miles north of the junction of Highways 372 and 28.

Killpecker Sand Dunes

Thirty-seven miles from Rock Springs is one of Wyoming's most unique natural wonders, complete with a herd of rare desert elk not found anywhere else in the United States. The 109,000-acre **Killpecker Sand Dunes** are the largest active dunes in the United States. The massive hills of white sand stretch more than 55 miles and offer a fun playground for hikers. There are two wilderness study areas in the dunes—Buffalo Hump and Sand Dunes—but elsewhere on the shifting sands, off-road vehicle enthusiasts can explore this natural playground. However, go prepared with water, food, a compass, and a map—people can easily get disoriented in the desert setting. If approaching the dunes from Rock Springs, you will pass the area office of the **Bureau of Land Management** (280 U.S. 191 N., Rock Springs, 307/352-0256); it's worth stopping in to get more information and a map of the area. Don't forget to ask about the wild horses and how you can have the best chance of seeing them in their desert habitat. Sightings often occur in the Leucite Hills area.

Also at the dunes, rock climbing enthusiasts will enjoy a visit to the volcanic plug known as **Boar's Tusk.** This towering rock formation measures 400 feet in height; Devils Tower is the only other geological feature like this in the state.

Fossil Butte National Monument

Known as "America's Aquarium in Stone," **Fossil Butte National Monument** (864 Chicken Creek Rd., Kemmerer, 80 miles west of Green River, 307/877-4455, www.nps.gov, free) sits in the middle of what was once a subtropical habitat. During the Eocene epoch, 50 million years ago, this was a large lake area, home to alligators, turtles, fish, and even palm trees. Over the eons, animal and plant remains sank to the bottom of the lake bed, where they were covered with sediment and fossilized. When the lake dried up and the bed was eventually pushed to the surface, some of the best-preserved fossils in the world were revealed.

The **visitors center** (9am-5:30pm daily May-Sept., 8am-4:30pm daily Oct.-Apr., closed holidays in winter) displays more than 80 fossils, including two types of bats, numerous species of fish, and even a 13-foot crocodile. There is also an area where visitors can handle the fossils and make rubbings of them. During summer, experts conduct fossil preparation demonstrations and take questions from the public. Two short trails take visitors through the unique history of the park and allow for some wildlife viewing. During summer, plan to visit 11am-4pm Friday-Saturday to assist paleontologists as they collect fossils at the research quarry.

★ Flaming Gorge National Recreation Area

The **Flaming Gorge National Recreation Area** is full of beautiful rock formations, spectacular land, and rich natural colors. The area was aptly named by a group led by Maj. John Wesley Powell, who started their famous journey down the Green River from where the town of Green River now stands. The explorers floated through the rocky canyons and were stunned by the striking red hues, particularly in Utah.

The area consists of more than 200,000 acres and crosses southwestern Wyoming into northeastern Utah. The landscape in Wyoming is primarily high desert, and the more impressive and dramatic sights are found over the border in Utah. Three roads—Highway 530, U.S. Highway 191, and Utah Highway 44—connect to form a loop around the national recreation area. The visitors center is on the Utah side at Red Canyon.

Activity in Wyoming is largely based around the 91-mile-long **Flaming Gorge Reservoir,** with more than 300 miles of shoreline. Constructed in 1964, the reservoir is a popular destination for water-skiing, fishing, camping, and boating. Its trout-filled waters make it an attractive year-round fishing spot; licenses may be bought in Wyoming or Utah. There are also campgrounds nearby (43 campgrounds with 700 individual sites and more than 30 group sites in the entire recreation area), and many boat launches around the reservoir.

If approaching the reservoir from Highway 530 south of Green River, the road follows the west side of the lake just a few miles from the shore. Various dirt-road turnoffs lead to the water, and many end at isolated beaches where you can camp

for free. There are also commercial services, including **Lucerne Valley Marina** (5570 E. Lucerne Valley Rd., off Hwy. 530, 435/784-3483, www.flaminggorge.com) and **Buckboard Marina** (Hwy. 530, 25 miles south of Green River, 307/875-6927, www.buckboardmarina.com), that take visitors to the recreation area's campsites and docks. If you continue south, heading to Utah, the road passes **Haystack Buttes,** rocky mound-like formations that resemble haystacks, and **Devil's Playground,** a barren badlands of rough terrain.

The loop can also be started at U.S. Highway 191, heading south from Rock Springs. This approach is more mountainous and therefore more scenic, but it is also farther from the reservoir. Early on, a paved road turnoff will take you to **Firehole Canyon.** Here you can see the rocky spires known as **North and South Chimney Rocks** and other interesting geological features. U.S. Highway 191 continues south, climbing 8,000 vertical feet, and has good views of the rolling hills and valleys to the east and west. From here the reservoir is about 15 miles from the road. However, when crossing Spring Creek, the water becomes visible, and there is a turnoff leading 4 miles to the shore.

Flaming Gorge National Recreation Area offers 200,0000 acres of high desert beauty.

Flaming Gorge National Recreation Area

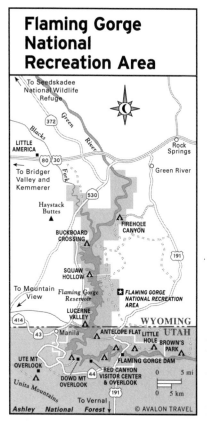

To Seedskadee National Wildlife Refuge

LITTLE AMERICA
Rock Springs
To Bridger Valley and Kemmerer
Green River
Haystack Buttes
FIREHOLE CANYON
BUCKBOARD CROSSING
SQUAW HOLLOW
To Mountain View
Flaming Gorge Reservoir
FLAMING GORGE NATIONAL RECREATION AREA
LUCERNE VALLEY
WYOMING
Manila ANTELOPE FLAT LITTLE HOLE UTAH
BROWN'S PARK
UTE MT OVERLOOK
FLAMING GORGE DAM
Unita Mountains
DOWD MT OVERLOOK
RED CANYON VISITOR CENTER & OVERLOOK
To Vernal
0   5 mi
0   5 km
Ashley National Forest
© AVALON TRAVEL

Both routes cross the Wyoming-Utah border and lead to Utah Highway 44, which takes visitors through the dramatic canyons. One other approach to the loop is from Highway 414, heading southeast from the town of Mountain View. This road traverses badlands, fields filled with sage and juniper, and large open pastures and leads to Henry's Fork, the site of the first mountain man rendezvous in the country.

ENTERTAINMENT AND EVENTS

Known as Wyoming's Big Show, the **Sweetwater County Fair,** held annually at the **Sweetwater Events Center** (3320 Yellowstone Rd., Rock Springs, 307/352-6789, www.sweetwaterevents.com, $13 adults, free

for children under 6), is a 10-day event that includes rodeo action, 4-H livestock competitions, entertainment, and a carnival. Comparable in size to the Wyoming State Fair, the event attracts some 80,000 attendees annually. The Sweetwater Events Center is also home to a variety of rodeo events and stockcar, motocross, and BMX racing.

Rock Springs has a healthy representation of the performing arts, including the **Sweetwater County Concert Association** (307/382-8251 or 307/382-5035), which produces four musical performances annually as well as fund-raisers that pair music with festive dining. The city also programs a solid lineup of musical performances with **Rock Springs Concerts in the Park** (Bunning Park, Evans St. between Elk St. and Noble Dr., 307/352-1500, www.rswy.net) throughout the summer, as well as **Movies in the Park** (Bunning Park). Also in Bunning Park in mid-August is the **Annual Sweetwater Blues 'n Brews Festival** (307/352-1434, www.sweetwaterbluesnbrews.com, $5 pp), which combines a daylong lineup of blues music with local hoppy libations.

As a nod to the town's 56 different ethnicities, the Rock Springs Chamber of Commerce hosts a free **International Day** (307/362-3771, www.rswy.net, free) in Bunning Park early-mid-July. The daylong family-oriented event includes international food and beer plus entertainment and activities.

In Green River, the biggest event of the year is **Flaming Gorge Days** (800/354-6743, www.flaminggorgedays.com), held annually the last weekend of June. The event includes a country concert and a rock concert along with basketball and volleyball tournaments, a parade, a festival in the park, and children's entertainment. Concert tickets are available in advance at discounted rates from the chambers of commerce in Rock Springs (1897 Dewar Dr., 307/362-3771, www.rockspringschamber.com) and Green River (1155 Flaming Gorge Way, 307/875-5711, www.grchamber.com), or at full price at the gate.

Another big event in Green River is the

Annual River Festival (307/875-5711, www. grchamber.com) held in late August. This three-day event includes an art show and auction, a Cajun shrimp boil, kids' games, concerts, nightly fireworks, a number of races including the Run with the Horses Marathon, a poker run, and plenty of food.

SHOPPING

With the major slump in both coal and oil prices, the economy in the region is hurting, and many of the local galleries and gift shops are shuttering (though Rock Springs is still the kind of place where you'll find a shop called Ammo Shack II). Little gems remain, however. **Tynsky's Rocks & Jewelry** (706 Dewar Dr., Rock Springs, 307/389-7246, 1pm-3pm Tues.-Thurs., noon-5pm Fri.-Sat., by appointment during non-opening hours) has a nice selection of locally quarried rock, fossils, jewelry, and tumbling supplies. **Busy Bee Bath Essentials** (535 N. Front St., Rock Springs, 307/851-9862, www.busybeebathessentials.com, 11am-6pm Tues.-Fri., noon-4pm Sat.) is known for its handmade body care and beauty products, but it also features handmade crafts by local artists including jewelry, home decor, blankets, and unfinished wood.

SPORTS AND RECREATION
Recreation Centers

Thanks to the energy boom around the turn of the 21st century and subsequent growth of the tax base, Rock Springs built plentiful facilities, so recreational opportunities abound. The **Rock Springs Family Recreation Center** (3900 Sweetwater Dr., 307/352-1440, www.rswy.net, 5am-7pm Mon.-Fri., noon-6pm Sat.-Sun., $6 adults, $3.25 students 6-18, free for children under 6) offers an indoor swimming pool with a fun splash area for little ones and slides for bigger ones; a full-size ice arena; a full gym with basketball, volleyball, racquetball, and handball courts; an indoor putting course; and various classes and fitness programs.

Golf

Golfers can tee off at the 27-hole championship **White Mountain Golf Course** (1501 Clubhouse Dr., 307/352-1415, www.rswy. net, sunrise-sunset daily late Mar.-early Nov.), considered among the best public golf courses in the state. Nonresidents pay $37 for 18 holes or $21 for 9 holes. There is also an 18-hole course in Green River, the **Rolling Green Country Club** (29 Country Club Rd., 307/875-6200, greens fees vary).

Hiking and Mountain Biking

Although this is wide-open desert, there are some interesting places to hit the trail. For starters, the **Green Belt** and **Scotts Bottom Nature Area,** running through Green River, offer lovely trails to stretch your legs and enjoy the views. The trails are easily accessed from **Expedition Island,** the launching point for Powell's famous river trips through the Grand Canyon.

For more of an adventure, Sweetwater County has more still-visible pioneer trails running through it than anywhere else in the country, and hikers and mountain bikers can follow the double ruts at a variety of points in the big open countryside. Trails in the region include the Oregon and California Trails, the Mormon Trail, and the Pony Express Trail. All adventurers need to be well prepared for the vast undeveloped stretches of land and should bring maps, adequate clothing, and plenty of water.

The mountain biking in the area is sublime, with hundreds of miles of trails ranging from the scenic to the gnarly. Green River is known for some of its hairier trails, including the extremely technical **Lunatic Fringe** and the slightly less insane **Macbones Trail,** both of which can be scouted on www.singletracks.com.

Among the most popular trails is the 20-mile **Cherokee Trail/Currant Creek Ranch Loop,** which starts and ends at the Currant Creek Ranch off County Road 33. It is part of a wider 250-mile network of trails on Little Mountain, south of Rock Springs.

For excellent advice or service, visit **The Bike and Trike** (612 Broadway, Rock Springs, 307/382-9677, www.bikeandtrike.com, 9am-5pm Mon.-Fri., 9am-3pm Sat.).

Without a doubt, the **Flaming Gorge National Recreation Area** offers the densest concentration of recreational opportunities, including miles upon miles of trails for hikers and mountain bikers. The scenic five-mile **Canyon Rim Trail** is accessible from the Red Canyon Visitors Center and is open to both hikers and mountain bikers. The **Dowd Mountain-Hideout Canyon Trail** is significantly steeper and is also open to both hikers and mountain bikers. A trail map for these and other trails in the gorge is available for free at the **U.S. Forest Service** offices in Green River (132 Buck Board Rd., 307/875-4641) and Manila, Utah (intersection of Hwys. 43 and 44, 435/784-3445). For a list of other hiking trails, visit www.flaminggorgecountry.com. For **mountain bike rentals** in the Flaming Gorge, visit the **Red Canyon Lodge** (2450 W. Red Canyon Lodge, Dutch John, Utah, 435/889-3759, www.redcanyonlodge.com, $12/hour, $20 half-day, $36 full-day), four miles west of the junction of Highway 44 and U.S. Highway 191.

Fishing

There are a couple of ways to fish this part of the state, but for anglers looking to hook the big one—a really big one—**Flaming Gorge Reservoir** is the place to go. The lake trout in the reservoir can grow to weigh more than 50 pounds, and 20-pounders are common. Lake trout generally like deeper waters and are more easily fished from boats. The rainbows in the reservoir, on the other hand, can be fished from shore. Other fish in the reservoir include smallmouth bass, kokanee, and burbot. The reservoir drops into Utah, and fishing licenses are required in both Wyoming and Utah; special-use stamps are available for fishing in both states.

The fishing on the **Green River** around its namesake town produces cutthroat, lake trout, and the occasional whitefish. For current conditions, information, and licenses, visit the **Wyoming Game and Fish Department** (351 Astle Ave., Green River, 307/875-3223, http://wgfd.wyo.gov).

For equipment and guided fishing trips on the Green River, contact **Trout Creek Flies** (1155 Little Hole Rd., Dutch John, Utah, 435/885-3355 or 435/885-3338, www.troutcreekflies.net, 7am-7pm daily) at the corner of U.S. 191 and Little Hole Road. In addition to being a full-service fly shop, Trout Creek Flies offers half-day ($375) and full-day ($475) float trips that are discounted in winter, plus lodging, shuttling, overnight camping trip options, and pretty much anything an avid angler might need.

Rafting and Boating

For a high desert, Sweetwater County has an awful lot of ways to enjoy the water. Kayakers get their thrills at the **Green River Whitewater Park and Tubing Channel** (www.cityofgreenriver.org) near Expedition Island in Green River. In addition to the splash park, there is a 1,200-foot-long tubing channel for beginning boaters and swimmers with a series of 4.5-foot drops and three pools. In the main river, a whitewater park with eight gates is geared to advanced boaters.

Most of the boating action in the area, however, happens at Flaming Gorge, and boats can be rented at three locations: **Buckboard Marina** (Hwy. 530, 25 miles south of Green River, 307/875-6927, www.buckboardmarina.com), **Cedar Springs Marina** (2685 Cedar Springs Boat Ramp, off U.S. 191, 2 miles from the dam, 435/889-3795, www.cedarspringsmarina.com), and **Lucerne Valley Marina** (1 Lucerne Valley Recreation Rd., off Hwy. 530, 435/784-3483, www.flaminggorge.com). All three marinas also offer lodging options.

FOOD

For a relatively remote Wyoming town, Rock Springs has an impressive number of international eateries, the origins of which date back to the town's population diversity. **Bonsai**

(1996 Dewar Dr., 307/362-1888, 11am-9pm daily, $8-16) feeds the community's appetite for Asian cuisine. In addition to Chinese and Thai specialties, the restaurant serves decent sushi.

For southwest Wyoming's favorite hamburgers, fries, and shakes, hit **Grub's Drive In** (415 Paulson St., Rock Springs, 307/362-6634, 6am-8pm Mon.-Fri., $4-10). It's not healthy, and you may have to wait in a good-size line, but the shamrock burgers are juicy, the fries come with a side of brown gravy, and the milk shakes are something to write home about.

Another local favorite in Rock Springs is **Cowboy Donuts** (1573 Dewar Dr. #4, 307/362-3400, www.cowboydonuts.com, 5am-2pm Mon.-Sat.), which serves 55 different varieties baked daily, from hand-chopped apple fritters to blueberry cake and glazed donut holes. It also offers an excellent selection of *kolaches*—slightly sweet butter bread stuffed with meat—and specialty coffee drinks.

Among the hippest dining options in town is ★ **Bitter Creek Brewing** (604 Broadway, Rock Springs, 307/362-4782, www.bittercreekbrewing.com, 11am-9pm Mon.-Sat., $9-32), which offers a large and varied menu—think chicken wings, Thai nachos, pizza, and mouthwatering baby back ribs—in a casual, fun, and family-friendly environment. It also has a nice selection of seasonal microbrews on tap.

Hungry diners head to **Penny's Diner** (1170 W. Flaming Gorge Way, Green River, 307/875-3500, 24 hours daily), adjacent to the Oak Tree Inn, a classic 1950s-style diner open 24 hours a day that serves up everything from omelets and sandwiches to burgers and pie.

ACCOMMODATIONS

Rock Springs has a number of chain hotels, but among the best is the pet-friendly **Best Western Outlaw Inn** (1630 Elk St., 307/362-6623, www.bestwestern.com, $100-156), which has a variety of room configurations, standard amenities, a pool, an on-site restaurant, and complimentary breakfast. Another

option in Rock Springs is the **Days Inn** (1545 Elk St., 307/362-5646, www.daysinn.com, $65-81).

The **Western Inn** (890 W. Flaming Gorge Way, Green River, 307/875-2840, $79-85) offers clean, basic accommodations with friendly staff, Wi-Fi, refrigerators, microwaves, and a nice continental breakfast included. Chains in Green River include the **Hampton Inn & Suites Green River** (1055 Wild Horse Canyon Rd., 307/875-5300, www.hamptoninn3.hilton.com, $106-185) and **Super 8** (280 W. Flaming Gorge Way, 307/875-9330, www.super8.com, $58-87).

The most appealing place to stay in the region is actually over the border near Dutch John, Utah. The ★ **Red Canyon Lodge** (2450 W. Red Canyon Lodge, Dutch John, Utah, 435/889-3759, www.redcanyonlodge.com, cabins $125-165) has attractive and cozy cabins with front porches perfect for enjoying the tranquil scenery. The resort offers excellent dining with stunning views and daily wild-game specials, plus a host of activities that range from horseback riding and mountain biking to boat trips and fishing tours.

CAMPING

The **Rock Springs/Green River KOA** (86 Foothill Blvd., Rock Springs, 307/362-3063, www.koa.com) is open year-round and offers tent sites ($34), RV sites ($36-43), and cabins ($68-135). The campground also has Wi-Fi, a swimming pool, a playground, and a variety of games. Pets are permitted.

There is phenomenal public camping in the Flaming Gorge Recreation Area. Among the favorites is the ★ **Red Canyon Campground** (early May-late Sept., $15), which offers front-row seats for the area's spellbinding sunsets. To reserve one of the more than 700 campsites throughout Flaming Gorge, visit www.recreation.gov or call 877/444-6777. To read more about individual campsites in the recreation area, go to www.flaminggorgecountry.com.

INFORMATION AND SERVICES

The **Rock Springs Chamber of Commerce** (1897 Dewar Dr., Rock Springs, 307/362-3771, www.rockspringschamber.com, 8am-5pm Mon.-Fri.) doubles as a visitors center. The **Green River Chamber of Commerce** (1155 Flaming Gorge Way, Green River, 307/875-5711, www.grchamber.com, 8:30am-5:30pm Mon.-Fri.) also operates as a visitors center.

There are **post offices** in Rock Springs (2829 Commercial Way, 307/362-9792, 9am-5pm Mon.-Fri., 9am-noon Sat.) and in Green River (350 Uinta Dr., 307/875-4920, 8:30am-5:30pm Mon.-Fri., 9:30am-1pm Sat.).

Medical care is available 24-7 at **Memorial Hospital of Sweetwater County** (1200 College Dr., Rock Springs, 307/362-3711, www.sweetwatermedicalcenter.com).

Wash clothes at the **Sweetwater Laundry** (2528 Foothill Blvd., Rock Springs, 307/382-6290, 7am-9pm daily) or **9th Street Laundromat** (1215 9th St., Rock Springs, 307/382-6092). Machines and drop-off service are available at **Springtime Laundromat** (520 Wilkes Dr., Ste. 11, Green River, 307/875-8134, 8:30am-8:30pm daily).

TRANSPORTATION
Getting There

The **Rock Springs-Sweetwater County Airport** (RKS, 382 Hwy. 370, 307/352-6880, www.rockspringsairport.com) has daily nonstop flights to Denver on **United** (800/241-6522, www.united.com).

Rental cars are available at the Rock Springs-Sweetwater County Airport from **Avis, National,** and **Hertz.**

Green River is 14 miles west of Rock Springs, 113 miles south of Pinedale, 209 miles southwest of Thermopolis, 240 miles southwest of Casper, and 247 miles south of Yellowstone National Park.

Daily bus service is provided by **Greyhound** (1695 Sunset Dr., Ste. 118, Rock Springs).

Getting Around

Public transportation across Sweetwater County is available through **STAR Transit** (307/382-7827, www.ridestartransit.com).

For taxi service in and around Sweetwater County, contact **All Time Taxi** (307/382-3183), **All City Cab** (307/364-0852), or **EZ Street Taxi** (307/922-0158).

Background

The Landscape

While Wyoming is well known for its spectacular mountains, rivers, and valleys, the eastern part of the state is remote, rural, and based on agriculture. The landscape also hosts Native American reservations and the stories that go with them—many of the West's greatest battles took place here.

GEOGRAPHY

Wyoming is the least populous state in the union with only 586,107 people as of 2015, but is 10th in land area—just over 97,000 square miles. One of only three states (Colorado and Utah are the others) that have borders along straight latitudinal and longitudinal lines, Wyoming is bordered on the north by Montana and on the south by Utah and Colorado. Nebraska and South Dakota border Wyoming on the east, while Idaho makes up most of the western border with a little slice of Utah. The western part of Wyoming is made up of mountainous terrain covered by coniferous forests, and similarly the Continental Divide continues its diagonal run through the state. Eastern Wyoming consists of the High Plains, an expanse of high-elevation prairie that is home to large cattle ranches and oil and gas wells. Wyoming is the third-highest state in the nation (behind Alaska and Colorado), with an elevation range of 3,125-13,804 feet. Gannet Peak in the Wind River Range is the highest point in the state at 13,804 feet.

GEOLOGY

The Greater Yellowstone ecosystem is widely regarded as the largest biologically intact temperate ecosystem in North America. Centered around Yellowstone National Park, this 31,000-square-mile area (nearly 20 million acres) consists of a diverse landscape with geothermal activity and native wildlife; it is considered by scientists as a natural laboratory for landscape ecology, geology, and wildlife preservation.

Visiting the Greater Yellowstone area provides the opportunity to see a natural environment much like it was hundreds and even thousands of years ago. Yellowstone National Park itself is on a high plateau, the remnants of a volcano that last exploded more than 640,000 years ago, leaving a giant caldera. Yellowstone is the most geothermic place on earth, containing a majority of the world's types of geothermal features, including geysers, hot springs, mud pots, and fumaroles.

If you are worried that Yellowstone could erupt during your vacation, you're not alone. Scientists are constantly measuring the amount of pressure in the magma chamber, which actually raises the floor of the caldera plateau—nearly seven inches between 1976 and 1984, and three inches from 2004 to 2008, or about the pace at which our fingernails grow. Since then, the rate of growth has increased to a record-setting seven centimeters per year. But as if the caldera could breathe, the growth is up and down. The dome rises and falls, then rises again. Theoretically, the volcano could erupt, but most scientists seem to think there is little evidence that a cataclysmic explosion will occur anytime soon. Due to its volcanic nature, the Yellowstone area experiences upward of 2,000 measurable earthquakes each year, but you are unlikely to feel one.

Outside Yellowstone Park, the rest of the ecosystem is mountainous and filled with large tracts of roadless land, jagged peaks, broad valleys, and flowing rivers—exactly why many people live here and even more

Previous: meadows in the Big Horns; bison in Grand Teton National Park.

choose to visit. Wildlife abounds, offering a rare glimpse into the lives of everything from the pine marten to the grizzly bear. Of course, people live here too, and the interaction between humans and nature is important not only historically but in contemporary matters as well.

In addition to mountains, there are large tracts of prairies that contain mostly dry grasses and shrubs. The iconic sagebrush plant can be found at nearly every elevation—more sage grows in Wyoming than anywhere else—and many land areas seem almost desertlike, right down to the tumbleweeds that roll along in the breeze. Wyoming actually includes two areas that are classified as desert: the Red Desert near Rock Springs, and a large part of the Bighorn Basin.

CLIMATE

Wyoming's weather is influenced predominantly by its diverse topography. Generally, summers are hot and dry, often punctuated by brief but intense afternoon thunderstorms. Winters are cold and see a healthy amount of snow, particularly in the western portions of the state. Daytime highs in a Wyoming summer are in the 80s and 90s, with triple digits occasionally setting in. July and August are the warmest months, while January and February are the coldest. Snow can fall at any time of the year, but most occurs November-March. May and June are often the rainiest

months of the year. Humidity is generally on the low side, making the hot summer days a little more bearable. It's important to realize that when engaging in outdoor activities during the summer, you should always plan for bad weather—it can happen almost instantly at any time, even during the hottest part of the summer.

Temperatures decrease with higher altitude, so it's not uncommon in the mountains for the weather to be drastically different from lower elevations. Storms can move in on a moment's notice and can often be fierce—driving hail in the summer and blizzard conditions in the winter. Rain in the valleys can often mean snow in the mountains, especially in the spring when a storm can dump several feet of heavy snow in a relatively short amount of time.

The state is on the windy side. Casper and Cheyenne rank among the top 10 windiest cities, and by some accounts Cheyenne is number 1. Winter winds can turn an average cold day into a bone-chilling one, while summer gusts often keep outdoor event planners working overtime. The unusually warm, dry Chinook winds blow down the east slopes of the Rockies and across the plains in the winter. They occur when moist Pacific air rises over the mountains, loses its moisture in the form of precipitation, and then warms rapidly on the leeward side. Chinooks can quickly melt snow and raise the temperature.

Plants and Animals

PLANTS

Wyoming encompass a variety of habitats, ranging from grasslands to forests and mountain meadows to alpine tundra. Though fairly arid, the state has some 2,200 plant species.

Trees

In Wyoming, forests account for roughly one-fifth of the state's land. In the lower-elevation mountains in the eastern part of the

state, ponderosa pine is the primary species. Farther west, **Douglas fir** is prominent in the lower elevations. Higher up, where the climate is cooler and wetter, **lodgepole pine, Engelmann spruce, subalpine fir,** and **aspen** are among the most common species. Timberline in the northern part of Wyoming is at about 8,900 feet, and at about 11,500 feet in the southern part of the state. Engelmann spruce, subalpine fir, whitebark pine—an

Indian paintbush is scattered across the West.

important and dwindling food source for grizzly bears—and **limber pine** grow at high elevations as shrubs, rather than trees. An infestation of mountain pine beetles has caused massive pine die-offs, increasing the threat of catastrophic forest fires.

Flowers

What it lacks in fall foliage colors, thanks to an abundance of evergreens, Wyoming more than makes up for with spring and summer displays of wildflowers. The state has more than 150 varieties including purple **New England asters, bluebells, California poppies, camas, black-eyed Susans, fireweed, wild blue flax,** and **sticky geraniums. Indian paintbrush** is the state flower of Wyoming.

Vegetation

In Wyoming's alpine tundra, found above timberline, are found a variety of grasses and other herbaceous plants that can tolerate freezing temperatures any time of

year. **Big sagebrush,** the most dominant of Wyoming's species of sagebrush, covers much of the western two-thirds of the state. Other plants with a wide range in Wyoming include **western wheatgrass, blue grama, needleleaf sedge, scarlet globemallow, fringed sagewort, phlox, milkvetch, rabbitbrush,** and **prickly pear cactus.** In the driest parts of the state, shrubs like **juniper, mountain mahogany, saltbush, winterfat,** and **spiny hopsage** occur alongside various species of sagebrush. The most abundant vegetation in this part of the state is found along rivers and streams and can include **cottonwood trees** and **willows.**

ANIMALS

Wyoming is known for its abundant wildlife, and it's only fitting that residents and visitors want to see them in their natural habitat. Both herbivores and predators roam the land, and with the right information a savvy traveler can seek out views of these animals. Keep in mind that it is not acceptable to approach wildlife for any reason—keep a safe distance away and never feed any animal.

Bison

Two herds totaling some nearly 5,000 bison roam within the borders of Yellowstone National Park, a far cry from the millions that once lived throughout central North America from Canada to Mexico. These massive creatures graze on grasses and can weigh more than 2,000 pounds. Bison can commonly be seen almost any time of the year in Yellowstone, often causing traffic jams as they stand on the road.

Elk

Elk are found throughout the mountainous region, and between 10,000 and 20,000 roam free in Yellowstone National Park in 6-7 herds. These regal creatures are fairly common and can be found at higher elevations in the summer and lower elevations in the winter. The Northern Yellowstone elk herd numbered about 4,844 animals during the winter of 2015, up nearly 1,000 animals since the 2013 count and the highest number since 2010; the herd spends its winters just north of the park. The National Elk Refuge in Jackson, Wyoming, is home to 6,000-7,000 wintering elk, as well as an educational visitors center and winter sleigh rides that travel among the herd.

Deer, Antelope, and Sheep

White-tailed deer and the large-eared **mule deer,** as well as **pronghorn antelope,** can be found throughout the region and are as often seen on the sides of highways as they are in the wild. **Bighorn sheep** are impressive, stocky animals. The rams (males) are known for their massive curled horns, which give the rugged creatures their distinctive look. Herds of bighorn sheep can be found in and around Yellowstone—near the north entrance of the park, in particular—and Wyoming's Whiskey Basin Habitat Area near Dubois.

Mountain Goats

Mountain goats inhabit many of the high peaks of Wyoming and can often be seen clinging to impossibly steep sides of rocky cliffs. They were introduced to Yellowstone in the 1990s and are one of 208 nonnative species in Yellowstone National Park.

Moose

Some of the largest animals you'll encounter are moose, which typically inhabit river bottoms, wetlands, and willowed areas and graze on grasses, brush, and leaves. Moose can surprise you on the trail, as they are typically quiet and private creatures. Their docile nature can quickly turn deadly if they charge; give them plenty of room, especially if you encounter a female with young.

Horses

The region is also home to a large herd of **wild horses,** located in the Pryor Mountains along the Montana-Wyoming border. One of just 10 herds left in the country, many of the Pryor Mountain horses have primitive striping on their backs, withers, and legs; they are thought to be descendants of colonial Spanish horses. In 1968, interested individuals and groups convinced the government to set aside 31,000 acres in the Pryor Mountains as a public range for the wild horses, which had been living there for more than a century. The Pryor Mountain Wild Mustang Center in Lovell, Wyoming, houses a museum where

Moose are most often seen where water and willows are nearby.

The Wyoming Jackalope

As much a design staple as statewide lore, the famed jackalope is to Wyoming what bigfoot is to the Pacific Northwest. Does it exist? Could it possibly? Stop into nearly any roadside tavern and you are bound to see a mount of the creature. Ask around and the locals will gladly play along.

Popularized by Douglas Herrick in 1939, the jackalope is supposed to be an extinct antlered rabbit species, a cross between a pygmy deer and some sort of killer rabbit. Among the beliefs surrounding these legendary creatures are that jackalopes can travel at speeds of 90 mph and can mimic human sounds when chased.

Sighted in Colorado, New Mexico, and Nebraska in addition to Wyoming, jackalopes have cousins in Germany (called the *wolperdinger*) and in Sweden (the *skvader*). Drawings of antlered rabbit-like creatures date back to the 16th century in scholarly European works, so it is not just the stuff of goofy Wyoming calendars.

Those who sit on the fence between believing and not believing cite a disease called papillomatosis, which indeed causes parasite-caused growths on the top of a rabbit's head to harden, perhaps resembling antlers.

For those who prefer lore to science, the story of Douglas Herrick, a taxidermist from Douglas, seems a believable origin. Herrick and his brother Ralph returned from a hunt one day and slid their catch onto the floor. A hare landed next to a set of antelope antlers, and a pop-culture idea was born. The brothers mounted the antlered bunny, and the rest is history.

Jackalopes became so popular in the 1940s that Douglas was known far and wide as the "Jackalope Capital of the World." The city has stayed true to the legend with public art and signage all over town, as well as an annual Jackalope Day in June. Each year the local chamber issues thousands of jackalope hunting licenses, which specify that hunters cannot have an IQ higher than 72 and can only hunt between midnight and 2am on June 31. In the works now? There's been talk for years of a giant 80-foot fiberglass jackalope sculpture to tower over I-25. This is a story so entwined with Wyoming culture that it will never fade away.

BACKGROUND
PLANTS AND ANIMALS

visitors can learn about the history, behavior, and life of the animals. The center can also direct visitors on where and how to catch a glimpse of these beautiful creatures running free in the wild.

Bears

Black bears can be found in forested areas and often see much more human interaction than their larger counterpart, the **grizzly bear.** Grizzlies once roamed the entire northern hemisphere, and when Lewis and Clark traversed the area, there were likely more than 50,000 grizzlies across the West. Although there are still healthy populations in western Canada and Alaska, grizzly numbers in the Greater Yellowstone Ecosystem dropped to as few as 136 animals by 1975. Since the U.S. Fish and Wildlife Service listed them as a threatened species, the population has recovered to include an estimated 700

bears in the region. But despite their successes, grizzlies in the region face enormous hurdles including habitat destruction and climate change, both of which put them in danger of human conflict. The U.S. Fish and Wildlife Service proposed delisting the grizzly in March 2016, but there is bound to be a long battle.

Wolves and Coyotes

The reintroduction of the gray wolf is one of the greatest—and most controversial—wildlife success stories of the 20th century. Numbers went from zero—gray wolves were last seen here in the 1930s—to more than 1,900 in some 300 packs living throughout Montana, Wyoming, Idaho, Washington, and Oregon by the end of 2015. Yellowstone National Park is the best place to catch a glimpse of the elusive wolf. The Lamar and Hayden Valleys are especially good places to view one of the 95 or so wolves that roam through Yellowstone in 10 different packs.

You'll often see coyotes walking along the roadsides in Yellowstone or strolling in an open meadow stalking their prey. These doglike predators have a longer and more pointed nose than wolves, and a much fluffier tail, and are noticeably smaller and more delicate in appearance. Their numbers in Yellowstone decreased substantially with the reintroduction of the wolf, thanks to food competition and conflicts between the two species.

Mountain Lions

Mountain lions, also known as cougars, are present in the region. Though their numbers dwindled to almost zero with the predator removal campaigns in the early 1900s, they managed to hang on thanks to their shy nature. These elusive cats are becoming slightly more common, and human confrontations have risen over the years. The largest cat in North America, with a length of up to 7.5 feet from nose to tail, male cougars can weight 145-170 pounds, and females generally weigh 85-120 pounds. If you see one in the wild, chances are it will be crossing the road on a late-night hunting excursion.

Pikas and Marmots

The high country is home to the smallish pika and the larger, fuzzier yellow-bellied marmot. Both can be spotted running along rocky outcrops and scree fields at higher elevations. Listen for their high-pitched chirp.

Birds

The state has numerous species of birds, including raptors. Attentive visitors can expect to see **bald** and **golden eagles, ospreys, hawks, falcons, owls, woodpeckers, grouse, herons, pelicans,** and more. Smaller species include **jays, mountain bluebirds, warblers, western tanagers,** and **magpies.** For information on the excellent birding opportunities, visit www.audobonwyoming.org.

Snakes

The **prairie rattlesnake** is found in the eastern part of the region, typically in open arid country. Prairie rattlesnakes tend to den on south-facing slopes with rock outcrops and consume rodents as their main meal. Wyoming also has an endangered population of its cousin, the **midget faded rattlesnake,** which lives only around the Flaming Gorge area.

A grizzly bear is distinguished by the hump of its shoulders and a dish-shaped face.

Environmental Issues

As in many Western states, the environment is a controversial topic. While the state is on the conservative side politically, many of the people who have moved here in the past two decades have a decidedly more liberal political view, particularly when it comes to land, air, and water issues.

AIR QUALITY

Air quality is a concern, in particular emissions from coal-fired power plants and, in places, ongoing tire burning. Proponents of banning snowmobiles in Yellowstone National Park have succeeded in lowering the number of machines allowed to enter, as well as requiring all snowmobiles to be the cleaner four-stroke variety. This has divided towns where the winter economy has traditionally relied on the snowmobile tourism industry. A significant problem for air quality during most summers is smoke from massive forest fires. The Department of Environmental Quality (www.deq.wyoming.gov) monitors air quality.

WATER QUALITY

Major environmental issues in Wyoming also include water quality, especially associated with coal-bed methane, a form of natural gas. Wyoming is the country's third-largest coal-bed methane producer, much of it coming from the Powder River Basin in the northeast part of the state. Wyoming is also the seventh-largest oil-producing state, with five large refineries and the fourth-largest volume of oil reserves. Wyoming faces issues with hard-rock mining and coal-fired power plants. And as is true around the country, and the world, the process of fracking—extracting natural gas from shale rock layers using hydraulic fracturing—is stirring up significant controversy in this resource-rich state.

FOREST MANAGEMENT

Perhaps nothing divides Westerners more than how to use and manage the forests. Whether it is the creatures that live in them, logging operations, forest fires, recreation, or potential wilderness, residents are passionate about their beliefs. Both sides of any issue typically have ardent followers, making legislation a painstaking process. Whether it's clear-cutting issues or motorized-vehicle access, forestry can be touchy subjects at the lunch counter. Check any newspaper in the state and you're bound to see articles and letters to the editor about these topics.

WOLF REINTRODUCTION

Another contentious issue is the government-sponsored reintroduction of the wolf, which started in 1995 when 66 Canadian wolves were transplanted to Yellowstone National Park and central Idaho. The population has rebounded and, in some people's minds, become a threat to humans and livestock. At last count, there were close to 1,900 wolves across five states and about 95 in Yellowstone National Park alone. Area ranchers say wolves decimate livestock and elk herds; environmentalists say the animals have a right to thrive on land that was once theirs. Wolves were relieved of their endangered-species status in Wyoming by 2012, but Wyoming wolves were re-listed in 2014 as a nonessential experimental population since the state could not abide by post-delisting rules.

Leave No Trace

Leave No Trace is an educational program that teaches outdoor enthusiasts how to protect the places they love from human-caused recreational impact. However, the Leave No Trace ethic extends far beyond backcountry and wilderness areas. As more and more people are recreating in "front country" settings, knowledge of how to apply Leave No Trace principles becomes increasingly important.

Planning ahead is the easiest way to protect outdoor places and to enjoy a safe visit. Use a map, bring a small first-aid kit, remember to bring additional clothing to keep you warm and dry, and wear suitable shoes or boots on the trails. When hiking, stay on designated trails, especially if they pass through private property. Shortcutting around corners causes erosion and damages trailside plants, especially if it's wet or muddy. Dispose of trash and biodegradable materials, such as orange peels, apple cores, and food scraps, in a bear-proof trash container. Remember, animals that become dependent on human food often have to be relocated or destroyed. Two easy slogans to remember are "Pack it in, pack it out," and "Leave it as you find it." By leaving the natural world as you find it, you will be protecting the habitat of plants and animals as well as the outdoor experience of millions of visitors.

In the backcountry, you must carry all trash out with you. Use a biodegradable soap when washing dishes, and avoid using soap within 200 feet of a stream or spring. Allow others a sense of discovery by leaving rocks, plants, archaeological artifacts, and other objects of interest as you find them. Minimize campfire impacts by instead using portable camp stoves or fire pans. Use designated fire grates if available, and always make sure the fire is completely out before you leave camp. If you make a fire ring with rocks, disperse the rocks before you leave camp, and try hard to "leave no trace" of your being there.

Finally, always respect wildlife and be considerate of other visitors to help protect the quality of their experience. The last thing you want to do is ruin somebody else's trip of a lifetime. Keep noise to a minimum and let nature's sounds prevail; everyone will be happier for it.

History

Wyoming is a young state with a long history. As the least populous state in the union, some parts of Wyoming have remained unchanged since the first settlers came into the area, allowing those who live and visit here today a glimpse into the state's rich and varied past.

Geology and Early Life Forms

Wyoming's geologic history includes the creation of the Rocky Mountains and the impact of glaciers on the landscape. Of course, Yellowstone National Park is the state's biggest geologic claim to fame, created when a series of three massive volcanic explosions—2.1 million, 1.3 million, and 640,000 years ago—spewed gases and hot ash across North America. Some experts suggest the most recent blast alone was more than 10,000 times larger than the well-known 1980 eruption of Mount St. Helens in Washington. Geothermal forces are still at work underneath Yellowstone's surface, giving the park its trademark geysers, hot springs, fumaroles, and mud pots, making it the earth's most active geothermal area.

Wyoming is also a hotbed for dinosaur fossils. A fossil of a giant *Allosaurus*—among the first meat-eating dinosaurs—was found in 1991, providing valuable insight into this carnivore that roamed the earth during the Jurassic period 130-190 million years ago. The excellent Wyoming Dinosaur Museum (www. wyodino.org) in Thermopolis features more than 200 displays and more than 30 mounted skeletons of various dinosaurs. Fossils of fish, insects, birds, plants, and reptiles are on display at the Fossil Butte National Monument, a 50-million-year-old lake bed near Kemmerer that holds the largest deposit of freshwater fish fossils in the western hemisphere.

By most accounts, humans have inhabited what is now Wyoming for at least 13,000 years. Stone fossils have been found that indicate the presence of early human cultures, including the Plano, a tribe of hunter-gatherers that inhabited the Great Plains 9,000-6,000 BC. There is also evidence of the Clovis culture, people that lived in the area nearly 13,000 years ago.

An interesting but still somewhat mysterious discovery in Wyoming was the Bighorn Medicine Wheel in the north-central part of the state. This giant stone ring is thought to have been sacred to indigenous people and is believed to have been used for astronomical, teaching, and healing purposes. Constructed between 900 and 700 years ago, the Bighorn wheel is 80 feet in diameter and is one of the best-preserved stone rings in the world.

Native Americans and Mountain Men

Plains Indians didn't move into the area until the early 1600s, when Native Americans around the Great Lakes and Canadian plains were forced west. The arrival of horses and rifles created nomadic hunters who followed the massive herds of buffalo, and the culture began to change as villages grew larger and tribes had more interaction. Indian society grew more turbulent by the 19th century, and it was soon greeted by early American explorers who sought control of the state's vast geographic and natural resources.

Although French explorers crossed into northern Wyoming in the mid-1700s, two of the most famous names in Wyoming's early history are John Colter and Jim Bridger. Colter, a member of the Lewis and Clark expedition, was most likely the first white American to enter the region in 1807, and he gave birth to the term *mountain man*. He explored what would become Yellowstone National Park and was one of the first non-natives to see the Grand Tetons, spending a winter alone in the wilderness as he recorded his discoveries. Colter's most legendary story is when he escaped from a group of Blackfeet Indians, running naked and evading capture for 12 days.

Another mountain man, Jim Bridger, had a profound effect on Wyoming's early frontier days in the 19th century. Bridger established the Rocky Mountain Fur Company in 1830 and spent the next 30 years in the West as a fur trader and guide, establishing a trading post on the banks of Wyoming's Green River. Bridger married Indian women—the last being the daughter of Shoshone chief Washakie—and discovered new trading routes, including shortcuts on the Oregon and Bozeman Trails. He later served as a U.S. Army guide and scout in their campaign against the Sioux and Cheyenne, who were attacking parties along the Bozeman Trail.

Blazing Trails Across the State

The famous Oregon Trail passed through central and southern Wyoming on its way from Missouri to the Northwest. Today, Wyoming contains the longest and least-changed stretch of trail—487 miles—that can be re-created by traveling on various state and federal highways. The Oregon Trail was one of the main trading routes for those migrating west and was used by an estimated 400,000 people. Large wagon trains left Missouri as early as 1841, and usage peaked in 1850, but the trail practically disappeared when the first transcontinental railroad was completed in 1869.

With the arrival of the railroad, population gradually began to increase, and the Wyoming Territory was created in 1868. Yellowstone was made the first national park in 1872, and visitors slowly started trickling in from the East. Coal was discovered near Rock Springs in 1885, but no large deposits of minerals like gold or silver were ever discovered. Wyoming's lack of a gold rush limited its population growth, but in 1890 the territory was officially recognized as the 44th state.

Wyoming played a large role in the women's suffrage movement, being the first to grant women the right to vote in 1869. Wyoming also had the first female justice of the peace, the first female court bailiff, and the first female governor in the country.

Livestock and Energy

The devastation of the West's bison herds and the subsequent placement of Native Americans on reservations led to the development of what would become Wyoming's hallmark industry in the late 19th century: cattle. Millions of cattle were driven into Wyoming in the 1870s and 1880s, and cattle barons soon dominated the natural and political landscape, basically buying off any and all forms of government. Sheep soon followed, taking advantage of vast tracts of grasslands, and by 1902 there were more than six million sheep roaming throughout Wyoming. Conflicts between sheepherders and cattlemen often escalated into violence, but these died down as the government enacted policies and divided up the land.

Wyoming's first oil well was drilled in 1884, and by the time of the first oil boom in 1908, the state was pumping out nearly 18,000 barrels per year. Production continued to climb, peaking in 1970, when more than 150 million barrels were pumped. It has mostly declined since then, leveling off at around 51-55 million barrels per year. But in 2014, another boom bounced production up to 69 million barrels of crude oil annually. The boom-and-bust oil cycle of the 1970s and 1980s had a profound effect in Wyoming as so-called oil-patch towns like Green River, Rock Springs, and Casper grew rapidly on the promise of high-paying oil jobs, then fell flat as the industry bubble collapsed in the early 1980s. The bust left many of these cities struggling to survive.

After its peak in the 1970s, the oil industry in Wyoming was surpassed by coal, of which the state is still the nation's leading producer. In 2012, the state provided 40 percent of the country's coal. Much of the coal is located in the Powder River Basin and is used for coal-fired power plants. The state produced more than 438 million tons of coal in 2011—a decrease from 2010—but still has billions, maybe even trillions, of tons in reserves. But the bust is obvious. Massive mine layoffs in 2016, plus bankruptcy filings for two of the largest coal producers, are in line with the 32 percent decrease in production from 2014 to 2015. Things don't look good for the mining industry in Wyoming at present.

The natural gas boom of the first decade of the 21st century seems to be over as well, with production falling six years in a row starting in 2009. Production decreases in Wyoming can be attributed to several things: plummeting prices for natural gas, increased stores nationwide, aging wells, and perhaps most of all, an inability to compete with the cheaper production costs back East via fracking.

Even wind power, on the rise nationally as a clean and cheap source of energy, has hit a wall in Wyoming as of 2015. Despite the state's natural windiness, no new capacity has been added since 2010 because of the expense of building transmission lines. The production is easy, but how to get it moved out of state? Other issues besides transmission have stalled further development of wind energy production. The U.S. Fish and Wildlife Service offered to not prosecute wind producers for eagle deaths that come as a result of the turbines. The permits they wanted to dole out would have been good for 30 years, but a federal judge in California said the repercussions of that had not been carefully analyzed and limited the permits to five years. There are also tax credits that have expired and other things that make profit from wind production less certain.

Just as people migrated west and settled in Wyoming hundreds of years ago, people today come to visit Yellowstone National Park, travel the Oregon Trail, or climb one of the majestic peaks of the Teton Mountains. Tourism is now the state's second-largest industry, worth more than $3.4 billion annually. Wyoming saw 10.5 million visitors in 2015, up from 10.1 million the year before and nearly doubling the national average visitation growth rate. Visitation in Wyoming has gone up 48 percent in the last decade. Towns like Jackson Hole and Cody reap the benefits of being adjacent to Yellowstone, while the park itself attracts more than four million visitors annually.

Wyoming's balance among energy development, agriculture, and tourism is the face of the New West, where people move for a better quality of life while still trying to preserve the cultural heritage. Just like the settlers who established trading posts hundreds of years ago, these new immigrants are chasing a dream of living in an unspoiled part of the world and doing anything necessary to pay the bills. As you explore Wyoming, you'll notice that history is never far behind, and that the future holds unlimited possibilities.

Government and Economy

GOVERNMENT

Wyoming Territory was formed in 1869, but the road to statehood did not begin until 1888. After a few statehood bills failed to pass, the House finally passed the bill on March 27, 1890, making Wyoming the 44th state after President Benjamin Harrison signed the bill into law soon after. Its capital is Cheyenne.

During the territorial era, the Wyoming Legislature played a pivotal role in the U.S. suffrage movement. In 1869, just 4 years after the Civil War and 35 years before women's suffrage became a highly visible political issue in the United States, Wyoming granted all women age 21 and older the right to vote; the territorial government was the first in the world to secure this right for women. Democrat Nellie Tayloe Ross became the first female governor in the country when she won a special election in 1924 after then-governor William Ross died in office. She later became the first woman to serve as director of the U.S. Mint, appointed in 1933 by President Franklin D. Roosevelt, a position she held until her retirement in 1953.

Wyoming remains one of the few states that has a true part-time citizen legislature, meaning its members don't enjoy the same accommodations provided to full-time legislators in larger states. As of 2015, for example, legislators were paid just $150 per day, when convening, and a proposal to raise payment to $175 per day was rejected. There are 60 state representatives elected for two-year terms along with 30 state senators that serve four-year terms. There are no term limits. The state legislature meets in odd-numbered years beginning the second Tuesday in January. The general session is limited to 40 legislative days. The offices of governor, secretary of state, auditor, treasurer, and superintendent of public instruction are all elected every four years.

The Wyoming Legislature passed a bill limiting the office of governor to two consecutive terms after Democrat Edgar Herschler served three terms in the mid-1980s. In 1992 voters approved term limits in a ballot initiative, but neither action constituted an amendment to the Wyoming constitution. In 2004 two state legislators challenged the term-limit law in the courts, and the Wyoming Supreme Court subsequently invalidated the limits in a unanimous decision, ruling that a constitutional amendment would be required to establish such a law. Popular Democrat Dave Freudenthal, who served two terms as governor after being elected in 2002 and 2006, did not use the same challenge to seek a third term.

Freudenthal's election and popularity—his approval rating was a staggering 82 percent in the months before the 2010 election—defy Wyoming's Republican nature. In fact, the governorship in general has seen its fair share of Democrats, but Republicans have dominated both houses of the legislature almost

Changing Politics

The political history of Wyoming is as colorful as the Wild West and has changed over the years to reflect the shifting population, economy, and culture that exists here.

Wyoming's political history is a study in contrasts. It was the first state to grant women the right to vote and the first state to elect a woman as governor. Yet the state remains largely conservative and has only voted for one Democratic president since 1960 (Lyndon B. Johnson in 1964). Even though more than half of Wyoming's residents consider themselves Republicans, and Republicans have held a majority in the state senate continuously since 1936 and in the state house since 1964, Democrats have owned the governor's seat for all but 14 years since 1975. Democratic governor Dave Freudenthal, in office 2002-2010, had one of the highest approval ratings in the country. Still, as recently as 2014, a Gallup poll ranked Wyoming the most conservative state in the country.

Like many states in the West, Democratic strongholds tend to exist in slightly more urban areas, or areas that have a large number of transplants and a younger population. In Wyoming, Teton County is the only reliably Democratic county, which is no surprise as it includes Jackson Hole. The town's population has boomed over the years, boosted by younger transplants from more liberal parts of the country who come for the skiing, fly-fishing, and outdoor lifestyle the town offers.

since statehood. Wyoming has only voted for one Democratic president in the last half century (Lyndon B. Johnson in 1964), and Republicans have held a majority in the state senate continuously since 1936 and in the state house since 1964. Despite its tendency to elect Democrats as governor—though current governor Matt Mead is a Republican—Wyoming is considered a red state at the national level, and was named the country's most conservative in a 2014 Gallup poll.

Dick Cheney is Wyoming's best-known political figure. Born in Casper, Cheney was the White House Chief of Staff during the Nixon and Ford administrations and was then elected to the U.S. House of Representatives in 1978. He served five terms and was then selected to be the Secretary of Defense during the first Bush presidency and later served as the vice president 2001-2009 under George W. Bush. His daughter, Republican Liz Cheney, tried to shake things up in 2014 by challenging incumbent Republican and three-term senator Mike Enzi, but dropped out of the race. In February 2016, Cheney announced her plans to run for Wyoming's lone seat in the U.S. House of Representatives, after Republican incumbent Cynthia Lummis decided not to run for reelection.

The Wind River Indian Reservation is home to the Eastern Shoshone Tribal Government, a sovereign government that operates under its own constitution. The Business Council of the Eastern Shoshone Tribe consists of a chair, vice-chair, and four additional council members who are elected by the tribe members. The Tribal Council Chair is the administrative head of the tribe and serves a two-year term with the vice-chairman and the other members of the council. Both the Eastern Shoshone and Northern Arapaho are represented.

INDIAN RESERVATIONS

The Native American population plays an important role in Wyoming government and politics. Tribal law prevails within reservation boundaries, and Indian reservations are federally recognized as independent political units with their own structure and legislation. As sovereign nations, tribes can have their own school systems, constitutions, police and court systems, and legislative councils. They can also regulate transport and trade within reservation boundaries. The state can't tax land or transactions that occur on reservations.

What does this mean to the visitor? Essentially, some state laws may not apply on reservations. Goods and services—mainly gasoline and tobacco—can be much cheaper on the reservations since there are no state taxes enforced. Not all land may be open to the public, and there may be additional fees for recreation, including hunting and fishing. It's best to inquire at a local store or gas station if you are traveling on reservation land.

ECONOMY

Natural resource extraction, agriculture, and tourism play major roles in Wyoming's economy. Oil production and coal and natural gas extraction fell dramatically in the middle part of the decade, making Wyoming's economy one of only four states in the country to see its economy shrink in the first half of 2015. Wyoming's GDP increased by 10.8 percent during the fourth quarter of 2014, before the oil and gas industry cutbacks began to take their toll. Reduced production and massive layoffs in the coal industry hit hard in early 2016. Sales and use tax collections in the first quarter of 2016 were down a whopping 16 percent—or $50 million—from the same period the previous year. Mining and logging numbers were down $27.5 million, or 42.5 percent.

While energy employment in the state was down by 4,400 jobs in October 2015 as compared to October 2014, the tourism sector grew by 3,100 jobs. Tourism is still the second-largest contributor of tax revenue to the state after natural resource extraction. Since 2005, tax revenues generated by tourism and hospitality in Wyoming have grown by 86 percent. In 2015, a record 10.5 million people visited the state, up from 10.1 million in 2014. Travel spending topped out at $3.4 billion in 2015, up $9 million over the previous year. Yellowstone and Grand Teton National Parks play a big role in tourism for the state, adding more than four million visitors annually.

Since most of Wyoming can be classified as rural, it's no surprise that agriculture plays a vital role in the state's economy—more than $1 billion in cash receipts annually every year since 2010. There are more than 11,700 farms and ranches operating in Wyoming, occupying 30.4 million acres. Wyoming ranks 11th nationally in total land in farms and ranches,

and 1st in the United States for the average size of farms and ranches. The number of ranches and farms peaked at more than 18,000 in the 1930s, then slowly declined, but the industry has leveled off in the past few decades and is now starting to grow again.

Hay is the leading crop in Wyoming, in terms of value, with $317 million produced in 2014, followed by sugar beets, barley, corn, wheat, and dry beans. Dryland winter wheat is grown primarily in the eastern part of the state. Other more specialized commodities in the state include oats, hogs, bison, and sunflowers. All crop production in the state totaled $473 million in 2014.

The cattle industry produces the largest agricultural commodity—mainly beef cattle—and dates back to the mid-1880s, when settlers first came to the West. After the Civil War, cattle ranching flourished, and Cheyenne became a world trade center for the beef industry.

Wyoming's high plains and mountain meadows are recognized for their role in producing high-quality sheep. According to the National Agricultural Statistics Service, in 2015 Wyoming ranked fourth in the country in stock sheep and the lamb crop, and third in wool production. Wyoming's wool is among the most desirable in the world.

The VA Newcastle Clinic in Newcastle is the largest employer in the state with 10,000 employees. The University of Wyoming is the largest government employer in the state with 2,800 jobs. The largest private employers are the Cheyenne Regional Medical Center with 2,500 employees, Wyoming Medical Center in Casper with 1,400 employees, and Powder River Coal LLC with 1,250 employees. In 2014, Wyoming's per capita personal income was $54,810, well above the national average (it ranked 13th in the United States), in large part due to the energy booms across the state. Wyoming's unemployment rate is usually lower than the national average, although the coal layoffs of 2016 hit the state hard. In June 2016, Wyoming's unemployment rate was 5.7 percent, compared to the national average of 4.9 percent.

Wind Power: Wyoming's Next Boom?

Having prospered from the boom and then endured the bust of energy production cycles count-less times over the last century or more, Wyoming is at the forefront of a new boom, this one based on what has for eons been at the center of the state's frequently harsh climate: wind. Wind power technology as we now know it started in the early 1980s. As the seventh-windiest state, according to the American Wind Energy Association, Wyoming ranks 15th in installed wind capacity, and the numbers are growing slowly but steadily—in 2011 the energy produced by wind was more than double the 2009 figures. In 2015, wind energy provided 7.7 percent of all in-state electricity production, or enough to power 345,000 homes. In addition to constant wind, the vast tracts of public land and low population density make Wyoming an ideal wind energy producer. Benefits of wind power to Wyoming include jobs and electricity produced without greenhouse gases. The DOE Wind Vision Scenario projects that wind energy from Wyoming could power the equivalent of 3.4 million average American homes by 2030.

However, the challenge is trying to sell that wind energy to major urban areas that need it, such as Las Vegas, California, and Arizona. The distances are vast, and as of 2016, there is still a significant lack of transmission capacity. A consortium of companies, some of them affiliates of the privately held Anschutz Corp., which is building the biggest wind farm in the country in Carbon County, are proposing the building of three major transmission lines—Transwest Express, Zephyr, and Gateway West—to send the energy to the Southwest and California.

Spend a few days in Wyoming, particularly in the southern half of the state, and you will agree it has some of the most consistent wind in the country. The state has the highest per capita wind-power capacity in the country. In 2015, there were 960 wind turbines installed in Wyoming, according to the American Wind Energy Association, and hundreds more were under construction. Estimates put the eventual tally as high as 10,000 towers across the state, which will clearly change the landscape of Wyoming.

Somewhat controversially, Wyoming is the first state to put a tax on wind energy production. Proposed by Governor Dave Freudenthal, the $1 per megawatt hour tax went into effect in 2012 after a sales tax exemption for renewable energy projects expired in 2011. In its first year alone, the tax generated roughly $2.6 million for the state. As of 2016, more than $15 million in revenue had been collected. Experts expect this number to grow significantly as the state's ability to sell and transport the energy expands. The crux of the controversy is that some feel this makes Wyoming unfriendly to wind power producers, but the governor and his supporters argued that the producers are going to make a lot of money but that Wyomingites will bear the environmental—primarily visual—and socioeconomic burden. They point to the benefits gained statewide by tax revenues from oil, gas, coal, and coal-bed methane.

As the wind power boom takes off, something of a land rush in southeastern Wyoming, where the greatest number of wind farms exist, is transforming the local agricultural and ranching culture. In an effort to prevent bad deals with a strength-in-numbers approach, ranchers and farmers have joined together to form associations to bargain collectively. One of a dozen or so such cooperatives, the Bordeaux Wind Energy Association asserts that everyone is going to be impacted, whether the turbines are on their property or not, so everyone should benefit. Just as the massive wind turbines are undoubtedly altering the landscape of Wyoming, so too are the proactive ranchers and farmers working together to transform the business of agriculture. Indeed, income from wind farms can often be the deciding factor in whether a family can hold on to their ranch or not. As a result, some argue that wind farms are in fact strengthening Wyoming's agricultural tradition by keeping farmers and ranchers on their land.

Local Culture

Since Wyoming is one of the newest states in the union (44th), it's no surprise that its people and culture are largely tied to the settling of the West and the Native Americans who inhabited the area. It wasn't until the 1860s that settlers started building permanent communities, as the gold rush, the railroad, and the Homestead Act lured those seeking a different and potentially lucrative way of life. Many areas were settled by immigrants and still retain their European heritage.

Wyoming is largely considered a conservative state. Its population is around 92 percent white. More than 9 percent of Wyoming's population is listed as Hispanic or Latino in origin.

NATIVE AMERICANS

Although farming, ranching, and natural resource extraction certainly contributed to the growing cultural landscape, it's the rich Native American history that gives the state a proud and colorful representation of the past that transcends today's modern American culture. Before trappers and settlers came west, Indian people roamed freely across the land, following the huge bison herds that once covered the plains. Each tribe has unique customs and traditions. While Native Americans have worked to adapt to the changing world around them, they have also tried to keep the culture and traditions of their past alive. Their culture is celebrated through dance, songs, games, language, and religious ceremonies. This rich heritage contributes to the distinct flavor of Wyoming.

There are several museums that pay tribute to the American Indian, and many reservation towns host annual powwows, rodeos, and celebrations. Today, 2.7 percent of Wyoming's population is classified as Native American.

Wyoming's Wind River Reservation, the seventh-largest in the country at more than 2.2 million acres, is home to more than 2,500 Eastern Shoshone and 4,500 Northern Arapaho. The Shoshones have been in Wyoming since the 16th century, and were some of the first Indians to have horses. The eastern part of the tribe was pushed back west of the Laramie Mountains when their enemies—the Sioux, Crow, and Arapaho—invaded their territory.

Fort Washakie is home to the Shoshone Tribal Cultural Center and the cemeteries where both Shoshone chief Washakie and Lewis and Clark's Shoshone guide, Sacagawea, are buried. Originally called Fort Brown, the name was changed in 1878 to honor the chief who negotiated the treaty establishing the reservation. Ironically, the Shoshones ended up on the same reservation as their former enemies, the Arapaho, after the U.S. government temporarily placed them together—which soon became a permanent situation, betraying Chief Washakie's wishes to end the arrangement.

The Arapaho ended up on Wyoming's Wind River Reservation along with their former enemies, the Shoshones, after the U.S. government placed them together, supposedly temporarily. Today, Wind River is home to more than 3,900 Eastern Shoshone and 8,600 Northern Arapaho.

Like many tribes, the Arapaho were forced out of Minnesota after the arrival of the settlers and migrated to the Great Plains in the late 18th century. After many years of trying to fight back against the settlers, the tribe was decimated by the late 1800s and ultimately forced onto a reservation with the Shoshones. The Heritage Center at St. Stephens and the Arapaho Cultural Museum in Ethete both provide insight into the tribe and its traditions.

THE ARTS

Wyoming is not just filled with cowboys and ungulates; in fact it boasts vibrant and varied

The Sacred Sun Dance

Very little is known about the Native American sun dance, a highly revered and often secretive traditional ceremony performed by various tribes in North America. The sun dance represents a spiritual rebirth and regeneration of the land. Participants acquire spiritual powers, often experiencing visions, and invoke blessings for the whole community. In 1875, Lakota chief Sitting Bull formed an alliance with the Cheyenne during a sun dance in which he had a vision of U.S. soldiers falling from the sky. Many saw his vision as foretelling the defeat of the U.S. Army at the Battle of the Little Bighorn in June 1876.

Although each tribe's sun dance has its own characteristics, there are some common elements. Sun dances involve construction of a lodge, dancing, singing, strict fasting among the dancers and subsequent feasting, the erection of a sacred pole, often body painting, and the sacrificial piercing of the chest or back. The sponsor of the dance, along with other leaders, works for months planning the event and performing certain critical rites beforehand. The sun dances themselves are known to last 3-8 days.

Before the introduction of reservation life, the sun dance ceremony provided an opportunity for the various hunting bands within a tribe to come together. Today, it serves a similar purpose in Native American communities. Often members travel from different regions of the country, and regardless of social status or religious affiliation, the sun dance provides an occasion for tribe members to reaffirm their cultural identity. Many would argue that important rituals such as the sun dance contribute to the longevity and preservation of Native American culture.

With the introduction of reservations and the determination of the U.S. government to assimilate Native Americans, many practices, including the sun dance, were banned in 1885. Some tribes did not continue with their rituals and ceremonies, and others did so in secret. When the Commission of Indian Affairs lifted the ban on ceremonies in 1934, certain tribes immediately returned to performing this sacred ceremony in public. The Shoshone in Wyoming had not lost the practice, for example, and they reintroduced it to the Crow.

art scenes with an interesting and colorful history. Jackson is a mecca for Western art, its quaint streets lined with galleries and shops, offering everything from locally made stationery to the finest in Western photography, sculpture, and painting. Two of the West's premier art events—Jackson's Fall Arts Festival and Cody's Rendezvous Royale—take place each September in Wyoming. Much of the Cody event is centered around the Buffalo Bill Center of the West, which houses the impressive Whitney Gallery of Western Art. Collections here include works from the early 19th century to contemporary times that commemorate the events, people, and landscape of the Rocky Mountain region.

Jackson's 10-day Fall Arts Festival is home to one of the region's largest auctions, and the Grand Teton Music Festival hosts some of the world's finest classical musicians each summer in nearby Teton Village. Jackson is also home to the National Museum of Wildlife Art, which boasts more than 5,000 works in its permanent collection, and to the Jackson Hole Center for the Arts, a vibrant community center that offers everything from nationally touring musical and dance acts to educational workshops.

Jackson's Off Square Theatre Company is a vibrant year-round company founded in 1998, and Casper's Stage III offers six productions each year September-June. In downtown Sheridan, the historic WYO Theater—which opened in 1929 as the Lotus—was saved from demolition and refurbished, opening again in 1989 as a nonprofit organization. Today it offers an array of musical concerts and theater productions that belie its small-town setting. The University of Wyoming is home to one of the most outstanding undergraduate theater programs in the country along with the

Tipis reflect Native American influence.

play was produced by the New York-based Tectonic Theater Project and was also made into an HBO film of the same name.

While towns in Wyoming certainly don't have the hip music scenes larger cities may offer, there are plenty of tunes around to keep your toes tapping, especially in the summer. Many communities have free music nights, and local bars and taverns are usually good for a fun country band and the occasional touring act. Casper and Cheyenne are home to big arenas, while Cheyenne's Frontier Days rodeo offers nightly performances by favorite country music stars each July. Wyoming's Grand Targhee Bluegrass Festival is one of the nation's best, and its Grand Teton Music Festival hosts classical concerts and workshops June-August.

Wyoming also has its share of literary standouts. Platte Valley resident C. J. Box is one of the top-selling mystery writers in the country, and Annie Proulx won a Pulitzer Prize for her novel *The Shipping News.* Other writers who call Wyoming home include Mark Spragg (*Where Rivers Change Direction*), and Kathleen O'Neal Gear (*People of the Longhouse*), and Alexandra Fuller (*Don't Let's Go to the Dogs Tonight*). In addition, Ernest Hemingway spent a lot of time in Wyoming, where he worked on several novels, including *Death in the Afternoon* and the *Green Hills of Africa.*

University of Wyoming Fine Arts Studio, where some of the region's finest facilities are located. Indirectly, Wyoming is probably best known in the theater world as the setting for *The Laramie Project,* an award-winning play depicting the reaction to the 1998 murder of gay University of Wyoming student Matthew Shepard in Laramie. The

Matthew Shepard and *The Laramie Project*

Born in Casper, Wyoming, in 1976, Matthew Shepard was a political science major and the student representative for the Wyoming Environmental Council during his first year at the University of Wyoming in Laramie. Long a champion for equality and an admired peer counselor in high school, Shepard was the kind of kid who wanted to change the world. Tragically, it was his brutal 1998 murder that effected the change Shepard worked to inspire during his short life.

On October 7, Shepard, who was gay, was abducted from a bar in Laramie by Aaron McKinney and Russell Henderson. The two men drove Shepard to a remote area east of town where they robbed and viciously beat their victim with the butt of a handgun. Likely unconscious from countless blows to the face and head, Shepard was tied to a fence and left to die. He was found 18 hours later by a bicyclist who at first mistook Shepard for a scarecrow. Matthew Shepard died on October 12 from his injuries without ever having regained consciousness. Both murderers confessed their crimes using a gay-panic defense strategy and are serving consecutive life sentences in unidentified prisons.

What was a horrific tragedy for the Shepards' tight-knit family was seen around the world as a hate crime, inflicted upon the 21-year-old because he was gay. Shepard's parents, Dennis and Judy, created the Matthew Shepard Foundation (www.matthewshepard.org) to honor the memory of their son and to "replace hate with understanding, compassion and acceptance" through educational, outreach, and advocacy programs. Judy Shepard has turned her personal tragedy into a crusade for justice as she travels the world over speaking on behalf of and advocating for lesbian, gay, bisexual, and transgender youth. To date, Judy has brought Matthew's message of acceptance to more than 300,000 people worldwide. In 2009, the Matthew Shepard and James Byrd Jr. Hate Crimes Prevention Act was passed into federal law, an expansion of the 1969 federal hate-crime law to include crimes motivated by a victim's actual or perceived gender, sexual orientation, gender identity, or disability. It was the first federal law to extend legal protection to transgendered people.

Another response to Shepard's murder was *The Laramie Project* (www.laramieproject.org), brought to fruition by Tectonic Theater Project. The small theater company traveled to Laramie and interviewed residents about the events surrounding Shepard's death. What they learned was transformed into a play, *The Laramie Project,* and eventually a movie of the same name that ran on HBO and was seen by more than 30 million people nationwide.

Ten years after the murder, Moisés Kaufman and other members of the theater company traveled back to Laramie to see if and how the community had been transformed by the passage of time. In October 2009, *The Laramie Project Epilogue* premiered across the country in major theaters, as well as at high schools and colleges. Another documentary project, *Matt Shepard is a Friend of Mine,* won an Emmy in 2016.

Essentials

Transportation

GETTING THERE

Flying into Wyoming is easier than you think, and it's by far the best way to get here. Flights into the larger airports are becoming increasingly frequent as the region gains ground as an incredible destination for visitors. Although getting here by train or bus is possible, it's not as convenient, and stops can be far from the main travel areas—best left to hardy travelers or those on an extreme budget. If you live in the West, driving to Wyoming is a great way to get here—major highways will get you into the state, and well-traveled back roads will lead you to your final destination.

By Air

Commercial flights are available to and from Casper, Cheyenne, Cody, Gillette, Jackson, Laramie, Riverton, Rock Springs, Sheridan, and Worland. Jackson has the best service, with jet flights from Atlanta, Denver, Salt Lake City, Dallas, Houston, Chicago, Minneapolis, Newark, San Francisco, and Los Angeles. Some flights only operate during peak times in the winter and summer, and many people choose to fly into Salt Lake City (275 miles) or Idaho Falls (90 miles) and pick up a rental car for the scenic drive to Jackson. Within Wyoming, Great Lakes Airlines (www.flygreatlakes.com) flies into Worland, Riverton, and Cheyenne. Major carriers with service to Wyoming include American, United, Frontier, and Delta. Allegiant Airlines offers direct flights to Las Vegas from Casper twice weekly.

If budget is your top priority, be sure to look into flights into nearby airports. That's not always the case; sometimes smaller airports can be even pricier with more limited schedules, but it's worth looking into. Keep in mind that drivers will often encounter wildlife on the roads, particularly late at night. And weather conditions can be sketchy, especially during winter. In other words, make sure the money saved on the flight is worth your time on the road.

GETTING AROUND
By Car

Driving around Wyoming is the most efficient way to experience the scenic grandeur of the state. I-80 runs across Wyoming from Nebraska to Nevada, while I-25 heads north from Colorado up to its intersection with I-90 in Buffalo, then on to Billings, Montana. U.S. Highway 89 is a popular and scenic route to Jackson from Salt Lake City, and heads up through Grand Teton and Yellowstone National Parks into Montana.

CAR RENTAL

If you plan on renting a car, it's a good idea to reserve one well in advance. Unless you will be driving entirely on paved roads, which is doubtful, a high-clearance or all-wheel-drive vehicle is a good idea. Many Forest Service campgrounds are located along gravel roads, and any time you venture off the beaten path, you're bound to encounter some type of gravel or dirt road. In the winter, all-wheel drive is a must. And be aware that rock chips on the windshield are common occurrences at any time of year. Make sure your insurance will cover it, or consider paying for added insurance from the car-rental agency.

Car rental agencies widely serving the area include **Alamo** (800/227-7368, www.alamo. com), **Avis** (800/352-7900, www.avis.com), **Budget** (800/527-0700, www.budget.com), **Enterprise** (800/261-7331, www.enterprise. com), **Dollar** (800/800-5252, www.dollar.

Previous: a historic Yellowstone bus; snowboarding in Wyoming.

Liquor Laws

Wyoming was born of the Wild West, and in many cases there still exists a hands-off, "we don't need no government" mentality. While this may work in some areas, some outdated laws and rules are being updated or eliminated. Believe it or not, it used to be legal to operate a vehicle in Wyoming with an open container of alcohol, whether you were driving or were just along for the ride. Wyoming passed a weak open-container law in 2002, which became known as the "Here, hold my beer while I talk to this officer" law, but passed a stricter version in 2007, making it illegal for drivers and passengers to have any amount of open alcohol. In a state where distances are often measured in "six-packs," this was a big deal. However, if you're taking a cab, bus, or limo, or riding in the back of a traveling motor home, you can still drink legally. Speaking of alcohol, Wyoming is one of the few states where you can still buy a bottle from a drive-through liquor store—just don't open it in the car. And they no longer serve "to go" cocktails.

com), **Hertz** (800/654-3131, www.hertz.com), **Thrifty** (800/847-4389, www.thrifty.com), and **National** (888/868-6204, www.nationalcar.com).

HIGHWAY SAFETY

A few considerations apply when you are planning a road trip. In general, interstates and major highways are in good condition across the region, although short summers mean road construction can be expected at any time of the day—or night, in some cases. State highways are often narrow and winding, not compatible with drowsy or inattentive drivers. Wildlife is a concern on any road, particularly at night, and fallen rocks can be a problem in mountainous areas. For Wyoming road conditions, the **Wyoming Department of Transportation** (888/996-7623, www.wyoroad.info) has a wealth of information.

Distances between settlements can be great, especially in the eastern parts of the state. As a rule of thumb, planning ahead is critical. Don't wait until your gas light is on to fill up your tank, and make sure your spare is inflated. Carrying emergency gear is recommended. Rest areas—even on major highways and interstates—can be hundreds of miles apart. Most major towns and cities have reliable mechanics and car dealerships, but don't expect to find parts for your old Porsche roadster in very many places.

In general, the speed limit is 80 mph on interstates and 70 mph on most two-lane highways in Wyoming, although it can vary quite a bit depending on location and time of day. Many two-lane roads have numerous turnouts, where slower-moving vehicles can pull over and let cars pass. Wyoming drivers are used to driving faster on these roads, so if you're getting tailgated by a local, just pull over and let them go by. Increasingly, passing lanes are being incorporated into many state highways, particularly on roads over mountain passes.

WINTER TRAVEL

Winter driving takes special care, focus, and—at times—lots of caffeine. Roads can be rendered impassable in a matter of minutes by snow and wind, and mountain passes are especially susceptible to fast-changing conditions. Because of the area covered, it may take a while before snowplows clear the roads. And be extremely cautious when driving behind or toward a snowplow, as visibility can be diminished to nothing. Be aware that because of wildlife, salt is rarely used on roads in Wyoming. Instead, the roads are graveled to provide better traction in icy conditions. Loose gravel often translates into cracked or chipped windshields, so drive with caution, and never get too close to a graveling truck.

Snow tires are a must in many places, and carrying emergency supplies is strongly recommended. A good emergency kit includes a shovel, a first-aid kit, jumper cables, a flashlight, signal flares, extra clothing, some food, water, a tow strap, and a sleeping bag. Don't rely on your cell phone to save you—although service is improving, there are dead zones.

The state transportation website (www.wyoroad.info) has links to current and projected weather patterns, and toll-free information numbers are updated regularly. It's a good idea to carry these numbers in your car. Occasionally weather information can be found on the AM band of your car radio—you'll notice signs along roads indicating when this is possible.

TRAVEL MAPS

Free road maps can be found at visitors centers and rest areas, while an excellent supplement is the **Delorme Gazetteer series** (www.delorme.com), available at bookstores and in many gas stations. These oversize companions are a must for those venturing off the beaten path, as they include topographic data, Forest Service roads and trails, camping and hiking information, fishing areas, scenic drives, and more. Sporting goods stores offer more specialized maps, from national forests and wilderness areas to Bureau of Land Management lands and mile-by-mile river guides. The free road maps you get when you enter the national parks are sufficient to use during your stay.

By Train

Although the state was quite literally built by the railroads, there is no train service in Wyoming today. Amtrak's **Empire Builder** (www.amtrak.com) travels in both directions daily through neighboring Montana between Chicago, Seattle, and Portland. Most of the stops are in the far northern part of Montana, which means rail passengers will still need a car to continue south into Wyoming.

By Bus

Greyhound (800/231-2222, www.greyhound.com) has service to all major cities and many smaller Wyoming towns, including Alpine, Buffalo, Casper, Cheyenne, Evanston, Gillette, Jackson, Laramie, Rawlins, Rock Springs, Sheridan, and Wheatland. Bus service is also available on **Jefferson Lines** (800/451-5333, www.jeffersonlines.com) from Buffalo, Gillette (stop is unstaffed), and Sheridan.

Alltrans/Jackson Hole Express (307/733-3135 or 800/443-6133, www.jacksonholealltrans.com) provides daily shuttle service between Salt Lake City, Idaho Falls, Pocatello, and the resort town of Jackson, as well as transfers to and from the Jackson Hole airport.

The Wind River Transportation Authority (307/856-7118, www.wrtabuslines.com) offers fixed-route shuttles in summer between Riverton, Ethete, Hudson, Lander, and Fort Washakie. In winter, it serves Kinnear as well.

By Bike

Wyoming has many options for those cycling through. Numerous back roads and accessible campgrounds make for some fun cycling trips, but be prepared for long-distance rides and not much company. The Wyoming transportation website (www.wyoroad.info) offers excellent information for cyclists. Information can also be found on www.cyclingwyoming.org.

Recreation

Wyoming offers some of the best recreational opportunities in the West, from mountain biking and fishing to boating and horseback riding. Vast areas of untouched land make for scenic beauty that can take a lifetime to explore, luring visitors back time and again to experience the outdoors.

In the summer, rivers come alive with white-water boaters, and smaller streams entice fly-fishers seeking solitude. Wilderness areas and national forests offer miles of hiking trails, while national parks host visitors from around the world. Surprisingly, excellent golf courses are to be found here and can be relatively uncrowded, even in busy seasons. Look for unusual forms of the sport like the mown-meadow version in Casper, where golfers share the course with pronghorn and prairie dogs at the Salt Creek Country Club for only $2 per round. Lakes buzz with the sound of motorboats, campgrounds are full, and everyone seems to be outside doing something. Summers in the West are short, so people take advantage of them.

It's no surprise, then, that winters are particularly long, but those that live in Wyoming take advantage of it by enjoying some of the finest and least-crowded ski slopes in the country. Great snow and majestic mountain trails make snowmobiling extremely popular, and Nordic ski centers and trails can be found in most mountain areas. Ice fishing, dogsledding, and backcountry skiing and snowboarding are other activities that keep folks busy when the snow flies.

NATIONAL PARKS

Although most of **Yellowstone National Park** (www.nps.gov/yell) is in Wyoming, three of the park's entrances are located in Montana. Just below Yellowstone is **Grand Teton National Park** (www.nps.gov/grte). Each park offers a different type of beauty, from Yellowstone's striking geothermal features and abundant wildlife to the majestic peaks of the Tetons. Visitors will find a variety of accommodations in the parks, including rustic cabins, grand lodges, and tent and RV campgrounds. Popular activities include hiking, boating, fishing, and wildlife viewing. Informational visitors centers and museums are located in each park and offer excellent resources for history buffs.

The entrance fee in the summer for each park is $30 for automobiles, which is valid for seven days. A combination pass for Yellowstone and Grand Teton, also valid for seven days, is $50 per vehicle. Campground and other lodging fees are extra. Annual passes are available for frequent park visitors.

Each state also has numerous national monuments, historic sites, trails, and recreation areas that fall within the national park system. Consult the National Park Service website (www.nps.gov) for more information on these areas.

STATE PARKS

Wyoming has **12 state parks** (www.wyoparks.state.wy.us) plus historic sites and landmarks, ranging from battlefields and museums to parks with hot mineral soaking springs. Daily use fees are $2 per adult for historic sites (kids under 18 are free) and $4 per vehicle for state parks. Overnight camping permits start at $17 for nonresidents and include the daily use fee. Camping cabins and yurts start at $40 per night. Sites can be reserved online no more than 90 days in advance for dates May 15-September 15.

NATIONAL FORESTS

Much of the public land in Wyoming's mountainous areas is administered by the U.S. Forest Service (www.fs.fed.us), including 9.7 million acres in eight national forests. The Forest Service is a branch of the United States Department of Agriculture (USDA)

Forest Service Cabins and Lookouts

Imagine waking up in your own rustic cabin, nestled in the woods next to a rambling stream. You stoke the fire, mix up a pot of cowboy coffee, and enjoy a sunny breakfast on the porch with a 10,000-foot peak looming overhead. There is no one else around. Now imagine that you have to pay less than $50 per night for this. Too good to be true? Well, thanks to the U.S. Forest Service cabin rental system, it isn't.

There are literally hundreds of these cabins in Wyoming, most situated in locations that some people pay millions of dollars to own a piece of. Many are old ranger stations, very few are still used by the Forest Service, and all have their own unique charms. Cabins come in all different shapes and sizes, from extremely remote backcountry sites and mountaintop fire lookouts to larger cabins with electricity and motor vehicle access. Either way, they offer an unparalleled way to enjoy the outdoors.

Each national forest has a number of cabins for rent. You can find a list for Wyoming (www.fs.fed.us/r2/recreation/rentals). All cabins must be reserved online (www.recreation.gov), where you can enter when you want to stay, and a list of available cabins will come up, or over the phone (877/444-6777 or 518/885-3639 outside the U.S.). Cabins range from $30 for small, two-room units to upwards of $180 for larger rentals that sleep up to 10 people.

Cabins typically have bunk beds (bring your own bedding), wood stoves, wood, and pots and pans. Some have more, some have less. Toilet facilities are usually outside, and potable water is not always available. When you make your reservation, you'll get a list of what to bring as well as detailed directions.

Some of the more interesting rentals are historic fire lookouts, perched high atop a mountain with commanding views of the surrounding peaks. Sitting inside these lookouts, you can imagine backcountry rangers gazing out over the land trying to spot forest fires. These lookouts are especially beautiful at night, when you're out among the stars feeling like you're on top of the world. It's a must-do experience for those who want to get off the beaten path—and one you'll remember for a lifetime.

and manages much of the nation's forest and rangelands. All national forests contain developed hiking and biking trails, and in the winter the roads and trails can often be used for cross-country skiing. Forest Service ranger stations are good places to obtain information on camping and recreation, while most sporting goods stores sell excellent maps that pertain to specific areas. **Beartooth Publishing** (www.beartoothpublishing.com) offers a popular series of waterproof maps that highlight national forest roads, trails, campgrounds, picnic areas, and fishing access sites for specific regions. Wyoming is located in Region 2 (Rocky Mountain Region) and Region 4 (Intermountain Region). You'll notice signs along the highways that indicate when you enter and leave a particular national forest.

Forest Service campgrounds are widespread and offer some of the finest camping available. Fees range free-$16, depending on the type of site and the amenities offered. Free sites are often very remote and offer limited services. The Forest Service also rents some rustic cabins and lookouts starting at $30 per night. These can be a great way to enjoy the outdoors, as most are in prime locations. These cabins, as well as most campgrounds, can be reserved in advance (with additional fees) at www.recreation.gov.

WILDERNESS AREAS

There are 15 federally designated wilderness areas in Wyoming. These are roadless and closed to mechanized use, including mountain bikes. Wilderness areas generally offer solitude and amazing scenery, although some areas may be more heavily used than remote non-wilderness areas. Some wilderness areas may fall under Native American jurisdiction,

Great Divide Mountain Bike Route

The Great Divide Mountain Bike Route is the longest off-pavement bicycle route in the world, running 2,768 miles from Banff, Canada, down to Antelope Wells, New Mexico. Developed by the Adventure Cycling Association, the trail is roughly 90 percent unpaved and crosses the Continental Divide as many as 30 times. The elevation gains and losses are equivalent to 200,000 vertical feet, which compares to riding up Mount Everest nearly seven times.

One stretch of the trail in southern Wyoming from South Pass City near Lander to Rawlins cuts through an area known as the Great Basin, since the water in this area does not drain into the Atlantic or Pacific but rather stays in the playa lakes here or evaporates in the heat. In fact, the Continental Divide splits and is on both sides of the Great Basin. It's the only portion of the route where the terrain is consistently level. But that doesn't make it easy. Riders will need to carry plenty of water on the 131-mile stretch and will likely have to deal with significant wind. Temperatures in this high desert can plummet quickly, and rainstorms can make the double-track nearly impassable. Possible wildlife encounters in this stretch of the trail can include prairie dogs, pronghorn, coyotes, and even wild horses.

The Great Basin is a starkly picturesque place that will appeal to those who love wide, open spaces. For maps and detailed route information, start online at www.adventurecycling.org.

so make sure you have the necessary permits before hiking, hunting, or fishing in these locations.

BLM PUBLIC LAND

The rest of the public land falls under management of the Bureau of Land Management (BLM), which offers everything from camping and boating to caving and backcountry scenic byways. The BLM manages multiple resources and uses, including energy and minerals; timber; forage; recreation; wild horse and burro herds; fish and wildlife habitat; wilderness areas; and archaeological, paleontological, and historical sites. There are nearly 18 million acres of BLM land in Wyoming. You can find out more about the BLM offerings at www.blm.gov.

HUNTING

Wyoming is a popular destination for those hunting elk, deer, black bears, bighorn sheep, pronghorn, pheasants, and mountain lions. In 2009, the state also implemented a wolf season, ending in 2014 when wolves were relisted on the endangered species list in Wyoming. For more information on hunting in Wyoming, contact the **Wyoming Game and Fish Department** (307/777-4600,

http://wgfd.wyo.gov). If you would like to enlist a hunting guide, check the websites for recommendations on established outfitters or contact the **Wyoming Outfitters and Guides Association** (307/265-2376, www.wyoga.org).

FISHING

Wyoming is known throughout the world as a premier fishing destination, mainly due to the popularity of fly-fishing on beautiful Western rivers that flow throughout the region. Legendary trout streams lure anglers looking for lunkers, especially June-September. These rivers can be crowded during the summer, but luckily there are literally hundreds of other rivers and smaller streams on which to wet a line. And for diehard anglers, plenty of secret spots are around—think spring creeks and alpine lakes—for excellent year-round fishing. The Flaming Gorge and Buffalo Bill Reservoirs offer lake trout, kokanee salmon, and smallmouth bass. In addition, hundreds of backcountry lakes offer solitude and great fishing in a wilderness setting, and ice fishing is becoming increasingly popular during the winter.

Nonresident fishing permits cost $14 for one day or $92 for a full year. Resident fishing licenses cost $24 per year or $6 per day. With the exception of a one-day license, you'll also need to purchase a Wyoming Conservation Stamp for $12.50, which is good for one calendar year. Youth under 14 do not need a license if fishing with an adult who has a valid fishing license. Check the state website (http://wgfd. wyo.gov) for specific stamps you may need when fishing in certain waters. Fishing outfitters and stores sell licenses, as do many gas stations and sporting goods stores.

It's important to remember that you need a separate license to fish in Yellowstone National Park. Anglers 16 years of age and older are required to purchase either an $18 three-day, $25 seven-day, or $40 season permit. Children 15 and under may fish without a permit if fishing with an adult who has a valid park permit. Permits are available at park ranger stations, stores, and many businesses in the Greater Yellowstone area.

Outfitters and guide services are abundant in Wyoming. Although it's not necessary, using one of these outfitters is a good idea if you're new to angling or want to hone your fly-fishing skills. Guides also know the hot spots on the rivers, can tell you what is hatching on any given day, and may have access to private sites along various streams.

An excellent private website for general fishing information and a good overview of the region is **Wyoming Fishing Network** (www.wyomingfishing.net). For detailed fishing information, contact the **Wyoming Game and Fish Department** (307/777-4600, http://wgfd.wyo.gov).

TOUR OPERATORS

Wyoming covers a large geographic area, so it can be difficult to choose what to see in the time you have. There are many tour operators with well-researched itineraries that can cater to your specific needs and wishes. Many of these tours cater to families or a particular interest: biking, cultural and history tours, wildlife, and more. **Austin-Lehman Adventures** (800/575-1540, www.austinadventures.com), for whom this writer used to

guide, offers numerous multiple-sport trips (think biking, hiking, horseback riding, and rafting on one trip) in the region, including Yellowstone and Grand Teton National Parks. The Montana-based **Adventure Cycling Association** (800/755-2453, www.adventurecycling.org) offers self-contained and supported bicycle tours in Yellowstone and Grand Teton National Parks. **Backroads** (800/462-2848, www.backroads.com) offers multiple-sport tours throughout Greater Yellowstone. **Big Wild Adventures** (406/848-7000, www. bigwildadventures.com) offers backpacking and canoeing trips in Wyoming, and in Yellowstone and Grand Teton National Parks. **Yellow Dog Fly Fishing Adventures** (406/585-8667 or 888/777-5060, www.yellowdogflyfishing.com) offers custom trips around the area. In addition, there are operators in nearly every town that offer specific adventures, such as white-water rafting, horseback riding, fly-fishing, hiking, biking, and more.

SPECTATOR SPORTS
Rodeo

Most communities in Wyoming have rodeos at least once during the summer, and some of the larger towns like Jackson and Cody have nightly or weekly rodeos that showcase the sport's nonstop action. Some of the best rodeos are the smaller ones, often called "ranch rodeos," that feature real cowboys and cowgirls from area ranches competing against each other in real-life ranch activities. Many rodeos offer events for kids, such as greased-pig contests or wild-sheep riding. Generally speaking, rodeos are great family-oriented events.

Frontier Days (307/778-7222 or 800/227-6336, www.cfdrodeo.com) in Cheyenne is the country's largest outdoor rodeo, with attendance of nearly 200,000 people each summer for the 10-day festival. The **Cody Stampede Rodeo** (307/587-2104 or 800/207-0744, www. codystampederodeo.com) in Cody has had bucking broncs since 1919, and the family-friendly **Cody Nite Rodeo** (307/587-5155, www.codystampederodeo.com) runs nightly June-August. Jackson Hole offers rodeos (307/733-7927, www.jhrodeo.com) twice weekly, on Wednesday and Saturday nights, Memorial Day-Labor Day, plus some Friday nights in July and August. The small town of Buffalo offers two weekly rodeos, including an all-women rodeo, the **Cowgirl Rodeo,** on Tuesday nights. West Yellowstone also hosts a rodeo (406/560-6913, www.yellowstonerodeo.com) during each weekend in the summer June-August, and the **Professional Bull Riders** tour (719/242-2800, www.pbrnow.com) stops in Wyoming at Cheyenne, Casper, and Afton.

College Football

With only one university in the state, it's no great surprise that the NCAA Division I **University of Wyoming Cowboys** (www.wyomingathletics.com) draw rabid fans to its home games in Laramie. The annual "border war" match between Colorado State and Wyoming has been going on since 1899 and is considered the oldest interstate rivalry west of the Mississippi River. Since 1968, the winner of that game takes home the Bronze Boot, one of the best-known and most highly sought-after traveling trophies in college football.

Travel Tips

TOURIST INFORMATION

Most chambers of commerce and visitors centers (listed for each town in this book) are good sources when driving around, but the online sites are where you should start your research. Visit **Wyoming Tourism** (307/777-7777, www.travelwyoming.com) for the latest information. You can check out the various towns, attractions, and events, as well as order a **free vacation guide.**

COMMUNICATIONS AND MEDIA
Cell Phones

Although Wyoming may be remote, cell-phone coverage is overall very good and getting better each year. That being said, rural and mountainous areas may have spotty coverage. Indeed, check the storefronts in some of the smaller towns in the region, and you'll see that cell-phone service is just being brought to the area. Verizon is the main carrier, although AT&T is increasingly available.

Internet Access

Many coffee shops and public libraries have computers available for Internet use, and most larger towns have business centers with computers and fax machines.

High-speed Internet connections are generally available, but the service is often slower and more problematic compared to larger metropolitan areas. Wireless Internet is frequently offered at coffee shops, libraries, hotels, and other public places.

Media

USA Today is the one national newspaper that can be found throughout the region, and the *Wall Street Journal* is also popular. If you want a national newspaper like the *New York Times* or the *Washington Post,* many towns still have smaller newspaper and magazine stores, but you may get a copy that is a few days old at best. Large grocery stores typically have regional dailies.

In Wyoming, the larger daily newspapers include the *Casper Star-Tribune* (the only statewide newspaper), the *Wyoming Tribune Eagle* in Cheyenne, and the *Laramie Boomerang.* Other popular papers include the weekly *Jackson Hole News & Guide* and Worland's *Northern Wyoming Daily News.* Other Wyoming publications to watch for include **Wyoming Magazine** (www.wyomingmagazine.com), which focuses on travel and adventure in the state, **Wyoming Lifestyle Magazine** (www.wyolifestyle.com), and **307 Magazine** (www.307magonline.com).

One of best sources of local and national

news is **National Public Radio,** which can be heard in even the smallest of towns. **Yellowstone Public Radio** (www.ypr.org) and **Wyoming Public Radio** (www.wyomingpublicradio.net) cover much of the state.

FOOD

One thing is certain: This is meat-and-potatoes country, which can be great for those craving a good steak, as you can find one in almost every town. Locally raised beef can be found on the menus of many restaurants, and bison is becoming increasingly popular as well. If you haven't had it, it's highly recommended, and beef lovers will generally enjoy bison. A good bison burger or tenderloin is hard to beat, but if you are asked how you like it cooked, never ask for anything more than medium. Wild-game dishes, mostly elk and venison, are also found at finer establishments, with pheasant and other regional game occasionally on the menu. If you enjoy trying new fare, this can be an exciting option.

With all the meat on the menu, you would think that vegetarians would be out of luck when dining out, but surprisingly, options abound, especially at higher-end restaurants. The "eat local" campaigns are in full swing out West, and many of the best restaurants get as much of their food as possible from local and regional growers. Despite being seriously landlocked, seafood is no longer a bad idea. Fresh seafood is flown in from Hawaii or Seattle daily in many places, and it is generally pretty good. Yes, there are even fresh sushi bars in Wyoming, and some are darn tasty. Innovative cuisine can be found in every major town, but certainly Jackson stands out.

Does Wyoming have a well-known meal? Well, not really. Rocky Mountain oysters (calf testicles) are usually breaded and fried—not exactly gourmet, and not exactly popular or necessarily worth trying. Delicious Indian tacos load the ingredients onto fry bread, and good Mexican and Chinese restaurants can be found throughout the region.

You'll also see the standard fast-food establishments, especially near the interstates, but avoid these and try a local restaurant instead. You'll find the best food at the most random of places—and it will certainly be a more culinary and cultural experience. And remember, folks out here are friendly—if you stop and ask someone about the best place in town, they will happily point you in the right direction and will probably know the owner.

If you are traveling the back roads and small towns and get tired of ordinary bar-type food (burgers, burgers, and more burgers), consider a quest to find the best chicken-fried steak or the best piece of pie. Sometimes a personal challenge can relieve the boredom of limited options. Plus, who doesn't want an excuse to eat homemade pie for breakfast, lunch, and dinner?

ACCOMMODATIONS

A wide variety of lodging options is available, from standard hotels and motels to luxury resorts and guest ranches. Generally speaking, all lodging is more expensive in the summer, and rooms fill rapidly—advance reservations are a must, especially around special events like Cheyenne's Frontier Days. Rooms, cabins, and even campgrounds in the national parks fill up several months—if not longer—in advance. Shoulder seasons (spring and fall) offer reduced rates and thin crowds, while rooms at the ski resort lodges fill up fast in the winter but may be wide open during the summer.

Most larger towns have numerous choices for chain motels, which are typically clustered around the interstate exits. Gateway towns to Yellowstone and Grand Teton National Parks also have chain hotels, as well as a number of mom-and-pop motels sprinkled around town. Travelers used to standard hotels will be happy with these choices, but those who seek a more unique experience will want to try some of the smaller boutique hotels located in towns around the West. It just depends on whether you would rather stay in the usual Super 8 or sleep in a room that once accommodated Ernest Hemingway or Annie Oakley.

An excellent resource is **Historic Hotels of the Rockies** (www.historic-hotels.com).

There are a number of bed-and-breakfasts, most of which are located in the higher-traffic tourist areas. Many are located on the banks of a river or nestled in the pine trees and are often great escapes from the busier hotel atmosphere. A fairly comprehensive listing can be found at **BnBFinder** (www.bnbfinder. com). Very few hostels exist in Wyoming, but **Hostels.com** (www.hostels.com) has a list of what might be available.

Guest ranches range from traditional horse-and-cowboy dude ranches to luxury "glamping" (a portmanteau of *glamorous* and *camping*) resorts that offer spa services and high-end cuisine. An excellent resource for those seeking a real Western working vacation is the **Wyoming Dude Ranchers' Association** (www.wyomingdra.com). Many of these are focused around horseback riding, fly-fishing, and family activities and are often booked in weeklong blocks. In the winter, many of these ranches offer cross-country skiing, snowshoeing, or dogsledding.

Higher-end guest ranches are becoming very popular, offering guests a chance to experience a more rustic atmosphere with upscale amenities. These are typically set in remote locations with beautiful surroundings and are private, in some cases gated from public access. Typically these are the priciest accommodations, ranging from several hundred to $1,000 and more per night.

Cabins and other vacation rentals are becoming increasingly popular, as many travelers are looking for that Western cabin experience. These can range from rustic—just beds, no plumbing—to luxurious—down comforters, a rock fireplace—and are perhaps the best way to stay. Sites like **VRBO** (www. vrbo.com) offer private homes and cabins for rent while many resorts offer nightly cabin rentals. For Forest Service cabins—which are quite primitive, but often set in phenomenal locations—travelers can check availability and make reservations at www.recreation.gov.

Plenty of RV and tent camping sites are available for those on the road. From national forest campgrounds to large private RV resorts, there is something for everyone. RV campers will find private campgrounds in most towns, and most national forest campgrounds have room for all but the longest RVs. It's generally legal to camp on national forest land, unless you see a sign indicating that overnight camping isn't allowed. For a real backcountry experience, drive on a Forest

Hamburger lovers will have much to sample in Wyoming.

Service road until you find a nice campsite, pull over, and set up camp. Not only is it often scenic, it's also free.

ACCESS FOR TRAVELERS WITH DISABILITIES

For the most part, Wyoming complies with state and federal guidelines for handicapped access. Most hotels offer accessible rooms, and the national parks and even some state parks feature accessible trails. However, it's important to remember that many parts of the state are rural, and some features may be outdated, less accessible, or nonexistent.

WOMEN TRAVELING ALONE

Overall, Wyoming can be exciting for a woman traveling alone. For the most part, the West is full of independent and strong women, and you won't seem out of place in most areas. Outgoing and talkative women—as well as men—will feel right at home. Folks are pretty friendly and accommodating around these parts, and in general they like to meet people from other places. Of course, there is always the occasional weirdo, so if a place or a person makes you uncomfortable, the best thing to do is just leave. Use the same precautions

and common sense that you would at home. And it's worth noting that bear spray can be just as effective on a creepy dude as it is on a curious grizzly.

GAY AND LESBIAN TRAVELERS

It's safe to say that many people in Wyoming are socially conservative, and same-sex public displays of affection are not very common. You shouldn't necessarily anticipate discrimination or hostility if you are gay, but you'll want to be aware of your surroundings. You might not think much of expressing yourself at a back-road bar, but you never know what the group of cowboys in the corner is thinking. Sadly, this is where Matthew Shepard was brutally murdered in 1998 for no other reason than because he was gay. Wyoming still has a long way to go in terms of recognizing and celebrating alternative lifestyles. In general, "don't ask, don't tell" is the safest policy to assume when traveling here.

That being said, there are thriving—although often underground—gay communities in many towns, particularly college town Laramie. An excellent resource for gay and lesbian travelers is the **University of Wyoming's Rainbow Resource Center** (307/766-3478, www.uwyo.edu/RRC).

Health and Safety

While medical services and health care in many of the larger towns are excellent—and in some cases on par with bigger cities—it's important to remember that when traveling around, you'll mostly likely be far away from emergency medical services. Rural and mountainous highways are especially troublesome, as cell-phone coverage can be spotty. Most small towns have a local clinic, and services are available in the national parks. Refer to specific areas of the text for emergency numbers, and remember that calling 911 doesn't always work in many rural areas.

In general, **weather, altitude,** and **insect bites** pose the greatest risk traveling here. The summer sun can get extremely hot, and it is easy to get dehydrated, so make sure to drink plenty of water during the day. Hiking—and just walking, for some people—can be a strenuous activity as the altitude increases. It's best to carry plenty of food and water, and take your time getting to your destination. Always let someone know where you are going and when you plan to be back. The earliest and most obvious sign of altitude-related health problems is a headache, and the best remedy is drinking water and moving to a lower elevation if possible.

The common insect nuisances are mosquitoes and ticks. Wyoming mosquitoes rarely carry any diseases, but they can be annoying at certain times during the summer. While West Nile virus is becoming an increasing threat to livestock across the West, human infection is less common. Still, it's a good idea to carry bug repellent with DEET, especially when hiking or camping near water. Ticks can pose a small threat of Rocky Mountain fever or Lyme disease, and they seem to have become more pervasive in the last 10 years or so. It's a good idea to check every part of your skin after a day of hiking or fishing outdoors—places where you might encounter underbrush, dense trees, and grassy meadows. If you find a tick with its head stuck in your skin, pull gently with tweezers or your fingers until the tick works its way out. Don't forget to check your pets too.

A common backcountry ill is **giardia,** sometimes called "beaver fever," a microscopic parasite that lives in mountain streams and can wreak havoc in your intestinal tract. Avoid drinking unfiltered or untreated water directly from streams, rivers, springs, or lakes. Carry a water filter or water-purifying tablets (iodine or similar products), and you'll have nothing to worry about.

If you're camping or staying in a cabin, **hantavirus** can be a concern. Hantavirus is a potentially fatal disease caused by contact with rodent droppings, particularly those of deer mice. Symptoms include fever, muscle aches, coughing, and difficulty breathing. Campers should avoid sleeping on bare ground, and avoid cabins if you see signs of rodents. For more information, visit the Centers for Disease Control and Prevention (www.cdc.gov).

Winter poses different types of health concerns, namely **hypothermia** and **frostbite.** If you or someone in your party shows any signs of hypothermia—uncontrollable shivering, slurred speech, loss of coordination—get them out of the wind and inside immediately.

If you're camping, a dry sleeping bag is your best bet. It's a good idea to dress in layers, avoid cotton clothing, always bring a hat, and—most important—make good decisions *before* you put yourself in a situation where you could be stranded in the wind and cold. If you're outside in the winter, a sign of frostbite is the whitening and hardening of the skin. The best way to warm the affected area is with other skin, but avoid warming it too quickly because thawing can be quite painful.

WEATHER

The old saying is a tad cliché but nonetheless often true: If you don't like the weather, just wait five minutes. What this means to the traveler is that weather in this part of the West can change dramatically in an unbelievably short amount of time. In the summer, extreme heat can dehydrate the human body rapidly, and in the winter, extreme cold can render your body useless in a matter of minutes. Sudden changes in the weather can happen at any time of the year in mountainous areas. It can snow, sleet, hail, and rain at a moment's notice. If you're heading into the backcountry or getting ready for a three-day river float, check the forecast, but don't rely on it; plan for the worst with extra gear and plenty of food and water.

In general, Wyoming has a semiarid climate. There is enough moisture at certain times of the year, but summers are typically dry and warm, with July-August being the hottest months. Mountainous areas see heavy snowfall during the winter (to the delight of skiers), while the eastern part of the state can seem downright desertlike much of the year.

WILDLIFE

Although many people visit Wyoming for the abundant wildlife, with so much human interaction, safety is a real concern. A general rule of thumb is *never* to approach wildlife, no matter what the situation is. It's just a bad idea, and each year people are hurt or killed because they ignore this basic rule. Not only are they putting themselves in harm's way, but they are often precipitating imminent doom for the animal as well. The old adage, "A fed bear is a dead bear," can be applied universally to wildlife. The problem of humans getting too close to animals, particularly in Yellowstone National Park, gets plenty of coverage these days, on YouTube and the evening news. Do not become a cautionary lesson for other travelers; keep your distance from wildlife. Period.

SAFETY IN BEAR COUNTRY

Grizzly bears and black bears live in many parts of Wyoming, and although encounters are rare, it is necessary to learn what to do in case it happens to you. It is also important to know how to avoid the situation in the first place. No method is absolutely foolproof, but with caution and attentiveness you can avoid most of the common mistakes that lead to bear encounters.

When out in the backcountry, it's the unexpected bear encounter you really want to avoid. The best way to do this is to let them know you are present. Make noise in areas of dense cover and blind spots on hiking or biking trails. Immediately move away from any animal carcass you come across, as there may be a bear nearby protecting it. Avoid hiking or biking in the early morning or at dusk, and travel in larger groups; the more of you there are hiking together, the more likely a bear will sense you and move away. Making noise is a great way to let bears know you are near, and in most cases they will be long gone before you have the chance to get a glimpse of them. Be aware that dogs can provoke bears and bring them right to you. And, of course, never leave food out.

If you're camping in an area frequented by bears, look for bear signs (waste, overturned rocks, decimated fallen timber, claw marks and hair on trees) around the campsite. Since bears are attracted to all kinds of odors—food, toothpaste, soap, deodorant—your cooking, eating, and food storage area should be at least 50 yards from your tent. It's tempting

Know what to do if you encounter a bear.

to bring tasty items like sausage, ham, tuna, and bacon with you, but these smell good to bears too. Freeze-dried foods are your best bet. Store foods in airtight bags, and be sure to hang all food at least 12-15 feet off the ground and away from tree trunks. Some designated campsites have bear storage containers or food storage poles.

Carrying **pepper spray** (sold in most sporting goods stores, but worth noting that the Grizzly and Wolf Discovery Center in West Yellowstone is the only place you can buy bear spray at cost) is a must in bear country, and it has been proven useful in fending off bear attacks. These sprays only work at close range (10-30 feet) and can quickly dissipate in the wind or sometimes blow back in your face. Carry the spray in a holster or on a belt across your chest for easy access. It's important to note that these spray canisters are not allowed on commercial airplanes, they expire after a certain date, and they should not be left in a very hot place like a closed car. Also, test your container every now and then in light or no wind to make sure it works.

If you happen to encounter a bear, and it notices you, try not to panic or make any sudden moves. Do not run—bears can run more than 40 mph in short bursts—or try to climb a tree. Make yourself visible by moving out into the open so the bear can identify you. Avoid direct eye contact with the bear, but talking in a low voice may convince the animal that you are human. If the bear is sniffing the air or standing on its hind legs, it's most likely trying to identify you. If it's woofing and posturing, this could be a challenge. Stand your ground if the bear charges; most charges are bluffs, where the bear will stop short and wander away.

If a grizzly does charge and knocks you to the ground, curl up in the fetal position with your hands wrapped behind your neck and your elbows tucked over your face. Keeping your backpack on may offer some protection. Remain as still as possible, as bears will often only sniff or nip you and leave. This is considered playing "active dead." If the bear rolls you over, as it will likely try to do, roll yourself back over on your stomach and keep your neck as protected as possible. Remain on the ground until you know the bear has vacated the area.

In general, black bears are more common and seem to have more interaction with people. In many places they can be a nuisance—getting into garbage, breaking into homes—but don't think that they are not dangerous. Black bears will generally try to avoid you and are easily scared away, but if you encounter an attacking or aggressive bear, this usually means it views you as food. In this case, most experts recommend fighting back with whatever means possible: large rocks or sticks, yelling, and shouting.

It's a rare event when a bear attacks sleeping campers in tents at night, as tragically happened at the Soda Butte campground near Cooke City in July 2010, but if you find yourself in that situation, defend yourself as aggressively as you can. In these circumstances, bears are viewing you as prey and may give up if you fight back. Never play dead in this case, and to thwart off an attack, always keep pepper spray and a flashlight handy.

Before you go into the backcountry, brush up on your **bear identification.** You can't tell what kind of bear you see by its color alone. Grizzlies are often larger and have a trademark hump at the top of their neck. Grizzlies also have more of a dish-shaped face profile, compared to a straighter profile of black bears.

OTHER WILDLIFE

Although bears get the majority of the press, there are other animals that you need to be aware of when traveling around Wyoming. **Moose** are huge animals that are prone to sudden charges when surprised, especially females traveling with young. If you travel through Yellowstone National Park, you'll encounter numerous **bison,** large animals with sharp horns. Although it may be tempting to walk up to them, avoid doing so. While they are not vicious, bison can charge if provoked and have maimed and even killed visitors in the past. Statistically, bison injure more people in Yellowstone than any other animal. Be aware that these lumbering beasts can sprint the length of a football field in six seconds and can leap a six-foot fence. Likewise, elk in the park can seem downright docile, but it's important to remember not to approach them.

Mountain lions generally keep a low profile, but as humans encroach on their habitat, encounters are becoming more frequent in the West. Most attacks have been on unattended children, and they rarely target adults. If you happen to find yourself in a situation with a mountain lion, be aggressive and fight back if necessary, or throw rocks and sticks to try to make it go away.

Rattlesnakes can be found in the central and eastern parts of Wyoming, especially in the drier prairies. Rattlesnake bites are rarely fatal (less than 4 percent when antivenin is used in time), and the snakes generally avoid humans. Be careful where you step when hiking around these areas, and pay attention if children are with you. If you surprise or step on a rattlesnake—chances are you'll hear its trademark rattle before you do—it may coil and strike. Any bite from a rattlesnake should be regarded as a life-threatening medical emergency that requires immediate hospital treatment by trained professionals.

With all of the incredible wildlife viewing opportunities, it can be easy for some people to get complacent when taking pictures or hiking around. Treat all wildlife with respect and care, and never feed or approach any type of wild animal. If you are lucky enough to see many of these critters, observe them in their natural habitat and then carry on. The last thing you want is to become a statistic.

Resources

Suggested Reading

THE NATIONAL PARKS
History

Black, George. *Empire of Shadows: The Epic Story of Yellowstone*. New York: St. Martin's Press, 2012. A fascinating look at the gripping and unexpected history of our first national park.

Haines, Aubrey. *The Yellowstone Story: A History of Our First National Park*. Yellowstone National Park, WY, and Niwot, CO: The Yellowstone Association for Natural Science, History, and Education and The University Press of Colorado, 1996. This comprehensive volume tackles the park's early years, from primitive exploration to early development.

Righter, Robert W. *Crucible for Conservation: The Struggle for Grand Teton National Park*. Moose, WY: Grand Teton Natural History Association, 1982. This gripping history makes one grateful that things worked out the way they did.

Righter, Robert W. *Wind Energy in America: A History*. Norman, OK: University of Oklahoma Press, 2003. Righter gives readers an excellent, in-depth look at the saga of wind energy across the West.

Saunders, Richard L., editor. *A Yellowstone Reader: The National Park in Folklore, Popular Fiction, and Verse*. Salt Lake City: University of Utah Press, 2003. This volume offers a core sample of historical literature that spans the late 19th century through the 1980s.

Whittlesey, Lee H. *Death in Yellowstone: Accidents and Foolhardiness in the First National Park*. Lanham, MD: Roberts Rinehart Publishers, 1995. Who doesn't love reading about a little gore and some good old-fashioned stupidity when traveling through Yellowstone?

Natural History

Johnsgard, Paul A., and Thomas D. Mangelsen. *Yellowstone Wildlife: Ecology and Natural History of the Greater Yellowstone Ecosystem*. Boulder, CO: University Press of Colorado, 2013. With stunning images by Mangelsen and detailed natural histories of the animals that call the park home, this is an outstanding book for wildlife lovers.

Mangelsen, Thomas, and Todd Wilkinson. *Grizzlies of Pilgrim Creek*. New York: Rizzoli, 2015. The project of famed photographer Tom Mangelsen and environmental writer Todd Wilkinson, this gorgeous, oversized book tells the story of grizzly bear #399, one of the most beloved and oft-seen bruins in Grand Teton National Park.

Murie, Margaret, and Olaus Johan Murie. *Wapiti Wilderness*. Boulder, CO: University Press of Colorado, 1985. A magnificent read by two of the region's now deceased but beloved conservationists, the chapters alternate between his work studying elk and her descriptions of their fascinating life together.

Peacock, Doug. *Grizzly Years: In Search of American Wilderness.* New York: Holt Paperbacks, 1996. A classic by one of Montana's favorite authors who was the model for George Hayduke in Ed Abbey's novels, this narrative tells of one man's 20-year quest to understand and appreciate this magnificent creature.

Phillips, Michael K., and Douglas W. Smith. *The Wolves of Yellowstone.* Stillwater, MN: Voyageur Press, 1996. Told with fabulous color photos and intimate details by the two men who oversaw the project, this book tells the story of the wolves' reintroduction to Yellowstone in 1995.

Schreier, Carl. *A Field Guide to Yellowstone's Geysers, Hot Springs and Fumaroles.* Moose, WY: Homestead Publishing, 1999. This slightly larger-than-your-pocket book is the authoritative guide to Yellowstone's best-known thermal features, with information about the origin of their names, regular and irregular activity, statistics, and anecdotal histories.

Schullery, Paul. *Searching for Yellowstone: Ecology and Wonder in the Last Wilderness.* Helena, MT: Montana Historical Society Press, 2004. A fascinating and compelling environmental history of the world's first national park.

Schullery, Paul. *Yellowstone Bear Tales.* Boulder, CO: Roberts Rinehart Publishers, 1991. Read this for hair-raising accounts of bear encounters by one of the park's most respected natural historians.

Wilkinson, Todd. *Yellowstone Wildlife: A Watcher's Guide.* Minocqua, WI: NorthWord Press, 1992. This is an excellent guide for where to see wildlife, with fascinating must-know information about each creature.

Recreation

Henry, Jeff. *Yellowstone Winter Guide.* Boulder, CO: Roberts Rinehart Publishers, 1998. This full-color guide is a must for travelers seeing Yellowstone in its quietest and arguably most magical season.

Lilly, Bud, and Paul Schullery. *Bud Lilly's Guide to Fly Fishing the New West.* Portland, OR: Frank Amato Publications, 2000. Written by the father of Western trout fishing and one of the West's most respected natural historians, this book weaves Lilly's personal history as an angler, guide, and conservationist with the history of fly-fishing in the region along with sage advice.

Lomax, Becky. *Moon Yellowstone & Grand Teton.* Berkeley, CA: Avalon Travel, 2016. This is the ultimate guide to what to see and how to see it in these two national parks.

Marschall, Mark C. *Yellowstone Trails: A Hiking Guide.* Yellowstone National Park, WY: Yellowstone National Park Association, 2008. Another great hiking guide, this one includes descriptions of more than 100 trails ranging from day hikes to backpack trips.

Nystrom, Andrew Dean, Morgan Konn, and Tim Cahill. *Top Trails Yellowstone & Grand Tetons: Must-do Hikes for Everyone.* Berkeley, CA: Wilderness Press, 2009. This book covers 45 wonderful hikes from half-mile jaunts to 30-mile treks.

Pitcher, Don. *Moon Yellowstone & Grand Teton.* Berkeley, CA: Avalon Travel, 2011. The ultimate guide to what to see and how to see it in these two national parks.

Schneider, Bill. *Hiking Yellowstone National Park,* third edition. Guilford, CT: Globe

Pequot Press, 2012. This excellent hiking guide offers short, moderate, and long hikes throughout Yellowstone.

Watters, Ron. *Winter Tales and Trails: Skiing, Snowshoeing and Snowboarding in Idaho, the Grand Tetons and Yellowstone National Park*. Pocatello, ID: Great Rift Press, 1997. Intertwining guide advice with great stories, you'll wish Ron was along for the trip.

WYOMING
Information and Travel

Fritz, William J. *Roadside Geology of the Yellowstone Country*. Missoula, MT: Mountain Press Publishing, 1985. Even though it was published more than 30 years ago, we're talking about rocks; a couple of decades doesn't make much difference, and this is a fantastic resource for anyone interested in the region's geology.

Kilgore, Gene. *Ranch Vacations: The Leading Guide to Dude, Guest, Resort, Fly Fishing, Working Cattle Ranches and Pack Trips*. Sonoma, CA: Ranchweb, 2016. The best resource for finding a ranch vacation perfectly suited to you and your family.

Pflughoft, Fred. *Wyoming Wild and Beautiful II*. Helena, MT: Farcountry Press, 2003. As in his first book in the series, photographer Fred Pflughoft captures the beauty of the Cowboy State.

Roberts, Stephen L., David L. Roberts, and Phil Roberts. *Wyoming Almanac*. Laramie, WY: Skyline West Press, 2001. Every factoid you could ever want to know about Wyoming.

Trevathan, Mary Ann. *More Than Meets the Eye: Wyoming Along 1-80*. Glendo, WY: High Plains Press, 1993. As a marvelous and unique approach to traveling, this book focuses on the people who live and work along the highway, and is imbued with the sense that people give places life.

History

Ehrlich, Gretel. *Heart Mountain*. New York: Penguin, 1989. This historical novel by one of Wyoming's best-loved writers is set in the Heart Mountain Relocation Camp.

Haines, Aubrey L. *Historic Sites Along the Oregon Trail*. St. Louis: Patrice Press, 1994. This volume gives readers a look at the historic sites along the trail written by a well-respected historian.

Harris, Burton. *John Colter: His Years in the Rockies*. Lincoln, NE: University of Nebraska Press, 1993. This book, first published in 1952, provides the best look at early explorer and legendary figure John Colter, considered the first nonnative to lay eyes on Yellowstone.

Larson, T. A. *History of Wyoming*, second edition. Lincoln, NE: University of Nebraska Press, 1990. This massive volume covers it all and is considered the best single-volume history of the state in print.

McPhee, John. *Rising from the Plains*. New York: Farrar, Straus and Giroux, 1987. McPhee masterfully parallels Wyoming's geology with frontier history.

Moulton, Candy. *Roadside History of Wyoming*. Missoula, MT: Mountain Press Publishing, 2003. An excellent guide, this book is organized by driving routes across the state.

Munn, Debra D. *Wyoming Ghost Stories*. Helena, MT: Riverbend Publishing, 2008. A fun read for ghost lovers, this short volume rounds up ghost stories from across the state.

Murray, Robert A. *The Bozeman Trail: Highway of History*. Boulder, CO: Pruett Publishing, 1988. Murray gives readers a short but meaty volume on the bloodiest settler route of them all.

Russell, Don. *The Lives and Legends of Buffalo Bill*. Norman, OK: University of Oklahoma Press, 1979. When it comes to biographies of the legendary figure, this is the bible.

Trenholm, Virginia Cole. *The Arapahoes, Our People*. Norman, OK: University of Oklahoma Press, 1986. First published in 1970, this compelling history of the Arapaho tribe follows their ways of life from prehistoric Minnesota and Canada through the 20th century in Montana, Wyoming, and Oklahoma.

Urbanek, Mae Bobb. *Wyoming Place Names*. Missoula, MT: Mountain Press Publishing, 1988. This is the best guide for those who want to know the stories behind names like Bessemer Bend and Tensleep Canyon.

Literature

Ehrlich, Gretel. *A Match to the Heart: One Woman's Story of Being Struck by Lightning*. New York: Penguin, 1995. Another masterpiece from Ehrlich, this one is a memoir about her near death and subsequent reawakening.

Ehrlich, Gretel. *The Solace of Open Spaces*. New York: Viking Penguin, 1985. Arriving in Wyoming to work on a PBS film in 1976, Gretel Ehrlich could barely extricate herself from the independent and hard-won life she created for herself there. This collection of essays is one of the best ever written about Wyoming's landscape, people, and culture.

Forbes, Jamie Lisa. *Unbroken*. Greybull, WY: Pronghorn Press, 2011. An award-winning novelist, Forbes writes about the harshness of Wyoming ranch life.

Fuller, Alexandra. *The Legend of Colton H. Bryant*. New York: Penguin Books, 2008. Though Fuller is better known for her memoirs set in Africa, her Wyoming stories are just as powerfully written. This one tells the true story of a young man swept up in Wyoming's energy boom, and the price he paid.

Galvin, James. *The Meadow*. New York: Henry Holt & Company, 1992. Part novel, part natural history, this poetic book tells the 100-year history of a meadow in the arid mountains that bridge Wyoming and Colorado.

Harrison, Jim. *The English Major*. New York: Grove Press, 2008. Perhaps known more for his poetry and dramatic fiction—like *Legends of the Fall*—this comedic novel about a 60-year-old, sad sack of a man traveling cross-country is a delight.

Proulx, E. Annie. *Close Range: Wyoming Stories*. New York: Scribner, 2000. Pulitzer Prize-winning Proulx is among the state's best-known writers, and for good reason. The tales are dark and the landscape unforgiving, but the characters in this collection are sublime. "Brokeback Mountain" is just one of the stories in this collection.

Schaefer, Jack. *Shane*. New York: Random House, 1949. It just doesn't get more Wyoming than this cowboy classic.

Shay, Michael. *Deep West: A Literary Tour of Wyoming*. Greybull, WY: Pronghorn Press, 2003. This anthology brings together 19 writers with roots in the state, including Annie Proulx and Robert Roripaugh.

Spragg, Mark: *Where Rivers Change Direction*. New York: Riverhead Books, 2000. A profoundly compelling memoir by one of Wyoming's most beloved contemporary authors, this book tells the story of Spragg's coming-of-age on a Wyoming dude ranch.

Twain, Mark. *Roughing It*. Mineola, NY: Dover, 2013. Published originally in 1872, this nearly 900-page work is an account of Twain's six years in the wild, woolly West.

Wister, Owen. *The Virginian*. Mineola, NY: Dover, 2006. This classic 1902 novel put Wyoming on the map.

Recreation

Birkby, Jeff. *Touring Montana and Wyoming Hot Springs*, second edition. Guilford, CT: Globe Pequot Press, 2013. A comprehensive guide to public and private springs across the region.

Downing, Paul. *Fly Fishing the Southern Rockies: Small Streams and Wild Places*. Fountain Hills, AZ: Majestic Press, 2016. This comprehensive guide by a longtime editor for *Fly Fish America* offers advice on where to fish and what to use, and includes waters in Wyoming, Colorado, and New Mexico.

Hunger, Bill. *Hiking Wyoming*. Guilford, CT: Globe Pequot Press, 2008. This guide carefully outlines 110 of Wyoming's best hiking trails.

Lewis, Dan. *Paddle and Portage: The Floater's Guide to Wyoming Rivers*. Douglas, WY: Wyoming Naturalist, 1991. Intended more for less experienced boaters, this book gives an overview of various waters around the state.

Lomax, Becky. *Moon Montana, Wyoming & Idaho Camping*. Berkeley, CA: Avalon Travel, 2010. Hands down the best guide for camping in the region.

Magazines

307 Magazine (www.307magonline.com) is a short but gritty look at life and recreation across the state.

A longtime literary publication covering Montana, Wyoming, and Idaho, *Big Sky Journal* (subscriptions 800/731-1227, www.bigskyjournal.com) is published five times annually and includes special issues devoted to fly-fishing and the arts. Regular features by well-known writers focus on ranching and rodeo, hunting, fishing, art, and architecture.

Wyoming Magazine (www.wyomingmagazine.com) focuses on adventure and travel opportunities across the state, with stories about communities, entertainment, and outdoor pursuits.

Wyoming Wildlife (subscriptions 800/710-8345, http://wgfd.wyo.gov) is an award-winning publication of the Wyoming Game and Fish Department.

Maps

Wyoming Atlas & Gazetteer. Yarmouth, ME: Delorme Publishing, 2013. The most indispensable map book you'll find, these topographic maps cover roads and trails all over the state.

Internet Resources

National Park Service
www.nps.gov
The NPS website is helpful for making plans to visit any of the national parks.

U.S. Forest Service
www.fs.fed.us
The Forest Service's website is helpful for pursuing recreational opportunities including multiuse trails, campgrounds, and cabin rentals.

Recreation.gov
www.recreation.gov
This government-run site allows visitors to make reservations at public campgrounds.

State of Wyoming
www.wyoming.gov
Wyoming's official website offers a wealth of information about the state and its government.

Wyoming Travel and Tourism
www.travelwyoming.com
The state's comprehensive offering for visitors, this is a great place to find information on towns, accommodations, shopping, and dining.

Wyoming State Parks, Historic Sites, and Trails
www.wyoparks.state.wy.us
Useful information on parks, recreation, and historic preservation.

Wyoming Travel Information
www.wyoroad.info
Up-to-date road information provided by the Wyoming Department of Transportation.

Park Camper
www.parkcamper.com
This site provides interactive camping maps for Grand Teton and Yellowstone National Parks.

Wyoming Game and Fish Department
http://wgfd.wyo.gov
The website offers much of what visitors need to know about fishing and hunting in the state.

Wyoming Outfitters and Guides Association
www.wyoga.com
A fantastic resource for planning guided outdoor adventures.

Wyoming Dude Ranchers Association
www.wyomingdra.com
An excellent place to look for dude ranch vacations.

Index

XYZ

List of Maps

Photo Credits

Title page photo: © Grand Prismatic Spring, Yellowstone National Park, Wyoming

All photos © Carter G. Walker except page 8 (top left) © Wyoming Office of Tourism; page 9 © Wyoming Office of Tourism; page 10 © Donnie Sexton; page 13 © Donnie Sexton; page 16 © Wyoming Office of Tourism; page 17 © Brian Flaigmore | Dreamstime.com; page 19 © Wyoming Office of Tourism; page 23 © Wyoming Office of Tourism; page 34 © Donnie Sexton; page 43 © Donnie Sexton; page 50 © Donnie Sexton; page 54 © Donnie Sexton; page 55 © Donnie Sexton; page 56 © Donnie Sexton; page 61 © Donnie Sexton; page 70 © Wyoming Office of Tourism; page 80 © Wyoming Office of Tourism; page 89 © Wyoming Office of Tourism; page 92 © Wyoming Office of Tourism; page 93 © Wyoming Office of Tourism; page 95 © Wyoming Office of Tourism; page 104 © Wyoming Office of Tourism; page 110 © Wyoming Office of Tourism; page 119 © Wyoming Office of Tourism; page 130 © Wyoming Office of Tourism; page 137 © Wyoming Office of Tourism; page 139 © Wyoming Office of Tourism; page 147 (top) © Wyoming Office of Tourism, (bottom) © Wyoming Office of Tourism; page 155 © Wyoming Office of Tourism; page 166 © Wyoming Office of Tourism; page 177 © Wyoming Office of Tourism; page 181 (top) © Wyoming Office of Tourism, (bottom) © Wyoming Office of Tourism; page 190 © Wyoming Office of Tourism; page 202 © Wyoming Office of Tourism; page 205 © Wyoming Office of Tourism; page 207 © Wyoming Office of Tourism; page 209 © Wyoming Office of Tourism; page 218 © Wyoming Office of Tourism; page 220 © Wyoming Office of Tourism; page 229 © Wyoming Office of Tourism; page 230 © Wyoming Office of Tourism; page 232 © Donnie Sexton; page 243 © Donnie Sexton; page 245 © Wyoming Office of Tourism; page 255 © Donnie Sexton; page 258 © Donnie Sexton

Acknowledgments

There is a bottle-top African proverb affixed to my computer screen. It reads, "If you want to go quickly, go alone. If you want to go far, go together." During my now years-long journey to create and update this book, I have never wanted for company. There are many people to whom I owe an enormous debt of gratitude.

First and foremost, thanks to the indefatigable Aparna Sundaram, my co-everything for as long as I can remember. Without her—and her patient and amazing family—this book would have been a mountain of notes and a bowl of salty tears at the edge of my cluttered desk. There simply aren't words enough to praise her diligent efforts and unfailing support. Nicole Wild was instrumental as both a meticulous fact-checker, an indispensable sounding board and, not least of all, the world's best distraction for two girls whose mama was sometimes glued to the computer. Alex White is just, well, why would I write anything, do *anything*, without Alex White? She makes everything more meaningful and more fun.

Thanks also to my conscientious and patient editors—Nikki Ioakimedes, Kevin McLain, and Kristi Mitsuda—and the whole team at Avalon Travel for taking the leap and working so hard on this book. Mike Morgenfeld is a map genius and Darren Alessi does magic with photography (and Luddite writers).

Thanks to Chris Mickey from Wyoming Office of Tourism, who helped get some wonderful photos into the book.

Last but certainly not least, I am grateful to my family, the one I came from and the one I made. You all have encouraged and supported and loved me well. I'm grateful too that you had the mettle and wisdom to let me go! Bjørn, Sissel, and Siri: You are what I love most about this spectacular place. Sharing the adventure with you is my life's greatest blessing.

Also Available

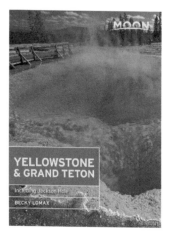

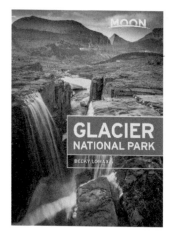

MAP SYMBOLS

▦ Expressway	★ Highlight	✗ Airfield	⚲ Golf Course
▦ Primary Road	○ City/Town	✗ Airport	℗ Parking Area
▬ Secondary Road	◉ State Capital	▲ Mountain	▰ Archaeological Site
┈ Unpaved Road	⊛ National Capital	✛ Unique Natural Feature	⬧ Church
┄ Trail	★ Point of Interest		⛽ Gas Station
⋯ Ferry	• Accommodation	⧓ Waterfall	◎ Glacier
⋯ Railroad	▾ Restaurant/Bar	▲ Park	⬚ Mangrove
▦ Pedestrian Walkway	▪ Other Location	☰ Trailhead	▨ Reef
⬚ Stairs	⋀ Campground	⛷ Skiing Area	▨ Swamp

CONVERSION TABLES

°C = (°F − 32) / 1.8
°F = (°C x 1.8) + 32
1 inch = 2.54 centimeters (cm)
1 foot = 0.304 meters (m)
1 yard = 0.914 meters
1 mile = 1.6093 kilometers (km)
1 km = 0.6214 miles
1 fathom = 1.8288 m
1 chain = 20.1168 m
1 furlong = 201.168 m
1 acre = 0.4047 hectares
1 sq km = 100 hectares
1 sq mile = 2.59 square km
1 ounce = 28.35 grams
1 pound = 0.4536 kilograms
1 short ton = 0.90718 metric ton
1 short ton = 2,000 pounds
1 long ton = 1.016 metric tons
1 long ton = 2,240 pounds
1 metric ton = 1,000 kilograms
1 quart = 0.94635 liters
1 US gallon = 3.7854 liters
1 Imperial gallon = 4.5459 liters
1 nautical mile = 1.852 km

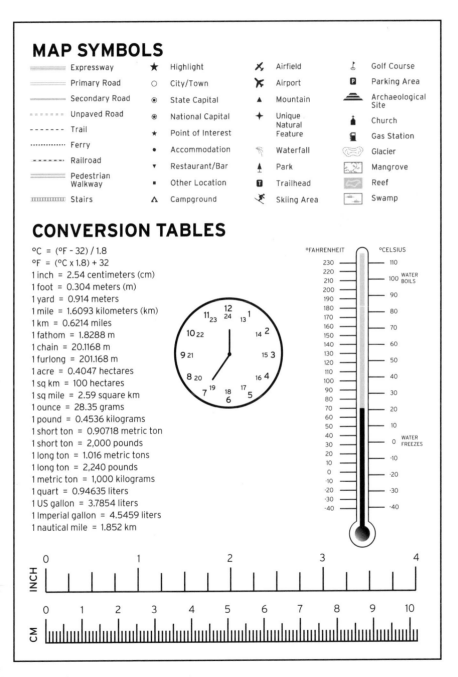

MOON WYOMING

Avalon Travel
An imprint of Perseus Books
A Hachette Book Group company
1700 Fourth Street
Berkeley, CA 94710, USA
www.moon.com

Editors: Nikki Ioakimedes, Kevin McLain,
  Kristi Mitsuda
Series Manager: Kathryn Ettinger
Copy Editor: Ann Seifert
Graphics Coordinator: Darren Alessi
Production Coordinator: Darren Alessi
Cover Design: Faceout Studios, Charles Brock
Interior Design: Domini Dragoone
Moon Logo: Tim McGrath
Map Editor: Mike Morgenfeld
Cartographers: Brian Shotwell, Austin Ehrhardt
Indexer: Rachel Kuhn

ISBN-13: 978-1-63121-580-3

Printing History
1st Edition — 2015
2nd Edition — June 2017
5 4 3 2 1

Text © 2017 by Carter G. Walker.
Maps © 2017 by Avalon Travel.
All rights reserved.

Some photos and illustrations are used by permission and are the property of the original copyright owners.

Front cover photo: Snake River in Grand Teton National Park © Niebrugge Images / Alamy Stock Photo
Back cover photo: Morning Glory Thermal Pool, Yellowstone National Park © Ramblingman | Dreamstime.com

Printed in Canada by Friesens

All recommendations, including those for sights, activities, hotels, restaurants, and shops, are based on each author's individual judgment. We do not accept payment for inclusion in our travel guides, and our authors don't accept free goods or services in exchange for positive coverage.